D0064771

UNFRIENDLY
FIRE

"Nathaniel Frank's indictment of the U.S. military's efforts to bar gays and lesbians from serving in the country's armed forces—better known as 'don't ask, don't tell'—is **searing and persuasive**. *Unfriendly Fire* peels away the falsehoods to reveal that at its core the policy has nothing to do with safeguarding military effectiveness and preserving unit cohesion, as its proponents insist."

—Professor Coit D. Blacker,
director of the Freeman Spogli Institute for International Studies,
Stanford University

Advance Praise for *Unfriendly Fire*

"Frank has written a fascinating account of the men and women, the motivations and the passions, surrounding the 'don't ask, don't tell' policy. Others have chronicled the efforts of advocates of gay service, but Frank delves into the minds, motivations, and strategies of those who sought to maintain the ban, providing a compelling indictment of the merits of their position. The heart-wrenching stories of those who failed to survive under the ban, which **Frank captures with both art and integrity**, provide the ultimate indictment of a flawed policy and practice."

—Chai Feldblum,
professor of law at Georgetown University

"Nathaniel Frank has written **the definitive text** on the 'don't ask, don't tell' policy. His treatise is **elegant** not only in its detailed historical accuracy, but in its **poignant** description of the impact of the current law on individual gay and lesbian service members."

—Rear Admiral Alan M. Steinman, USPHS/USCG (Ret.)

"Thanks to Nathaniel Frank's **rigorous, precise, and insightful research**, we now understand the true costs of 'don't ask, don't tell.' "

— Johnny Symons,
Emmy-nominated filmmaker,
Ask Not and *Daddy & Papa*

"**Nathaniel Frank has written an astonishing tale** of 'don't ask, don't tell.' No other book reaches as far, or as deep, to explain the origins and consequences of this misguided policy."

—Elizabeth L. Hillman,
professor of law at University of California Hastings College
of the Law and former U.S. Air Force Captain

"No intellectually honest American general or flag officer can read *Unfriendly Fire* and continue to support the failed 'don't ask, don't tell' policy."

—Major General Dennis Laich,
U.S. Army (Ret.)

UNFRIENDLY FIRE

——•——

HOW THE GAY BAN

UNDERMINES THE MILITARY

AND WEAKENS AMERICA

——•——

NATHANIEL FRANK

THOMAS DUNNE BOOKS ✦ NEW YORK
ST. MARTIN'S PRESS

THOMAS DUNNE BOOKS.
An imprint of St. Martin's Press.

UNFRIENDLY FIRE. Copyright © 2009 by Nathaniel Frank.
All rights reserved. Printed in the United States of America.
For information, address St. Martin's Press, 175 Fifth Avenue, New York,
N.Y. 10010.

www.thomasdunnebooks.com
www.stmartins.com

Library of Congress Cataloging-in-Publication Data

Frank, Nathaniel.
     Unfriendly fire : how the gay ban undermines the military and weakens America /
Nathaniel Frank.—1st ed.
          p. cm.
     ISBN-13: 978-0-312-37348-1
     ISBN-10: 0-312-37348-1
     1. Gays in the military—Government policy—United States.   2. Gays in the
military—United States.   I. Title.

     UB418.G38 F73 2009
     355.0086'640973—dc22

                                                            2008035886

First Edition: March 2009

10 9 8 7 6 5 4 3 2 1

Make us to choose the harder right instead of the easier wrong, and never to be content with a half truth when the whole truth can be won.

—Cadet prayer, United States Military Academy at West Point

CONTENTS

ACKNOWLEDGMENTS

————

THIS BOOK HAS been a collective project in the best sense a writer could ever imagine. The Palm Center at the University of California, Santa Barbara, fostered a community of supportive scholars who were dedicated to making their—and one another's—work see the light of day instead of collecting dust in university archives. I thank the Palm Center for its humanity and its intellectual and financial support, and for its flexibility, especially during the months that I was given extra time to work on the book.

I owe an unpayable debt of gratitude to Palm's founder and director, Aaron Belkin, who literally plucked me from academic obscurity and helped me cultivate a life doing what I love—engaging with ideas that matter. His selflessness, work ethic, patience, and friendship mean the world to me and have been constant sources of support, without which this book would probably not have been completed. The Palm Center has also been blessed with a large roster of staff, friends, and supporters who gave generously of their time and talents over the years, particularly Indra Lusero, our capable and fearless assistant director, Jeanne Schepper, our creative and thoughtful research director, and Shivaun Nestor, our Web designer. The Palm Center is deeply indebted to the Evelyn and Walter Haas, Jr., Fund, the Gill Foundation, the Wells Fargo Foundation, the Arcus Foundation, Andrew Tobias, Henry van Ameringen, Steven Gluckstern, and numerous other generous foundations and individuals for their support. For their time and assistance, I also thank Bob Witeck, Ethan Geto, Robert Raben, Mark Glaze, Bridget Wilson, Christopher Neff, Jesse Klempner, Tobias Wolff, Gary Gates, Elizabeth Hillman, Melissa Embser-Herbert, and Laura Miller.

The passionate work of the entire staff at the Servicemembers Legal Defense Network (SLDN) has been invaluable in compiling useful information about this issue and in raising its visibility, as well as in representing service members affected by "don't ask, don't tell." I am grateful for SLDN's cooperation in my efforts to tell the story of this policy. I thank Dixon Osburn, Aubrey

Sarvis, and especially Kathi Westcott, whose careful reading of the manuscript and helpful and informative critiques were essential as I worked to ensure that the story of this policy was described in proper detail.

Founders and organizers of several other groups committed to educating the nation about the experiences of gay, lesbian, and bisexual service members were also an enormous help to my research efforts: American Veterans for Equal Rights, Servicemembers United, the Military Equality Alliance, Military Community Services Network, USNA Out, and Gay and Lesbian Servicemembers for Equality.

My heartfelt thanks go to my agent, Carol Mann, who believed in this project from the moment she read the proposal and helped me navigate the bookmaking process in a realistic and encouraging way; to the entire team at St. Martin's Press/Thomas Dunne Books, who have been nothing but lovely: my highly responsive chief editor, Rob Kirkpatrick; my spirited lunch partner, Tom Dunne; my savvy publicist, John Karle; and the rest of the sharp and ever helpful editing clan: Lorrie McCann, Julie Gutin, Martha Cameron, and Amber Husbands.

My editing experience with my personal editor, David Lobenstine, was a dream. David often rearranged his schedule to do exactly what I needed, and to do it quickly, but he cut no corners and offered the ideal blend of support and constructive criticism. The book would simply be an inferior product if it weren't for his steady guidance.

Research is so often a solitary affair and, while technology allows collaborators to remain geographically apart, it was a source of not only priceless practical assistance but also ongoing social edification to have had the aid of so many talented and committed researchers on board. For their assistance, I thank Cindy Gorn, Josh Vandeburgh, Dominick Mach, Michael Freeman, Caroline Hong, and the inimitable Cassie Peterson.

For the sake of narrative flow, I have kept to a minimum the mention of other scholars and journalists who have done tireless work in uncovering the stories of gays and lesbians in the military. Here I would like to acknowledge a few on whose pathbreaking research and writing I have heavily relied for my historical understanding of this issue. Their job of gathering information and insisting it was important enough to write about was particularly tough and heroic in the days when discussing this issue still made most people queasy or uncomfortable. The late Randy Shilts and Allan Bérubé are foremost among them. Chris Bull and John Gallagher's chronicle of the role of the religious right in the battle over gay service in the 1990s was especially helpful, as was Anne Loveland's primary research on the relationship between American evangelicals and the U.S. military. I am grateful to her for sharing her papers on that topic with the Palm Center.

Of course, this book could not exist without the service and cooperation of the many named and unnamed service members, both here and abroad, who shared their stories with me, helped host my research trips, and put me in touch with others affected by "don't ask, don't tell." I am especially appreciative of the efforts and assistance of Alan Steinman and Alex Nicholson.

Thanks also go to Peter Dangerfield, who gave generously of his time to read and critique the manuscript, and to Christopher Rhodes, Ed Hall, Chris Rizzo, Dan Koenig, Johnny Symons, Chris Laidlaw, Matthew Brown, Miranda Beverly-Whittemore, Amanda Selwyn, Thaddeus Rudd, James Latham, Sarah Kitson, and the guys at Outpost Café in Clinton Hill, Brooklyn, where I wrote much of the manuscript.

My parents, John and Elaine Frank, my grandparents, and my entire family have been incredibly supportive throughout the writing process, showing enthusiasm for my work, respect for the subject, and thoughtful ideas and editing tips along the way. My grandfather, the late Gerold Frank, gave me cause to believe that I could be a writer like he was, as did my cousin Emily Rosenblum. My grandmother, Mollie Greenberg, generously expressed her interest in a way that prodded me to soldier on. My love for them all has no bounds.

Finally, my deepest gratitude goes to Richard Latham. He has encouraged, comforted, and moved me for six years; he patiently supported my interests and gently spurred me to work when I didn't always feel like it; he has taught and inspired me with his own commitment to his art; he has amused me and taken the piss out of me and helped me laugh at myself, always keeping the right perspective about what's important as he willingly inhabited a world that was sometimes foreign to him. For all this I am forever grateful.

"DON'T ASK, DON'T TELL" refers to a 1993 government policy, together with its implementing regulations and directives, and to a federal statute that Congress passed the same year. This marked the first time restrictions against gay troops were ever written into federal law. The policy and the law are distinct but overlapping entities. While I endeavor to make these distinctions clear whenever necessary, I also use the word "policy" as an umbrella term for the entire set of government restrictions against openly gay service. This usage has become common since the policy was formulated, although some observers have emphasized the differences between the Pentagon policy and the federal statute, noting, for instance, that while the Pentagon policy includes a "don't ask" provision, the actual law does not, and that the law was never formally named "don't ask, don't tell."

It is true that the policy and the law are different in important ways, yet the two do not conflict. The policy does nothing that is forbidden by the law, and there is nothing the policy fails to do that is mandated by the law. While the law does not force the Pentagon to stop asking recruits about their sexuality, for instance, it does not bar it from doing so, either, and in fact legislators made clear in a "Sense of Congress" that they supported doing away with the questioning of recruits about their sexual orientation. My interpretation, then, is that the policy and law are close enough that they can accurately be referred to as "don't ask, don't tell." When their differences become germane to a particular discussion, I try to make those distinctions clear.

To an extent, I sometimes place responsibility for the final outcome on the military itself because of the key role that military leaders have played in the political process. It is important to remember, however, that because the policy is now a matter of federal law, it will require an act of Congress to end the ban on openly gay servicemen and -women.

As we shall see, subject to certain exceptions, the policy requires the discharge of anyone found to have engaged in "homosexual conduct," which is defined to include statements declaring one's homosexual identity. Because the policy has been cast as a restriction on conduct, and not on the status of being homosexual, some suggest it is not accurate to refer to it as a ban. I argue that it is, in fact, a ban because it defines conduct so broadly as to include the most basic revelation of homosexual identity. In any event, whether or not you view the policy as a ban on gay people, it is, by all accounts, a ban on openly gay service, and when I use the term "ban," that is how I intend it.

I use the terms "gay" and "homosexual" to refer inclusively to people who identify themselves as gay, lesbian, or bisexual. I realize this does not fully comport with common usage. To me, however, the terms "gay" and "homosexual" refer to men and women who have an erotic and physical attraction to people of the same sex, whether felt exclusively or occasionally. For that reason, and to avoid awkward and bulky phrasing, I am hoping you will find the usage appropriate. Note, also, that the "don't ask, don't tell" policy does not encompass transgendered people, but refers only to homosexuals and bisexuals, which is why I don't include transgendered people in this analysis. This is not meant to neglect or exclude the experiences of transgendered people in the military, but the specific analysis of those experiences lies outside the scope of this study.

One final note: I often use the word "discharge" to refer to administrative separations under "don't ask, don't tell." Technically, "discharge" is the term used any time a military member leaves the service, whether prematurely or because his or her contract term has expired, whereas an administrative "separation" normally refers to removal for any of a number of reasons, including a finding of "homosexual conduct." In most cases for our purposes, I use "discharge," "separate," "dismiss," "expel," "fire," "oust," and "boot" interchangeably. It is also helpful to note that criminal convictions under military law, which governs offenses such as sodomy and adultery, are distinct from the territory of "don't ask, don't tell," which can only result in an administrative separation. Normally, "don't ask, don't tell" discharges are characterized as "honorable" unless the conduct is performed by force, with a subordinate or youth, in public, for money, on a ship, or otherwise has an aggravating impact on discipline, good order, or morale.

PROLOGUE

CHARLIE MOSKOS WAS proud of his contribution to the English language: coining the phrase "don't ask, don't tell." It was fall of 1992, and the Northwestern University professor was knee-deep in the latest hot-button social issue to confront the U.S. military: whether it should finally let gays and lesbians serve. "The phrase and the policy just came to me one night at my house when I was at the watercooler," he recalled in an interview in the year 2000. "Obviously, it was perking around in my subconscious."[1] Professor Moskos, then considered the most influential military sociologist in the United States, was not engaged in idle speculation or academic posturing. Over the last four decades, he had gained an international reputation as an academic expert on social issues in the military—racial integration, conscription, national service, women in combat—and had contributed ideas and policies that affected thousands of lives.

And now this: homosexuality. The presence of gay men and women in the military had long been a subject of sweeping pronouncements and endless compromises. It had been a persistent thorn in the Pentagon's side since the Vietnam War era, but by 1992, as Bill Clinton geared up for the presidency and religious conservatives geared up to save America's soul, the gay troops issue was becoming a public relations nightmare.

Moskos spent years building his credentials as a military sociologist. After graduating from Princeton in 1956, he was drafted into the U.S. Army and spent two years as a company clerk in Germany. Although he served there with the army's combat engineers, he made a name for himself not as a soldier but as an academic. After earning a Ph.D. from the University of California, Los Angeles, he became an expert field researcher on military personnel issues and soon took a job as a sociology professor at Northwestern University, developing a popular introductory course where, with a self-deprecating demeanor, he humbly presented his ideas and then finished with the words Churchill once used to describe democracy: "It's the worst system possible," he told the five hundred students in his 9:00 A.M. course, with a gradually widening grin. "Except for all the others." It's a maxim he would invoke with equal delight years later in describing "don't ask, don't tell." Since his eureka moment at the watercooler, Moskos's phrase has evolved into "don't ask, don't tell, don't pursue," a law that helps determine how the military trains and treats its men and women. The military's policy on gays and lesbians has been transformed from a residual hodgepodge of a bygone era to a carefully articulated modern legal morass that wreaks havoc with the lives of service members and with the capacity of our nation to defend itself—all courtesy of an administration that promised it would make things better. And Charles Moskos was among a small and powerful group of people who were largely responsible for this debacle.

Moskos had the ears of the highest military and civilian decision makers in part because he had spent his career analyzing a problem that many considered similar: racial integration of the armed forces. In 1957, while still serving in the army in Germany, he published his first article on the topic, striking a tolerant, optimistic tone. "In the final outcome," he wrote, "the experience of the Army's integration program offers to the international audience the true measure of America's world leadership." In later works, he wrote that the authoritarian structure of the military made it "uniquely suited" to implement and enforce policies that might not be immediately popular, such as desegregation. Because of how the military was organized, with its focus on hierarchy and obedience, the institution was perfect for "mitigat[ing] tensions arising from individual or personal feelings." He went on to write extensively about integration throughout the tumultuous decades of the Vietnam War. His scholarship was eventually translated into sixteen languages.[2]

As a researcher on the workings of military forces around the world and a veteran academic policy wonk in key historic debates, Moskos was a natural candidate to take on the issue of gays in the military. But he was a less natural choice for the nation to enlist as an authority on sexuality. With a charming affability, he glibly recalled his military days, revealing in interviews an almost adolescent view about sex. "I had a gay commander once," he quipped in 2000. "He didn't hit on me much because I wasn't good-looking enough." He chuckled and clarified his point: "Let's just say he was always too close with the college-educated enlisted men." Citing alarming statistics about sexual abuse among convicts, Moskos failed to grasp the most basic differences between sexual behavior among the incarcerated and among gays. He noted, for instance, that prison rapes are more common than all the male-female rapes in the country. "This does not speak well for gays," he said, "when they are in a dominant position." Never mind the subtleties of life be-hind bars; to Moskos, men who have sex with other men even while in jail were homosexuals all the same, never to be fully trusted. He regarded gay men as virtually interchangeable with women, explaining that the ban on openly gay soldiers is based, in part, on closely comparing the two: "We do separate men and women in the military in intimate living conditions. If you had open gays, you'd probably have the same harassment problems as you do among men and women." That is, if women can be legitimately separated from men, gays can be, if not separated, at least denied recognition. The solu-tion, then, was to pretend everyone was straight.[3]

It is this pretending, or, to be more precise, the legal institutionalization of such pretending, that distinguishes the policy from its predecessor. "Don't ask, don't tell," which is both a Pentagon policy and, in somewhat different form, a federal law, requires the discharge of service members found to have engaged in homosexual conduct. It was cast—and is routinely reported—as a compromise that allows gays and lesbians to serve in the military while regu-lating only their behavior, not their identity. That is, it is supposed to punish conduct, not status. But as we will see, the policy actually bans gay people, not just homosexual acts. This is because the policy prohibits conduct that gay people, by definition, engage in, while allowing straight men and women who engage in the same conduct to serve.

In fact, the law does not even require that a person engage in sexual con-duct to prompt a discharge—it's enough for two men to hold hands or engage in "any bodily contact" that a "reasonable person would understand to dem-onstrate a propensity" to satisfy sexual desires with someone of the same sex. It's even prohibited to make a "statement" that one is attracted to a member of the same sex. And statements don't require spoken words—e-mails, letters, tapped phone calls, romantic photos, the possession of gay-themed videos, or anything the military's "reasonable person" finds incriminating can be—and have been—considered admissible evidence of wrongdoing.

By defining conduct as including a statement of status, and defining a statement of status to include any indication that one may have a "propensity" to engage in homosexual conduct, the military was able to get around the legal objection that they were targeting people for who they were and thus violating the constitutional rights of gays and lesbians. And by insisting that the policy does not punish people for being homosexual, only for engaging in homosex-ual conduct, the government implies that anyone who is fired under the policy has willingly chosen to break the rules. In reality, the policy targets same-sex desire itself, and bans what gay people, by definition, do, while allowing straight people who engage in occasional gay fun to go right on serving. It is no more conduct-based than a rule that bars people from praying to Jesus—this is what Christians *do,* just as having sexual relationships with people of the same sex is what gays do. Is banning people who pray to Jesus any different from banning Christians? Is a restaurant that bars creatures that bark not a restaurant that bars dogs? Is a policy that bars people who engage in homosexual behavior not a policy that bars homosexuals?

The U.S. military has never quite known how to deal with sex, straight or gay. The Pentagon prides itself on cultivating a culture of discipline, command, and obedience. Sexuality, by its very nature, chafes against such strictures. And so the Pentagon has floundered when forced to recognize and govern the animating passions of its rank and file. A crucial part of military culture has also been its self-definition as a realm of strong men. Resistance to allowing women in combat, reluctance to discipline sexual harassment, refusal to accept homosexuals into the service—it often seems that command leaders would rather not acknowledge the presence of anyone but straight males in their midst. For the military, the current policy on gay and lesbian soldiers was thus a triumph not because it protected combat performance but because it forced the issue of sexual desire—and the gays in the barracks—securely into the closet. At least, that's what it was supposed to do.

But the truth cannot be hidden away so easily. And the true nature of "don't ask, don't tell" is increasingly coming to light. The reality is that the United States no longer needs—if ever it did—a ban on openly gay troops. But more important, our nation can no longer afford it; we can no longer afford to be stuck in the quagmire of "conduct" versus "status." Quite simply, we need every last soldier who is willing to sacrifice for his or her country.

The U.S. military is in crisis. The terrorist attacks of September 11, 2001, were a watershed moment in American history. The role of the U.S. military, like so much of American life, has been radically altered and our forces have been stretched dangerously thin. The U.S. Armed Forces have engaged in everything from peacekeeping to monitoring elections to deadly combat missions on a scale not seen since Vietnam. What has not changed, however, is the situation of gays in the military.

Yet despite "don't ask, don't tell," we now know that hundreds—and probably tens of thousands—of gays and lesbians have participated in battle not only discreetly but as openly gay soldiers, sailors, airmen, and Marines. And so, at this crucial juncture, as the United States sinks its military resources into Iraq and Afghanistan and other trouble spots throughout the world, and as gays continue to serve, despite being told they are not wanted, we must ask:

How has the presence of gays sapped the military? What has been the cost of openly gay service to military effectiveness? Answer: It hasn't sapped the military, and the costs have been nil.

What *has* drained the military, what *has* cost hundreds of millions of dollars and wrecked careers and stained the lives of tens of thousands of gays and lesbians serving their country, is the "don't ask, don't tell" policy itself. So we must ask: How did we get here? How did the most powerful nation on earth, a product of the Age of Enlightenment, with its celebration of freedom, science, knowledge, progress, and human rights, create a policy at the end of the twentieth century that brings these grand aspirations to a halt by legally mandating ignorance, denial, and repression? And how did this happen in the United States at the very moment when our major allies were ending the ban on gay and lesbian troops and finding that the move helped, rather than harmed, their militaries? Indeed, this and mountains of other evidence have been wholly ignored in the debate over gay service in the United States. Instead, in the hands of a vocal, anti-gay movement, the nation was presented with a false choice to support either gay rights or national security.

Yet it turns out that granting gay rights is good for national security. So we ask: How important have the needs of the military really been in the battle over gay service? Was "don't ask, don't tell" really the result of a reasoned discussion, based on available evidence, about what was best for the military? Or was it a result of the fears, emotions, moral qualms, and outright prejudice of military brass and political leaders who were more concerned about being "soft" on homosexuality than about ensuring that the best people were serving in the armed forces? What was the role of the American public, with their often ambivalent feelings about homosexuality? How fervently did ordinary individuals and particular interest groups campaign to prevent openly gay service or acquiesce in the debate swirling around them?

"Don't ask, don't tell" was the result of a bitter battle over the acceptability of homosexuality in the United States. Its final outcome was supposed to allow gays and lesbians to serve quietly, minimize troop loss, and protect the privacy of all service members so they would not be distracted from defending the nation. What has happened, however, is the exact opposite: It is the United States that needs to be defended from the inanity of "don't ask, don't tell." Expulsions swelled, privacy was compromised for gays and straights alike, and the trust and cohesion of fighting units were torn apart by forced dishonesty, suspicion, and unnecessary troop losses.

———

OVER THE PAST ten years I have conducted extensive academic and field research on gays in the military. As a scholar at the Palm Center, a research institute at the University of California, Santa Barbara, I visited U.S. bases and service academies; toured aircraft carriers; spent time with gay and straight service members working and socializing, on base and off; and met with foreign military members abroad. In total, I discussed the question of gay service with hundreds of people—officers and enlisted personnel, policy makers and scholars, government personnel and civilian advocates on both sides of the debate. And I reviewed thousands of pages of military, government, political, scholarly, journalistic, and personal documents pertaining to gays in the military.

In addition to exploring the origins of this policy and its impact on our armed forces, I conducted this research with another central question in mind: Is it possible to view "don't ask, don't tell" as the product of anything other than prejudice, defined as "blind intolerance"? Could military necessity truly have dictated that some form of gay exclusion rule must be retained in order to preserve unit cohesion and combat readiness? Could questions of privacy and modesty have made the gay ban reasonable, somehow justifying its discrimination as a proper bow to the cultural expectations of the majority? Is it possible this policy is somehow not "anti-gay"?

As a historian trained to do my best to "walk in the shoes" of my subjects, I have a commitment to fairness and intellectual honesty, even as I came to this issue as a gay man skeptical of the fairness and wisdom of "don't ask, don't tell." My research has, indeed, borne out this skepticism. As hard as I have tried to appreciate the positions of those who had a hand in shaping this dishonorable policy, when you scratch at the surface of every last, roving rationale for the gay ban, and when you learn about the lives, thoughts, and behaviors of the bulk of individuals who insisted on gay exclusion, what you find at the bottom is prejudice.

This conclusion—that the gay ban is based on prejudice, not military necessity—isn't exactly news. Many of my colleagues have been saying so for years. But I am hoping that the extensive and rigorous process by which I came to this conclusion and the story—together with the evidence and research—that I present in the following pages will help make that point even more persuasively for those who are not yet convinced.

In other words, this book does not simply assume that the policy is anti-gay because it discriminates against gays; it seeks to prove it. It is with the perhaps immodest assumption of my ultimate success in this effort that I refer to the policy, at times, as "anti-gay." One way or the other, the policy is based on the view that homosexuality is bad—morally wrong, to be precise. When you study all the evidence, including the experiences of other nations, and when you consider that American troops have always served with gays, but that opponents of gay service simply seem to not want to know about it, and when you examine the political drama and the cultural rhetoric surrounding the formulation of "don't ask, don't tell," you will, I believe, come to the inescapable conclusion that this policy springs from either anti-gay animus or, at best, a deep-seated need to repress the reality of homosexuality—and hence is still, ultimately, anti-gay.

Yet it is important to note that not all opponents of gay service were malicious or bigoted, and I want it to be absolutely clear that I am not arguing they were. While many social conservatives have expressed venomous attitudes toward homosexuals, some of the most articulate military experts, both inside and outside the military, who spoke up against lifting the ban sincerely believed that doing so would undermine the armed forces or at least sufficiently feared the consequences that they felt compelled to oppose change. Many of these people wished gays no harm, and some may even have avoided the subtle, often unconscious anti-gay animus that is all too frequent in American life. The sincerity of their beliefs, however, does not mean the policy was based on good reasons that ought to have been heeded—even then. Opposing change based on unfounded fear or ignorance does not change the fact that support for "don't ask, don't tell" meant sanctioning prejudice and intolerance, and history must hold all these players accountable.

THIS IS A work of nonfiction. Absolutely nothing has been made up, composited, switched around, or changed. It is based on extensive personal interviews and communications as well as published sources. Because of the strictures of the "don't ask, don't tell" policy, there are occasions when I have been unable to give supporting details, ranging from names to dates to details of a story, because they describe active-duty service members whose identification would put their jobs, careers, benefits, and families at risk. This reality can, unfortunately, sap the richness of the narrative in a few spots. The mild damage to my prose, however, pales in comparison to the impact this policy has had on the tens of thousands of gay and lesbian troops who served their country under its peculiar burden. This book is dedicated to them.

UNFRIENDLY
FIRE

1

The Long History of the Military Closet

E VER SINCE THE REVOLUTIONARY WAR, men have been drummed out of the U.S. military for homosexual acts. The first recorded incident of a discharge for homosexuality was that of Lieutenant Gotthold Frederick Enslin in 1778. Caught in his Valley Forge bunking cabin with a male private, Enslin was found guilty of sodomy, defined broadly as "unnatural" sexual penetration, but most often enforced against men who had sex with men. He was ushered out of the army in an elaborate ceremony in which an officer's sword was broken in two upon the soldier's head. But while punishment for such sexual transgressions is older than the nation, the targeting of gay men and lesbians as members of an identifiable—and threatening—group, a class of people who must be regulated and even stigmatized, is a surprisingly recent phenomenon. An awareness of how and why this gay "threat" emerged is essential to understanding how we ended up with a policy on homosexuality in the military that was doomed to fail.[1]

The taboo against same-sex desire is hardly new. But homosexual identity—the conscious investment of enduring meaning in one's same-sex desire and the structuring of major life determinations around homosexual relationships—is a product of the modern age. As a result, it is inaccurate—and from a historical perspective, nonsense—to speak of the regulations of homosexuals before this period. Indeed, the term "homosexual" was not used before the late nineteenth century, and "heterosexual" was coined even later. Not until certain economic and social conditions evolved was there even the possibility that men and women would regard themselves as primarily homosexual in how they identified themselves and lived their lives, even though sexual contact and love relationships had long existed between people of the same sex.[2]

Lacking a key component of modern psychology—that individuals possess an essentially permanent sexual identity—the Revolutionary Army punished the act of sodomy rather than the status of homosexual. But military regulations did not even address sodomy explicitly. Instead, it fell under the rubric of broader offenses like "perverted" or "unnatural" acts, or conduct "prejudicial to good order and discipline." When sodomy needed to be identified more precisely, it could be called "the unmentionable vice" or "wickedness not to be named." But the taboo against sodomy—for all people—reflected an understanding of the time that the act was something everyone was prone to engage in during moments of moral weakness, not just the characteristic behavior of one type of person called a "homosexual."[3]

Why was such behavior banned in the armed forces? The moral and legal strictures against same-sex intimacy in the military mirrored those of Western society, and reflected the wider proscription against any sex that was not procreative. Contraception, masturbation, fornication, even having sex in the wrong position, were all banned or punished in the colonial era. These norms were themselves an outgrowth of religious taboos that had been incorporated into English common law and adopted without fanfare in the original thirteen colonies. (Sodomy was even punished by execution in several colonies in the seventeenth century.) But they were also rooted in the prevailing belief that the heterosexual family structure was the primary source of production and social stability. Any sex not geared toward reproduction was regarded as a barrier to the social and survival goals of increasing the population, dividing up labor, consolidating family wealth, and preserving the family lineage, including lines of blood, race, and religion. Both within and outside the military, these beliefs took the form of efforts to control people's behavior, maintain social order, and protect existing relations of power. They revealed a recognition that sexuality was a powerful force that could lead to both very good and very bad things.[4]

Yet despite the taboos against it, same-sex love has simultaneously been knowingly tolerated—and even deeply relied on—in the military throughout history. It has been so from the Sacred Band of Thebes in the fourth century BC, where martial valor was said to rest on the love of each soldier for the other, to the American Revolution, where Friedrich von Steuben, a brilliant gay Prussian captain who was considered a genius at training men, joined the war effort and wrote an indispensable drilling manual called *Regulations for the Order and Discipline of the Troops of the United States*. He is considered by historians to have been invaluable to the war's success, despite the fact that "order" and "discipline" are precisely the qualities gays are now said to impair.[5]

Indeed, the indebtedness of the armed services to same-sex love cannot be underestimated. There are two reasons for this. First, though it doesn't exactly broadcast the fact, the military relies on gays to make up its fighting force. An estimated sixty-five thousand gay and lesbian Americans currently serve in uniform, a small but significant portion of the nearly 3 million U.S. service members. The role of lesbians is particularly vital. Without women, who make up 15 percent of all personnel and 20 percent of junior personnel, the military would simply not have enough bodies to complete its missions; and without lesbians, there would be far fewer women in uniform. According to statistical analyses of the U.S. census and other data, the proportion of female service members who are lesbian is 5.2 percent, nearly twice the estimated proportion of lesbians in the general population.[6]

The exact number of gay men in uniform is trickier to estimate. While it's possible that anti-gay law and attitudes in the military have kept the number of gay men lower than their proportion in the general population, some evidence suggests that gay men are equally or even more likely to have served in the military than straight men.[7] There are two reasons to believe there could be a higher percentage of gay men in the military than in the general population: As an institution that segregates the sexes, the military is a homo-social environment, and may draw men who, as it's said, prefer the company of men. And because military service relies on individuals who are willing to leave home for extended periods of time, it can be more appealing to those who are not living with partners and children, a category that still includes more gays than straights.

The second reason the military is indebted to same-sex love is psychological. Without homosexuality as its foil, the military would not be able to be "straight," just as without the concept of femininity, it could not function as a proving ground for manhood. The U.S. military would therefore be unrecognizable if it weren't for homosexuality. If the very self-image of the American warrior is straight, the counterimage of the homosexual is essential to its existence. As we'll see, the heterosexual self-image of young male troops is also quite fragile, and this vulnerability plays a central role in explaining the powerful opposition to openly gay service. The point here is not to offer a laundry list of the contributions of homosexuality and gay people to military service. But recognizing the indispensable place of both gay people and same-sex love in the armed forces is essential to understanding Americans' ideas about the perceived relationship between sexual expression and social order, and how it ultimately gave birth to "don't ask, don't tell."

Until the end of the nineteenth century, that relationship seemed simple enough: Sex outside of heterosexual marriage was a transgression against God and society—both a sin and a crime—and a danger to the structured order of things. Nonproductive sex was a waste of precious energy and an invitation to put pleasure above duty and order. All individuals were thought to have the capacity to engage in such misbehavior, and it was thus important to punish it whenever it was discovered, so as to discourage masses of people from transgressing at will.

By the twentieth century, new models of sexuality had begun to emerge, ushered in largely by the medical and psychiatric community. Instead of regarding homosexual conduct as a transgression anyone could choose to commit, it was increasingly viewed as the characteristic behavior of distinct personality types. The developments in the first half of the century were fitful and complex, and they defy easy categorization. But the changing interplay between psychiatric understandings of sexuality and the evolving needs of the U.S. military had a profound influence on many of the assumptions and policies that continue to govern our understanding of homosexuality today.

The early efforts to reform views about homosexuality in the years leading up to World War I were largely spurred by the fledgling psychiatric profession. While the practitioners of the new analyses were products of their time, and sometimes reflected moralizing biases that can sound hostile to modern ears, most were seeking to better understand people with homosexual tendencies with an eye toward alleviating suffering and even integrating them into society. Their assessments built on a disease model, which viewed homosexuality as a neurological defect that was either congenital or the result of bad habits that actually damaged the central nervous system. As such, it was a mental disorder, and one that might be regarded as a moral defect in cause or effect. Yet its classification was not part of an attempt to condemn, but to understand and treat. Homosexuality was normally screened out of the military only when it manifested itself in overt conduct or glaring nonconformity.[8]

The psychiatric profession itself was not of one mind in its thinking about homosexuality. Sigmund Freud, for instance, believed that homosexual orientation was neither a moral weakness nor a disease, but a "variation of the sexual function." The father of psychoanalysis famously wrote that homosexuality was "nothing to be ashamed of, no vice, no degradation, it cannot be classified as an illness." In the United States, however, the psychiatric community was more hostile to homosexuality. "The homosexualist is not only dangerous but an ineffective fighter," said a San Francisco psychiatrist during World War I. He advised the military to seek out and separate homosexuals to protect the "combative prowess of our forces" during the war. Another American psychiatrist argued that only heterosexuality was natural and that homosexuality was a phobic response to the other sex. American psychiatrists increasingly viewed homosexuality as a degenerative personality disorder that had to be stopped to preserve optimal mental health. It was this kind of thinking that created a pathologizing characterization of gays and lesbians in the United States that was pitted against the normative vision of exclusive heterosexuality. Like the military's policy on homosexuality, this outlook frequently masked the scientist's own moral or religious animus to gay and lesbian people.[9]

It was during World War I that sodomy—though still not homosexual identity—was explicitly banned in the military. In 1917, when the Articles of War were revised, sodomy was named for the first time as a military crime, but only if committed as part of an assault. A second revision three years later made consensual sodomy a crime in the military. While the sodomy regulation applied to both homosexuals and heterosexuals, its formulation reflected a new understanding that "sodomists" were a group of people with a coherent identity, who were more prone than "normal" people to practice the unmentionable act, and were sometimes defiant in their insistence that there was nothing wrong with their behavior, much to the chagrin of medical, military, political, and cultural leaders.[10]

By the end of World War I, the military was increasingly intolerant of a gay presence. In 1919, the U.S. Navy conducted a purge of its installation in Newport, Rhode Island. It was headed by Chief Machinist's Mate Ervin Arnold, who said he could spot "degenerates" a mile away by their clothing, walk, and effeminate manner. In Newport, he worked in Ward B of the Naval Training Station hospital, where young gay sailors revealed their life and subculture to him, including girlish nicknames, women's clothes, and orgies. Repulsed and yet compelled to learn more, he started to informally collect gossip and take down names of suspected sailors, eventually expanding his activities to include an investigatory crew of volunteer "operators" who spied on suspected homosexuals. Securing authorization to formalize his investigation from Franklin D. Roosevelt, then assistant secretary of the navy, Arnold formed a group of enlisted sailors to take the next step beyond spying: At the local YMCA, they entrapped suspected gay sailors by soliciting and having sex with them. With amnesty from the navy, Arnold's operators were instructed to go as far as necessary to obtain evidence, but not to take a "leading part." They claimed to have been motivated by a belief in the mission to rid the navy of unwanted sexual perversion, regarding themselves as "normal" and dutiful service members. A dozen sailors were ultimately arrested, court-martialed, and convicted of sodomy; they served several years in prison.

It was not lost on many observers, including the U.S. Senate, which censured the navy for its "shocking" and "indefensible" investigative tactics, that the military had no trouble rounding up its own men to sleep with other men as part of a sting operation to rout out gays. In its reprimand, the Senate panel wrote that "perversion is not a crime, in one sense, but a disease that should properly be treated in a hospital," reflecting the changing outlook of the era.

The investigation and its censure had great historical significance. The young sailors who volunteered for the entrapment operation, who the senators acknowledged might have been gay, were nevertheless cast as victims. Perversion had been "practically forced upon boys who, because of their patriotism and the patriotism of their parents, had responded to the call of the country to defend their flag and their homes." Outraged over the "iniquitous procedure" that seemed to have corrupted wholesome young American men, the senators recommended a ban on ever using enlisted personnel to investigate immoral conduct again. A better approach, they suggested, would be "the arbitrary wholesale discharge of suspected perverts" from the navy, as well as the ejection of all suspected civilian homosexuals from the town of Newport. What this meant was that actual sexual conduct could no longer be the required proof for screening gay people out of the military; from that moment on, the focus would be on personality types that, simply because of who they were suspected to be, were considered threats to the moral purity and operational capacity of the armed forces. It was the beginning of the rationale for banning gay *people*, since the task of banning gay *conduct* had proven to be perilous, and had inadvertently thrown light on how easily "normal" men could end up in the jaws of a homosexual rapport.[11]

As psychiatrists sought to circulate their ideas around the country, struggling to earn respect for their young science and maximize its influence, they readily offered their service to the military. Instead of sending sensitive boys to the military to become men, they counseled, "Send them to us!" Some in the psychiatric community still felt they were looking out for the interests of both homosexuals and the military; even when recommending screening gays out, their objective was to minimize the level of "psychiatric casualties" resulting from combat, so as to save both gays and the military the trouble of a bad match. But others increasingly spoke of gays in pejorative and moralizing terms. During the interwar years, the situation worsened, as the military bureaucracy took the process out of the hands of psychiatrists and relied on the most crass and slapdash characterizations of gay people. Military officials went far beyond psychiatrists' efforts to classify, treat, and protect gays and lesbians from prison or psychological harm. They began to exclude men from service whose bodies they deemed feminine, as evidenced by "sloping narrow shoulders," "broad hips," or a "female figure," as well as those with "degenerate" psychological traits that were believed to prevent individuals from properly joining the civilized world. Between the wars, purges, crackdowns, and persecutions of homosexuals increased. Often service members were dismissed or incarcerated for "moral perversions" or "conduct tending to the destruction of good morals." At the same time, however, a sizable underground culture of gay men thrived in the military, partly a product of the mobilization and concentration of military men in port cities during World War I.[12]

If World War I began the process of punishing homosexual conduct, World War II systematized discrimination against homosexual people. The massive war mobilization sent an unprecedented volume of recruits through the military's accession offices, prompting a new effort to make the process efficient and discerning. Some service branches excluded not only gays but blacks and women as well. The crucial difference was that, of the three groups, the identities of blacks and women were readily discernible, while gays had to be *detected*. The need to screen nearly 20 million young people to determine who was suitable for the exacting demands of defeating totalitarianism meant the creation of an elaborate apparatus designed to separate the worthy from the unfit. In the process, the military helped to solidify views about homosexuality, and the impact spread far wider than just the armed forces. These views included not only the notion that homosexuality was a distinct identity, and a dangerous one at that, but that gay people could—and should—be identified by relying on stereotyped characteristics that were often unrelated to whether one was actually gay.

Psychiatrists played a lead role in this effort. In 1940, an advisory committee of psychiatric consultants to the new Selective Service System began giving lectures on how the military should screen for mental health. Homosexuality was only one among many traits included, and it was not singled out as a particular threat to the military. But as the training spread throughout the bureaucracy, quality control suffered. Poorly trained psychiatrists, for instance, relied on examinations of limited pools of mentally troubled subjects to draw sweeping conclusions about the mental state of homosexuals, failing to realize that most gays were living well-adjusted lives far from these clinical samples of people seeking psychiatric help.

Based on these skewed conclusions, in the early 1940s the military began to issue new regulations that, by the end of the war, had formalized the exclusion of gays by distinguishing them from "normal" people. The rules used the language of identity and mental illness and the philosophy of preemption: "persons habitually or occasionally engaged in homosexual or other perverse sexual practices" were to be separated, as they suffered from a "constitutional psychopathic state" that made them "sexual psychopaths." The mark of a homosexual person was the identification of "tendencies" or "proclivities" toward homosexual conduct. This formulation lingers today in the anti-gay policy's use of the word "propensity," as if describing an impulse that just can't quite be controlled. And it remains as ineffective now as it ever was in identifying true threats to order, discipline, and cohesion in the military.[13]

Because it was difficult to pin down what it meant to have a proclivity to engage in homosexual conduct, authorities came to rely heavily on stereotypes, especially on the pseudoscientific association of effeminacy with homosexuality. With limited time and, ultimately, inadequate tools to conduct psychiatric evaluations of the masses of new recruits, World War II examiners scrutinized not only those they deemed effeminate, but anyone who indicated in occupational questionnaires that he might want to pursue interior decorating or dancing after the war. Such classifications were not always instances of homophobia, but could be expressions of concern over the impact of nonconforming men on the morale and cohesion of the group. One military medical team advised in 1942 that "sissy" men should not be allowed to serve, even if they were heterosexual, because their "appearance and mannerisms" would subject them to scorn that would undermine the good of the group.[14] But the subtext that enabled such distinctions was always deviant sexuality, rooted in the belief that such nonconformity signaled a personality disorder that kept individuals from being team players. Gender inversion— adopting or displaying gender roles that were typically associated with the opposite sex—was just as feared as homosexuality, and the two were often mistaken for one another.

The specific elements feared most by the authorities are instructive, as many continue to form the basis of opposition to gay military service. As sexual psychopaths, gays and lesbians were seen to suffer from an excess of desire, as individuals who compulsively eroticized aspects of life that well-adjusted, civilized people would never regard as sexual. Not only did homosexuals feel such desires, but they were unable to restrain themselves, to grow fully to maturity and assume the adult responsibilities that were the mark of healthy people and the sine qua non of an ordered civilization and a functioning military. The threat of these alleged sexual deviants ranged from gender nonconformity, whose presence could embarrass "normal" military men and provoke hostility, to the insistent expression of homosexual desires, which could violate the privacy of heterosexuals and even result in sexual predation.[15]

The evolving anti-gay outlook of this military-psychiatric axis involved circular logic at its most senseless. With lots of gut feelings but no credible evidence, officials nevertheless came to believe that gays were dangerous to the military; but because that danger seldom seemed to yield the consequences they feared it would, it became necessary to spin out a narrative of the "homosexual menace." In so doing, they created images of sexual and gender deviants that rationalized exclusion, even, in many cases, of those who were not homosexual but were merely nonconformists. And because the world did not always share the certainty of doctors, generals, and other self-styled experts that gays and lesbians were a threat to military order and discipline, these narratives had to be explicit and damning. Simultaneously, in order to ensure that people could not avoid the draft by claiming to be gay, it was necessary to enforce and even intensify the stigma of homosexuality, both in the military and in society at large: Gay inductees will "contaminate our young boys," just as they had in Newport; they will be "subject to ridicule and joshing, which will harm the general morale" of the unit; they will lower the quality of the force and drive good men away. The more military officials denigrated homosexuality, the more they and others believed the narrative of danger that had largely been of their own making. It's a tale whose resonance remains far stronger today than reason can possibly dictate. But, then, reason has only a limited role in the formation of prejudice.

The policies created by this irrationality have had equal staying power. Throughout World War II, the different branches of the military issued dozens of revisions to their regulations governing the fate of gay and lesbian troops. By the war's end, gays and lesbians were deemed "unsuitable for military service" and were officially banned from all branches, whether or not there was any evidence of homosexual conduct.[16]

The cold war did nothing to liberalize views toward homosexuality in the military. In 1949, amid growing fears of subversives in government and as part of a postwar congressional reorganization of the armed forces, the newly created Department of Defense sought to apply a single policy across all the branches of the military. The new regulation stated: "Homosexual personnel, irrespective of sex, should not be permitted to serve in any branch of the Armed Forces in any capacity, and prompt separation of known homosexuals from the Armed Forces is mandatory." As part of the reform, each branch was asked to give homosexuality indoctrination lectures in order to facilitate the ferreting out of gays.[17]

The following year, in an effort to reform and standardize disciplinary procedures in the military, Congress created the Uniform Code of Military Justice, which made "unnatural carnal copulation" in the armed forces a crime punishable by five years of hard labor and dishonorable discharge without pay. This sodomy ban remains military law to this day. The ban criminalizes both heterosexuals and homosexuals engaging in anal or oral sex (or sex with animals), despite a 2003 Supreme Court ruling that states may not outlaw sodomy between consenting adults. As a separate society, the courts have ruled, the military is exempt from the decision.[18]

The gay ban continued to face a hodgepodge of revisions in the second half of the twentieth century, the most significant of which came during the Carter administration. Following the embarrassing Iranian seizure of American hostages in 1979, Carter sought to strengthen his record on national defense. He vowed to reinstitute draft registration, increase spending, and get "tough on gays." Several new court cases had recently challenged inconsistencies in the implementation of the homosexual exclusion policy. On January 16, 1981, one week before he left office, Carter's deputy secretary of defense managed to push through a servicewide ban on gays and lesbians in uniform, removing any discretion that different branches or individual commanders previously enjoyed. The new policy, perhaps in a vague gesture toward destigmatizing gay individuals, but mostly in an effort to avoid legal challenges, modified the language that had dubbed gay people "unsuitable for military service." Instead it stated that "homosexuality is incompatible with military service." It explained the reason for the ban as follows: "The presence of such members adversely affects the ability of the armed forces to maintain discipline, good order and morale; to foster mutual trust and confidence among servicemembers; to ensure the integrity of the system of rank and command; to facilitate assignment and worldwide deployment of servicemembers who frequently must live and work under close conditions affording minimal privacy; to recruit and retain members of the armed forces; to maintain the public acceptability of military service; and to prevent breaches of security" by the threat of blackmail. It offered no evidence that any of the foregoing was actually true, but simply provided a list of alleged homosexual dangers—emanating from the specter of the "homosexual menace"—whose sheer length appeared to create an airtight rationale for exclusion.[19]

Despite the new policy, the 1980s were marked by increased tolerance of gays and lesbians in uniform, mirroring the greater awareness and acceptance of gay neighbors, friends, and family members in civilian society. On and around certain bases and ships, hundreds of gay service members gathered to socialize in storage rooms, cafeterias, apartments, and even "gay discos," and met shrugs and affectionate joking and only minimal anxiety from peers and superiors of all stripes.[20]

But hostile sentiment toward overt homosexuality remained the norm, and despite the presence of fairly open gay subcultures, in some ways it was scarcely less trying or dangerous to serve in the military as a gay man or woman in 1985 than it had been in 1955. Discharges, abuse, evacuations, and prison sentences continued, and in the 1980s, the military lost seventeen thousand of its troops to gay exclusion.[21] The majority of these losses were men, as the majority of uniformed personnel were male. But discharges of women were far out of proportion to their numbers, a fact that highlights the incidence of lesbian-baiting—threatening to tar as lesbian any woman who resisted or reported sexual harassment. It's one of many examples of how fear of homosexuality works to bolster the power of heterosexual men.

During the late 1980s, women represented a quarter of gay discharges even though they were only a tenth of the military population; in the Marines, they accounted for nearly a third of gay discharges while representing only 3 percent of the force. These discharge figures reflect several conditions, some of which will be addressed in later pages. But one unavoidable reality was the rising level of tension during this period between gay and straight servicewomen; some straight women complained that lesbians formed their own faction within the unit, a charge that confirmed institutional fears about homosexuality as a disruptor of order, and that also helped these women demonstrate that they themselves were not gay.[22]

Complaints, rumors, accusations, and gossip began to build. They came to the fore early in 1988, when the Naval Investigative Service (NIS) began a sweeping purge of suspected lesbians at the Parris Island Marine training center in South Carolina. Threats, naming names, informants, revealed affairs, broken promises of immunity—these were the order of the day. By the end, after interrogating half the female drill inspectors at Parris Island, the navy ousted eighteen women and incarcerated three others. One suspect committed suicide while under investigation.

It was the Parris Island purge that prompted a small group of gay and women's organizations to form the Gay and Lesbian Military Freedom Project (MFP) late in 1988. Seeking to end discrimination against gays in uniform, MFP worked to coordinate the different groups and individuals fighting to end gay exclusion in the military, to assist service members who were directly affected, to bring national attention to the ongoing witch hunts and their impact on the military, and to lobby for a change in policy. They were soon joined by other civil rights organizations, legal groups, and aides to members of Congress. The question was whether this new effort would be enough for the battle that lay ahead.[23]

Advocates of gay service were buoyed over the next few years by the perception that public opinion was turning in their favor. Because of the military's anti-gay discrimination, college students ratcheted up their protests against the presence of ROTC on campus, bringing the policy "under assault," as Professor Charles Moskos of Northwestern University complained in a piece in the *Navy Times*. Talk in the corps of military lawyers was that the gay ban was on its last legs and would imminently become a casualty of a legal culture quickly catching up to the times. Bold legal challenges from pioneering gay service members like Leonard Matlovich, Miriam Ben-Shalom, and Perry Watkins had put the government on notice that the gay ban was increasingly vulnerable to court action. Dick Cheney, then secretary of defense under George H. W. Bush, had a gay daughter and was reported to be no fan of the ban on gay troops. In 1990, Barney Frank, one of only two openly gay members of Congress, pressed Cheney privately on repealing the gay ban. Cheney acknowledged that he was not a supporter of the policy, but made clear that scrapping it was not a priority, though his words left open the possibility that he might, at some point, become a force in opposing gay exclusion: "I pilot a big ship," he told Frank. "It takes a long time to turn it around."[24]

Many thought the 1991 Gulf War would finally blow the military's sails in the right direction. Troops known to be gay were sent to this brief war, only to be discharged upon their return. In the six months following the conflict, over a thousand gays were fired, including many whose sexuality had been fully known to their superiors.[25] The hypocrisy did little to change the Pentagon's tune, but it revealed further cracks in the old story about how gays undermined the military. After all, if commanders truly believed that homosexuality was incompatible with military service, would they let gays serve during wartime, when security and cohesion mattered most? Anger at the inconsistency added to the feeling among gay rights advocates that the ban was a policy in search of a rationale, and that little more than prejudice and inertia was keeping it afloat. They resolved to keep up the fight.

They received unexpected help when *The Advocate*, a gay magazine, outed a high-ranking civilian Pentagon official, referred to as a "senior spokesperson" for the defense secretary. The official, Pete Williams, an assistant secretary of defense, did not deny the allegations. Speculation was that Cheney had to have known he was gay. Williams had a high-level security clearance and had been a major spokesman during the Gulf War. Cheney had a choice to make: If he kept the aide, he risked further undermining the rationale for the ban by holding on to someone that his own military defined as a security threat; if he fired Williams, he would lose a trusted aide and compromise the loyalty he held dear. Matters were further complicated by the leak of a major military study written by the Pentagon's Defense Personnel Security Research and Education Center (PERSEREC), located in Monterey, California. The study found that only 6 out of 130 espionage cases since 1945 were committed by gays, and concluded that being gay, on its own, was not a security risk at all. Blackmail, it said, becomes a concern when someone has an important secret, but many straight people have secrets and many gay people are out of the closet; security threats must be evaluated on a case-by-case basis.[26]

In Cheney's response, he first distinguished between civilian service and uniformed, where order, discipline, and morale were crucial, thus laying the groundwork for a continued defense of the military ban rooted in the alleged effect of a gay presence on unit cohesion. But he also admitted that gays do serve in the military, the first time a defense secretary had publicly made this obvious point. He further distanced himself from the discriminatory policy, saying he had "inherited" it from the previous administration. Ultimately Cheney decided to stick by Williams. In so doing, he helped dismantle the argument that gays in the military were a security risk, calling the notion "a bit of an old chestnut."[27]

Without the security risk rationale, it became harder to simply assert that homosexuality was "incompatible with military service." Yet many—probably most—military men continued to believe it, even if no actual argument backed it up, and even if the reason was an instinctual or moral opposition rather than a rationally derived concern for military effectiveness. Charles Moskos was one of these military men. A friend of Sam Nunn, the conservative Democrat from Georgia who had flirted with running for president in 1988, Moskos was hoping to have his friend in the White House come 1992. Unfortunately, Nunn once again disappointed supporters. After losing popularity by leading the Senate opposition to the popular Gulf War, in the spring of 1991 Nunn decided that he would not run for president. Moskos and Nunn had known each other for years, and had worked together on developing a national youth service corps, which Nunn eventually sponsored in the Senate. They also shared views on women in combat, expressing their opposition in the press when the issue came up. "It's a cultural issue in this country," said Moskos, "that women shouldn't be compelled to go into combat, shouldn't kill people."[28] Statements like these were another small indication of what drove him, and others, in their opposition to the military service of gays: not the demands of military effectiveness but a cultural and moral belief about the place of men and manhood in American society.

With Nunn out of the game, a little-known governor of a southern state named Bill Clinton began to pick up momentum as a Democratic rising star to take on George H. W. Bush. Although polls showed tiny name recognition in the summer of 1991, Clinton headed the well-organized Democratic Leadership Council, a group that Nunn had helped to found in an effort to win back centrist voters, especially in the South. It was a controversial organization, criticized by some traditional liberals as too right-wing, a "second Republican Party." But it also generated excitement among those convinced that Democrats could only take power if they moderated their image as old-fashioned tax-and-spend liberals. By the year's end, Sam Nunn had formally endorsed Clinton.[29] Moskos's influence would not be as direct as he had hoped. He would now have to catch the ear of Bill Clinton.

The evolution of Clinton's role in the eventual enshrinement of "don't ask, don't tell" was irrevocably linked with an old friend, David Mixner. The two had met at a Martha's Vineyard retreat in 1969, where a group of bright young anti-war activists had gathered to socialize and discuss tactics. Mixner remembers Clinton as irresistibly appealing and genuinely warm, while also appearing so smooth as to elicit some suspicion.[30] The men bonded quickly as they learned how much they had in common: their small-town origins, their aspirations to have an impact on a troubled world, their unprivileged backgrounds, which made them outsiders in the world of New England's liberal elite. But there were other reasons for their marginal status in the anti-war movement: Mixner was gay, and even the free-love ideology of the 1960s student movement failed to extend to overt tolerance of homosexuals; Clinton, for his part, was obligated to dwell around the edges because he harbored strong political ambitions and knew that vocal opposition to the war could derail them in a flash.

By the time these ambitions culminated in his presidential bid in the 1992 election, Mixner and Clinton had taken different paths but remained friends. Smart and politically astute, the two men both understood their distinct life courses as a kind of division of labor, which helped them avoid taking it personally when their positions clashed. As a young gay man who determined that he could not realistically hope to hold high office, Mixner, though often angered by his lot, felt freer to act on his beliefs than Clinton, whose every action since youth seemed calculated to avoid offense. The question was whether their friendship could survive a test as large as what lay ahead, and whether it could help both men to, at least in their own minds, do the right thing.

Since their anti-war days in the late 1960s, Mixner had come out of the closet, become a successful political and strategic consultant, and earned a reputation as an effective fundraiser for gay and lesbian causes. So he wasn't surprised when Bill Clinton reached out to him for help in his 1992 presidential run. The call came in early September 1991. Clinton asked for his support, a somewhat ambiguous request that suggested Mixner might help generate both gay dollars and gay votes. Mixner never doubted Clinton's genuine empathy for the plight of gays and lesbians, and appreciated his willingness to take political risks to show—and earn—support of the gay community. He had demonstrated this most publicly when, in 1980 as the young governor of a conservative, rural southern state, he boldly appeared at a reception hosted by Mixner and other openly gay supporters in Los Angeles. He eventually supported the passage of a gay rights bill in Arkansas.[31]

On the other hand, Arkansas had passed a law banning same-sex sodomy in 1977. As the state's young attorney general, Clinton was in a position to make a statement on the law, but he remained silent. This would haunt him during the 1992 campaign when some skeptics pointed out that he seemed eager to win gay dollars and votes even though his record was unproven.[32] In 1989 Clinton refused to issue a statement for National Coming Out Day as governor of Arkansas. Clinton's request gave Mixner pause. The response of a savvy organizer and fundraiser was tactical: He'd love to help, but Clinton would need to build a public record of commitment to issues of concern to the gay community. When Clinton asked what positions he would need to endorse, the first one Mixner mentioned was the right to serve in the military.

Clinton's relationship with Mixner was part of the reason why gays in the military became a priority of the new Clinton administration. But given the hurdles the new president faced in addressing this issue, many have continued to wonder just why he focused on gays in the military so early, especially considering the political costs for the White House and the alternate priorities of many gays. Indeed, for most of the gay and lesbian community, the AIDS plague was a far larger concern than military service. After a decade of passionate political work on behalf of the countless friends dying of AIDS around them, work that had galvanized a generation of radical and nonradical gays alike, it was unthinkable that the issue championed by the first president to court the gay community would be one that seemed marginal and unimportant to many, even one to which some were downright hostile. Many gay activists were appalled as they watched the debate over military service grow throughout 1992 and then burst onto the pages of mainstream newspapers in 1993—it was all about the right of gays to fight in wars that many politically active lesbians and gay men, like Mixner himself, had opposed for years while cutting their activist teeth in the anti-war movement.[33]

In reality, this issue affected millions of working-class, female, and minority citizens by institutionalizing their second-class citizenship. Still, the issue of military service seemed to many to be one that was pushed to the front of the agenda by a small group of inexperienced, wealthy, white, male Johnny-come-latelies suddenly eager to support gay issues, now that their political viability made them trendy.[34]

For the Clinton White House, its priority status also made little sense. Support for gays and lesbians was still highly controversial and by no means a sure vote-getter. While Clinton was the first "gay-positive" president, he had carefully crafted his pro-gay message to avoid offending those who saw things differently. He cast his support for gay rights as part of a more general commitment to tolerance and meritocracy, while making calculated statements designed to signal to more socially conservative voters that he understood their concerns. For instance, he said that he did not favor teaching about homosexuality in schools and would not seek to force the Boy Scouts, a private organization, to lift its ban on gay scoutmasters.[35]

But to Clinton the issue of gays in the military probably seemed like an easy win: AIDS could not be cured with a snap of the fingers, and the research that was needed cost money; private intolerance and discrimination could not be ended overnight; and same-sex marriage was not on the agenda in a serious way. But ending overt government discrimination against gays in the 1990s seemed, by comparison, almost simple, and long overdue. Harry Truman had desegregated the military over a generation earlier amid even greater hostility against blacks, and had done so, according to some, "with the stroke of a pen" in an executive order. (In truth, effective racial integration in the military took many decades.) Indeed, though deeply traditional, the military was known as an institution that was, at times, on the forefront of social change, especially when military necessity demanded transformation, as with sending known gay troops to fight in the Gulf War. And as Charles Moskos had clearly argued, the hierarchical nature of military authority meant that, with strong leadership, social change in the armed forces could be carried out in fairly straightforward and highly effective ways.

David Mixner knew all of this as he bargained with Clinton. Then, too, Mixner's focus reflected the emboldened atmosphere created by several years of hard work by groups like the Military Freedom Project. Its member organizations, particularly activist women with military ties, had helped to develop legal challenges, educate the public, and generate publicity. They also lobbied Congress to introduce legislation to lift the ban and worked with university students and administrations to mobilize opposition to the presence of ROTC programs on campuses.

In that sense, prioritizing the gay ban was no accident but rather the deliberate choice of gay rights activists, such as those who started MFP, who were all too aware of the systematic government persecution of gay troops, the daily harassment and indignity they faced at work and on the battlefield, and the powerfully destructive message of second-class citizenship that the gay exclusion rule sent to all Americans. Whenever they could, they engaged political leaders and hopefuls in discussion of the military ban as one of the major issues of concern to gay Americans.[36]

Bill Clinton seemed to think he could accomplish both what was right in his heart and what would help him politically by winning the support of gays and liberals who opposed the military's discrimination. "That's done," Clinton glibly told Mixner, referring to his pledge to lift the ban. "What else?" As they discussed the issues Clinton must endorse to earn gay support,[37] Mixner said the candidate would need to show he'd fight hard for AIDS research and demonstrate that he understood gay lives and could speak comfortably about a subject that many found distasteful to even mention. The next step would be to meet with a larger group of Mixner's friends and associates, gay Los Angeles donors who had recently become a force in political fundraising. It would be an important meeting, as most politically active gays at this point had already thrown their support to Paul Tsongas, the liberal former senator from Massachusetts who, in 1979, had sponsored the first gay rights bill in the history of the Senate.

The October meeting impressed Mixner's group. Whereas Tsongas had seemed to take their support for granted, Clinton engaged those present with his knack for listening and his trademark empathy. As he heard the stories of those who had lost so much in the AIDS epidemic and endured such pain in a country that still scorned them, his eyes misted. When Clinton finished listening and began to share how moved he was by their stories, he seemed to say all the right things. Among them was a commitment, once he was elected, to lift the military exclusion rule by executive order. When he left the group, he promised them he would not let them down.[38]

At the end of October, Clinton was asked at a talk at Harvard's John F. Kennedy School of Government what his position was on the ban on gay service members. Without missing a beat, he said he opposed it and would lift it if he became president. It was the first public indication that the candidate intended to lift the ban. In classic Clintonian fashion, the little-known presidential contender framed his position in terms of meritocracy: The nation, he said, was ill served by banning capable citizens from helping their country just because some might not like them. Clinton later said that when he was asked this question, he had never before given it any thought, a claim that conflicts with Mixner's account of discussing the topic in detail with Clinton the previous month.[39]

During the final year of George H. W. Bush's presidential term, and as Clinton's campaign slowly gained momentum, the plight of gay soldiers splashed repeatedly across the front pages. More and more service members came out publicly and challenged the exclusion policy in military hearings and federal court. Four separate rulings came down in the final six months of the campaign, lending a sense of momentum to reform, but also offering the opportunity for those against change to refine and publicize the grounds for their opposition.

That year started, really, in December 1991, when a ruling was issued in the case of Joseph Steffan, a former Annapolis midshipman booted out just weeks before his graduation, who then sued the U.S. Naval Academy for discrimination. Steffan was a battalion leader and soloist for the school's glee club. He was one of the ten highest-ranking midshipmen at the academy. He had excellent performance and conduct records, and his training had cost an estimated $110,000 in taxpayer money. When the military decided to dismiss him, it claimed that as a homosexual, he had "insufficient aptitude for military service." At his hearing, the superintendent of the academy told him they didn't feel there was anything they could do to retain him, as the regulations were clear. Although he pleaded to be allowed to graduate (he was only weeks away), he faced blank stares from the superintendent and the averted eyes of the rest of the board. After his request was denied, his battalion commander told him, "You were a great midshipman, Joe. You could easily have been the brigade commander. You can do anything you want in life."[40]

So Steffan sued. The legal arguments the government deployed to defend the ban involved the creation of an elaborate apparatus designed to foreclose on the possibility of genuine debate. It was part of an astounding legal, political, and ideological defense of gay exclusion created over many decades by opponents of gay service who were committed to ignoring the considerable evidence showing that the gay ban was unjustified and unnecessary. The effect was to build an ideological wall of opposition to gay equality, which rational arguments would repeatedly fail to penetrate.

Ironically, the legal arguments simultaneously involved claiming the mantle of rationality while carving out a space to ignore it. The challenge for the government's lawyers was to convince the courts that the military's gay ban was rational and hence unchallengeable, but the easiest way to do this was to claim that the courts must not make a judgment on the workings of the military at all. To do this, lawyers built their argument around three points, each of which was rife with assertions that were not only vague and unproven but simply false, many based on the same stereotypes and pseudoscience that had been created to prop up World War II–era discrimination.

First, they argued that the navy's gay exclusion rule was not based on prejudice but was "rationally related to a permissible end," and that legal precedent allowed discrimination if it had a "rational relationship" to a "legitimate government interest"—a legal standard known as the rational basis test. Second, they insisted that courts must defer to the military's judgment on matters relating to gay service, as no civilians could be trusted to know what was best for the armed services. Finally, they claimed that gays and lesbians were not entitled to the same kind of rigorous legal protection due African Americans or women, and that the government was therefore allowed to discriminate against them.[41]

The question in a rational basis test is this: What constitutes a sufficiently compelling rationale to permit the government to limit individual rights that would otherwise be protected? In the case of the military's gay exclusion rule, on what basis could the government argue that it must deny gays entry in order to defend the nation? In answering this question, the government simply cut and pasted the never-proven rationales from the past. Banning gays from the military, they claimed, "serves legitimate state interests which include"—and the gay menace list from the 1981 Pentagon policy was inserted here: maintaining discipline, good order, and morale; the trust of soldiers; and the integrity of the armed forces. Few would disagree that these were, indeed, legitimate aims of the military. But on what basis could the government claim that banning gays was necessary to forward these aims? "We believe," wrote their lawyers in a memorandum in the Steffan case, "that the policy requiring discharge for homosexual conduct is a rational means of achieving those legitimate interests."[42] No evidence was required.

The other prongs of their case were equally irrational. Relying on a precedent from the conservative Rehnquist Court, the government sought to insulate the military's policy from civilian challenge by insisting that the judiciary should defer to whatever the military said in these kinds of matters. Again, the Department of Justice cited earlier court decisions giving the military virtually free rein to discriminate, with no need to explain its justification to civilian society. They quoted a 1986 case that upheld the military's right to ban its troops from wearing yarmulkes: "The military need not encourage debate or tolerate protest to the extent that such tolerance is required of the civilian state. . . . Courts must give great deference to the professional judg- ment of military authorities concerning the relative importance of a particu- lar military interest" since they are "ill-equipped to determine the impact upon discipline that any particular intrusion upon military authority might have." On the question of constitutional protection, government lawyers cited a 1990 case called *High Tech Gays* in which a court ruled that homosexuals lacked certain constitutional guarantees because, unlike African Americans and women, gays and lesbians could change their sexual orientation if they wanted to. According to a doctor's testimony, the lawyers argued, "changes in sexual orientation have frequently occurred as a result of therapy."[43]

The judge in the Steffan case, an eighty-five-year-old man named Oliver Gasch, ruled in favor of the military, denying Steffan's charge of discrimina- tion. Like the decision of other courts before and since, Gasch's ruling was built on the raw assertions of military and political leaders who claimed the gay ban was rational because it was necessary to preserve order and discipline in the military. But neither Gasch nor earlier courts bothered to answer the question: How does banning gays preserve order and discipline? The most they did in addressing this question was to say that the military and Congress have deemed it necessary, and that the courts believe them. Indeed, Gasch accepted the claim uncritically in his opinion, saying, "Surely the govern- ment has a legitimate interest in good order and morale, the system of rank and command, and discipline in the Military Services."

With equal enthusiasm, he determined there was a rational basis to ban gays from service in order to promote these interests. Rejecting the claim that the ban was founded in prejudice, Judge Gasch wrote that if straight troops found gay soldiers "morally offensive," then it is not prejudice that is respon- sible for the regulations, but rather a "standard of morality." Shockingly, what he wrote next implied that he actually believed the navy could be fully purged of gays: "The quite rational assumption in the Navy is that with no one present who has a homosexual orientation, men and women alike can undress, sleep, bathe, and use the bathroom without fear or embarrassment that they are be- ing viewed as sexual objects."[44] To call this assumption rational was a remark- able window into the thinking of the entire legal, political, and cultural front aligned against gays in the military. The reality, of course, is that gays have al- ways been in the military and always will be; even if the most draconian mea- sures were taken to purge them, some portion would slip in before they even knew they were gay, and continue to escape detection for some time. But this exaggerated threat of homosexual desire imperiling the safety and virtue of an idealized military rank and file has continued to loom over the debate about gay service right up to the present.

Gasch's insistence that the ban was not grounded in prejudice is ironic, if unsurprising, coming from him. In responding to Steffan's lawyers' requests to admit government studies on gays in the military that Defense Secretary Dick Cheney was seeking to withhold, Gasch said he would only admit what relates to the plaintiff before him, and "not every homo that may be walking the face of the Earth." Steffan's lawyers sought to have Gasch removed from the case given his obvious bias, but, as Gasch was the one to decide whether he'd be removed, he not surprisingly found that his own remarks did not indicate bias: this from a man who believed that an individual "chooses his sexual orientation," and who compared gays and lesbians to illegal aliens since both groups willingly choose to break the law. Gasch also fully accepted the government's argument that gays and lesbians were in need of judicial protection of constitutional rights because they were politically powerful. After all, he said, the mayor of New York had marched with gay activists in the 1991 St. Patrick's Day Parade and thirty-two members of Congress had signed a letter concerning the Steffan case. In reality, the lawmakers had not taken a position in the case, but simply urged Dick Cheney to cooperate in providing the documents he was refusing to release. Nevertheless, these examples were enough for Gasch to conclude that homosexuals, as an earlier court put it, could "attract the attention of lawmakers" and therefore were "not without growing political power." The fact that gays were too politically powerless to end discrimination against them in the military (and in civilian society) did not seem to enter Gasch's calculus.[45]

When he finally ruled against Steffan, his reasoning for upholding the ban also introduced an entirely new rationale that neither the military nor the government's lawyers had offered in their carefully constructed arguments to defend the policy: The policy is "rational," said Gasch, since it would help to reduce the risk of AIDS spreading throughout the force. "The interest we as a nation have in a healthy military cannot be underestimated," he explained. The Pentagon, in fact, had been screening all recruits for AIDS since 1985, six years before Gasch's ruling.[46]

AS BILL CLINTON crisscrossed the country in the spring of 1992, spreading his message of equal opportunity and investment in the nation's people, the stakes were being raised in the halls of the Pentagon. In May 1992, Petty Officer Keith Meinhold, a flight systems instructor in the navy, announced his homosexuality on *ABC News*. He acknowledged no homosexual conduct, but merely said he was gay. Meinhold's superiors said he was one of the best flight instructors they knew. But the navy gave him a discharge. Alongside Meinhold came Lieutenant JG Tracy Thorne, an A-6 bombardier-navigator, who announced on *ABC News* that he, too, was gay, and would challenge the ban as discriminatory, unnecessary, and unconstitutional. The navy quickly discharged him as well. The same day as Meinhold and Thorne appeared on TV, Representative Patricia Schroeder of Colorado introduced legislation to overturn the gay ban. The bill had little chance of getting out of committee and onto the floor of Congress, but a matching bill was soon put forward in the Senate by Senator Howard Metzenbaum, who, at a press conference attended by Thorne, called the policy discriminatory and "a little bit un-American." As Thorne appeared before a military board to challenge his discharge, Air Force Staff Sergeant Tom Paniccia appeared on *ABC News* to put yet another human face to the military's policy, saying the ban was based on unsubstantiated fears, and that he, too, would take it to court.[47]

At his hearing, Tracy Thorne wanted to know why he was "not as qualified as the aviators from the Tailhook gauntlet." His reference to the sexual assault of scores of women and a few men at a 1991 aviators convention was a sharp rebuke to military hypocrisy. Sponsored by the Tailhook Association, the Las Vegas event was organized to connect naval officers and civilian contractors. But despite the presence of top military brass, including the secretary of the navy, aviators were given free rein as they groped, pinched, felt, and assaulted the private parts of women and men. Additional activities included "ball-walking," where men walked with their pants lowered to expose their testicles, streaking, mooning, and chicken fighting. At a raucous party, American sailors and Marines undressed a teenage girl whose resistance was weak from drink. The Naval Investigative Service, so adept at routing out gays from the military for their alleged threat to the sexual privacy of straight men, found nothing worthy of disciplinary action in its investigation of the Tailhook melee. This was the same NIS that had tried to blame the 1989 explosion on the USS *Iowa* on a gay suicidal sailor before retracting its charge in the face of evidence that it had been trumped up. After coming up short on Tailhook, the NIS was found to have engaged in a coverup in its investigation of wrongdoing by senior navy officials. Only a string of brave whistle-blowers and press inquiries eventually exposed the wanton disregard by straight service members of the privacy rights of others, rights they insisted were inviolable when it came to themselves.[48]

Thorne had trouble understanding why he was a greater threat to the military than the perpetrators of Tailhook. He told his board that he was a qualified aviator who simply wanted to serve his country. "But all you want to know," he lamented, "is whether I'm a homosexual." After a tearful statement to the Navy Discharge Review Board, in which he said he was "not a sexual predator with some sort of hormonal imbalance," the navy recommended an honorable discharge, even though his commander had called him "exemplary" and a "hard-charging young lieutenant" with great "professional ability to do the job." A navy attorney accused Thorne of "publicly attacking the military" by criticizing the policy on television while in uniform. He sinisterly suggested that Thorne was not to be trusted and that his commander had not realized who he really was. "You don't really know much about him at all, once he leaves the doors of Jefferson Plaza," he said ominously.[49]

As in so many cases that challenged the gay ban, the government did all it could to keep facts and evidence from coming to light. The navy board successfully argued that seventy-nine witnesses and exhibits that Thorne's legal team tried to introduce were inadmissible, including scientists who sought to testify about the significance of sexual orientation in the military. Navy lawyers also told Thorne's former roommate, Lieutenant JG Todd Suko, that if he testified, people might think he was gay, prompting charges by Thorne's lawyers that the government was intimidating a witness. Suko testified anyway, calling Thorne "one of the finest Navy officers I ever met." The navy's tactics played on a basic fear ubiquitous in military culture: that any tolerance or support of gays and lesbians would call into question the sexuality and manhood (and, to a lesser extent, the womanhood) of straight soldiers. It was circular logic once again: If the military didn't go out of its way to demonize and bar homosexuality, it would matter far less if someone was suspected of being gay; but the military deployed this fear of being gay to continue to perpetuate anti-gay sentiment and then to insist that that sentiment necessitated gay exclusion.[50]

On the heels of Thorne's case, the military announced it would discharge Margarethe Cammermeyer, a fifty-year-old grandmother who was chief of nursing for the National Guard in Washington state. On the day of her discharge, which took effect on June 11, 1992, and made her one of the highest-ranking military officers to lose her job because of the policy, she filed suit in U.S. District Court in Seattle to overturn the ban.[51]

Colonel Cammermeyer was exactly the kind of person Bill Clinton touted as a model American citizen. Her family had supported the anti-Nazi resistance in Norway during World War II, hiding guns in Cammermeyer's baby carriage and members of the resistance force in nooks in their apartment. Her father, a doctor, publicly protested the Nazification of the medical profession in Europe. Later, Margarethe joined the U.S. military to repay her new country for welcoming her family after the war. Earning a doctorate in nursing, she served in the military for twenty-seven years, won a Bronze Star for her service in a Vietnam field hospital, was adored by her commanders, who repeatedly stated they were discharging her against their will, and was in line to become the top nurse for the entire National Guard. Standing poised and upright at over six feet tall, she was literally a model of professional, selfless service to her country.

Cammermeyer had scrupulously kept her sexual orientation to herself until she was up for a security clearance that was required to be considered for the post of top nurse for the National Guard. Consistent with her belief in honesty and personal integrity, and not unaware of the perils of lying in a security clearance investigation, when asked that spring of 1989 about her sexuality, she told the truth. She recalls that moment, the one when she first uttered the reality of her experience as a human being fully loving another human being who happened to be of the same sex, as the first time she really knew who she was. At the time, she had no idea that admitting she was a lesbian would end her career, a remarkable reminder of just how little the topic was talked about in public before 1993.[52]

The security clearance investigation was also a reminder of the circular logic of gay exclusion: Gays are a security risk because their shameful secret could subject them to blackmail—so they must never tell anyone they're gay, thus forcing them to carry the secret that they are then punished for having. It's another example of how the cure is worse than the disease: Because the policy forbids gays from coming out—indeed requires them to carry a secret and insists that it is shameful—it creates the very security risk that it blames, and punishes, gays for causing.

Shortly after her discharge, Cammermeyer spoke directly with Bill Clinton. He was struck by her story, which exhibited all that was wasteful and un-American about the gay ban. He went on to praise her publicly, citing again the Pentagon's own PERSEREC study showing the ban to be unnecessary, and reiterated his promise to end it.[53]

Cammermeyer's discharge galvanized opponents of the gay ban, including many who had not been gay activists, as well as gays and lesbians who were politically engaged but had not focused on the right to military service. That a fifty-year-old grandmother who was the epitome of the dedicated, capable, selfless public servant could be rooted out of the service, her career crushed and her integrity impugned simply because of the gender of her personal partner, was too much even for many Americans who previously hadn't given the policy a second thought. Her commanding officers, as well, were among those who began to find the knee-jerk opposition to gay service increasingly irrational. They, more than anyone, lamented her discharge as a needless waste of talent and a blemish on the honor of the armed forces. The major general who informed her of her dismissal, adjutant general of the Washington National Guard, actually wept during their conversation.[54]

MEANWHILE, THE BURGEONING relationship between Bill Clinton and gay donors culminated in a West Hollywood gala event in May 1992, which raised $100,000 for his campaign. The Clinton camp had set up more meetings with gay donors and supporters with the help of David Mixner, who assured all involved that Clinton's promise was good and that lifting the ban would come with the simple "stroke of a pen." In his emotional May address, Clinton talked about uniting the country, his abhorrence of discrimination, and the need for America to use all its people's capacities. Citing the PERSEREC study showing gays were not a security risk, he vowed to act on that research and end discrimination in the armed forces. In a memorable finale that drew thunderous applause from the six hundred gays and lesbians gathered, he told the crowd that he would give up everything, including his presidential bid, if he could wave his arms and cure AIDS overnight. With help from an estimated $3 million in gay donations, as well as votes from gay men and women that totaled 4 percent of all ballots cast, Clinton won the California primary, the Democratic nomination, and, on November 3, 1992, the White House.[55]

2

Christian Soldiers: The Morality of Being Gay

T HE MILITARY ESTABLISHMENT," wrote a budding sociologist early in his career, "has means of coercion not readily available in most civilian pursuits. Owing to the aptly titled 'chain of command,' failures in policy implementation can be pinpointed." Written in the *American Journal of Sociology*, the article was an evaluation of the widely celebrated racial integration effort in the U.S. Armed Forces. "Desegregation," he explained, "was facilitated by the pervasiveness in the military of a bureaucratic ethos, with its concomitant formality and high social distance." He concluded that "whatever the internal policy decided upon, racial integration being a paramount but only one example, the military establishment is uniquely suited to realize its implementation." The author was Charles Moskos. The year was 1966.[1]

A generation later, the military's special capacity to put new personnel policies into practice had become far less clear in Moskos's eyes. If racial integration was "only one example" of the military's ability to execute controversial policies, there must have been others. But gay service, apparently, was not among them. In several articles written in 1993, he soundly rejected the comparison of racial integration to gay service, echoing the concerns of prominent black generals such as Colin Powell and Calvin Waller. "Policy makers," wrote Moskos, "should think twice before invoking a misleading analogy between the dynamics of racial integration and the proposed acceptance of overt homosexuality." Before Congress, Moskos suggested that comparing racial segregation to the ban on openly gay soldiers "trivializes the black experience. The black struggle, an enslaved people, is quite different, I think, from the gay/lesbian analogy."[2]

Moskos's principal point was that military effectiveness, not fairness for gays and lesbians or abstract principles of equality, must be the paramount concern. "The driving force behind integration of the armed forces," he wrote, "was not social improvement or racial benevolence but necessity (notably manpower shortages in World War II and the Korean War)." Racial integration had increased military efficiency (although not immediately). But "the acceptance of declared homosexuals will likely have the opposite effect, at least for a time," argued Moskos. If lawmakers did not face the "possible cost to military effectiveness" of letting gays serve openly, "we can only hope that our postmodern military never has to face the uncivil reality of war."[3]

Why did Moskos lose faith in the military? He didn't, exactly. "We could adjust to it," he said in 2000, referring to lifting the gay ban. While the professor argued in public that lifting the ban would undermine "unit cohesion," his commitment to discrimination in the military was not actually grounded in the needs or capacities of the armed forces but in his view of morality, of what's right and what's wrong. Discussions and interviews with him are peppered with talk of "universal law" and "natural law" and the "moral right" that he believed straight people have not to share close quarters with people who might fancy them. "I'm just against that," he said of letting gays serve openly. "I should not be forced to shower with a woman. I shouldn't be forced to shower with an open gay. If you choose to, that's your business."[4]

Despite Sam Nunn's disappearance from the national scene after the 1992 election, Moskos remained influential in military circles. His position on the cultural imperative of discrimination continued to find its way to key opinion leaders and policy makers. Indeed, his impressive academic credentials gave them cover to argue that the United States must not move too quickly toward equality. Moskos shared with top military brass a traditional worldview that placed men, and a form of rugged masculinity, in positions of social power. This was the foundation of his belief that it was a "cultural issue" that women "shouldn't kill people."[5]

For Moskos, the ban on openly gay soldiers was grounded in a similar cultural concern to the one raised by women in combat. Invoking the analogy of sex integration, he asserted that the gay ban was necessary to protect "modesty rights for straights." He asked, "What if you put three heterosexual men living in a unit of say, 100 women, and say, by the way, if you misbehave we're going to do something, would somebody want that or not?"[6] For Moskos, this privacy right appears to have been a sincere expression of his deeply held beliefs, a moral system he held so dear that he'd say almost anything to find a rationale for it.

Americans have long been reluctant to fully embrace the rights of gays and lesbians. As a sociologist, Charles Moskos felt that, in opposing an end to the military's gay ban, he was simply articulating the truth of national sentiment and linking it to concerns about what impact a radical change in military culture could have on the armed forces. But Moskos's academic and military credentials gave cover to a diverse group of opponents to gay military service, each of whom had their own reasons for their position. None of them, in the end, relied on empirical evidence or sound logic. All of them, including Moskos's own reasons for defending the ban, were rooted in different varieties of moral beliefs about the place of homosexuality in American life.

Looking back, we can see that "don't ask, don't tell" was the result of three different forces operating together and reinforcing one another—and all three rested on a belief that homosexuality was morally objectionable. The first was the conflicted feelings of the American public and, even more so, the military population. However committed both were on paper to tolerance and equality, many, if not most, were ultimately sympathetic to the traditionalist worldview that looked suspiciously upon homosexuality and resisted its full integration into mainstream society. The second was the powerful empire of conservative Christian groups that made maintaining the gay ban into their cause célèbre. The extraordinary alliance of the religious right laid the elaborate groundwork for the successful campaign that convinced America that it would let gays serve their country at considerable peril. And the third source was the personal opposition to gay service of academic, political, and military leaders such as Charles Moskos, Sam Nunn, and Colin Powell. The first two reasons are discussed here, and the third in subsequent chapters.

IN THE ABSTRACT Americans favored concepts like tolerance, equality, freedom, fairness, and civil rights. But polls showed sharp limitations on how far they would go in translating such abstractions into support for real rights. In 1992, according to Gallup, only 48 percent of Americans thought homosexual relations should be legal, and only 38 percent thought homosexuality should be considered an "acceptable alternative lifestyle." When it came to gay service, Americans were fickle and impressionable. In August of that year, as Margarethe Cammermeyer tried to figure out what to do next with her life, 59 percent of Americans had supported letting gays serve, just before the national debate heated up. Three months later, that figure had dropped to 48 percent, the first time since 1977 that support to end the ban actually fell. In December 1992, 46 percent favored lifting the ban. By mid-January 1993, only 42 percent wanted to let gays serve, and by late January, following some of the most heated rhetoric about the gay troops issue, only 35 percent of Americans supported Clinton's effort to lift the ban. Within the military itself, opinion was more consistent: solid majorities opposed letting gays serve, and stated that they "feel uncomfortable in the presence of homosexuals."[7]

Why did so many Americans oppose letting gays serve in the U.S. military? What were they against? What were they afraid of? And what were they hoping for or trying to accomplish? Beneath the instinctive hostility to gay soldiers, what was the real source of opposition to officially welcoming gay and lesbian Americans into the armed forces?

The short answer is, in a word, morality. Millions of Americans found (and still find) homosexuality either viscerally repugnant or at least vaguely wrong. It logically follows that if something is bad, it should not be inflicted on an eminent American institution, particularly one that relies on discipline and a heightened sense of its own virtue as an antidote to the unavoidable fact that it's ultimately about killing people. But part of the power of morality is the deep tug it has on our hearts; one's belief about right and wrong is often not a rational position, but a gut instinct. And if homosexuality were to be approved by the U.S. defense forces—a bastion of conservative values, including traditional notions of masculinity—it might force the country to confront its deep discomfort with same-sex intimacy and sexuality. That discomfort could remain underground as long as no one had to talk about it; this is one reason why "don't ask, don't tell," despite its bizarre and convoluted requirements, sounded like the natural solution.

Why were so many uncomfortable with homosexuality? The reasons can be numerous: they ranged from the "ick" factor of contemplating sexual intimacy that is unfamiliar and culturally reviled to the penetration anxiety of straight males; from the heterosexual fear of discovering one's own complex desires to a fierce attachment to traditional norms of gender and sexuality, and to the social hierarchy it helped preserve. The ensuing taboo against homosexuality was expressed, for religious Americans, in doctrinal narratives that condemned homosexual desire and practice as sinful and socially destructive. Often, this understanding of the gay life as sin produced feelings of anger and hostility rather than quiet judgment or reasoned questioning. Few anti-gay activists, for instance, stopped to challenge the selective use of religious doctrine. After all, most religions condemned divorce far more squarely than homosexuality, yet marital breakdown, while lamented by the religious right, yielded nothing like the obsessive machinery of hate and damnation faced by gays and lesbians, perhaps because too many conservative Christians had been unable to avoid divorce in their own lives. For others, whether grounded in religious faith or not, anti-gay sentiment reflected, and perpetuated, a need to humiliate a vulnerable group, to capitalize politically or financially on such

humiliation or to protect, through clinging to tradition, the power and prestige of those who had grown comfortable with their privilege. Some simply
associated homosexuality with sex and thus believed that it was an impolite
subject of conversation. For still others, stereotypes of gay promiscuity meant
that homosexuality represented pleasure unbounded by responsibility or the
giving of life, ungovernable hedonism whose powerful hunger for pleasure
seemed to threaten either people's sense of self-control or their faith in the ability of society to control its members' behavior.

No one is exempt from uncomfortable feelings, and most of us at one time
or another deal with that discomfort by pushing its source out of our minds:
don't confront, don't consider, don't discuss. But in 1992, as Bill Clinton began
his momentous, if troubled, presidency, it became far more difficult to avoid
the discussion of gays in the military. And though gay advocacy groups helped
to push the issue onto the table, it was the organizational skills, and ferocity,
of the religious right that turned an issue that most Americans hadn't thought
all that much about into one that—according to many—heralded the demise
of America itself. What made homosexuality in the military a unique battleground in the 1990s was the looming train wreck of vocal gay rights advocates
facing off against an even more vocal, and stunningly effective, coalition of
religious conservatives convinced that their world—and the next one—hung
in the balance.

AS TALK OF lifting the military's gay ban picked up in the early 1990s, the religious right emerged as a potent force in the dialogue. Sometimes called the
New Christian Right, this vast missionary empire was built up in the 1970s by
evangelical Christian leaders such as Jerry Falwell, Pat Robertson, and James
Dobson who had ties to segregationist, anti-Semitic, and anti-feminist cru-
sades from earlier in the century. Encompassing a range of socially conservative religious groups, from traditional Catholics to fundamentalist Protestants,
in the 1980s the religious right turned its attention to politics, with a particular
focus on blocking abortion rights. Amassing huge fortunes from believers,
books, church dues, and television shows, these groups shared mailing lists,
held political strategy sessions, referred to one another in their broadcasts and
mailings, and ultimately spread their message of God, family, and country to
tens of millions of American homes.

Their focus on a strong military was a natural fit. The religious right and
the military establishment both shared a commitment to conservative values
like a strong, hierarchical social order and traditional notions of virtue and
honor. They also believed in the nation's destiny as a godly mission to spread

freedom to the world. As a result, the military drew legions of religious conservatives to its ranks, thus positioning them to play an influential role in the debate over gay military service. Often the religious right and the military establishment were one and the same.

It was the powerful leaders of the New Christian Right who had the greatest hand in mobilizing their flocks to oppose Clinton's effort to lift the gay ban. First, there was Jerry Falwell. In 1979, the Baptist televangelist with a megachurch in Virginia and his own Christian university founded the Moral Majority, designed largely to mobilize Christian voters to support conservative political candidates. Falwell's radio and television broadcast, *Old-Time Gospel Hour,* grew into a formidable force by the end of the 1970s, reaching millions of listeners and raising tens of millions of dollars. When Ronald Reagan assured the National Association of Religious Broadcasters that he opposed the separation of church and state, he won millions of evangelical hearts and enough votes to take the White House, a feat that was credited in part to Falwell's efforts.[8] Falwell would later blame the terrorist attacks of 9/11 on feminists, abortionists, and homosexuals. His operation was just one part of an empire of conservative Christian venues for the preaching of anti-gay sentiment that rallied together in 1993.

There was also Pat Robertson, host of the Christian Broadcasting Network's *700 Club,* the powerhouse fundraising broadcast in which Robertson linked natural disasters to homosexuals and Jewish bankers to government subversion plots. When Robertson entered politics directly, running against George Bush for the 1988 Republican nomination, he announced that his campaign would focus on battling abortion and homosexuality. That a religious leader fond of speaking in tongues could beat Bush, the future president, in the Iowa caucus spoke volumes about the influence of evangelical Christianity in American politics by that time. While Robertson's political fortunes were limited, his material ones grew to an estimated $200 million on the success of his particular blend of fundraising and preaching about the gay-liberal-feminist menace. After his unsuccessful bid for the White House, Robertson parlayed his contacts to found the Christian Coalition, one of the most powerful grassroots political organizations in the nation, which by the early 1990s had a virtual lock on the Republican political agenda.[9]

Yet even the Christian Coalition was dwarfed by the Christian powerhouse, Focus on the Family, founded by Dr. James Dobson. He became a household name in 2005 after darkly suggesting that the cartoon character SpongeBob SquarePants was gay and a tool of homosexual activists. A child psychologist, Dobson started his ministry in 1977, and it grew into a social and political behemoth, with millions of names on its mailing list. By some accounts, his radio broadcasts reach 220 million people every day on two thousand stations in 160 countries, and the group, with an annual budget of $150 million, fields ten thousand inquiries a day from believers seeking Dobson's wisdom. (Focus on the Family gets so much mail that it has its own zip code.) Throughout the 1980s and 1990s, every Republican presidential candidate who wanted a chance at winning had to visit with James Dobson.[10]

In 1979, recognizing his burgeoning power, Dobson finagled an invitation to the White House by asking his radio listeners to recommend him for a presidential conference on the family. Eighty thousand calls later, he was on the list and on his way to starting the political arm of his ministry, the Family Research Council (FRC). In 1988, Dobson tapped Gary Bauer, a Reagan policy adviser and sometime "family values" presidential candidate, to head FRC. The current president of FRC, Tony Perkins, is a graduate of Falwell's Liberty University. In 1996, he was tied to the Ku Klux Klan after he managed a Senate campaign that struck a deal to share the mailing list of the Klan's former grand wizard, David Duke. Although Perkins denied any wrongdoing, the campaign was fined by the Federal Election Commission for trying to conceal the paper trail.[11]

Clinton's election to the White House in November 1992, alongside the bubbling gay troops issue, proved an inspiring combination for social conservatives. Exactly one week after Clinton's victory at the polls, a federal judge in San Francisco ordered the navy to reinstate Keith Meinhold after a homosexual discharge under the existing ban on gays in the military. The next day, November 11, 1992—Veterans Day—reporters asked Clinton to react to the decision, and he said he agreed with it. He reiterated his commitment to ending the ban and said he planned to "consult with military leaders about it."

His announcement made for a powerful rallying and fundraising tool for social and religious conservatives who felt their way of life was under siege by a liberal, secular worldview that, with Clinton's election, seemed to be gaining sinister momentum. The religious right viewed Clinton as a threat to everything they held dear: a strong military, a government sympathetic to religion in public life, the rights of the unborn, and traditional values that placed the heterosexual male at the top of the social hierarchy. And they regarded ending the ban as akin to official approval of homosexuality in the eyes of the state, a potentially irreversible move on America's path toward becoming a godless nation.[12]

But as much as evangelicals felt the need to oppose the growing acceptance of homosexuality in American culture, they were also aware of an upside to the trend: Christ's reign on Earth would be precipitated, they believed, by a calamitous period of tribulation, when the faithful would be severely tested by the evils around them. According to their interpretation of the Bible, the precipitating events would include death, suffering, and destruction, perhaps through war. But in the absence of a true war, a culture war might do the trick. Thus, fundamentalists had an incentive to exaggerate—and even create—the harms that homosexuality could birth. While the situation was dire, it was also welcomed as an opportunity by leaders of the right to consolidate their own resources and power, and to gain national attention, political strength, and money.

Christian conservatives grasped these opportunities at once. "Clinton has done us a great favor," said Randall Terry, founder of the anti-abortion group Operation Rescue, in January 1993, just weeks after the new president had taken office. "This is going to help us mobilize people to take action for the next four years." Terry, who called his opposition work "the resistance," said his group was "avalanching Congress with phone calls and letters" in a "rebellion against President Clinton because sodomy is against God's law, just like baby-killing is against God's law." In fact, the matter of homosexuality "galvanizes our public more than right-to-life," said the Reverend Louis Sheldon of the Traditional Values Coalition, because the injunction against homosexuality was even more clear-cut in the Bible than that against abortion.[13]

The campaign orchestrated by the religious right to mobilize social conservatives against gay service was extraordinary, and is widely credited with helping turn public and political opinion against Clinton's proposal to lift the ban. It helped take a public that was divided and somewhat apathetic about the issue and rally among ordinary people a hefty opposition to ending the long-standing ban on gay service. Within weeks of Clinton's election, church leaders began to deploy their full arsenal: They approached millions of foot soldiers with open wallets, reaching into communities from the southern village chapel to the midwestern megachurch, and using their massive communications network spanning television, radio, and eventually the Internet. By the 1990s, the religious right was one of the most powerful political interest groups in the nation, and part of the reason was the proven ability of its leaders to mobilize tens of thousands of people to action literally within moments of airing a plea on television. Even before Clinton's inauguration in January 1993, Falwell began a "dial-a-lobby" operation, using his *Old-Time Gospel Hour* program to generate 24,000 signatures on a petition against gay service in a matter of hours. As a result, the week after the inauguration, Congress was besieged with 434,000 phone calls in a single day, overwhelmingly against letting gays serve. The number of calls was more than five times the daily average of 80,000.[14]

Unlike previous culture war battles that had generated large but spontaneous public involvement, the gay ban precipitated the most deftly organized, effective mobilization of religious conservatives. Groups like the Family Research Council, Focus on the Family, Concerned Women for America, the Christian Coalition, and the Traditional Values Coalition urged their constituents to jam phone lines at the White House, Congress, and the Pentagon. Their radio programs spent hours whipping up anger and resistance among their millions of daily listeners. Reverend Sheldon of the Traditional Values Coalition, which had twenty-five thousand member churches, crowed, "We're the ones that shut down the phone lines at the Capitol." His phone drive was so effective that when Sheldon called, he couldn't get through, and had to trudge to Congress in person to lobby his friends in government. These friends were considerable. He was able to assemble a press conference on Capitol Hill with a string of lawmakers and retired military officers, which he then used in his "action alert" asking church members to keep calling, keep lobbying, and keep giving money to the sacred cause of banning gays from the military. Indeed, the issue of gay service soon overtook abortion as a fundraising tool for the religious right. Oliver North, who was indicted on sixteen felony counts for his role in the Iran-contra weapon and drug smuggling scandal (his three convictions were overturned on appeal), made a direct-mail plea to hundreds of thousands of social conservatives for "a special contribution of $15 or $22 right away" to support his Freedom Alliance lobbying campaign against gay service. James Kennedy's Florida-based Christian ministry sent appeals to his substantial following with an urgent message: "Dear Friend in Christ: July 15, 1993," said the letter, referring to the deadline Clinton eventually set to lift the ban, "may well be a day of moral infamy in the United States—unless you and I and other caring Christians across this country do something to stop it." Kennedy exhorted his clan to send "the most generous gift you can" to help fund the battle against Clinton's godless ambitions. By the end of 1993, the Christian Coalition had raised its budget and membership by 20 percent.[15]

The issue of gay service was the perfect battle for the Christian right, not only because social conservatives and military officers shared ideological beliefs, but because they shared members. Indeed, this was a war that, in many ways, was taking place in the conservatives' own backyard. The influence of the religious right on many aspects of American culture was vast and growing in the 1980s and 1990s. But perhaps nowhere was it as strong as in the armed forces. Since early in the cold war, evangelicals had made systematic inroads into military culture, organizing methodically to increase their numbers and sway in the armed forces. In the 1960s, their efforts began to yield fruit, as military leaders, many of whom were themselves conservative Christians, liaised with evangelical groups to increase the number of chaplains representing evangelical denominations. By the beginning of the Reagan era, the New Christian Right was firmly entrenched in the halls of political power, as the president consulted with their leaders to help sell the country on his nuclear buildup. Evangelicals like Falwell and Robertson hoped that Reagan's vision of the "evil empire" could revive the moral and military strength of the nation. They became willing warriors in an effort to shape a foreign policy that would save the United States through the twin pillars of military might and cultural superiority.[16]

Christian conservatives viewed their opposition to homosexuality in the armed forces as part of a larger effort to preserve and expand the Christian character of the military and the nation. While the coordination of opposition to gay service among military officials and Christian conservatives began modestly, it would grow into a marvelously choreographed and stunningly successful affair. Yet sometimes, little coordination was needed: Many of the most vocal and influential military leaders were evangelicals themselves, who came to the services with an unyielding belief in the sinful nature of homosexuality and who violently opposed its acceptance on religious grounds. The existence of such connectors meant that outfits like FRC were not just preaching to the choir. The venomous misinformation they printed found its way into the center of the debate, as senior military officials took up their call to action, secured slots to testify before Congress, and entered their publications into the *Congressional Record*.

Under Gary Bauer, the Family Research Council played a lead role in the battle against gay service. Beginning in 1992, it fixated on the issue and disseminated position papers that cast gay rights as a threat to the family. The idea was to mobilize their constituency to fight reform while simultaneously convincing the rest of the country that, whatever they believed about God and morality, gays had no place in the nation's armed forces. This plan involved rallying around the argument that straights had the right not to associate with known gays, that forcing the acceptance of gays in the military meant victimizing the nation's upright and moral sons and daughters, and that the military would be dangerously weakened by lifting the ban. In "How Lifting the Military Homosexual Ban May Affect Families," Robert Knight, director of "cultural studies" at FRC, argued that condoning "open homosexuality" would threaten "a particularly vulnerable group within the military: military families." Convinced that the fight for access to military service was nothing more than a tool of homosexual extremists bent on foisting their sinful ways on an innocent society of families and churchgoers, Knight painted a picture of a military—and a society—brought to its knees by militant homosexuals. Gays were sure to further press for equal access to base housing "without regard for the impact that their open embrace of homosexuality might have on children," and so families, Knight warned, had cause for concern. Military bases already had waiting lists for family housing, "so mothers and fathers with children now face additional competition from homosexual couples." In short, lifting the ban "would create a less wholesome environment for military families."[17]

Knight listed a host of other perilous consequences to gay military service, including the possibility that military base magazine suppliers would be pressured to carry homosexual pornography. Gay nudie magazines would then be placed on shelves beside *Penthouse* and *Hustler,* staples of military reading since they first burst onto the American cultural scene. He likened gay people who "indulge in homosexual behavior" to alcoholics, saying neither should be placed in a "specially protected category of civil rights." The analogy fanned his indignation at comparisons between race and sexual orientation, since it was impossible to "change your skin color, but you can choose to act or not on your inclinations. Ask any recovered alcoholic—or former homosexual." Indeed Knight, and much of the Christian conservative empire, held the belief that there was actually no such thing as a homosexual; instead, we were all heterosexuals, and unfortunately some of us had to battle against evil impulses, ranging from alcoholism to theft to adultery to sodomy. "Sexual orientation can be changed," he concluded. How could society, and the military in particular, give its endorsement or protection to people who proudly advertised their habitual choice to commit sin?[18]

But the clearest danger to the military and their defenseless families was the threat of gay disease. Citing alarming statistics about the number of HIV cases that were caused by homosexual behavior, Knight wrote that lifting the ban "would add to the burden on medical facilities in disproportionate numbers." Linking gays to a "higher incidence of sexually transmitted diseases," he claimed they would "compete disproportionately for services" in the military's medical system. "Families," he stated incredulously, "may find one of their children, suffering from chicken pox, standing in waiting room lines behind homosexuals suffering from diseases they incurred during homosexual activity."[19]

Knight's appeal to the country's base fears—of an army of infectious homosexuals waiting to physically and morally taint the innocent, wholesome institutions of American life—became the modus operandi of the religious right. Dozens of Christian organizations, whose influence reached literally hundreds of millions of people worldwide, combined efforts to promote their dark vision. Knight's argument, while morally and religiously based, was linked to a social and ultimately political claim: that giving state approval to homosexuality would undermine the cultural norms that nudged people to form heterosexual families, whose consequent decline would pull down American society. "Undermining military families by placing homosexual behavior on a par with marital fidelity," he concluded, "would provide devastating evidence that our government no longer recognizes the importance of strong families in cultivating the virtues that enable us to be a free, self-governing people."[20]

Perhaps no one was more instrumental in consolidating evangelical and military opposition to gay service than Lieutenant Colonel Robert Lee Maginnis, who would soon become Knight's colleague at FRC. In 1990, Maginnis left a combat tour in Alaska to take a position with the U.S. Army Inspector General, where he investigated allegations of officer improprieties. The experience gave him firsthand lessons in the ethical challenges faced by military officers. Maginnis was something of an essayist, arguing to anyone who would listen about the dangers of letting women into combat positions in the military. In 1992, he began researching a series of articles to share with military leaders about the similar perils of letting gays serve in the military. He went to gay hotspots, including the Washington, D.C., gay bookstore Lambda Rising, and trolled through the pages of *The Advocate* to collect information to use against the movement to lift the ban.[21]

Maginnis worked tirelessly to ensure that the armed forces were not tainted by homosexuality. As the military weighed how to respond to the prospect of openly gay troops, each service branch appointed a study group to examine the issue and report to senior officials. These service task forces would eventually report to a Pentagon working group that would produce a direct recommendation for the secretary of defense. Some of the service groups, like the air force group, accepted as a fait accompli that gays would be allowed to serve, since that was what the president ultimately instructed in January 1993, before backing away from the order that summer. The task for these military study groups, then, was to advise how, not whether, to make the change. But the army group set about trying to resist the order altogether, an effort that some critics regarded as insubordination. The group's working papers, which were leaked to the press, warned that lifting the ban would "force the military to experiment with profound cultural and life-style changes not accepted by the majority of Americans," and that it could so hurt recruitment that "the country may be forced to consider abandoning the all-volunteer force and returning to conscription."[22]

The force behind the army study group was, predictably, the religious right. According to Maginnis, all five of the group's members were religious conservatives, himself included. Recognizing, along with other leaders of the religious right, that biblical citations might not be enough to win the battle of hearts and minds, Maginnis decided to focus on secular research for what he called "political reasons." He knew there was widespread support for the gay ban in military circles, but he also suspected that the "moral repugnancy" of many military personnel toward homosexuality could not be the sole basis of their argument.[23] Teaming up with the Family Research Council while still an active-duty officer, he coauthored a policy paper that appeared in FRC's newsletter, and eventually made its way to both the Pentagon and the Congress.

Yet the bulk of Maginnis's anti-gay venom was contained in another paper he wrote around the same time, which was also entered into the *Congressional Record*. "The Homosexual Subculture" was a six-part profile of a typical homosexual, meant to combat "ignorance about homosexual practices" and "educate the Congress and the American people" so they would be more likely to support gay exclusion. Maginnis's strategy, now time-tested by the religious right, was to make quack statistics look credible by piling up footnotes, most of which cited the same small group of discredited anti-gay researchers. The fact that more credible scholars and journalists eventually published exposés of the fake evidence rarely made its way to the countless Americans who gobbled up the initial "studies" and leaned on them to confirm their own worldview.[24]

"The Homosexual Subculture" cast the gay community as permanent rebels who scoffed at authority and could never conform to society. Gays use their "raw political power" to make a string of demands including "laws to prohibit discrimination," pro-gay sex education, the "decriminalization of private sex acts between consenting 'persons,'" and acceptance of military service. This agenda, wrote Maginnis, amounted to a "homosexual assault." In his counterassault, he launched into a tirade about the homosexual's destructive sexual and health practices. His obsessive attention to detail makes Ken Starr's later report on Bill Clinton's affair with Monica Lewinsky look like Romantic poetry. According to Maginnis, studies showed that gay people "typically live a dangerously promiscuous lifestyle": 43 percent had over five hundred sexual partners and 28 percent had over a thousand. "Some of their favorite places are 'gay' bars, 'gay' theaters and bathhouses." The quotations around "gay" seemed to imply that the whole torrid affair was anything but happy and festive.[25]

Maginnis described in graphic detail what the typical homosexual alleg-edly did in bathhouses, right down to the clothes-checking procedures. Ac-cording to "medical literature," these environments were "contaminated with fecal droppings because many homosexuals can't control themselves due to a condition called 'gay bowel syndrome.' They've exhausted their anal sphincter muscles by repeated (93 percent) acts of sodomy, thus becoming incontinent." Many gays, wrote Maginnis, enjoyed fisting, which he also described in min-ute detail, as well as rimming, fellatio, scat, and golden showers. Their frequent sadomasochistic practices included the use of "Nazi like insignia and the use of whips" and gays "often model their actions after the Nazi party."[26]

Maginnis insisted that these practices were "commonplace" and were documented in "authoritative scientific journals." In other sections of the six-part profile, Maginnis explained the gay penchant for reproducing them-selves through recruitment, including the common seduction of vulnerable teens "still developing their sexual identity." Gays were eighteen times more likely to have sex with minors, often when teachers molested their students. Three-quarters of gays had sex with underage boys. In all this, protested Maginnis, the national media was maddeningly complicit, casting homosex-ual lifestyles as simply "different," rather than "wrong." He lamented that talk shows even treated gays and lesbians as "normal people."[27]

Finally, Maginnis indicted the mental health of gays and lesbians. "Homo-sexuals are a very unstable group," he wrote, whose lifestyle "breeds enormous amounts of guilt" over their promiscuity, dishonesty, and failed relationships. "They are restless in their contacts, lonely, jealous, and neurotic depressive," concluded the amateur psychiatrist. "As a category of people, homosexuals have a greater indiscipline problem than heterosexuals," he stated, citing as evidence for this "indiscipline"—for reasons that are unclear—a greater likeli-hood of being murdered.[28]

Maginnis's research was chock full of footnotes, an effort to present his preconceived notions of homosexual danger and immorality as sound social science. But his "research" was profoundly dishonest. It relied on the un-founded assertions of extremists in both the pro- and anti-gay camps. These "sources" ran the gamut from gay radicals writing intentionally provocative treatises like "Rimming as Revolutionary Act" to discredited homophobic re-searchers who made grandiose conclusions based on miniscule, skewed, and uncontrolled sample pools. In other words, Maginnis relied on research prac-tices that even eighth-grade science students learn never, ever to engage in.

The most notorious of these sources was Paul Cameron, who in 1983 had been expelled from the American Psychological Association; condemned by the American Sociological Association for ethical violations, including misrepresenting social science research; and slammed by courts for being unprofessional in previous testimony. And it's no wonder. One of Cameron's studies yielded conclusions about homosexuals based exclusively on interviews with serial killers. Another concluded that lesbians were inclined to purposely infect their partners with sexually transmitted diseases. It was based on a sample of seven. Cameron famously declared that gay men in the United States would live to an average age of forty-three. This theory was derived from perusing random obituaries of gay neighborhood newspapers as the AIDS epidemic peaked. These obituary pages were hardly a representative sampling of all deaths of gay American men.[29]

Cameron was the chief source for Maginnis's anti-gay "statistics." Another source was Judith Reisman of the Institute for Media Education. Reisman studied classified ads in *The Advocate* and compared them to mainstream and ethnic magazines, concluding that only gays sought to entrap underage boys, engage in prostitution, and solicit violence. Arguing preposterously that the *Advocate* classified ads reflected "prevailing" gay norms, she claimed that "the evidence reveals a repeated pattern from 1972 to 1991 of man-boy sex and 'boy lovers' as a prevailing cultural homosexual/*Advocate* value." Her work was quoted by Concerned Women for America (with a "warning" saying its report made "occasional reference to repulsive homosexual sex acts" that were "necessary to accurately convey the nature of 'gay' behavior-conduct"), as well as the Family Research Council and numerous other conservative Christian organizations. Eventually they also found their way onto the congressional floor, when allied officers or lawmakers entered them into the record.[30]

Maginnis's strategy was to paint gays and lesbians as, by definition, selfish and indulgent, unable to be virtuous participants in American society, and thus the perfect foil to his military culture of selfless service. "National security demands that individual notions and desires always be subordinate to military readiness and cohesion," he insisted. American society, he believed, was becoming increasingly weak, selfish, and centered around individual desire, and he saw the military as a bastion of traditional values that was the last hope for keeping such indulgent individualism at bay. "Soldiers," insisted Maginnis, "are expected to adhere to unforgiving organizational values and behaviors. Instead of embracing military culture, 200 years of military experience has found that homosexuals want to subject the military's best interests to their lifestyle choices. That's why the military has long held to the principal statement that 'Homosexuality is incompatible with military service.'" For Maginnis, the military is "not a job, but a way of life," marked by "little individuality" and great "self sacrifice." But this way of life was not for everyone. The "rough-and-tumble, predominantly male military," Maginnis wrote, "is neither for shrinking violets nor for homosexuals." On television he repeated that the military "is about selfless service," which is why "homosexuality and the military are incompatible." The implication is that homosexuals cannot engage in selfless service, but can only indulge in their own desires. And ultimately, this selfishness would have disastrous consequences. If the United States continued to lose the selfless service ethic that was the foundation of military service and thus the defense of the nation, the result would be "a chain reaction that, ultimately, threatens our national security." Thus, for Maginnis, "Our moral strength is directly related to our combat strength."[31]

What Maginnis seemed to care most about was safeguarding the symbolic space of military culture as a bastion of traditional male values. The real reason he opposed gays in the military was because it allowed traditionalists to carve out a fantasy realm of undisturbed masculinity, a realm in which idealized male virtues could be preserved and could exert their strengthening influence on the wider culture. As he said in 2002, quoting James Dobson of Focus on the Family, "Nations that are populated largely by immature, immoral, weak-willed, cowardly, and self-indulgent men cannot and will not long endure." Somehow, a gay-free military was essential to stop this dangerous turn in American culture. Never mind the abundant instances of straight male vices—from the abuses at Abu Ghraib and Guantánamo to waterboarding, Tailhook, and legacies of prostitution and drug abuse that have long characterized the real military. If Maginnis actually cared about the military's strength and virtue, he would have howled when each of these incidents occurred. Instead, he fixated on the gay menace. And in homosexuality, the religious right found a perfect bogeyman against which to cast themselves as normal and virtuous—the only Americans capable of defending the nation against threats both moral and military.

In addition to Maginnis, the army study group included Major Melissa Wells-Petry, a fellow evangelist and active-duty lawyer in the U.S. Judge Advocate General's Corps (JAG) who worked closely with Maginnis to disseminate anti-gay literature under the guise of legitimate social science. With Wells-Petry on board, the study group had easy access to military legal records and convinced the JAG office to conduct an army study of courts-martial for homosexual misconduct. The study concluded that the sex crime rate of gay service members was higher than the army's overall crime rate. The study was so biased—it never even bothered to look at rates of heterosexual misconduct, giving it no basis to compare sex crimes of gays and straights—that the army launched an investigation into the release of the data, and in April 1993 Wells-Petry was hauled into the office of the secretary of defense for a scolding. But it didn't stop Wells-Petry from taking time out of her busy work schedule to criss-cross the country opposing gay service—all as part of a publicity campaign to sell her book *Exclusion: Homosexuals and the Right to Serve*, which came out that same year.[32]

In the book, which was sent around to as many members of Congress and the military leadership as would accept their free copy, Wells-Petry argued that it was not anti-gay to discriminate against gay people, any more than it was "anti-overweight people" to bar those who were too heavy for military service. For Wells-Petry, it was simply a question of who could do the job.[33] Never mind that in the case of gays and lesbians, no serious critic had claimed they couldn't do the job. Rather, gays were banned because straights allegedly could not do the job when gays were present.

For Wells-Petry, it was also proper to ban gays because other countries where service members might be stationed, such as Saudi Arabia, were intolerant of homosexuality. Some even executed people simply for being gay (and many would never allow someone like Wells-Petry—a woman—to don a military uniform). Such deference to medieval attitudes toward sexual freedom, she maintained, is not "countenancing prejudice. It is using common sense to compose a fighting force that can operate anywhere in the world without provoking unnecessary social controversy or opposition."[34] It was a remark that looks painfully hollow and naïve in the years after the U.S. invasion of Iraq, which many observers regard as a far more serious instance of American service members "provoking unnecessary social controversy" in a foreign nation.

Despite claims that her opposition to gay service was rooted in military necessity and genuine meritocracy rather than prejudice, *Exclusion* was full of moral condemnations against gays, and even defenses for why such animus was appropriate. Resorting to all the tired stereotypes that her evangelical colleagues deployed, Wells-Petry cited studies saying gays were promiscuous (one found that the mean number of lifetime sexual partners among gay men was 1,422, and some had up to 7,000), raised health-care costs because of risky behavior that caused illness, and were unduly privileged and therefore did not need special "protection"—never mind that lifting the ban would not create special protection, but merely end unequal treatment. But Wells-Petry was also unabashed in citing a moral basis for the ban. "The homosexual exclusion policy has a moral dimension," she wrote. "It is important to recognize that morality is not the law's poor cousin," but rather a legitimate foundation for law and national policy. She even cited the notorious 1986 *Bowers v. Hardwick* case, in which the Supreme Court upheld laws banning sodomy. That decision had said the law is "constantly based on notions of morality," and rightly so—if laws representing "moral choices" were unconstitutional, said the Court, "the courts will be very busy indeed." *Bowers* was reversed in 2003, when Sandra Day O'Connor wrote that imposing "moral disapproval of a group cannot be a legitimate governmental interest" under the Constitution and that any law rooted in moral opposition "raises the inevitable inference that the disadvantage imposed is born of animosity toward the class of persons affected." Indeed, wrote O'Connor, "We have never held that moral disapproval, without any other asserted state interest, is a sufficient rationale under the Equal Protection Clause to justify a law that discriminates among groups of persons."[35]

Though Wells-Petry's legal manifesto looked more thoughtful and professional than some of the sloppier screeds of her peers, nowhere did it make the case for why the damning (and intellectually dishonest) statistics she cited about homosexuals meant they must stay out of the military. In fact, her position was that defending the gay ban did not require empirical evidence, proof, or research, so long as it jibed with the commonsense assumptions of enough people. "Based on the reasonableness of . . . assumptions, presumptions, and commonsense propositions—though not proof proper," she concluded, laws have been upheld by the Supreme Court as having "obvious" justification. Thus the gay ban "clearly does not require proof of the factual merits" of the military's judgment.[36]

THE INFLUENCE OF Maginnis and Wells-Petry on the debate over gay service was direct. In April 1993, Defense Secretary Les Aspin appointed a Pentagon task force called the Military Working Group (MWG), which drew on the study groups of the individual services and conducted its own further research. Its purpose was to provide options to reform the policy that would be consistent with Clinton's pledge to lift the ban. The MWG consisted of a panel of six flag officers and a support staff of other Pentagon personnel, including Wells-Petry and, unofficially, Maginnis, who provided research and advice.[37]

In June, after just a few weeks of consultation, the MWG completed its report. It was promptly leaked to the press, some said in an effort to force Aspin's office to embrace its approach before it was thoroughly evaluated.[38] The report said that homosexuality was "incompatible with military service," just as the 1981 Carter policy asserted. But President Clinton had directed the group to come up with a policy that would end discrimination against gays and lesbians simply because of who they were. In nominal deference to this order, the recommendations called for a policy that regarded sexual orientation as "a personal and private matter." But the group wanted to ban people with a homosexual orientation. Since it was, they concluded, impossible to determine one's homosexuality unless it was revealed in speech or action, they decided that, "for practical reasons," service members would be discharged "only when their homosexuality is manifested by objective criteria—homosexual acts, homosexual statements, or homosexual marriages."

These exact phrases would be adopted as part of the final "don't ask, don't tell" policy the next month. And both the Pentagon and, soon after, Congress accepted the MWG's rationale for maintaining a ban on open gay service: "The presence in the military of individuals identified as homosexuals would have a significantly adverse effect on both unit cohesion and the readiness of the force—the key ingredients of combat effectiveness."[39]

The MWG also made clear that the real basis for its opposition to openly gay service was moral. "The core values of the military profession would be seen by many to have changed fundamentally if homosexuals were allowed to serve," the report explained. "This would undermine institutional loyalty and the moral basis for service, sacrifice, and commitment" for the bulk of straight soldiers. Although it cast its policy recommendations in terms of the need to respect the values of the rank and file, the report's authors did little to contain their own moral opposition to homosexuals. Lifting the ban would leave the military's image "tarnished," said the report. "The homosexual lifestyle has been clearly documented as being unhealthy. Due to their sexual practices, active male homosexuals in the military could be expected to bring an increased incidence of sexually transmitted diseases," including AIDS, which could create the perception of an "enemy within."

The moral basis for the policy was undeniable. For Maginnis and fellow conservative Christians, the debate over gay service was really about something larger. It was an opportunity to protect a fundamentalist worldview they regarded as threatened by modernity. Religious crusaders like Maginnis and Wells-Petry and cultural crusaders like Moskos all had direct influence on what would soon become the military's final policy. With their encouragement, military leaders made the case not simply that lifting the ban would be a threat to cohesion, but that it would be such a threat because the "core values" of the institution were—and should rightly remain—anti-gay. Changing this fact would require changing the culture, something these men and women were not willing to sanction.

Maginnis's tireless work on behalf of the gay ban so solidified his relationship with the Family Research Council that, three weeks after retiring from the army, Maginnis was made a full-time FRC policy analyst and, eventually, the organization's vice president.[40] Nor did FRC policy papers, such as the ones written by Maginnis, sit on office shelves gathering dust. While it is clear that the moral imperatives of evangelical Christianity were the source of the strongest opposition to gay service, the concrete consequences that conservative Christians tried to tie to gay equality revealed their understanding that citing biblical damnation of homosexuality would not, in itself, be enough to sway their countrymen. The United States, they thought, was generally a religious and morally conservative nation. Yet they recognized that they would face objections or indifference from large segments of the population if they relied on religious injunctions alone to oppose gay rights. As a result, the religious right developed two powerful messages to deploy alongside their religious rhetoric: that gay equality represented a threat to families, and that it was equally a threat to national security. While the former was largely a creation of conservative Christians, the latter—that gay military service would undermine the armed forces and thus the security of the nation—was not their invention, but tapped into the old narrative of "homosexual incompatibility" described in Chapter 1. The contribution of the religious right was to spread that message with phenomenal efficiency and, most important, to insinuate the argument into the national debate by pressing powerful military leaders to make it their mantra.

The argument, of course, was one already shared by many military officials, some of whom were evangelicals themselves. But strategists at groups like FRC had quickly become experts at casting their reflexive disgust with homosexuality as a well-considered assessment of whether gay service would be good or bad for the military. The "military effectiveness" argument and the "homosexuality is sin" argument shared a reliance on the moral danger of homosexuality, and each gave the other the missing credibility that it lacked by itself. This marriage was, far and away, the most important factor in orchestrating the eventual defeat of the effort to lift the ban. For the religious right, it was a conscious, explicit, if not broadly advertised, campaign to give national standing to sectarian moral beliefs by enlisting the cache of military leaders whose opinions were widely respected and routinely shielded from civilian skepticism under the rubric of national security. And the connections were greased by the long-standing presence of evangelical Christians in positions of power in the armed forces.

So religious groups and the "research" wings they had erected began adding to their social and moral laments the argument that the military itself would be broken by a homosexual presence. FRC position papers noted that lifting the gay ban not only threatened to undermine families and destabilize innocent children but actually "could cost lives." "Promiscuous, anal sex, which is practiced by the typical homosexual male, has proved to be the most efficient way to transmit" the HIV virus, wrote Knight in yet another 1992 policy paper. Military life, he continued, "is not a pristine environment. People get cut and scratched while in intimate proximity. In real battle, blood can flow freely." Surely it was an unfair threat to place a heterosexual "in mortal fear for his life in case his homosexual comrade suffered a bleeding wound of any kind." Knight had slipped into using gay men and HIV sufferers completely interchangeably.[41] Again, the military's AIDS screening program, instituted in 1985 for all recruits, had been uniformly considered a success.

Having declared their "revulsion toward homosexual[ity]" stemming from "an appreciation of the natural relationships between men and women," FRC researchers tried to claim in the very same article that their actual concern was with the needs of the armed forces: "The real issue is military readiness, and whether the inclusion of active or self-avowed homosexuals would have a detrimental effect on military efficiency and fighting ability." In a refrain they shared with conservative military leaders, Christian conservatives chose buzzwords that allowed them to fuse professed military concerns with the language of moral propriety, insisting that openly gay service "would lower morale, disrupt order and discipline and harm combat readiness."[42]

The religious right was highly effective in getting its message out to the military brass and, through them, to Congress and the American public. By the 1990s, according to historian Anne Loveland, evangelicals had become the consummate military "insiders, who had the ear of the military leadership." Interviews she conducted in 1993 and 1994 with evangelicals inside the military suggested that high-ranking generals viewed gays in the military as, in the words of one, "the biggest moral issue in the century." Even Colin Powell reportedly was "concerned about the moral issue" and had written a "moral argument" against gay service that was distributed to top brass. Loveland concluded that the relentless efforts of military evangelicals "surely made an impression on the military leadership" and "undoubtedly played an important role in fueling the leadership's determination to maintain the ban."[43]

But military evangelicals complained that they had been told by allies involved in the political negotiations on gay service not to express their opposition in moral terms—a source of endless frustration and anger to Christian conservatives who felt called to oppose any violations of their religious beliefs.[44] Licking their wounds, they did all they could to oppose the admission of gays into the military, even if it meant making secular arguments instead of religious ones.

Whether religiously motivated or not, the moral question entered the debate at almost every turn. Rear Admiral John Hutson was a captain in the U.S. Navy JAG in 1993 when "don't ask, don't tell" was formulated, serving as the JAG's executive assistant. This meant he participated in high-level discussions among top navy officers about how to implement Clinton's plan. In 1997, he became the JAG himself, and it fell to him to enforce the policy.

In discussions about how to handle the gay troops issue, Hutson recalled, there was a "push to make this a question of morality rather than the question of just unit cohesion." Hutson said the navy brass "declined that option, sort of." He said "sort of" because it was "implicit in the unit cohesion" argument that homosexuality was immoral. "We never said that it's OK to be gay," he said. "We were arguing that it would disrupt unit cohesion; implicitly, then, it wasn't OK to be gay because if it were, it wouldn't disrupt unit cohesion. To some extent we wove [the moral] argument in by what we weren't saying rather than what we were saying."[45]

The influence of conservative moralists did not stop there. In May 1993, a group of retired officers formed the Defense Readiness Council, dedicated to preserving the ban on gay troops and disseminating information about homosexuality in the military. The group claimed a hundred members consisting of former and active-duty military personnel, such as Wells-Petry, who championed the group by appearing on a videotape that it distributed to members of Congress and at the Pentagon.[46]

Another supporter was William Weise, a virulently anti-gay retired Marine brigadier general, who released a report modeled after the army JAG study on homosexual criminal misconduct. Through his military contacts, Weise secured a slot to testify before Congress on the gay ban, where he said that letting gays serve would turn the military into a "wishy-washy force" that would "needlessly cost thousands of American lives," all because militant activists were demanding "special rights." General Weise said that his report found there was "much higher criminal activity among the homosexual than the heterosexual population in the military," even though, like the JAG study, his "data" consisted exclusively of homosexual court-martial records and a made-up figure for how large the gay population was in the military.[47]

Like many military men, Weise insisted that gay service would "degrade combat effectiveness" but failed to offer a whit of evidence for his claim. Not that he didn't try. He contended that unit cohesion would suffer if gays were admitted because of the "clearly-stated agenda and objectives of homosexual organizations." According to Weise, the real goal of gays and lesbians in the military fight was to change society's behavior, indoctrinate children, stop HIV screening, repeal age-of-consent laws, secure federal funding for explicitly sexual art, and protect abortion rights. He was indignant that gay groups wanted to prevent discrimination in employment, cure AIDS, prevent anti-gay hate crimes, and, indeed, secure statehood for the District of Columbia![48]

Weise also included a litany of gay sex crime cases that he had thoroughly researched for his report. Many of the gay crimes were only crimes because homosexuality was itself criminalized. But his report also involved graphic depictions of shower rape, public sex, fraternization, abuse of power, and harassment. Weise's research cited all the usual suspects, including Wells-Petry, Maginnis, concerned military mothers, and a Korean War vet who described a bloody war scene from his combat tour in 1951, which, he claimed, showed how AIDS today required the exclusion of gays from service. His congressional testimony included as enclosures all the FRC scare studies penned by Maginnis and Knight, along with pictures of showers and toilets and crowded bunks and squad bays. His statement and report, appearing on Family Research Council letterhead,[49] were also submitted to Aspin's Military Working Group.

ONE OF THE clearest indications of the extraordinary impact of the religious right on the gay troops debate was the dissemination of tens of thousands of copies of an anti-gay video. *The Gay Agenda* showed footage of nudity, spectacle, and simulated sex from the 1992 San Francisco gay pride parade. It was produced by Bill Horn, a conservative Christian who published the anti-gay newsletter *The Report*. An outgrowth of his church in Lancaster, California, *The Report* dedicated itself, starting in 1992, to opposing gays in the military by publishing information and interviews and hawking "educational" material, such as the video. In addition to the gay pride scenes, which pictured scantily clad gay men writhing on floats, the twenty-minute film featured representatives of the "ex-gay" movement describing graphic sex practices that they claimed to have disavowed when they finally bested their homosexuality; a physician explaining graphically the purported health dangers of homosexual behavior; and children crying while, according to the narrator, they were watching footage of leering homosexuals.[50]

In June 1993, *The Report* merged with *Lambda Report,* a newsletter edited by Peter LaBarbera, a former writer for the conservative *Washington Times.* *Lambda Report*—devoted exclusively to "monitoring the homosexual agenda"—

was filled with lurid tales of gay rape, sadomasochism, and conferences on other fetishes often held on public property like state universities, "flogging and fisting" shows, and examples of general decadence and subversion culled from parades, marches, and performances. Satirical entertainment, in which performers and writers parodied right-wing paranoia about gay conspiracies, were a staple resource for the anti-gay movement. It is often unclear if the authors were aware they were drawing on comic exaggerations of the "gay lifestyle"—using them dishonestly to imply they are representative of all gays and lesbians—or simply oblivious. Either way, the result was an amusing but damaging spectacle of earnest social conservatives quoting from parodies of their own paranoia—as proof that their most extreme visions of homosexuality were correct! At the end of the day, the impact was the same: countless more Americans exposed to wildly exaggerated depictions of gay life and quietly confirming that their unloveliest suspicions of what it meant to be gay were indeed true.[51]

In the spring of 1993, Horn distributed over fifty-five thousand copies of *The Gay Agenda*. By Horn's account, the video "kind of rocked the Pentagon." He got it in the hands of numerous officers who began distributing it to colleagues and even showing it to troops at military bases across the country. Among those who viewed a copy were members of the Joint Chiefs of Staff, including the head of the Marines, General Carl Mundy Jr., who, despite the obviously hysterical and unrepresentative nature of the video, copied it and circulated it to his colleagues. "The military has really pushed this video to the forefront," said Horn, who also gave copies to members of Congress.[52]

THE MILITARY CHAPLAINCY was another key source of the increasingly aggressive evangelical presence in the armed forces. In 1993, there were 243 religious denominations represented in the armed forces by 3,152 military chaplains.[53] To become one requires securing an endorsement from an agency of a recognized religious entity, and the number of chaplains representing each religion is determined proportionally to the religious representation in the military population. While military chaplains therefore represented a wide variety of faiths, the predominance of Christian religious leaders in the chaplaincy meant a strong—and growing—culture of conservative cultural values.

Not surprisingly, many chaplains were adamantly against openly gay service. And they were not inclined to keep to themselves. As early as August 1992 the senior leadership of the Marine Corps distributed an official position paper written by the U.S. Navy's deputy chaplain, Commander Eugene Gomulka, explaining that lifting the ban would threaten the physical and psychological health, and even the lives, of straight service members. The paper insisted that homosexual behavior was a "choice" that "most people do not view as normal," and worried that the military would "pose a major challenge to gay men who might wish to arrest their behavior." Gomulka dwelled on the prospect of open homosexuality, writing that "homosexuals do not consider their orientation a private matter, but are inclined to seek public affirmation for their lifestyle." The disclosure itself, he wrote, amounts to a "demand for a social infrastructure to support the behavior." Like so many opponents of gay service, Gomulka seemed less concerned by the existence of homosexual behavior than by the recent effort to normalize it. The government, he concluded, had a "legitimate role to play in checking the spread of homosexual behavior," especially among "innocent" young soldiers, whose minds are still in their "formative stages," and thus especially vulnerable to the sexual predations of gays and lesbians.[54]

Gomulka's paper spread rapidly throughout the senior leadership, winning praise from Mundy, as well as from Rear Admiral Roberta Hazard, the highest-ranking woman in the navy, and Captain Larry Ellis, the top Marine Corps chaplain. Ellis sent the paper around to senior officers and chaplains of the army, navy, and air force in order to "stimulate their thinking" on the issue of gays in the military, breaking a long chaplaincy tradition of avoiding public comment on such controversial issues.[55]

The early rhetoric of opposition to gay service did not distinguish between open and concealed homosexual service. Once the distinction was made, however, the rhetoric of opponents continued to betray a troubling lack of reasoned thought. Gomulka wrote that because homosexuality "can threaten the lives, including the physical (e.g., AIDS) and psychological well being of others," it was essential to bar "*acknowledged* homosexuals" from the military. Yet if the risk of HIV infection was truly increased by the presence of gay soldiers, surely the best way to combat it would be to identify the sources of the disease, not to drive the infected underground and out of sight.[56]

One of the largest, most powerful of the chaplain endorsing agencies was the Commission on Chaplains of the National Association of Evangelicals. The NAE had been a powerful religious interest group since World War II, but it gained national notoriety well after "don't ask, don't tell" had been enshrined. In November 2006, Ted Haggard, the NAE's president, resigned following revelations that he paid for sex and drugs from a male prostitute. Less than a month after the story broke, Haggard, married with four children, announced through spokespeople that he had received counseling (from, among others, James Dobson) and was now "completely straight." The comment reflected the worldview of the 15 million constituents the NAE claimed to represent: that with faith in Jesus, people with homosexual inclinations could cleanse themselves and live happy, healthy heterosexual lives. The NAE represented fifty thousand churches from seventy denominations across the United States. In 1993, over seven hundred of the military's chaplains had been endorsed by member churches.[57]

Starting late in 1992, the NAE worked feverishly behind the scenes to ensure the continuation of the gay ban, even if, ultimately, it meant emphasizing secular rationales in place of religious ones. The NAE estimated that it met with one hundred military groups to discuss the issue and it devoted enormous resources to developing an effective approach to defeat Clinton's campaign promise. Paying close attention to polls, the NAE discovered that only a third of those who opposed gay service did so on the grounds of "moral judgments." In response, strategists shifted their tactics to highlight the "practical concerns" of gay service, in line with what groups like FRC had determined was the most effective way of fighting gay service. Brigadier General Richard Abel, head of the Campus Crusade for Christ's military ministry, said his group was taking an "operational" rather than a moral or religious approach "on purpose—because most people are not Bible-believers." Part of Abel's approach was to distribute as many copies of Horn's *Gay Agenda* video as he could. He gave them to active-duty service members and veterans, tossing it into whatever laps he could find. He believed that if enough people saw what the homosexual lifestyle was like, up to 90 percent of the public would oppose gays in the military. He also met personally with colleagues in the Pentagon as well as retired officers to shore up support for the ban, calling the visits "informational" so as to skirt restrictions on formal lobbying.[58]

Abel's Military Ministry became a resource center for military officers working out how to respond to the gay service issue. In 1992, it moved its offices from San Diego to the East Coast, where it served as a coordinating headquarters for over a thousand like-minded groups. Its leader, General Abel, led morning Bible study at Langley Air Force Base and helped facilitate other military Bible study groups, whose members "find many ways and places to use our training in evangelism and discipleships." Set up to give "hope and help" to active-duty service members and their families, the Military Ministry worked full-time to spread the gospel throughout the armed forces.[59]

In a paper written by General Abel, the familiar view of homosexuality—as a matter of choice and a harbinger of AIDS—emerged as the predictable basis for opposition to gay service. But above all, Abel equated homosexuality with selfishness, and cast gay inclusion in the military as the death of selfless service. Anti-gay activists spoke as though the gay struggle for inclusion and the right to be honest about sexual identity was more than a quest for equality but an insistence on "special rights," an elevation of self-interest above that of the whole. This was the point of the widespread rhetoric that spoke of militant homosexual activists forcing their lifestyle on others. In reality, it was not just the effort to assert equal rights that bugged social conservatives; homosexuality itself was, for them, inseparable from uncontrolled pleasure, the epitome of self-interest and thus a grave threat to the social norms of self-restraint on which social stability depended. "Subordination of self-will to the greater good of the unit," wrote Abel, is essential for military readiness. Discipline "is the antithesis of self-serving self-advancement." He ended his paper by driving the point home: "One final word may be good to keep in mind: 'Selflessness.' It forms the bedrock supporting the very concept of military or civil service and is inseparable from the personal and corporate sacrifice which national service—in or out of uniform—is all about."[60]

Ultimately, groups like the NAE decided on a two-pronged approach. They would continue to stress moral and religious outrage whenever they could, hoping to galvanize their base to oppose gay equality in the political realm; but they would simultaneously push their military liaisons to the front lines and encourage them to make their case in terms of military effectiveness—in line with the tactic embraced by social conservative groups in the civilian world such as the Family Research Council. "We thought that the best strategy was to allow those with military experience to speak to this issue, rather than one of us in the NAE Office of Public Affairs," acknowledged NAE director Robert Dugan, Jr. "None among us had military experience."[61]

The NAE targeted both military and political leaders. On the day of Bill Clinton's inauguration, Ted Edgren, director of the NAE's Commission on Chaplains, wrote to the new president, with accompanying letters to Sam Nunn, chairman of the Senate Armed Service Committee, and Colin Powell. As Edgren claimed he was helping the political leaders to bring "reason and caution" to the issue of gay service, his tone was one of desperation more than caution. Imploring political leaders to defeat the proposal to lift the ban, he argued that openly gay service would be "bad for the services." "May I ask you, in fact, beg you, to intercede," he wrote to Nunn, hoping the senator would press Clinton to delay any action until hearings were held. "May we ask you to attempt *one more time* to personally talk with" Clinton, he wrote to Powell, to assure gays would not stain the military. "For us," he wrote, "this *is* ultimately a moral issue!" But in case that didn't convince, he reiterated, this time to Clinton himself, that it was also a "military readiness" issue but "with moral-spiritual implications."[62]

With the letters, the NAE enclosed its statement, "Homosexual Behavior and Military Service," which sought to distinguish between homosexual behavior, which it said was "against God's law," and a homosexual "tendency, proclivity or orientation toward such behavior," which were "not under condemnation." The statement said that the military's Uniform Code of Military Justice criminalizes "homosexual acts" and that it was crucial "to be consistent in dealing with all forms of sexual sin" so as not to discriminate against any particular group." The statement was astonishing in either its ignorance or disingenuousness, since the UCMJ does not mention "homosexual acts" but bans "sodomy," which includes both anal sex and oral sex among gays or straights. To be "consistent" and "not discriminate" would mean to punish roughly 80 percent of the military, the estimated portion of Americans who engage in oral or anal sex.[63]

Despite the statement's fuzzy distinction between behavior and proclivities, in its own literature the NAE was adamantly anti-gay. Its newsletter, *Insight,* which shared a name and graphic with FRC's newsletter but was reportedly unconnected, counseled conservatives to prepare to respond to gay demands for equality with arguments about "showers, barracks, blood banks, and AIDS." It advertised videotapes that purported to tell the truth about the threat of the "homosexual perversion."[64]

Like FRC, the NAE sent contradictory messages about whether military necessity or morality dictated the gay exclusion policy. "Homosexuals insist that the issue is discrimination," said one newsletter, "but the real point is the purpose of the military—fighting and winning wars." Seven lines down, however, a quite different rationale was offered. The letter called the "homosexualization of the military" a "counter-cultural assault on the last major American institution to resist the attack on traditional values." It concluded: "How can God bestow His favor on an army or a nation which condones that which He declares to be an abomination."[65]

In testimony before the House Republican Research Committee, a resource group for the Republican leadership chaired by Representative Duncan Hunter of California, Edgren let his homophobia run free. Offering an idealized narrative of traditional heterosexual purity, he complained that "It is *not fair* to the mothers of America to subject their sons and daughters to immoral influences." To Edgren, discrimination was the only fair thing to do. "To continue to exclude homosexuals from military service is to do 'what is fair to *all* the citizens of our nation.'" Edgren formulated his views by drawing from "my own personal experience" with homosexuals, although he never made clear what that experience was. His diagnosis of the homosexual was that he had been turned gay through molestation and ensuing "arrested development," has low self-esteem, and "views himself as worthless, trapped in a pattern of behavior from which he cannot escape." He is "often borderline suicidal, since he is well aware that he is an object of scorn and revulsion over what he does." He is found "betraying the petty character traits and actions of a small child, and is capable of perpetrating actions upon others that will enhance his self-esteem at their expense," including recruiting and molesting straight men. "Finally, this obsession overtakes him, blotting out all other considerations, dominating his life, such as it has become, and rendering him incapable of sublimating his own desires to the good of the unit, the service, the nation, or his fellow man. He is a tragic figure," Edgren concluded, and "he needs treatment, he needs compassion, he needs hope, he needs the love of Christ. He is *not* a combat-ready soldier."[66]

Keeping gays out of the military became such a fixation for some conservative Christians that entire new careers emerged out of the issue. Early in 1993, Edgren tapped Brigadier General James Hutchens to become associate director of the Chaplains Commission. Hutchens, retired from the army in 1992 after thirty-seven years of service, was a spokesman for the Presbyterian and Reformed Joint Commission on Chaplains and Military Personnel. He wrote in *The Centurion,* the newsletter of the Commission on Chaplains, that he had been moved to take the position at the NAE because of the gays in the military issue. His duty was to "buil[d] the house of the Lord," and for him, that meant "saying yes to Jim Edgren's invitation" to strengthen the body of Christ "as we seek to give visibility from an evangelical viewpoint to the issue of homosexuals in the military."[67]

When it learned that Congress would hold hearings that spring on the issue of gays in the military, the NAE requested to testify, hoping to keep the nation focused on the moral dimension of gay service. In May, the NAE would get its wish, securing for Hutchens the opportunity to testify before the House of Representatives (see Chapter 4). He was one of several influential religious figures who were able to use the halls of government to spread their message that homosexuality was a dangerous "moral virus" that must be stopped.[68]

Working alongside the NAE was the Chaplaincy of Full Gospel Churches, another powerful endorsing agency. Representing over 5 million people and more than a thousand churches, the CFGC was equally vociferous in its quest to keep gays out of the military. In January 1993, the group wrote an open letter to President Clinton and sent copies to over five thousand fellowship groups, churches, and senior leaders in the Pentagon and Congress. Letting gays in the military, said the letter, "would do more than just undermine discipline and morale, although they would do that as well. Homosexuals are notoriously promiscuous." They are "perverted," "aggressive recruiters," and "going for the young—pedophiles." Should "innocent soldiers" be forced to serve "with someone lusting after them?" Should they be required to aid injured comrades "whose body fluids may be spilling out, without the benefit of latex gloves?" The rest of the letter was filled with biblical references to homosexuality, noting passages condemning sodomites to death and lumping them with prostitutes, thieves, drunkards, and "the greedy."[69]

The CFGC letter contained an essential ingredient in the thinking that would eventually birth "don't ask, don't tell." As Christian witnesses to the kingdom of God, the religious right was at its most indignant not so much when the word of God was neglected but when such neglect was not properly sanctioned. "Though they know God's decree that those who do such things deserve to die," quoted the letter, citing the New Testament on sodomy, "they not only do them but approve those who practice them." Military officers, said the letter, would be obliged to resign if the ban were lifted because to continue to serve would mean being "blind" to violations of moral absolutes.[70]

Such beliefs were echoed in Bible study material disseminated by and circulated among military leaders throughout 1993. A document entitled "What the Bible Teaches About Homosexuality: A Study of Scripture Passages" emphasized that God's anger focused on "communities that, like Sodom and Gomorrah, tolerate and support homosexuality." Indeed, "the haughty 'parading' (i.e., the public celebration) of their homosexuality by the residents of Sodom seems to have increased the urgency of divine judgment on their community." The scripture condemned in particular those who "parade their sin like Sodom; they do not hide it. . . . They have brought disaster on themselves." This study material was included in a packet sent to researchers by Ted Shadid, an editor of *Command*, the magazine of the Officers' Christian Fellowship.[71]

By summer, the CFGC had, along with other evangelical military groups, become obsessed with the issue of gay troops. Its annual conference that June was consumed by sessions on gays in the military. Ultimately it adopted a policy paper condemning homosexuality as "socially destructive behavior" (along with substance abuse, adultery, and fornication) and making clear that "only through the redemptive power of the Gospel [of] Jesus Christ can every person fulfill his or her own ultimate potential." It sent the policy paper out to the usual list of thousands of members and national political and military leaders, urging its membership to "take a public stand to MAINTAIN THE BAN" by becoming politically active.[72]

The CFGC also sent to each of its chaplains a book by retired colonel Ronald Ray called *Military Necessity and Homosexuality*. The newsletter announced that Ray's book "presents the truth about homosexuality" and makes a compelling case for retaining the "375-year-old ban against homosexuals openly serving in the military services." Ray's depiction of gays and his case against letting them serve recycled the unhinged stereotypes and extremist rhetoric of his anti-gay evangelical colleagues. His book contended that gays were addicted to sex, that they engaged in practices that "are inherently degrading or humiliating and are rarely practiced by heterosexuals," that pedophilia was "close to the heart of homosexuality," and that gays acted compulsively to obtain sex, especially once they come out of the closet. "In coming out," he wrote, "a homosexual throws off most social and moral restraints on sexual behavior and embraces and surrenders entirely to the 'gay lifestyle,' which, for most male homosexuals, is extraordinarily promiscuous."[73]

Like so many social conservatives, Ray used homosexuals as a symbolic stand-in for all that was immoral, uncontrolled, and unconnected to old certainties. "The gay community," he wrote, was "seized by a deadly fatalism that sees life as absurd and short." They do not care about the future or about others, only about the pleasures of the moment. "They have no direct links with the next generation, no reason to invest in the future, no reason to defer gratification. Their lives consist of little more than having an exciting time while life lasts and seeking 'self-fulfillment,' a modern euphemism for selfish gratification and ambition."[74]

THE IMPACT OF the religious right's organizing was profound. The new Clinton White House and the existing cadre of gay advocacy groups were totally unprepared for the opposition they would encounter in achieving what some had said was already a "done deal."[75] And it was the conservative Christian leadership, a sometimes loosely connected but devastatingly effective consortium of individuals and research centers and media outlets, that caused this issue to explode on the American stage. The consistency, passion, and vehemence with which conservative military officials methodically set about to inject themselves into what might have been a relatively minor discussion over military personnel regulations was unusual even in the heated history of military-political disagreements and is further evidence of the success of the social conservative crusade.

While General Abel never reached his goal of convincing nine-tenths of

America to oppose gay troops, the polls mentioned earlier—showing sliding support for gay service between November 1992 and February 1993—suggest the effects of anti-gay religious rhetoric on American sentiment. Moskos's comments and behind-the-scenes work to keep the ban in place added to the mix. His views on homosexuality, while often immature, suggested no animus against gay people, and he never expressed a belief that homosexuality itself was immoral or inferior, beyond quips about a gay commander he had in the 1950s who couldn't keep his hands off the enlisted men. Yet his opposition to gay service was nevertheless grounded in morality, as he had said, in the "moral right" of heterosexuals to privacy. Of course, few people actually believed there were no gays in the military, and the eventual policy of "don't ask, don't tell" merely offered military members a hand in pretending to a privacy that was in no real way achievable. In any event, in the hands of the religious right, Moskos's privacy concerns quickly morphed into sweeping homophobic declarations that homosexuality threatened to destroy the military and, ultimately, Western civilization. With the help of Sam Nunn and Colin Powell, Christian conservatives were about to stave off Armageddon for a little while longer.[76]

3

The Powell–Nunn Alliance

A S PROPONENTS OF GAY equality worked to bring increased visibility to the gay troops issue in the early 1990s, and as opponents in the church and the military advocated against Clinton's pledge to overturn the ban, the matter sparked the attention of Congress. In fact, political and military leaders had already begun to tackle the question several years before Clinton made his fateful promise to David Mixner in September 1991. The result was a series of parallel paths that occasionally intersected and often branched away from one another. If the work of gay rights advocates and ousted troops to overturn the ban is one strand in this trajectory, and the work of the religious right another, then the calculated deliberations among politicians and members of the military mark a third, intermediary trail through these confusing woods.

Starting in the late 1980s, the offices of Barney Frank and Gerry Studds, the two openly gay members of Congress, became call centers for gay service members terrified of losing their jobs or worse. Studds and Representative Patricia Schroeder of Colorado had worked to force the release of the PERSEREC study in 1989, which had concluded that gays were not security risks and could serve without compromising the military. When the report was made public, Pentagon leaders were suddenly on the defensive. In July 1991, Frank asked Dick Cheney about the policy at a congressional committee hearing and he appeared to have virtually no defense for the ban. "I have not spent a lot of time on the issue," he said by way of explanation. Cheney went on to note that he knew of times when the policy had "not been administered in a fair fashion." It was then that he made his now-famous remark, calling the security risk rationale "a bit of an old chestnut." The issue turns, he said vaguely, "upon the need of the department to maintain the combat effectiveness of our military units, and that our sole mission in life is to be prepared to fight and win wars."[1]

That fall, Democrats in Congress introduced a resolution opposing the gay ban. The measure would have been nonbinding, and thus unenforceable, but it kept a small degree of momentum going in the fight for equality. By early 1992, General Colin Powell was in the hot seat, taking questions from the same congressional panel that had prodded Dick Cheney the previous summer. Powell seemed more equipped to field the challenges.

Testifying in February 1992, Powell—then one of the most admired men in the United States for his role in the first Gulf War—agreed with Cheney that the gay ban was not justified by the old security risk rationale. Luckily, there was a new one: "privacy, good order and discipline." Powell started out by say-ing that in a military setting, there is "no privacy," an oft-mentioned point that begs the question: Why is it justified to exclude gays in order to protect something—privacy—that doesn't even exist to begin with? He then went out of his way to praise gays and lesbians. This step may have been an effort to avoid appearing homophobic, and there is no evidence in the public record that Powell was prejudiced or homophobic, beyond his endless willingness to accommodate other people's negative judgments of homosexuality. But the general's language—referring to gays as "proud, brave, loyal, good Americans, but who favor a homosexual lifestyle"—dated his outlook. Already by 1992, the "lifestyle" phrase was generally used by those who were either over sixty or homophobic, a code to suggest that being gay was essentially a series of care-free choices about how one wished to spend one's days—at brunch, at the gym, in boutiques, or on the beach. And finally, Powell made his case: Letting such people into such a setting "with heterosexuals who would prefer not to have somebody of the same sex find them sexually attractive" would be "prejudicial to good order and discipline."[2]

While Powell was scrupulous about remaining high-minded, he never succeeded at explaining how the presence of gays would undermine order and discipline, and he never marshaled any actual evidence that gays hurt the often invoked notion of "unit cohesion." In fact, he barely even tried, opting instead to simply assert the point as a given. Without proof that open gays harmed the military, Powell's argument boiled down to this: Many straight people prefer not to be considered attractive to gay people.

Of course, military life was all about doing things you might prefer not to: wandering through a hostile war zone in the Iraqi desert in stratospheric temperatures; dismantling deadly improvised explosive devices (IEDs) block-ing the path of your convoy; literally giving up a limb to defend your country. Service members don't generally enjoy this stuff, even as they may embrace it as a part of their duty. Some might even regard these grim realities as quite a bit worse than showering with an admirer. By fixating on this particular hardship and suggesting that this alone would break morale, Powell gave his imprimatur not only to the preferences of straight soldiers not to serve with gays but to the notion that there was, indeed, something wrong, something unacceptable, about homosexuality. Otherwise, serving with gays would have become just one of the hundreds of things men and women are required to do to become good, disciplined soldiers.

There was another glitch to Powell's argument. Gays already served. Powell knew this and admitted it publicly. His testimony in early 1992 came before the nation began to absorb Moskos's distinction between open and closeted gay service. That means he wasn't speaking here about banning *open* gays, but *all* gays; a total ban was required by the principle he was defending. It may have sounded nice to say that gays must be banned to protect the privacy of straights. But since Powell admitted gays were already in the showers with straights, it wasn't clear how a rule saying they weren't allowed to be there accomplished anything. Later, when the distinction was made between serving openly and serving in the closet, that problem remained unresolved: If straight men didn't like to have "somebody of the same sex find them sexually attractive," what would be achieved by forcing gays to conceal themselves? Would anyone really take such silence to mean there was no one in the shower finding them attractive?

To astute observers, Powell's argument—which echoed through all branches of the armed forces—sounded eerily familiar. "The Army is not a sociological laboratory," one army official said. "Experiments to meet the wishes and demands of" every group and ideology in the country "are a danger to efficiency, discipline and morale and would result in ultimate defeat." Such pronouncements were part of a rising chorus of opposition to the push to modernize the armed forces. "The close and intimate conditions of life aboard ship," read a navy memo from the same year, "the necessity for the highest possible degree of unity and esprit de corps, the requirement of morale, all demand that nothing be done which may adversely affect the situation. Past experience has shown irrefutably that the enlistment of" certain groups "leads to disruptive and undermining conditions."[3]

But this chorus was sung not in the 1990s but in the 1940s about a similar yet also very different issue—the integration of African Americans into the military. The resemblance of the language from that battle to the current culture war is unmistakable: The presence of homosexuals, claimed the U.S. military in its 1982 regulation, "adversely affects the ability of the Military Services to maintain discipline, good order and morale," and "to facilitate assignment and worldwide deployment of members who frequently must live and work under close conditions affording minimal privacy." It wasn't true with black soldiers and it isn't true with gay soldiers. Racial integration was a challenge, but not an impossibility. In fact, desegregation was ordered and implemented *even though* it caused enormous problems with cohesion, morale, and discipline. Moskos himself, despite arguing that racial integration was prompted by military necessity, has pointed out that racial tension and hostility plagued the military throughout the Vietnam War. As late as 1972, race riots broke out aboard the USS *Kitty Hawk* and the USS *Constellation* as sailors wielding wrenches, chains, and brooms pummeled each other and left one another bleeding, wounded, and terrorized. As Barney Frank put it, "Saying we can't have gay people in the military because heterosexuals won't like them, regardless of how they behave, is like saying we can't have black people around because white people won't like them. That was wrong, and this is wrong."[4]

Yet in the 1990s, when it came to gays, who were already integrated into the military, the very same language that had been used to justify racism was deployed to justify homophobia. Senator Richard Russell of Georgia had opposed military integration in 1948 because it would "increase the rate of crime committed by servicemen" since "Negro troops," according to him, committed rape thirteen times more often per capita than whites. Likewise, General Norman Schwarzkopf worried that if openly gay troops were allowed to serve, they would sexually assault straights, citing "instances where heterosexuals have been solicited to commit homosexual acts, and even more traumatic emotionally, physically coerced to engage in such acts."[5]

Russell had cast African Americans as disease-riddled outsiders who threatened innocent young white boys with deadly health risks, particularly sexually transmitted diseases. Syphilis, gonorrhea, chancre, and tuberculosis, he said, are "appallingly higher among the members of the Negro race than among the members of the white race." (During World War II, the military insisted that the Red Cross maintain separate blood banks for whites and blacks.) In the 1990s, the joint chiefs and the chaplaincy said the same about gays in the military when they complained to lawmakers that openly gay service could increase the spread of AIDS.[6]

In 1942, Vice Admiral F. E. M. Whiting testified to the General Board of the navy: "The minute the negro is introduced in to general service . . . the high type of man that we have been getting for the last twenty years will go elsewhere and we will get the type of man who will lie in bed with a negro." In 1992, a four-star general insisted that "good people will leave the military in droves" if gays were allowed to serve. During World War II, the chairman of the navy's General Board claimed that, compared to blacks, "the white man is more adaptable and more efficient in the various conditions which are involved in the making of an effective man-of-war." Colonel Ronald Ray must have been consulting the same "science" half a century later when he asserted: "It has been proven in the scientific literature that homosexuals are not able-bodied" as heterosexuals.[7]

The echoes didn't end there. In the 1940s, Americans were told that whites would not respect or obey commands by an African American; that integration would prompt violence against a despised minority that the military would be helpless to stop; that integration would lower public acceptance of the military and the federal government; that the military should not be used for "social experimentation"; that military integration was being used to further a larger minority rights agenda that would ultimately break the armed forces; that the military is unique and is not a democracy; and that integration would thwart God's plan to keep whites above blacks. Every last one of these arguments was used, in some instances with frightening similarity, against letting gays serve.

Powell's arguments were so similar to those made fifty years earlier against racial integration that some younger officers actually thought he was joking. But the joke was on history. Colin Powell was the first black chairman of the Joint Chiefs of Staff. He was the beneficiary of the postwar racial integration and of years of affirmative action programs in the military since.[8] He was also tall, large-framed, distinguished-looking, even-tempered: the very emblem of American military might. And his very existence was the perfect symbol of the country's triumph over discrimination, its deliverance, to an impressive but still limited extent, from a history of bigotry and ignorance into a newer tradition of equal opportunity for excellence—for individuals and therefore for the nation as a whole.

But it was hard to miss the symbolism of the nation's top general endorsing exclusion of a whole group of people using the very same language of fear and disruption that was used to mark his own people as inferior in the very same fighting force. In May 1992, Patricia Schroeder called him on it: "I am sure you are aware," she wrote in a letter asking Powell to reconsider his position, "that your reasoning would have kept you from the mess hall a few decades ago, all in the name of good order and discipline."[9]

Schroeder's language set Powell up to settle the issue. "I know you are a history major," he wrote back in rather dignified anger, "but I can assure you I need no reminders concerning the history of African-Americans in the defense of their nation and the tribulations they faced. I am a part of that history." Powell then forcefully rejected Schroeder's comparison, saying that skin color was "a benign, non-behavioral characteristic" while sexual orientation was "perhaps the most profound of human behavioral characteristics. Comparison between the two is a convenient but invalid argument." He concluded with as much weightiness as he began: "As chairman of the Joint Chiefs of Staff, as well as an African-American fully conversant with history, I believe the policy we have adopted is consistent with the necessary standards of order and discipline required on the armed forces."[10]

Rear Admiral John Hutson recalls that moment as a definitive early victory sign for proponents of the ban. "Powell put a hole in the analogy to racial integration," says Hutson, "not particularly logically, but just by force of his personality and who he was. That provided a bulwark behind which the rest of us could hide." It allowed other defenders of the ban to say, "This isn't the same as racial integration. This is different, and General Powell says so."[11] Schroeder went on that May to introduce legislation to lift the ban, but Powell's opposition made its passage increasingly unlikely. Having confronted and handily dismissed the racial analogy, Powell managed to win the high ground. In so doing, he gave respectability to opponents of gay service, including those whose resistance was unabashedly rooted in moral animus against homosexuality.

What drove General Powell to come down so adamantly against gays in the military? Powell was a team player, a company guy whose willingness to put loyalty above principle was masked by a charismatic personality that made what can be a vice seem like a virtue. It was a trait that would become much clearer in the years following the passage of "don't ask, don't tell." For the second U.S. invasion of Iraq, Powell, as secretary of state, helped bolster a shaky case for going to war, even though he later admitted he had strong private doubts. It wasn't the first time Powell molded his own position to that of the big kids. After Operation Desert Storm in 1991, journalists learned that Powell had actually supported containment, not invasion, but was perfectly willing to become a chief salesman for George H. W. Bush's war. And in 2000, Christopher Hitchens accused Powell of two "shameful cover-ups" in failing to come forward with knowledge of atrocities in the Vietnam War and illegal arms deals in the Iran-contra affair. Powell, charged Hitchens, "acted to gratify immediate superiors and to short-circuit any unpleasantness," placing the "prestige of the military above any inconvenient ethical or legal concerns."[12]

Powell's commitment to keeping the military free of gays appears to have been rooted in this same loyalty to the beliefs, the traditions, and, above all, the men of the institution he loved. Powell had no evidence to support his arguments. He had admitted that the security risk rationale was discredited and that gays had served well throughout the nation's history. Yet he simply repeated, ad nauseam, that reform would harm "order and discipline" and that it would be "difficult to accommodate" homosexuality in a military setting with little privacy, platitudes that resonated well with the views of anti-gay Americans who already regarded gays as, by definition, disordered and undisciplined. So what was his position based on? His soldiers, his officers, his military simply didn't want this change. It was all he had left in an arsenal of weapons that even he admitted failed to make the case that the armed forces genuinely could not absorb the change Clinton was proposing.

While Powell set the tone of high-minded debate, he was essentially reflecting, and legitimizing, the opinion of military officers across the nation. Many of them, usually older, usually male, echoed the same concerns about discipline, morale, and cohesion. They said they had enough on their plate molding a group of testosterone-charged nineteen-year-olds from wildly different backgrounds into a disciplined, effective fighting force; they didn't need one more thing to worry about. It was an unsurprising position: Ask a teacher in a large, rowdy, diverse classroom if she favors or opposes adding to her volatile mix a bunch of kids from one of the most unpopular minority groups in the country, and guess what she'll say.

Some senior military officers managed to keep their language just above the fray of anti-gay rhetoric. But almost all, including Powell, eventually betrayed with their words a worldview that regarded homosexuality as either harmful, predatory, immoral, or sinful. General Gordon Sullivan, army chief of staff, cast his concerns in terms of "difficult management problems," but added that he owes his soldiers "a certain amount of privacy and security." It's not clear how banning gays protected soldiers' security, unless gays are viewed as innately predatory. For others, this view was simply implied. Letting gays serve "could upset the good order and discipline of the unit," said a Marine Corps general. He described "standing in this shower tent, naked, waiting in line for 35 minutes for a 5-minute shower." Then he raised the question: "Would I be comfortable knowing gays were there standing in line with us? No. It just introduces a tension you don't need."[13]

The four-star general who said that if the ban is lifted, "good people will leave the military in droves," was sending a clear signal of support not just for opposition to gay service but for the moral rectitude of anti-gay sentiment. After all, if you resigned in protest at the acceptance of homosexuals, and were singled out as "good people," your position must be morally sound. As a senior military officer said, in a rare example of public (albeit anonymous) dissent from the united military opposition to gay service, "We have been allowed—by law—to become homophobic."[14]

The sentiments of Admiral Thomas Moorer, former chairman of the Joint Chiefs of Staff, would be amusing if they weren't so repugnant. Saying he had no doubt that gays in the military would cause problems, he predicted a scenario: "I can guarantee you that these young people . . . will spot a homosexual a mile away as soon as he comes in, and they'll have to name him Tessie or Agnes, or whatever, and then subsequently he'll get caught in some kind of sexual activity and then he's discharged." Moorer found the issue of gay service "the most disturbing that I've ever encountered in war or peace because what is going on here is an effort in effect to downgrade and demean and break down the whole structure of our military forces."[15] Moorer, not surprisingly, authored the preface to Wells-Petry's book, *Exclusion*.

Sean O'Keefe, the acting navy secretary, said that even debating the issue had already hurt morale. Like Powell, he acknowledged that gay service would not break the military. "It's not so severe as to suggest that the basic objective of what they're asked to go do is threatened by it," he said of gay service. But his resistance was absolute nonetheless—based on his judgment that pleasing the majority of his force on this issue was the higher imperative than fairness or inclusion. "Is anybody happy out there that [the navy] is being used as a public debating society for all manner of societal issues?" he asked. "No."[16]

The navy gave free rein to its officials to denigrate gays and lesbians in defense of the ban. "Homosexuals are notoriously promiscuous," said a navy spokesman, Commander Craig Quigley, one more repetition of what, by the early 1990s, was nearly a military mantra. If gays are allowed to serve openly, Quigley continued, straight men would have to take showers with the "uncomfortable feeling of someone watching." Navy officials cited the court-ordered return of Keith Meinhold as evidence that gays hurt morale, as his squadron had to spend "many hours dealing with issues created by his return." Of course, Meinhold would never have had to "return" to the navy if he hadn't first been kicked out by an anti-gay policy.[17]

Indeed, as with virtually all the stories offered as evidence for disruptions caused by gay troops, the problems in Meinhold's squadron were actually caused not by Meinhold but by the homophobia that had caused his ouster in the first place. But navy personnel seized on the story to fan the flames of anti-gay sentiment. The press reported in January that Admiral Frank Kelso, chief of naval operations, was "deluged with angry questions from sailors and officers about the lifting of the ban." His own defense of gay exclusion was vehement. (Kelso, who was accused by a navy judge of lying about his role in the Tailhook scandal, struck a deal with the Pentagon in 1994 to retire early in exchange for an exoneration by the secretary of defense.)[18]

Powell, too, was hit with anxious queries about the prospect of gay service in the navy. After a long and jovial speech in January 1993 at the Naval Academy, in which Powell regaled the midshipmen with talk of virtuous sailors and "charming young ladies," the very first question, met with loud applause from the audience, was on the gay ban. If the ban is lifted, a cadet wanted to know, what should be done by "the majority of us who believe that homosexuality is an immoral behavior?" Powell's revealing answer was an effort to continue the diplomatic tone he had struck since beginning to field queries on this issue a year before. But he slipped. "We're all Americans," he said, "and there are some Americans who are homosexual. That is a choice they have made." Perhaps realizing he had waded into moral waters that inflamed instead of defused the controversy, he quickly added, "Or it may have been made for them, I don't know." Powell dwelled for a bit on the moral aspect, as if trying to find his bearings. He said that in his professional capacity he could not "make a moral judgment as to whether that is a correct lifestyle or not." As Americans, everyone is free "to make our own moral choice about that." In fact, his final answer to the question was less than inspiring: "If you find it so morally unacceptable that you could not serve in that capacity," then the only alternative to conforming is to resign.[19]

The upshot of Powell's answer was not to advise people to resign, but simply to lay out the existing options for service members struggling with the issue. When an order conflicted with your moral beliefs, either you gulp and swallow or you leave. But like the "don't ask, don't tell" policy to come, the significance of his answer lay between the lines of what was said. If being gay was not benign, then it must be—at least a little bit—malignant; if gay service would cause disorder and indiscipline, then homosexuality must be harmful and obviously undesirable.

AS THE GAY service issue made headlines at various points throughout 1992—in response to Powell's remarks, growing legal challenges, inchoate gay lobbying, and the rather glib way in which promises of reform rolled off of Bill Clinton's tongue—Charlie Moskos had an idea. His friend Sam Nunn had opted not to run for the White House, but the senator remained one of the most powerful members of Congress. That spring, Moskos dashed off a fateful memo to Nunn, outlining a plan to let gays serve in the military as long as they remained in the closet. After Clinton entered the White House, Moskos sent copies of his memo to Secretary of Defense Les Aspin and, through George Stephanopoulos, to the president himself. Moskos would meet with Nunn half a dozen times over the next six months to discuss the issue, which landed him a starring role in Nunn's Senate hearings in March 1993. "Don't ask, don't tell" had been born.[20]

In his memo, Moskos acknowledged that gays had long served effectively in the military. "What is at issue," he wrote in a commentary piece in the *Army Times,* "is allowing declared gays and lesbians into the military." Putting on his sociologist's cap, he elaborated in a string of op-eds early in 1993. Open service, he wrote, "is an entirely different kettle of fish from the service of discreet homosexuals in uniform." Moskos knew his idea would not be popular. But it didn't seem to bother him much, and indeed almost seemed to drive him. "Yes, you are treating gays as second-class people by saying they can't identify their sexuality," he acknowledged. "And so be it. Who says life is fair?" In another piece in *The Washington Post,* he cast his compromise as a pragmatic approach to an intractable problem, one best resolved with a dose of realpolitik. To condone "discreet homosexuality" while codifying an official ban on known gays, he wrote, "is to set oneself up for the charge of hypocrisy. And it probably does no good to say that a little hypocrisy may be the only thing that allows imperfect institutions to function in an imperfect world." But returning to his preferred tone of folksy common sense, he offered up yet another analogy, which betrayed a troubling inattention to the most basic modern understanding of sexual identity. Adultery, he pointed out, was also illegal in the military. "You could say adulterers are being repressed because they can't wear an 'A' on their sleeves. What about adulterers' rights?"[21]

That an old-school Democrat like Charles Moskos would come out so heavily against openly gay service spelled trouble ahead. In the very first weeks after the election, Clinton had fielded press inquiries about his intention to lift the gay ban. He repeatedly assured reporters that his plans had not changed. "Status alone, in the absence of some destructive behavior," he said on Veterans Day, November 11, 1992, should not disqualify people from military service. On Monday of the next week, he was asked about the issue again. And again, he reiterated that the nation did not have a person to waste. More to the point, there were already gays in the armed forces, he said. "We know there have always been gays in the military," he answered. "The issue is whether they can be in the military without lying about it." Referencing his commitment to meritocracy, he emphasized there would be a code of conduct that applied equally to all service members, and again distinguished between the simple fact of being gay and the prospect of disruptive behavior. "There is a great deal of difference between people doing something wrong and their status or condition in life," he said.[22]

These answers sounded reasonable enough, echoing as they did his campaign theme of judging actions rather than identity. But Clinton left open the thorny question of just what kind of behavior would be allowed and what kind punished, if gay and lesbian soldiers were officially allowed to serve. Would they be admitted so long as they avoided the sexual conduct that defined their status as homosexuals? Would they have to be celibate? Was Clinton hinting that he would welcome gays and lesbians so long as they didn't do what homosexuals do?

For the moment, such niceties troubled neither the White House transition team nor the reporters trailing them around. The mixture of guns and sex made for racy copy, and the larger question of gay service quickly became something of an obsession for the media. An outpouring of front-page and lead stories clogged the major papers and television news shows for the next eight months. While many newspapers editorialized in favor of letting gays serve, the American public was decidedly mixed, and would grow more opposed to the idea the more they heard the scare stories of military brass and the religious right on national security, the spread of disease, and the decline of the American family.

When Clinton was elected, many gays were overjoyed. They saw it as a sign that their exclusion from respectable spheres of politics and society was finally coming to an end. After all, their increasingly effective political organizing had helped elect the first president who publicly courted them during the campaign. In electing Clinton, their fellow Americans seemed to them to have rejected the overtly anti-gay rhetoric of the Republican Party's presidential bid, lowering a major barrier to reform. Gays and lesbians now had little reason to doubt Clinton's promised intention to lift one of the last remaining instances of legal discrimination against a minority group in the United States.

For their part, the president-elect and his advisers began the Clinton years with a strong sense of momentum on the issue. Hanging in the air was Truman's virtuous legacy of desegregating the armed forces with what appeared to be a simple executive order. (In reality, not surprisingly, the racial integration of the military was slower and more complicated than it has often been depicted.) The Republican National Convention in August had seemed to add to this momentum by creating a minor backlash against gay bashing. When Patrick Buchanan opened the convention with an inflammatory tirade de-

claring a culture war "for the soul of America," the Houston Astrodome re-
acted with wild praise; Pat Robertson estimated that a third of the delegates
were members of the Christian Coalition. But mainstream Americans responded poorly and the speech added to the GOP's reputation for being intolerant and out of touch. The convention did less than expected to raise the
sagging fortunes of the Bush campaign.[23] Chastened by voter disapproval of
the convention's tone, mainstream Republicans briefly backed away from the
nastiest anti-gay rhetoric.

But Republican reticence on the issue, it turns out, was a boon to anti-gay
forces. It added to the false confidence of Democrats who believed they could
expand gay rights without great resistance. It encouraged them to let down
their guard only to be pummeled by a surprise attack shortly after the election at the hands of social conservatives and their military and political allies. Once Clinton was in office and ready to act, Republicans would hammer
Democrats as soft on gays and untrustworthy with issues of national security,
a line that would gain traction with an emerging narrative that Clinton and
his supporters actually aimed to bring down a military they had opposed
since the early days of Vietnam.[24]

Barely a week had passed since the election victory when trouble began.
Hoping to focus on the stagnant economy and other issues of great importance to the nation, Clinton found instead that much of his time was devoted
to defending his campaign pledge to let gays serve. The issue became priority
number one for much of the media, who questioned the president-elect whenever they could, particularly in the wake of the court order to reinstate Keith
Meinhold. Press reports typically quoted military people as solidly against
lifting the ban. "We're 100 percent against it," said a recently retired master
sergeant in the army to the Associated Press. "I believe this sailor is entitled to
his rights," said another, referencing Meinhold. "He just shouldn't be in the
military. It was a hidden issue before and that was all right, but knowing about
it is going to be disruptive. Now that it's out, there are going to be fights—and
somebody's going to get hurt." Some acknowledged that their opposition was
cultural or moral and had little to do with military readiness. "No, you just
can't have gays in the military," said an army sergeant. "It's just the principle of
the thing—the long tradition." Another worried about her safety: "You're in
such close quarters and would literally have to take showers with these
women," she said. "You get dressed, sleep, do everything together. Will I be
protected? That's what I wonder."[25]

As Clinton was pushed onto the defensive, Powell led a unified front by the Joint Chiefs of Staff to make public their opposition to gay service. "The military leaders in the armed forces of the United States—the Joint Chiefs of Staff and the senior commanders—continue to believe strongly that the presence of homosexuals within the armed forces would be prejudicial to good order and discipline," he told reporters. "And we continue to hold that view." To avoid any appearance of insubordination, he added that the decision was ultimately "a judgment that will have to be made, and appropriately so in our system, by our civilian political leaders—the president of the United States, Congress." At the end of the day, he said, "the armed forces of the United States will do what we are told to do."[26]

The Joint Chiefs also made the Clinton team aware privately that their resistance would remain fierce so long as the president-elect continued on a course to letting gays serve. The chiefs acknowledged that gays already served, but said that if such service were formally allowed, gays might become open about their sexuality, which could undermine morale and discipline.[27] With no evidence tying gay service to undermining readiness, the officers could only speak in hypotheticals—gays *could* become more open, which *could* cause problems with cohesion and morale. When pressed, they could only offer isolated anecdotes in which the disruptions were actually caused by the actions of homophobic military men, or recycled fear stories about how sexual advances by gay men—a problem of misconduct, which no one was proposing to make legal—had hurt morale.

Aware that a confrontation could be brewing, Clinton met in person with Colin Powell two weeks after Election Day at the Hay-Adams Hotel in Washington, D.C., to discuss this and other military matters. Chief among them was Clinton's plans to downsize the Pentagon, including a major cut to the defense budget. As the first baby boomer president, and the first president to be elected since the fall of the Soviet Union, Clinton came to office representing the hopes of millions of liberals to finally yield a "peace dividend" by reversing the costly military buildup of the previous generation. Money from the military budget was needed to fund Clinton's ambitious domestic policy agenda. The defense community was aware of such plans and understood that it would be increasingly challenging to explain to the public the need to keep open cold war military bases and fund expensive and controversial programs like the Star Wars missile defense system. Some in the military faced the arrival of the new administration with a sense of dread, a feeling that social, cultural, and fiscal pressures were conspiring to marginalize them. They worried that their livelihoods, their lifestyles, and their beliefs, including their unique perception of the dangers that would continue to threaten the

United States, were increasingly neglected or mocked by a misunderstanding public.

From Clinton's anti-war days, he had gained a reputation as no friend to the armed forces, once describing his generation's "loathing" of the military. As David Mixner tried to explain to the press, Clinton was hardly a strident member of the anti-war community. In fact, he was considered a relative outsider to the cause, almost a dabbler in the movement when many young liberals had become greatly radicalized around their opposition to Vietnam. There was both virtue and vice in Clinton's actual feelings around the war. Mixner recalls the future president had genuinely struggled with his moral position on the war, which is more than can be said for many. But his wavering also reflected his desperate need for approval, his wish to please everyone, sometimes at the expense of failing to commit passionately to a principle and fighting for it at great cost, as so many of his generation had done around Vietnam. Clinton's mixed feelings about authority also appeared to have shaped his ambivalent relationship with the military and the activities of his antimilitary peers. Mixner even sensed that in Clinton's adult life, he had developed a kind of "awe" for the military that reflected this conflict between his youthful instinct to resist power and his later wish to grab its reins.[28]

But politics is not about appreciating the complex layers of a person's psyche or his emotional effort to come to terms with the subtleties of issues like war and peace. Instead, Clinton's opponents painted him as a draft dodger, and worse. His decision not to go to Vietnam and his criticism of the military buildup of the Reagan years fit perfectly into his detractors' image of the naïve, weak-willed liberal who is both too ignorant and too cowardly to defend and strengthen the country. The construct played right into the hands of the conspiracy theorists who wrote tracts about Clinton's plans to break the military and hand the country over to the communists. But it didn't take a conspiracy theorist to hate Bill Clinton and what he seemed, to some, to stand for: imposing a selfish, irresponsible, decadent, dangerous lifestyle throughout the country, which would leave the nation vulnerable to life-threatening military and moral weaknesses.

Clinton was aware of his damaged reputation in military circles that Thursday when he met Powell at the Hay-Adams Hotel. He knew that his public promises to lift the gay ban using executive power sounded to many military men like one more prong in a misguided effort by young liberals to impose a radical social agenda on a traditional culture they did not understand or respect. And Clinton was determined to finesse the situation at their meeting that afternoon. Not backing down, he repeated to Powell his intention to lift the ban but signaled that he wanted to include top military leaders in the process. Powell repeated his opposition, but said that military leaders would offer greater cooperation if they were consulted over the next year. The general suggested that the president move very cautiously to study the issue, rather than simply issue an executive order to mandate the change.[29]

Though both men dug in their heels, the meeting appeared productive. By the beginning of December, the press was reporting that Powell had "softened" his opposition. Powell said that he and the Joint Chiefs were pleased that Clinton had agreed to consult them on the issue. He also made it very clear that his concerns about the impact of gay service were qualified: "I've never been of the view it will break the armed forces of the United States if we went in this direction," he said, adding that if the president lifted the ban, the military would follow orders. "Nor will there be large resignations" if gays are allowed to serve. "I hope we can keep some of the emotionalism out of this issue," he concluded, in an apparent plea for rationality, "until we have time for a full debate."[30] Once the debate began in earnest, presumably, emotionalism was fair game.

Clinton's willingness to "consult" the Joint Chiefs of Staff seemed like a natural gesture toward cooperation. But coming in the context it did—amid fierce resistance and questions about Clinton's level of commitment—it was also an early sign of difficulty for the anti-ban forces. The decision was both a reminder of the Clinton team's failure to reach out to the Pentagon brass early enough and the first step toward what would become a months-long delay, allowing the opposition to fester and snowball. In any event, the détente did not last long. In mid-December, *Newsweek* reported, Powell and the Joint Chiefs warned Clinton's aides that the lot of them would resign if the new administration forced their hand on the gay issue.[31]

Clinton's "consultation" effort was led by John Holum, a friend and aide to Clinton who had been a defense adviser to George McGovern during his failed 1972 anti-war presidential bid. Holum's name was being floated as a possible secretary of the navy, which made the navy brass apoplectic. Holum was still known as a McGovernite. He had advised McGovern when the candidate pushed for a retreat on Vietnam as well as major funding cuts for defense. Now Holum was Clinton's point man on how to let gays infest the military.[32]

Holum spent the Christmas season meeting with top military brass and gay rights advocates in an effort to eke out a compromise. He also visited ships and military bases, where he was surprised to find a "live and let live attitude" from enlisted personnel. "What I drew from my consultations was that it was doable," Holum said, but he encountered resistance from some of the military brass. Colin Powell gathered the other members of the Joint Chiefs who served under him and made a clear show of force, telling Holum in front of them what a bad idea it would be to lift the ban. Individually, some of the Joint Chiefs displayed a reluctant "problem-solving" approach, saying they didn't approve, but would weigh the options for how to lift the ban if it was so ordered. Carl Mundy, head of the Marine Corps and the most outspoken opponent of gay service on moral grounds, gave Holum a copy of Horn's film. Despite this opposition, Holum drew from his consultations that lifting the ban was "doable, that the military is probably better than the rest of society in dealing with social change."[33]

In January, Holum sent the Pentagon and the president his recommendation. He suggested the president issue an executive order, but not one that would lift the ban immediately. Holum had heard again and again from military brass that they didn't feel adequately consulted, and he could sense that his own role as a former McGovernite go-between didn't butter the biscuit. So Holum proposed that the executive order should delay any substantive change until the matter could be studied for up to a year. Eventually, a "memorandum of instruction" from the president to the Defense Department could lift the ban, once the early opposition died down. Holum never got a formal reply to his recommendation. And he was happy enough to leave the ball in the White House's court, as he had already taken too much time away from his law practice.[34]

Into the void stepped Nunn, Bob Dole and the new secretary of defense, Les Aspin. On Sunday, November 15, 1992, Dole, the Republican leader in the Senate, and Nunn, the Democratic chairman of the Senate Armed Services Committee, went on the Sunday talk shows to warn Clinton publicly that Congress would not watch idly as he let the gay lobby push around the world's most powerful military. Dole said that lifting the ban "would cause real problems in the military," but his most vocal opposition was grounded in politics: Letting gays serve could "blow the lid off the Capitol," he cautioned. He suggested that the incoming president put the issue on the back burner and appoint a commission to study it. "In my view he's going to get in more trouble than he can add up right now if he starts with an executive order on that issue." Dole made clear that if Clinton went forward as planned, Congress would take a vote on whether to override the president, "and I'd be surprised if he won that vote."[35]

If the Republican Dole's opposition to Clinton was unsurprising, Sam Nunn's was only slightly less predictable. In the spring of 1992, having twice considered and aborted a run for the White House, the Democratic senator watched as Bill Clinton edged slowly toward the world's most powerful job—the same post Nunn had once thought could be his. While Nunn had given up on the presidency, he still hoped to hold at least one of the reins of power, perhaps as secretary of state or defense. The latter ambition was telling. When the first President Bush took the White House in 1988, Nunn led Senate opposition to Bush's choice for defense secretary, former senator John Tower. One of his main objections was that Tower was alleged to have a drinking problem. As the battle heated up, Nunn was forced to admit that he himself had a drunk-driving accident in his past, which involved leaving the scene of the crime.[36] It was perhaps a partial explanation for why Nunn opposed Tower's nomination—the projection of his own, even minor, moral failings lent an added layer of competitiveness to the political rivalries for which Washington is famous—and offered a disturbing window into Nunn's modus operandi.

Nunn's interest in becoming secretary of defense hardly seemed an idle ambition. Although his own military experience consisted of only one year in the Coast Guard,[37] he represented a state with many military bases and had spent twenty years building a reputation as Mr. Defense. Nunn was considered so powerful in military circles that he was thought to have been the only person capable of stopping the first George Bush from invading Iraq. Of course, he failed. (The fact that he took a beating in opposing a Republican president's plan to go to war suggested either that he was a man of great principle or that he was determined to assert his prowess in military matters against the GOP.) Nunn was even rumored to have been considered by the first President Bush to be named defense secretary. Ultimately, went the joke, such an appointment was unnecessary; in practice, he already was. "Nunn's numbers," his suggestions for each year's proposed defense budget, were considered sacrosanct in military circles and often accepted uncritically in Congress, even as Nunn's attachment to cold war weapons and strategies became as dated as his views on homosexuality.

After Clinton's election, as Nunn's name was floated around for secretary of defense, gay rights groups became angered. A conservative southern Democrat who had backed the fiercely segregationist George Wallace in 1972, Nunn was no friend of gay rights. "He seemed to have bought into the 1950s line that there was some kind of disconnect between being gay and being of good moral character," said Urvashi Vaid, who was head of the National Lesbian and Gay Task Force in 1992. In fact, Nunn's unabashed antipathy to gay equality—which would become even more obvious with his hostile questioning during Senate hearings on gay service that he would lead the following spring—rendered his opposition to lifting the ban a foregone conclusion. He had backed Senator John Glenn's bid for the White House in 1984, citing his courage in expressing his "strongly held moral belief that homosexuals should not be the role models for our children." Nunn had also dismissed two political aides because they were gay. He defended his actions by blaming the military's anti-gay policy, saying the aides could not work for him effectively on classified matters because the military and intelligence agencies considered them a security risk. But the crusade he was about to lead to protect that very same anti-gay policy gave the lie to his effort to pin his discrimination on the policy. Mainstream gay groups clamored that someone so outspoken against the rights of gays should not be secretary of defense. The activist group Queer Nation even staged a kiss-in at his office to protest his homophobia.[38]

It was clearly with horror that, partly due to the opposition of gay groups, Nunn watched another longtime rival, Les Aspin, step over him to become secretary of defense. Aspin, the Wisconsin Democrat who chaired the House Armed Services Committee, was an Ivy League economist, while Nunn was a small-town southern lawyer. Aspin had ultimately opposed the Vietnam War and was far more ready than Nunn to support cuts in the defense budget. He was known as a supporter of gays in the military, and his nomination was greeted with relief by gay groups. But he was also respected by many Republicans, despite his support for Pentagon budget cuts. Aspin's early comments on the gay ban seemed to straddle the two constituencies fairly well, while remaining firm and decisive. The current policy, he said, "has got some serious flaws," and must be dealt with "head-on." There would be no chance to "try and patch up the old program or sideslip the issue," he said. But he also tried to lower the temperature of the debate, saying the Clinton administration was only doing what public pressure or the courts have forced the Pentagon to do anyway. The idea, he said, is "to deal with this thing very, very carefully, but to deal with it very, very deliberately."[39]

With Aspin's acceptance of the post, the stage was set for a mammoth battle of wills between Aspin and Nunn, one that, at times, had far more to do with the power struggles and personal psychology of individual personalities than with what was best for the military or for the country. One top Pentagon official close to Nunn said the senator viewed the skirmish over gay service as a *"mano a mano* test of manhood about who runs defense policy." For Nunn, it was a chance to "take Les Aspin down a notch or two." In the view of Democratic politicos, "Nunn was not given the deferential treatment he expected during the transition." In response to this and other perceived slights, Nunn sought "to embarrass Clinton."[40] Indeed, keeping gays out of the military became a way for Nunn to pay back those he felt had disrespected him and to bolster his commitment to moral purity.

Of course, like Powell, Nunn sought to take the high ground, maintaining a firm but decorous public face on the issue that avoided the most vituperative anti-gay rhetoric. Yet Nunn could scarcely conceal his antipathy toward gays. "We've got to consider not only the rights of homosexuals," he said days after Clinton reiterated his promise to lift the ban, "but also the rights of those who are not homosexual, and who give up a great deal of their privacy when they go into the military." He said he thought "there could be some very emotional feelings," and that if things changed too quickly, "I fear for the lives of people in the military themselves."[41] Nunn was a master of language that sounded superficially fair but was actually not: Here he asked the nation to respect the rights of those who were so hateful toward an innocent minority that they might be driven to murder if this minority were granted the same rights as everyone else. Could Nunn have gotten away with considering the rights not only of blacks but of those who hated blacks enough to kill them?

Nunn's willingness to scuttle Clinton's first major initiative was curious. The new president was the first person from Nunn's party to occupy the White House in twelve years, and a product of the moderate Democratic Leadership Council, a group Nunn himself had helped start after Walter Mondale's loss in 1984. (Mondale had supported laws protecting gays from discrimination, one of the inspirations behind Nunn's effort to push the Democratic Party rightward.) Once Nunn had bowed out of the 1992 race, he had worked hard to help get Clinton elected, and had helped advise Clinton on military issues during the campaign.[42] But their relationship was also awkward and brittle. Clinton viewed Nunn's support as unpredictable and sometimes fair-weather. He was highly sensitive to perceived snubs, while Nunn was equally sensitive to congressional prerogatives and the threat of executive overreach.

Gay rights groups would come to see Nunn's stalwart opposition to gay service as a product of these sensitivities and resentments. "Nunn's basic problem with this issue was not the issue but that he was passed over for a job," said Urvashi Vaid, "and he turned his fury on the administration as a way of punishing them." Perhaps Nunn's opposition to gay rights should not have been surprising, Vaid said, but his vehemence on this topic didn't seem explainable even by his record of anti-gay sentiment. "Why did Sam Nunn suddenly become a crusader against this, holding hearings, going to submarines to talk about close quarters?" she asked rhetorically, suggesting that it was motivated in large part by his sense of being snubbed.[43]

But as Vaid has also acknowledged, gay rights groups faced several challenges that they did not meet successfully during the war over gay service. They underestimated both the vehemence of opposition to homosexuality in the United States and the organizing will and know-how of the religious right, and they consequently took insufficient steps to formulate a successful battle plan. Their overconfidence was exacerbated by assurances from Clinton and his team, conveyed through David Mixner, that lifting the gay ban "won't be a big deal." Yet the well-oiled machinery of the religious right outnumbered, outflanked, outspent, and overwhelmed any semblance of organized lobbying by the gay movement. The methodical anti-gay organizing by Christian conservatives, which took off nationally starting just days after Clinton's election, would prove impossible to best. Gay groups developed their own coalitions, but even their Hollywood dollars and political know-how, buffed by decades of anti-war organizing skills, could not match the spiritually and culturally inspired tactics of the anti-gay lobby and the vast telecommunications technology of the New Christian Right. As one gay rights organizer put it, gays were lobbying "the old-fashioned way," writing letters and setting up meetings with their members of Congress.[44] They had nothing like the three to four hundred thousand American churches on which the religious right could draw to mobilize voters and rein in recalcitrant politicians. Liberals had been shut out of the White House for a generation, and their sudden return to power meant a double whammy: overconfidence that the road to justice was suddenly an easy ride and inadequate experience in how to actually navigate the halls of power.

Short on money, broadsided by resistance, and low on numbers, the anti-ban forces belatedly scrambled to organize, unable to avoid the attendant turf wars that so often accompany shifts in power, tactics, and strategy. It wouldn't be until February 1993 that Mixner hastily brought together the Campaign for Military Service, an alliance made up of the Human Rights Campaign Fund, National Gay and Lesbian Task Force, and a dozen other pro-gay groups. With talented gay rights lawyers like Tom Stoddard and Chai Feldblum at the helm, the group did all it could to work privately and publicly to build support for reform. They hoped that, whatever was happening in Nunn's dramatic hearings, they would be able to convince enough Democrats to go with a plan that would keep the reins of control in the executive branch and not relinquish it to Congress, where a statutory gay ban would be far harder to reverse down the line.[45]

But it was too late. Supporters of gay service could not build the momentum they needed, and ultimately no effective strategy emerged to revive their cause after the first round had been lost. Instead champions of reform were dismissed by at least one commentator as "career activists, urban reformers, marchers in whatever good cause needs a champion, liberated women and men, AIDs [sic] demonstrators, a fair number of members of Congress and the trailing media band," and if that wasn't enough, they were "politically correct groups and individuals whose military experience and insights are about the equal of Clinton's." Even the few retired military officers who supported letting gays serve admitted privately that pressure from former colleagues in the military was too much for them to brook and they were unwilling to publicly oppose the military brass.[46]

In January, Clinton's advisers acknowledged to the press that they'd been surprised by the strength of the opposition. In response, aides were exploring alternatives to an executive order. As soon as Clinton appeared to be wavering, opponents smelled weakness and prepared to pounce. Clinton had repeatedly said that lifting the ban was not open to negotiation—only to discussion over how to do it. But things got worse from here. Holum's presence on the front lines of the battle gave Nunn and military leaders a new reason to resent the forces of reform. Over the next few weeks, conservatives rallied around a "thorny questions" strategy designed to overwhelm the debate with the specter of uncontrollable change and the full-scale imposition of the "homosexual lifestyle" on the military.

Nunn introduced these thorns in a passionate Senate speech late that month. "Too many times," he said, "we in the political world send down edicts and don't think about the implications of the things that have to follow." There are numerous "questions that have to be thought about, and every military commander will tell you that they have to go through each one of these things, probably, and plus a lot more." Nunn then served up over forty questions in rapid succession, as if from a machine gun: "What would be the impact of changing the current policy on recruiting, retention, morale, discipline, as well as military effectiveness? Should there be restrictions on homosexual acts with other military personnel, or only with nonmilitary personnel? What restrictions, if any, should be placed on conduct between members of the same sex? Should such restrictions apply in circumstances in which conduct would not be prohibited if engaged in between members of the opposite sex? What about displays of affection between members of the same sex while they're out of uniform? What about displays of affection that are otherwise permissible while in uniform, such as dancing at a formal event?" What about "pay and benefits and entitlements? Should homosexual couples receive the same benefits as legally married couples? If homosexual couples are given such benefits, will they also have to be granted to unmarried hetero-sexual couples? Will there be a related requirement for affirmative action re-cruiting, retention, and promotion to compensate for past discrimination? If discrimination is prohibited, will there be a need for extensive sensitivity training for members of the armed forces? Who will carry out this sensitiv-ity training?" How will the military handle demands for "back pay, reinstate-ment, promotions, and similar forms of relief?" Nunn said he did not "pretend to have the answers to these questions, but there are too many people talking on this subject now who haven't even thought of the questions, let alone the answers."[47]

Military leaders and political commentators took to the pages of major papers to magnify the angst Nunn was spreading, adopting his "thorny ques-tions" strategy. John Marsh, Jr., secretary of the army under President Rea-gan, wrote in *The New York Times* that ending the ban by presidential decree "would raise thorny problems" about privacy, benefits, and the Uniform Code of Military Justice's ban on sodomy. "Military commanders and administra-tors," he wrote, oppose "a sweeping order" because "known homosexuals threaten established values and create tensions that can undermine a unit's spirit and confidence."[48]

Robert Novak and Rowland Evans used their *Chicago Sun-Times* column to echo the thorny questions. "Should the same-sex 'spouse' of an Army man be provided with joint living quarters on the base?" they wrote. "Should same-sex spouses be given equality in pension and survivor benefits, which could add high cost to the Pentagon's shrinking budget? Should gays have equal rights with non-gays to dance in the officers' club or hold hands in the enlisted Marines' slop shoot?" By all appearances, they wrote, those trying to overturn the ban are "not close to deciding these hard-core issues. Their cur-rent thinking is limited."[49]

Novak and Evans thought that Nunn's planned hearings could be "devas-tating." To them, the central issue was not what was best for the military but "the cultural question: whether gays can be admitted to the military without also bringing their lifestyle onto the base and into the barracks." It would be surprising, they concluded, if the "gay lobby does not have other, quite differ-ent ideas" beyond simply equal treatment in the military. "Indeed, the presi-dent may discover that the right to serve is only the first of many rights that the gay community will expect him to supply."[50]

As Nunn worked to weaken Clinton's pledge, he deftly anointed himself the control valve between the GOP and the White House. If Clinton would agree to hold off on an executive order lifting the ban, Nunn proposed, he would close the tap on Republican efforts to write the policy into law, over Clinton's head. If not, he would join it, virtually assuring its passage and tying Clinton's hands. "Let's don't legislate on something," he said, "and in exchange, let's have the Executive show some restraint." Nunn's reference to "restraint" had special resonance: Hillary Clinton had accused Nunn of ditching her the day news broke of Bill Clinton's affair with Gennifer Flowers. The first lady was in Nunn's state of Georgia that day, and the senator was scheduled to keep her company for media appearances, but he never made it. Nunn, who considered himself a champion of moral propriety, may have disappeared on purpose, seeking to distance himself from Clinton's indiscretions.[51]

Later, when the Lewinsky scandal broke, Nunn complained that Clinton had "placed his own personal interests far above the national interest," resulting in a "lowering of our moral discourse" and "the exposure of our children to a negative role model," the same phrase he'd used in backing John Glenn's opposition to homosexuals as moral guides for young people. Nunn even suggested that Clinton's irresponsible actions, along with the inattentiveness of the American people, could cause dangerous international conflicts, and concluded that Clinton should engage in "personal sacrifice," including possibly resigning from office.[52] Even in 1993, "restraint" was a pointed effort to link Clinton and his fellow liberals to a lifestyle of license and irresponsibility.

The first of two chapters in the battle over gay service climaxed in the last third of January 1993, the first full week of Clinton's presidency. The topic so dominated the meetings of top military and political leaders that they only "spent a few minutes on Iraq," according to one of the Joint Chiefs of Staff. On January 21, Les Aspin met with the JCS for two raucous hours of debate in the "tank," the soundproof chamber inside the Pentagon where the JCS gather to discuss strategy. Both parties restated their positions. Aspin reiterated the president's commitment to overturning the ban. The JCS insisted that doing so would undermine morale, hurt recruiting, force devout people to leave the military, and spread AIDS by increasing sexual promiscuity that could ultimately bring heterosexuals into contact with the virus.[53]

As news stories overflowed with the drama of the battle, the Joint Chiefs and other senior officers increasingly expressed outrage that they had not been sufficiently consulted. And then, the issue spun out of control. On Sunday morning, January 24, Bob Schieffer of CBS's *Face the Nation* obtained a copy of a confidential memo from Les Aspin to the president; it outlined a strategy to both compromise on Clinton's pledge and press the JCS and congressional opponents of reform toward letting gays serve.[54] How could they do both? Though they hadn't yet named it as such, Clinton and Aspin were hovering on the brink of Moskos's "don't ask, don't tell" plan. By focusing on the vague realm of "status," and by continuing to restrict "conduct," the White House team thought (correctly, as it would turn out) that they could strike a compromise that would avoid a revolt by Congress and the Joint Chiefs. They hoped it would appease gay rights groups, too. In the former, they were essentially correct, but in the latter, they were very wrong.

The leaked memo wrought havoc. In it, Aspin warned the president that congressional and military opposition to reform was too strong to overcome. He recommended that Clinton meet with the JCS, saying "this is not a negotiation" but simply the "consultation that you have promised." Aspin appeared to be caught totally off guard when forced to explain to the nation, without any preparation, why he was encouraging the Joint Chiefs to consult with the administration if the president's mind was already made up. It made it seem like he was prodding the president to feign consultation with military leaders even though he had no intention of listening to their objections. Rumors surfaced that Powell was threatening to bolt. There were "reports all over Washington this week," said Schieffer on *Face the Nation*, "that General Powell, the chairman of the Joint Chiefs, has said that he may resign if this is forced upon him." Aspin's reply: "Not going to happen."[55]

As angry as the military leaders were, gay groups were no happier with what they heard. The public discussion of the memo contained the first known suggestion that the White House might accept a plan that required gays to conceal their sexual identity and avoid any sexual activity while in the service. Aspin spoke of "trying to get the gay rights groups to do a little compromise" in order to ward off congressional action. He hinted what that compromise would be. "The president has said that he wants to eliminate the discrimination against gays in the military based upon status," said Aspin on *Face the Nation*, but he would like "to have strict controls, or prohibitions, against people's behavior." Aspin said that the question of conduct was "at the heart of the ability to make this thing work" as a compromise between the military and the gay community. Some gay rights advocates wondered if Aspin had leaked the memo himself as a way to end the battle.[56] Indeed, Aspin would later say publicly that he was trying to preserve political capital for other battles. And it seemed peculiar that a brand-new defense secretary would somehow lose control of a private memo to the president like this. What better way to avoid a drawn-out battle than to concede defeat before the fight had ever really begun?

Meanwhile, George Stephanopoulos, then White House director of communications, reiterated in a press conference the following day the president's "commitment to ending discrimination against gays in the military solely on the basis of status, and to maintain morale and cohesion in the military."[57] But the language was quickly becoming code for the limited right to serve as closeted, celibate gays. The administration, which had hoped to execute its plan in private, was wounded by the perception that it was taking neither the Joint Chiefs nor gay groups seriously.

Nunn was also furious. First, Aspin was speaking on TV about a plan that Nunn did not feel he had been consulted about. Worse, Nunn learned from the leaked memo that Aspin had cited him by name as one of the chief impediments to the White House's plan to end the ban. Already sensitive over matters of military and political prerogative, thick in an ideological and personal battle with two powerful men whose jobs he once coveted, Nunn dug in his heels. He held a news conference on Capitol Hill the day after the *Face the Nation* revelation, in which he complained that the White House had not consulted enough with him and with other congressional and military leaders. "I'll just say that if there's a strategy there, that it hadn't been explained to me," Nunn said. "Does that mean you're dissatisfied?" asked a reporter. "No," said Nunn, "it just means what I said. I just am not part of the strategy."[58]

The day after the leak, the Joint Chiefs met with Clinton himself. Although it was their first meeting with Clinton as president, they never even discussed the evolving trouble spots in Iraq, Bosnia, or Somalia. Instead, they focused on whether a certain variety of love—instead of a certain variety of hate—could bring down the world's strongest military. (Ironically, that week GOP senator Phil Gramm said, by way of opposing gay service, "We're not going to let politics destroy the greatest Army the world has ever seen"—even as politics was doing all it could to distract the nation's leaders from pressing issues.) While the meeting was described as cordial and lacked the kind of outrage that characterized the previous week's tête à tête with Aspin, both sides reiterated their commitments to seemingly opposite positions and the men left quickly when it was done.[59]

Then it was on to Congress, where Bob Dole threatened to write the ban into law and Senator George Mitchell, the Democratic leader, informed the White House that, without Nunn's blessing, Democrats would be powerless to stop the rest of Congress from overriding the president's efforts. After meetings on Capitol Hill, Clinton held his ground. The words of Stephanopoulos this time did not even betray an intention to compromise on the status versus conduct distinction: "The president is sticking by his commitment to ending discrimination against homosexuals in the military," he said.

Either the White House still thought full success was possible, or its definition of "ending discrimination" had become woefully corrupted. After all, no one would seriously regard it as an end to discrimination if gays were permitted to serve while they were required to conceal their identity and remain celibate twenty-four hours a day. Still, as Aspin had done in his memo, Mitchell and other allies of the president were now warning the White House that its power was not limitless. "Any executive order can be overturned by act of Congress," Mitchell said. As a backdrop to the frenzied negotiations, hundreds of thousands of calls came into the Capitol, with the vast majority opposing gay service—largely courtesy of the furious organizing of the religious right.[60]

The rest of the week consisted of frantic meetings, often lasting deep into the night, in which Clinton and Aspin engaged Nunn and other lawmakers to figure out a way to tamp down the national uproar. The compromise that became "don't ask, don't tell" was essentially formulated that week, though its details and permanence would not be worked out until July and beyond. Powell and Nunn, his main ally in Congress, insisted that no homosexual conduct—which would come to include saying you were gay and even holding hands off base—be permitted by service members anytime anywhere. Congress appeared to have more leverage in this area, because the Uniform Code of Military Justice, which was controlled by Congress, banned sodomy. How could the nation permit the president to issue an executive order to allow something that was criminalized in the military justice system governed by Congress? Sure, the UCMJ banned sodomy for everyone, gay and straight alike. But the average American viewed gays alone as defined by sodomy, and the ultimate policy defined "homosexual conduct" as any physical activity that a "reasonable person would understand to demonstrate a propensity or intent to engage in homosexual acts."[61]

President Clinton, for his part, held firm through the end of the month. He appeared to be motivated by both the principle of equality and the recognition that abandoning this campaign promise threatened to brand him as untrustworthy, as the White House was already taking heat for failing to deliver on middle-class tax relief and spending reductions. But in light of Aspin and Mitchell's advice that the White House might not be able to surmount congressional opposition, his options were drying up. That week, the president and his advisers began to hint that their commitment to nondiscrimination would only extend to status, not conduct.

On Thursday, Clinton began to make it clear that the compromise would involve only welcoming gays who did not engage in homosexual conduct, although the meaning of this was still being debated. "The principle behind this for me is that Americans who are willing to conform to the requirements of conduct within the military services in my judgment should be able to serve in the military and that people should be disqualified from serving in the military based on something they do, not based on who they are," Clinton said. "That is the elemental principle." He said he had won agreement from the Joint Chiefs that recruits would no longer be asked if they were gay, but said "the narrow issue on which there is disagreement is whether people should be able to say that they are homosexual without being . . . severed."[62]

That "narrow disagreement" ended up delaying the formation of a final policy for six months—similar, in the end, to what Holum's recommendation had been, but with no executive order. On Friday, January 29, President Clinton held a news conference to announce that no final plan would be decided on until July, enough time for Nunn to hold congressional hearings on the matter. Immediately, Bob Dole, in an effort to embarrass the president and launch his own presidential campaign for 1996, sought to write the full gay ban into law. Nunn as part of his compromise with Clinton and in an effort to control the six-month study period offered a softer bill to write the delay itself into law, a bill that prevailed over Dole's. Nunn's success solidified his role as lead man on the issue. The six-month study period would enable the pro-ban forces, under the leadership of Nunn and with the eager assistance of the religious right, to rally still greater support for holding the line on gay troops.

As part of the two-step plan outlined by Secretary Aspin, the military would, in the meantime, stop asking recruits about their sexual orientation and suspend discharges based on homosexuality. But investigations of homosexuality would continue, and if they were found out, gays and lesbians would be transferred into the "standby reserves," where they would receive no pay or benefits, and where their careers would be frozen until the final plan was in place. The standby reserves were a last-resort cadre of reservists who did not even train for deployment.[63]

Clinton acknowledged the compromise was not everything he wanted, but tried to claim it as a victory, calling it a "dramatic step forward." He said it would allow gays to serve "who are prepared to accept all necessary restrictions on their behavior, many of which would be intolerable in civilian society." He also insisted he still planned to sign an order that summer allowing gays to serve in some capacity. While he hinted he might veto any legislation that sought to maintain the ban, part of the January compromise was that he would invite Congress to vote on whatever proposal he came up with in July. And there were still several arrows Congress had in its quiver, including writing an amendment banning gay service and attaching it to a larger bill that would be even harder for Clinton to veto.[64]

Senator Bob Dole, the minority leader, called it "a de facto lifting of the ban and therefore a sham," and Senator Dan Coats, Republican from Indiana, called the plan a "dangerous mistake." Yet even Nunn's aides acknowledged that the interim policy was essentially unchanged from the status quo, since being relegated to the standby reserves was little better than being sacked.[65] Plus, refraining from asking about sexual orientation at accession made little practical difference, because for decades, gays and lesbians had entered the military by lying in answer to that question (or by answering truthfully because they didn't yet identify as gay). The new rule could mean one less lie to a bureaucrat at the beginning of a career, but gays would still have to hide the truth from those who really mattered, their closest comrades, if the ban wasn't lifted outright.

The compromise gave Nunn and Powell essentially everything they wanted. Senator Nunn had the president "in a vice," recalled Ruth Marcus of *The Washington Post*. By the end of that agonizing week, the administration was asking Nunn what language he wanted in the compromise plan, which Nunn literally faxed to the White House. For the substance of the plan Nunn credited Powell. "Gen. Colin Powell," he said, "chairman of the Joint Chiefs of Staff, has stated that in view of the unique conditions of military service, active and open homosexuality by members of the armed forces would have a very negative effect on military morale and discipline. I agree with Gen. Powell's assessment."[66]

4

Listening to Nunn: The Congressional Hearings on Gay Service

W HEN NUNN CAME OUT against lifting the ban in 1992, he did it with
the typical political savvy of a seasoned Capitol Hill veteran. He called
for "comprehensive hearings." He urged "caution." He insisted the issue be
"studied," that nothing be done "overnight." He said he wanted to "hear a lot
more evidence" before any change was incorporated.[1] All of it sounded emi-
nently reasonable, except that those who knew how these things worked knew
that Nunn would use the "study" period not to assess the evidence but to build
an arsenal of weapons to defeat the effort to lift the ban.

Even a close confidante of Nunn's acknowledged that he often formed
positions based on quick judgments made before all the evidence was in.[2] The
so-called cooling-off period demanded by Nunn would be a time to seek out
evidence for a position he had already reached. Studies would be buried when
they didn't support his views. Hearings would be stacked against Nunn's political opponents. Time would be used not to learn, but to let opposition fester
and grow.

Both Clinton and Nunn had publicly promised a thorough investigation
of the matter, even though they had made clear that they already knew exactly what they planned to do. Was the study period, then, a joke? Were the
hearings just a performance? "The funny part of the story," recalled Tim Mc-
Feeley, then head of the Human Rights Campaign Fund, the nation's largest
gay rights group, "is that we even argued over this for six months. The inter-
esting part is that [Clinton] even kept hope alive for six months," when it
quickly became clear that the new president was already prepared—by
January—to drastically water down his commitment. If Aspin did, indeed,
leak his memo on purpose, this would be the reason: Conceding there was
insufficient support in Congress to push the change through was a way of
admitting defeat—and blaming it on others—without having to spend much
effort on the fight while there still might be time to change minds. Indeed by
March, the president was publicly entertaining a plan to create segregated

fighting units for gays and straights, though some congressional staffers argued the purpose of this inflammatory proposal was simply to ward off enshrinement of the outright ban into law, leaving control in the hands of Clinton and the Department of Defense.[3] Still, Clinton perhaps believed he could come out in July with something he could call a victory. Gay groups who worked tirelessly on the issue seemed to believe that Clinton remained genuine in his commitment to make it work.

Along with Nunn's Senate hearings that spring, Clinton would direct Defense Secretary Les Aspin to oversee the six-month study period. Aspin would respond by commissioning two studies. One was to be conducted by the Military Working Group, the panel of generals and admirals who drew on the services of military insiders like Robert Maginnis and Melissa Wells-Petry. The other would be handled by the Rand Corporation, a global policy think tank created by military brass after World War II. That both groups had long-standing ties to the military did not give much comfort to gay rights groups, who increasingly felt cut out of the picture. But the Rand Corporation, which conducted the far more extensive and rigorous study of the topic, came up with a surprising result. In the end, Nunn's Senate hearings were more of a performance than a fair and open inquiry. Their stunning drama helped shape the contours of the ultimate policy and provide a revealing window into the nation's feelings about both the military and the place of sexuality in the larger culture.

BEGINNING ON MARCH 29, 1993, Nunn made good on his promise to hold hearings on gays in the military. The Senate Committee on Armed Services met at 9:30 A.M. at the Hart Senate Office Building. The twenty-two members sat at a wraparound table, with Chairman Nunn at the center and the press corps stooping, kneeling, crawling, and creeping alongside the table skirt. Facing the senators was a smaller, rectangular table where witnesses sat, selected by members of the committee, but only if approved by Nunn. Over eight days of hearings, spread across four months ending on July 22, men and women would sit at that table, first reading a prepared statement and then responding to questions.

On the first day of hearings, consistent with the strategy Nunn and Powell had deployed since 1992, the senator framed the discussion around military readiness: "Our primary focus and concern must be on the implications of any change in current policy on the effectiveness of our armed forces to carry out their mission to defend our nation." But he also acknowledged that, for many people, this was "a moral issue, touching upon deeply held religious and philosophical beliefs," and that for still others, it was a "civil rights issue involving the fair and equitable treatment of individuals with a particular sexual orientation." He promised the hearings would be "fair, thorough and objective" and that every witness would be "treated with dignity and respect."[4]

It soon became clear, however, that Nunn had strange definitions of both objectivity and respect. "When the interests of some individuals bear upon the cohesion and effectiveness of an institution upon which our national security depends," he said, already hedging his bets, "we must, in my view, move very cautiously. This caution," he added with a touch of defensiveness, "is not prejudice; it is prudence." (His language was yet another eerie replay of the words used to justify racial segregation four decades earlier, when a Korean War commander said, "There is no question in my mind of the inherent difference in races. This is not racism—it is common sense and understanding."[5])

There was no evidence that the "interests" of gays and lesbians—the wish to be treated just like everybody else—had any bearing upon the effectiveness of the military. But Nunn set up the hearings as though that assertion were a fact. He seemed to fully embrace the idea—promulgated by the religious right— that the fight for gay equality was another instance of inherently self-centered homosexuals putting their own interests above the common good. As he would say on television later that spring, "You can't put individual rights above the mission. . . . If you don't put the mission first, we're going to lose an awful lot of young people." The implication was that letting gays serve would so demoralize the ranks that they would lose wars and American lives—all to acquiesce to the selfish demands of a dangerous and despised minority.[6]

The first testimony was given by David Burrelli, a sociologist at the Congressional Research Service. Nunn explained that the responsibility of the CRS was to "provide Congress with neutral and objective research without bias." But Burrelli's discussion of gay service, which raised the question of what caused homosexuality, right there alongside mention of "asexuality, fetishes, and other paraphilias," reflected a pathologizing orientation toward homosexuality. After all, no CRS expert was ever called into Senate hearings to explain the "causes" of heterosexuality, as part of a discussion of toe-sucking and telephone scatalogia. Burrelli acknowledged that the homosexual exclusion policy was a form of discrimination but said that the military also discriminates against people with "learning defects," criminal records, drug and alcohol dependence, and "other sexual conditions other than homosexuality, including transsexualism and other gender identity disorders." Much of what he said was taken from a series of reports he wrote for CRS that quoted liberally from Moskos on "hanky-panky" in the military, "discreet homosexuals" versus "declared" ones, and the importance of military "values and norms" capable of "transcending individual self-interest," which gays presumably, by definition, could not do. Burrelli also gave testimony that did not favor the ban, perhaps in an effort to appear neutral. He pointed out that if gays were forced to conceal their identity, there was a greater risk of blackmail than if they were allowed to be open. "In other words," he said, "the policy itself actually may serve to create the security risk issue that you raise."[7]

Burrelli was followed by other witnesses who sounded as though Senator Nunn had literally fed them his favorite lines through an earpiece. David Schlueter, a law professor at St. Mary's University, seemed to replicate Nunn's "thorny questions" strategy to raise fears about privacy, morality, and discipline. Letting gays serve, said Schlueter, "advances their personal private interests," but what might it unleash? "Could military boards be required to adopt affirmative action for homosexuals to make up for past discrimination?" Could they be forced to provide the same housing, health care, and base privileges to gays as to straights? Schlueter then returned to the moral question, as had Burrelli, Nunn, and Moskos. "The law is grounded on deeply rooted and firmly held moral and religious values," he said. "A key question before Congress is whether the military, as a paradigm of a law-and-order society, should be required to accept or accommodate a status or conduct which some service members, civilians, and potential service members would find unacceptable on moral or religious grounds." His words were gleefully quoted by Chaplain James Hutchens during his House testimony five weeks later for the National Association of Evangelicals.[8]

Each of these testimonies seemed eagerly digested by the conservative senators of the Armed Services Committee Strom Thurmond, John Warner, John McCain, Trent Lott, Dan Coats, and John Glenn—who displayed a united front against gay service that reflected both the careful strategizing of the pro-ban delegation and the personal animosity of each of them to gays and lesbians. Senator Trent Lott, who later would step down as Republican leader amid accusations of racism after he praised Strom Thurmond's 1948 segregationist presidential bid, made a halfhearted attempt to wrap his anti-gay animus in the mantle of military effectiveness. The American people, he insisted in his brief written statement entered on that first day of hearings in March, "do not believe the Federal Government should *endorse* homosexuality as a lifestyle—and that is exactly the message we will send if we lift this ban." In the very next sentence, as though realizing he had forgotten to abide by the script, he suddenly changed tacks, jutting away from the issue of government approval and toward military performance: "These hearings must seek to answer one fundamental question: Will lifting this ban improve or hurt our ability to fight and win future conflicts? I say, 'It will hurt.'" Senator Jim Exon, Democrat of Nebraska, conceded that he was "not completely . . . open-minded" on whether homosexuality could be "open and approved in the service."[9]

Senator John Warner, a former navy secretary, framed his comments by saying that Clinton's proposal would "compel the U.S. military to accept openly and acknowledge the existence of a class of people whose lifestyle is found by many Americans to be unacceptable."[10] It was a rather extraordinary admission—to concede that the military ranks were refusing to acknowledge what everyone actually knew to be true. Then there was the peculiar singling out of gay Americans. Tens of millions of different kinds of people had served in the U.S. military over the centuries, and many Americans would take issue with the "lifestyles" of many of them. But no law ever required a referendum on how those millions of people lived their lives before they'd be admitted to serve their country. Unless they were gay.

Warner suggested lifting the ban would be unfair to straights who signed up for military service believing that they would not have to ever encounter a gay person. Like many high-minded supporters of the ban, Warner insisted that he had no problem with homosexuality. "I have tolerance," he said. "I have no prejudice." But Warner said he must shelve his own tolerance and distinguish his outlook from that of a "young 17-, 18-, 19-year-old just coming into the military," who might be less tolerant. It was for *him* that the ban must remain in place. Recruits like him are "coming out of what are usually small towns, and high school environments, coming out of the security of the town and the family and the school and all of a sudden being confronted with all of these new problems." They are being "thrust into military life and asked to take on tremendous responsibilities, including risk of life." Warner used this idealized—if patronizing—vision of small-town America, presumably free of the messy burdens of homosexuality, to endorse the intolerance he claimed not to have. "In their own simple way of thinking it through," said Warner of these hypothetical young Americans, "they may just be right. And we have to listen to them and respect their views."[11] Intolerance of homosexuality was, for Warner, respectable.

Once again, the line in the sand around gays and lesbians was nothing short of remarkable. Imagine if it were considered acceptable for service members to break their contracts and receive benefits because our nation's leaders decided to invade Iraq, when some troops opposed the decision. Yet Senator Warner considered a policy measure with far less impact on life and limb so radical and so objectionable that he sought to excuse enlisted personnel from service over it.

Despite Warner's general resistance to lifting the ban, he was willing to tether his position largely to the whims of public opinion. From his research of foreign militaries, Warner concluded that open gay service "will work in a military organization if it works in society. If society is prepared and does, in fact, accept the openness of a professed homosexual or a lesbian, then it will work in the military." The upshot, he said, was that he had seriously considered supporting an end to the ban, in part because he had heard that other countries had lifted their bans without problems. But after traveling throughout Europe and Canada, he concluded that what he saw "does not provide a basis for lifting the ban." Only two nations, he said, have a policy of full nondiscrimination, Canada and the Netherlands. Canada had just lifted their ban six months before. The Dutch military was small and the Netherlands was more open to homosexuality than the United States. "It works for them," Warner said. But that didn't mean it would work for us. Warner's position left him open to reconsidering the American ban should public opinion evolve toward significantly greater tolerance of homosexuality, or should the Canadians or Dutch prove themselves in future combat. But for the moment, "the issue of homosexuality has not reached a sufficient level of acceptance in American society for us as lawmakers to impose it as a matter of law on the young men and women coming into the military of the United States."[12]

Not all senators on the committee were hostile to gay service. Senator Carl Levin of Michigan asked Burrelli if there were any studies or evidence that homosexuals in the military would be more likely to "engage in improper sexually related conduct than heterosexuals?" Burrelli answered cryptically, "There is no evidence that they will or that they will not." Outside military life, Burrelli said, there is evidence that gay men are more promiscuous. If sodomy is illegal, then gay men, by definition, would "be involved in more illicit behavior." Levin responded that married heterosexuals can commit sodomy as well. "I do not believe that sodomy between a husband and wife fits the definition of . . . ," began Burrelli, before pausing and finally conceding, "well, yes." "It does," reaffirmed Levin, presumably referring to the fact that sodomy practiced by married heterosexuals was still illegal in the military. Burrelli tried to wiggle away: "I am going to start getting into something that I do not want to get into." But Levin pressed on: "Is there any evidence in civilian life that homosexuals commit sodomy more often than heterosexuals, including husband

and wife?" The twenty-two-member committee of his peers was silent. Neither Burrelli nor anyone else could answer.[13]

Levin concluded that there was no evidence for the ban against gays: "In terms of a rational basis, then, if you are looking at the likelihood of engagement in a prohibited sexual act, we do not have the data to substantiate that rational basis. Is that accurate?" Schlueter answered yes, and also acknowledged that he knew of no other cases where the antipathy of a unit toward an individual based on that person's identity or beliefs served as grounds for limiting that person's rights. Only gays.[14]

One day in April was supposed to be devoted to testimony from academics. The witness list included two professors of sociology, a professor of political science, and Lieutenant General Calvin Waller, a retired general with no academic background. Waller, who was deputy commander of allied forces for Operation Desert Storm, was fiercely anti-gay, and seemed to be on the panel for balance—apparently not enough academics opposed gay service.

"I was invited to be on the academic panel," recalled Judith Stiehm, a professor of political science at Florida International University, several years later. "When I got to the capital, I found Charles Moskos in consultation with Nunn. It was all rigged. Moskos and Nunn had already found an agreement. The hearings began and Moskos stood up and said, 'Well, what about the showers? What about the privacy rights of straights?'" When the time came for the academic panel to testify, Stiehm remembers, "in walks what looks like a six-foot, nine-inch black general, not an academic at all, and most of the questions were directed at him. So the academic panel wasn't even an academic panel."[15]

Waller's defensive testimony made it clear that he was upset about larger issues than just gay service. First among these was resentment over military budget cuts. "As we downsize our armed forces," he said, "we must also consider how important it is to maintain our readiness and our deployability." Waller bristled at suggestions that handling the gay issue was a question of leadership. Commanders, he complained, "are already working 12 to 14 hours a day; they are in the midst of one of the most difficult things that we have ever had to put upon them, that is, to downsize this military." And yet here we are trying to "throw one more thing on their plate. Why in the name of God, are we willing to tell those great young captains and lieutenants, or whoever is in command of those units, that this is your problem: You have to deal with it?" Waller said he was "equally concerned about the healthcare budget of our military forces." He said that up to a thousand military persons were nondeployable "for health reasons," a clear reference to AIDS.[16]

While insisting that as an African American he sympathized with what gays were facing, Waller finally let loose with his homophobia. "To compare my service in the America's [*sic*] Armed Forces, which I submit to you is not a deviant force, with the integration of avowed homosexuals, is personally offensive to me." The key for Waller was that he could not turn his racial identity on and off, as gays could. "I cannot come in and out at my own free will to decide what it is that I want to be. Do I want to be African American today? Do I want to be a China man tomorrow, or do I want to be a Caucasian the next day? I cannot do that." Following the "China man" comment, Senator McCain thanked Waller for his testimony and expressed his "appreciation for your service to our Nation."[17]

For Waller, the worst part seemed to be that gays "want to openly foist their lifestyles upon" other service members. In his view, this was another instance of selfish gays demanding permission "to do as they want," and if the country yielded to their indulgences, the U.S. military would become "a second-rate Armed Forces" and "good young men and young women" would not want to be part of it. His evidence? "I have done a lot of surveys, not scientifically done, but in talking to young men and young women." Waller had found that U.S. soldiers, sailors, airmen, and Marines did not want gays in their military. They would not be able to trust any individual who "proves to be a liar, a thief [or] openly homosexual."[18]

Waller apparently based his views of homosexuals on "the platforms of some of our gay activists." Too many, he said, want not just "to serve" but "to convert you." And then, down came his guard, and out came a full range of insecurities that helped explain his resentment toward gay rights. When an individual "starts getting up on his high horse and saying you are going to be damned for the rest of your life unless you believe in my particular religion, then we cannot have that kind of nonsense in the military forces. And that is where I draw the analogy for people saying, I want to be able to do this, and if you knew what was right, and if you had an open mind, and if you were not so downtrodden, and if you were enlightened as I am enlightened, you would believe the way I believe."[19]

The session ended with Waller complaining about a *60 Minutes* segment showcasing the Dutch army's tolerant policy toward gays, while not making clear how different the Dutch and American militaries were. A gay lieutenant colonel in the Dutch military, Waller accused, even winked at the camera at the end of the segment, putting to rest any doubt about the gay conspiracy. The Dutch army, Nunn chimed in, doesn't even have a dress code. "Absolutely not!" said Waller. "It's sort of—you know, made up as you go." "Wear whatever you please, whenever, and so forth?" offered Nunn. "That is correct, sir."[20]

AFTER THEIR START in late March, the hearings then recessed for a month and resumed at the end of April, with several days of testimony continuing into May. On May 7, the committee allowed other senators to join the debate by adding their own testimony to the mix. Senator Frank Murkowski focused on the risk of AIDS not only to the military but to the health-care system of the Veterans Administration. "There is simply no question about" it, said Murkowski. "By opening the door to gays," the nation would be adding "po-tentially enormous proportions of exposure" to the VA system. According to the Centers for Disease Control, said Murkowski, among "men who have sex with men, there is an exposure factor of 69 percent." The suggestion that over two-thirds of all gay men contracted the HIV virus was totally false. What Murkowski might have said—had he been either more honest or less sloppy—and what he did say elsewhere, was that two-thirds of current AIDS patients in the United States were gay men, a wholly different and far, far lower figure.[21]

He assured the audience that his "input is based on the obligations of us to take care of our military personnel after they have served their tour of duty." The HIV screening process in place was apparently not enough for Murkowski. The senator simply did not want to fund any health-care costs associated with gay service members. And since that budget was currently fixed, he suggested that AIDS treatment would come at the expense of health care for veterans with other medical needs.[22]

The scare tactic was typical of anti-gay rhetoric. Murkowski's thinking relied on a capacity to block out similar health costs incurred by heterosexual behavior. Senator Barbara Boxer made the point: After the Vietnam War, she reminded the committee, the Philippines was dotted with fatherless Eurasian children—the result of fornication and, in many cases, adultery by U.S. sol-diers. "This Congress voted hundreds of millions of dollars to look after those children," said Boxer, "so obviously there are costs associated with hetero-sexuals serving. Let us stop living a lie." She went on to cite the Tailhook fi-asco as another example of the damage and costs resulting from heterosexual behavior. Eighty-eight women were "grabbed, groped, pinched, fondled and bitten. Women were knocked to the ground, their clothing ripped, forcibly removed." One assailant wore a shirt reading WOMEN ARE PROPERTY. "Did anyone ever suggest that we kick all heterosexuals out of the military because of the despicable behavior of 117 officers?" Boxer asked.[23]

Howard Metzenbaum, the Democrat from Ohio who had previously introduced a bill to lift the ban, framed his discussion in terms of civil rights. It was a strategic mistake that too many gay rights supporters made in the battle over gay service. "The issue of whether homosexuals should be permitted to serve is not as complicated as many people would have us believe," he began, appearing to make light of the enormous resistance of so many military members. For Metzenbaum, the issue was solely one of "civil rights" and "equal opportunity." In his view, the government was propping up an "outdated, unjustified, and arbitrary policy of discrimination," and it was time for it to stop. He said there was no real evidence that homosexuals in the military would undermine the military, and that the rationale was "limited to the emotional argument we keep hearing from the troops that they do not want to serve with homosexuals." He said that military leaders had never before taken orders from the troops, and that if the leadership endorsed and enforced a policy of nondiscrimination, "you can be darn sure that [it] will be obeyed right on down the line." If lifting the ban became a problem, he said, "it will be because the brass made it so by neglecting, willfully or otherwise, to enforce discipline."[24]

Metzenbaum was right, but he was also wrong. Opponents of gay service were, indeed, trying to make the issue more complicated than it was. This was the point of Nunn's "thorny questions" strategy, which he continued in the hearings to the point of obsession. Yet by casting the issue as one only of civil rights and equality, instead of military effectiveness, Metzenbaum lost ground in the court of public opinion, and alienated, not surprisingly, the military leadership whom he seemed to be both neglecting and burdening. Metzenbaum's tone seemed cavalier to the concerns of military folk. The majority of service members supported the ban. "So what?" asked Metzenbaum. "Why is that significant? Did we take a poll of our armed personnel" when we ended discrimination against African Americans or when we let women serve in the military?[25] The senator's focus on leadership also rang hollow: To many Americans, the idea that good leadership could be strong enough to protect them from the perils of homosexuality, however they imagined them, was unrealistic—a liberal delusion that failed to recognize the power of human sexuality. Many further believed it was unfair to the leaders to add this "problem" to their plate, as Waller had complained. They wished it would simply go away.

Senator John Kerry, along with Barbara Boxer and Dianne Feinstein, joined Metzenbaum's critique of the ban that same day in May. Kerry appealed to Americans' better angels counseling against tolerating the "licensed hate" of the gay exclusion rule, and suggesting that our strength, our values, and our capabilities could make equality work. "We are making much more of this than we need to or than we ought to be," he said. "A country that can defeat Hitler is a country that can deal with people, whether it is a question of holding hands on base or otherwise." "If somebody wants to walk around holding hands, we are big enough to tolerate that," said Kerry. "I mean, for God's sakes, men were dancing with men in the war when they did not have any women around."[26] But Kerry was wrong—we couldn't deal with it. He underestimated the gut resistance to such displays of same-sex intimacy, and he failed to see that men dancing together at war was precisely the reason for the ban: So long as the military denied that gays existed in its ranks, same-sex intimacy could not threaten young men as something that was actually, truly gay; once the presence of gays was acknowledged, intense bonding that was previously safe was suddenly suspect.

Kerry said it was "fundamentally wrong" to deny gays the right to serve, and that there was nothing about gays that made them unsuitable. Repeating a powerful argument from the days of racial segregation, Kerry asked how the U.S. military can "properly or righteously or morally protect freedom if its own policies deny freedom to a significant minority of citizens." The current policy of "intolerance," he said, "either diminishes us or dishonors us."[27]

Kerry also argued that gays should not be required to "deny a fundamental part of their being" as a condition of service. Indeed, during his testimony Kerry and Nunn sparred repeatedly over which approach was an honest one and which was rooted in denial. "What do we gain," Kerry wanted to know, "by continuing to codify a lie that there are no gays in the military? You cannot turn your backs on the reality of everyday society in America." Anyone who believes they can "avoid somehow living and working with homosexuals simply by avoiding service in the military is avoiding reality."[28] But Americans could, and did, turn their backs on reality every day of their lives. This was the only way proponents of the ban could insist that housing gays with straights was an invasion of privacy analogous to housing men with women; in reality, gays and straights had long shared intimate quarters, in the military and elsewhere, but denial allowed people to avoid thinking about it.

Nunn, in response, had his own charges of denial to hurl. Lifting the ban, he suggested, would mean inviting people to violate the UCMJ's prohibition of sodomy. How could we tell avowed homosexuals—a phrase he apparently, but incorrectly, considered interchangeable with avowed sodomists—that they were welcome in the military when the military banned sodomy? It would require looking the other way. "I thought you were trying to get away from the hypocrisy and lies," Nunn said to Kerry. Passing one law that invites the tacit violation of another "gets right back to it."²⁹

Nunn was only correct, of course, if one assumed that all homosexuals practiced sodomy, and that no heterosexuals did. As Kerry pointed out, heterosexuals also practice sodomy. And some homosexuals don't. No one on the Senate floor knew what percentage of homosexuals practiced sodomy. But certainly it was less than 100.

In this august Senate chamber, there was a great deal about human sexuality that the lawmakers and "experts" alike did not know. But chances are, Strom Thurmond knew less than anyone in the room. Born in 1902, Thurmond had run for president in 1948 on a segregationist ticket, saying there were "not enough troops in the army to force the Southern people to break down segregation and admit the nigra [sic] race into our theaters, into our swimming pools, into our homes, and into our churches." Over fifty years later, the nation was briefly transfixed, if not thoroughly surprised, when the Thurmond family acknowledged that this segregationist giant, like Thomas Jefferson before him, had fathered a child with an underage African American maid. Hypocrisy, it seemed, was Thurmond's specialty. And it was on unabashed display at the Senate hearings. "Heterosexuals do not practice sodomy," he called out, during Kerry's testimony. "Or do not admit they do. Homosexuals do admit they practice sodomy. How do you reconcile that with the Code of Military Justice?"³⁰ Notwithstanding everything Nunn had just said about ending the lies and hypocrisy surrounding sex and military law, Thurmond was focused solely on what people admitted, and on punishing those who told the truth—even while he acknowledged that heterosexuals, as a class, lied about their sexual behavior.

Kerry tried to set the Senate straight. Surely, many heterosexuals did not practice sodomy, said Kerry. Some abhor the notion. "But in reality, I do not think you will find a sex therapist or a psychiatrist or a psychologist or most people who are experts in the issue who will tell you that heterosexuals do not practice sodomy." "You do admit that homosexuals practice sodomy, do you not?" came Thurmond's reply. "Yes, sir," said Kerry. "That is against the Code of Military Justice, is it not?" continued Thurmond. "And against the laws of many states, is it not?" As Kerry began to answer, Thurmond cut in, "I have no further questions."³¹

Nunn and Thurmond were simply dedicated to finding a reason to continue to exclude gays, no matter how irrational a string of thinking it required. Kerry tried again: "Mr. Chairman," he said, "let us be honest and fair." Everyone knows, he continued, that the anti-sodomy law is today broken by heterosexuals, and they seldom get in trouble for it. Nunn: "Well, if you are going to be honest and fair, somebody had better introduce the change in the Uniform Code of Military Justice to go along with the lifting of the ban, because the two are directly related." It was another nonresponsive response: The sodomy ban related to heterosexual behavior and identity, too, but Nunn and Thurmond refused to see it. It was simply a moral issue for them that homosexuality must not be approved. "Most States of the Union have criminal behavioral statutes that go back into the moral beliefs of the country," said Nunn. How could we just "sweep all that away?" Plus, said Nunn, maybe the military should have a higher standard than civilian society. "I am not sure we ought to go for the lowest common denominator approach," said Nunn.[32]

Kerry agreed—he just didn't think gays were the lowest common denominator. As a legal matter, he explained, an admission of homosexuality is never taken as a cause for arrest even in those places, including Washington, D.C., at the time, where sodomy is illegal. "For instance, today you have gays working in the workplace. You have them right here in the Senate. Is this against the law? Has Senator Thurmond or have the Capitol Police arrested anybody because we have people up here that we know practice sodomy? No." "Well," Thurmond chimed in, "do you want them arrested for that?" It wasn't really a question of what Kerry wanted. "Well, do you, sir?" asked Kerry. "If they are practicing sodomy," replied Thurmond, "and it is against the law, why should they not be arrested?"

The truth was that the military simply did not round up heterosexuals for violating those aspects of the UCMJ that banned private, consensual sex such as sodomy and adultery. And it was not just that military commanders neglected to enforce the law; rather, orders came from the top to neglect the law. The Pentagon's top lawyer, Jamie Gorelick, general counsel for the Department of Defense, would admit as much in a press conference later that year, saying "we haven't been using our criminal resources that way for heterosexuals" when it comes to consensual sexual conduct because "we just don't think it's a good use of our resources."[33]

For Kerry, the equation was simple. The UCMJ currently banned behavior by both gays and straights that everybody knew was consistently, routinely, repeatedly violated. Either you should change the UCMJ "to reflect reality," argued Kerry, or you should try to enforce it consistently, "but you will never wind up enforcing it unless you invade everybody's privacy of their bedroom." There was simply no rationale for basing a law on the false assumption that only gays committed sodomy even if common sense suggested they did so more often than straights. And sodomy was far from the worst of it. "I mean," continued Kerry, "there is not a Marine or a sailor or anybody who went to the Philippines during the Vietnam War who cannot tell you a story about hetero-sexual behavior in public that was in violation of the Code of Military Justice. So let us be honest about this and not apply a double standard to it."[34]

Worse than the double standard of Nunn's rationale for the gay ban was his own blindness to the reality of what he was supporting: a halfway mea-sure where, as he put it, "no one would ask questions about anyone's sexual orientation and people could serve as long as they keep their private behavior private." What would be wrong with this? Nunn wanted to know. The prob-lem, Kerry answered, is that even if recruiters did not ask about sexual orien-tation, anyone else might. Nunn spoke of privacy as though, in his emerging "don't ask, don't tell" plan, it would be protected equally for gays and straights. But what he really meant was that when "private" behavior became public, it would mean discharge if you were gay, and would mean nothing if you were straight. "You are still going to have a policy of exclusion if you learn that some-body is gay," explained Kerry. "Well," replied Nunn, "you would not learn they were gay unless it was by their own admission, unless it was by conduct."[35]

Nunn's ignorance was striking. There were countless ways, well short of an "admission," that a person's homosexuality could become clear—at least clear enough to worry anyone concerned about showering with gays. (Indeed some service members had said that "just the mere suspicion of homosexual-ity" could wreak havoc. According to one person who testified at Nunn's field hearings, sailors broke regulations by stealing the mail of a shipmate they suspected was gay.) No less a Nunn ally than John McCain once said that he knew he served with gay people in the navy by their "behavior and by atti-tudes."[36] But Nunn simply could not envision the daily reality of gay life in America. For all his professed concern about creating a policy that was free of lies and hypocrisy, for the scores of questions Nunn asked under the banner of formulating clear direction for the military leadership, what he would ulti-mately endorse was a law that couldn't have been more confusing, more mis-understood, or more predicated on concealment, innuendo, gossip, pretense, and dishonesty.

NUNN'S MAY 10 "field hearings" at Norfolk Naval Complex, in Virginia, were a master stroke. The idea was to listen directly to the views of service members and to illustrate to the civilian world just how close the quarters were on ships and submarines. In the bowels of the USS *Baton Rouge* and the USS *John F. Kennedy*, with cameras rolling and microphones piled high, fresh-faced recruits from wholesome states swore they were not anti-gay but could simply never brook serving with gays. Sailors climbed into tiny submarine berths piled on top of each other to show how little privacy they had. They even simulated how they used the showers and toilets. It was a string of deft performances that, no doubt, reflected both the depths of discomfort in the ranks and the success of the campaigns by religious and social conservatives to whip up fear and opposition to lifting the ban.

The field hearings were designed to give cover to the political and military leadership that was all too eager to back discrimination as the only viable path—practically, morally, or otherwise. A majority of service members were against lifting the ban, but Nunn acknowledged he was surprised by the number of men and women who said they had no objection to serving with gays. Indeed, while formal witnesses—those who appear on the roster of published Senate testimony—were overwhelmingly against gay service, the cameras caught a sizable number of young people saying, "I don't have any problem with it" and "What I want is someone who does his job."[37]

The rhetoric of opponents of gay service—sometimes downright venomous—reflected the widespread absorption by service members of standard talking points that had been pushed for months by social and political conservatives. For many, gay exclusion was a moral requirement, normally rooted in religious belief. "This issue comes to the moral fiber of all of us," said U.S. Navy Petty Officer Second Class Al Portes. People "like me believe in a God and believe that we are going to be judged." He said he found homosexuality "morally incorrect. This is an act of rebellion. This is an act of rebellion against the God I believe in." Portes said he entered the military because he knew that open gays were not allowed, and if the ban were lifted, "Al Portes will refuse, and this is not a call to mutiny or to massive disobedience, but I will refuse to serve with gays in the military." He ended his comments saying, "Do not come blaming me" if more incidents occur like the "Iowa accident," the 1989 explosion aboard the USS *Iowa* for which navy personnel falsely blamed a murderous, suicidal homosexual sailor who, they said, was acting out after rejection by a shipmate. Master Chief Harry Schafer agreed: "It is the belief and known practice of those people that is morally wrong. And that belief, that knowledge of what we traditionally—religious values, Mom and Dad raised us through the church and through society, for my 19 years, before I got 26 years of professional Navy experience, that's wrong, just bottom-line wrong. And I will never accept that."[38]

Much of what was expressed during the field hearings had this quality of reflexive moral opposition, with no reason for gay exclusion offered beyond a straight service member's own tradition of disapproval. But many, like the leaders above them, tied their moral opposition to practical costs they claimed gay service would incur. Lifting the ban, said Master Chief Tommy Taylor, "has got so much against it, so many bad things as far as morale, readiness of our navy, you are going to go right to the readiness of our navy." Captain Gary Fulham of the Marines said, "The adverse effects of those persons openly engaged in behavior that a majority of our society and our species finds abnormal and repugnant will in fact be adverse to the military." Master Chief Schafer said that having to serve with gays would dramatically undermine effectiveness. While civilians were free to tolerate "these sexually oriented homosexuals," the close quarters of military life meant that open gay service would "be totally disruptive to good order and discipline." Seldom were service members able to be any more concrete about how, exactly, the presence of gays would destroy the military. Senator Lott even had to ask, at one point, for examples of what would happen, saying, "I do not want a graphic explanation, but give me a couple of ideas of what you are envisioning here," to which the answer was simply that "people will leave" and "reduce our mission capability."[39]

Sometimes the rationales given for gay exclusion strained credibility. Lieutenant Fred Frey claimed that "to be able to put your life on the line for somebody requires you to know that he has the same moral foundation you do," that your comrades "believe the same things you believe," and would conduct themselves "as you conduct yourself professionally and privately.[40] It is hard to believe that any service members thought they shared the same beliefs with all of the nearly 3 million men and women in the U.S. Armed Forces. But to Frey, the homosexual "lifestyle is so objectionable to so many people currently serving in the United States military and the civilians of this country that there is no way that unit cohesiveness will not be detrimentally affected."[41]

The showers, not surprisingly, were also an area of concern. Petty Officer First Class Ginger McElfresh said she could have "a perfectly fine professional relationship" with a gay person, but "the very next day I may have to shower with that person. In the back of my mind, I am thinking, yes, they are acting professionally with me, but what are they thinking about me as I stand here in the shower naked?" Commander James Pledger said he had "never witnessed such an emotional response to any issue in my 21 years of active duty." He said he had taken "an admittedly unscientific poll" and found that 98 percent of his crew opposed lifting the ban because of a combination of concerns over privacy and morality. "They are repulsed by the prospect of having to shower in view of homosexual shipmates, as well as sleep no more than 2 feet from homosexuals," he said, acknowledging that his crew was "basically a group of conservative Christian young men."[42]

Not all the testimony from the field hearings was from people opposed to gay service. But most of the remarks in favor came, not surprisingly, from declared gays and lesbians. The most striking moment of the day came when Lieutenant Tracy Thorne announced, "I am the person you have been talking about." "My sexuality is part of me, but it is not all of me," he said. "Mr. Chairman, members of the committee, I am Lieutenant Junior Grade Tracy Thorne, and I am a red-blooded American. I am the member of a family, the son of a doctor from Mississippi and a mother from South Carolina, a member of the Methodist Church. I grew up in a small town in south Florida. I lived the all-American boy's life, going to school on weekdays and fishing on weekends." Thorne said that simply because he told the truth, a shipmate "was ordered to climb a ladder with a rag and a can of paint thinner and he wiped my name from the side of the jet I once flew."[43]

The eloquence of Thorne's speech made no dent in Nunn's armor. Doesn't tolerance flow "both ways" here, he wanted to know. Doesn't Thorne also have to tolerate those who won't tolerate him? Perhaps Thorne should admit that he had "some degree of intolerance for those who believe that they have a right of privacy too, and they have a right to be in quarters that are not in any way connected with people who find them sexually attractive." While Nunn dwelled on privacy, he didn't conceal his wish to accommodate the moral animus of troops who believed that homosexuality was simply unacceptable. Tens of thousands of enlisted personnel "have been taught from early childhood that homosexuality is immoral." Don't they have rights? "You decided that you had to come out in the open," Nunn told Thorne sternly. "Could you tell us why you felt that you had to come out in the open? And did you take into account by doing so, whether they are right or wrong, you were really making an awful lot of other people feel very uncomfortable in their surroundings?"[44]

Thurmond elbowed his way in. He wanted to know if gay service members who came out in their unit retained the respect of their peers. Thorne and Lieutenant Richard Selland, another gay lieutenant junior grade in the navy, both replied that they did, even if some people had questions or reservations. Thorne said he was "pleasantly surprised." He began to explain: "The reaction that I received when I . . ." but was interrupted by Thurmond. "You do not have to make your answer too long," said the senator. "Just come to the point." Keeping his composure, Thorne explained that the response to his revelation had been entirely positive until his unit was dressed down by Vice Admiral Anthony Less, the commander of Naval Forces Atlantic Fleet. The vice admiral had reprimanded his commanding officer for supporting Thorne over navy policy. The officers in his squadron, said Thorne, were "ordered to toe the Navy line. And from that day on, good order, discipline and morale suffered heavily. It did not suffer because of the fact that I had declared I was homosexual. It suffered because the Navy policy was enforced from above." Thorne said that resolving the issue of gay service was about leadership, and cues from above. "My squadron disavowed me when they were ordered to do so," he said. "When they [are] ordered to treat me just like any other American, they will do so. That is all it is."[45]

Senator Thurmond could no longer contain himself. "I would like to commend you both for your desire to serve your country," he said. "However, your lifestyle is not normal. It is not normal for a man to want to be with a man or a woman with a woman." A round of applause broke out. Thurmond then asked the two gay sailors "if either of you has considered getting help from a medical or psychiatric standpoint, or do you want to change?" Both said they did not wish to be heterosexual.[46]

If the ban is lifted, asked Senator Richard Shelby, won't the result be "open and defiant homosexual behavior" throughout the military? Of course, if open homosexuality were tolerated, it could not be called "defiant." But Shelby's remark raised the question of what value there might be in requiring gays to serve in the closet. What was wrong, in short, with Nunn's idea of asking gays to keep their private lives private? Thorne had watched Kerry and Nunn spar on that very question three days before. So he turned to Nunn to answer the question. "What is fundamentally wrong with that, Senator Nunn, with all due respect, is that . . . most of you men who sit up there, you wear a wedding ring on your left hand, and at your office you may have a picture of your wife that sits behind you on your desk. And I pose the question to you: Have you ever cared about someone so much that you come into the workplace and you talk about that person that you care so much about?" Thorne told the senators that they themselves did not, and could not, keep their private lives wholly separate from their work lives, even in civilian society. "By asking me to keep my private life private, you are saying it is okay that you may be gay, it is okay that you may have someone that you care about, but when your ship pulls in after six months at sea, that person that you care about has to stay at home. And when you get letters while you are out at sea, you cannot read them out in the ready room because somebody may come over and find out that that person is not a woman." Thorne finished by saying that "in order to live life as you would under this presumed 'we will not ask if you do not tell,' you would have to constantly fabricate lies, and it is just not right to ignore the truth in such a way." But the senators would have none of it. The "overwhelming majority of people who are heterosexual" have rights, too, suggested Shelby. It was no wonder the Congress, and eventually the nation, yielded to the pleas of Master Chief Kelvin E. Carter, when he begged, "Don't do it, please. Keep our Navy strong and proud."[47]

There were a few more days of hearings in July. Once Clinton announced his policy, Congress had to question Powell, Aspin, and other officials about the final proposal before lawmakers decided whether they could support it or would seek to reverse it in law. But by the May field hearings, most of the damage was done. Nunn had promised his hearings would be "fair and objective," but the claim strains credibility. When Nunn found out that the planned testimony of a retired army colonel, Lucian Truscott III, would describe the experiences of openly gay service members seamlessly integrated into their units, he removed Truscott from the roster of witnesses. When he realized that the father of modern conservatism, Barry Goldwater, was also planning to testify that gays ought to be allowed to serve openly in the military, he replaced him, too. Indeed, gay rights groups charged that Nunn was stacking the deck by choosing witnesses friendly to his position and silencing opponents, and by the way he conducted the hearings.[48]

A prime example was how he ended the field hearings. In response to a question from Thurmond about how military families felt about lifting the gay ban, a string of sergeants and captains said their wives, girlfriends, mothers, fathers, and in-laws were strictly opposed. They said it was a "major concern" for their families. Their wives had told them it was worth missing Mother's Day to testify against gay service. Families were concerned that openly gay service would lead to married gay couples living on bases, "and quite frankly that is nothing they want to expose their children to." Trent Lott praised the sentiment, prompting a round of hearty cheers. And Nunn, who had brought the chairman's gavel down several times to halt forbidden applause, this time said he would "not bang the gavel on that applause because I think we all agree" on this one.[49]

That May, Nunn went on NBC's *Meet the Press* to try to convince Americans that he was not allowing moral opposition against homosexuality to affect his position on gay service or the way he was running his Senate hearings.

But his performance was unconvincing, and put to rest any doubts about whether Nunn was anti-gay. "I can tell you that I have my own moral beliefs," he said, "but that's not playing a role in my hearings," which he again insisted were fair and objective. Americans needed to be "tolerant of people who have different lifestyles," he said, but he added that we must not "endorse the sex behavior of people that are lesbian and gay." Nunn claimed he refused to "endorse different lifestyles" with "government policy" even as he sought to inscribe in law a policy enshrining the acceptability of heterosexuality over homosexuality. About this point, Nunn was pleased to be explicit. Asked by Robert Novak if he was "saying the heterosexual lifestyle is superior, is morally superior, to the homosexual lifestyle," Nunn answered that he was "not only saying that," but that "American family deterioration is one of the biggest problems we face in our culture, and government programs cannot solve that," implying that somehow tolerance of homosexuality was a leading cause of the problem. Nunn's statement might pass as an odd non sequitur, except that social and political conservatives had, for years, been linking homosexuality with family breakdown as often as possible, no matter how illogical the connection.[50]

That same month, the U.S. House of Representatives held their own less publicized and shorter hearings. Not surprisingly, the two days of testimony before the House Armed Services Committee (a subcommittee would hold three more days of hearings in July) were a replay of all the same arguments contained in the Senate hearings, and included the now-familiar invective of the religious right and their champions in both the military and the Congress. The May hearings were chaired by Representative Ronald Dellums of California, who supported lifting the ban. Dellums said that to the extent the issue was truly one of unit cohesion, "what you really are saying, unfortunately, is that people have a problem with homosexuals." But despite the leadership of Dellums, the House hearings were marked by some of the most virulent homophobia yet voiced in public debate. Representative Robert Dornan of California said, "You gentlemen all know that the best of your troops can never respect and thereby follow orders totally from someone who likes taking it up the bum, no matter how secret he keeps it. Once it leaks out, they think this person is abnormal, perverted, and a deviant from the norm." It's unclear if "leaks out" was a deliberate pun.[51]

In both the May and July hearings, Duncan Hunter, also of California, broached the topic of morality unabashedly. In so doing, he helpfully clarified the upshot of political leaders' support for the moral opposition to gay service. "Service leaders," said Hunter, addressing top military officers at the July hearings, "have a duty to protect the values of your troops—if you consider them to be legitimate values." A majority of military men and women, he said, do not want the ban lifted. Yet "you have not once used the term 'value.' You have not once accorded legitimacy to the feelings of people who serve in the armed forces who feel that because of their values, because of their faith, because of their traditions, homosexuality is repugnant and they do not want to serve in intimate quarters with homosexuals." A lot of people, said Hunter, "have read the same Bible, they have read Romans and Paul and have repeated Paul's statement which stated that homosexuality is wrong, wrong, wrong!"[52]

Colonel John Ripley, a retired marine, called gay people "walking depositories of disease." Under the "queers, cowards, and thieves" rule, which according to Ripley was a mainstay of the Marine Corps, anyone falling into any of these categories would be cordoned off from the group. On one ship, someone known to have been gay reportedly "went over the side." Ripley said the military was "so supercharged and electrified over this that they are prepared to take matters into their own hands." Charles Johnson, also a retired Marine, said the ban could not be lifted—not because "middle America will not accept this," but because "a superior power, God, will not accept this."[53]

The May House hearings also provided a forum for Brigadier General James Hutchens, the associate director of the NAE's Commission on Chaplains. Hutchens viewed himself as a spokesman for the moral warriors on this issue, and he used the opportunity of his congressional testimony to make the case that homosexuality was a "moral virus" that was threatening to infect the military and society at large. "I come to speak to that aspect of the homosexual issue represented by the *M* word," he said, "the word that for one reason or other has not been surfaced with sufficient visibility to allow for adequate debate." The *M* word was "morality," the word that "has been tiptoed around by many in our military and political leadership, for fear of unleashing the wrath of the homosexual movement of this country."

In his testimony, he cast gay equality as "an infringement on the religious rights of service members." "To require service members to serve with those whose status and thus their behavior is in direct opposition to their own religious and moral beliefs," he said, "is to show a gross insensitivity to and disregard for those beliefs, and to provide a climate where those beliefs and values are institutionally 'trashed.'" Hutchens argued that lifting the ban would put the government "in the position of establishing what is right and wrong. That, I would submit, infringes on the First Amendment to the Constitution, that becomes an establishment of religion issue."[54]

Apparently his bombastic stance didn't work the other way around: Given Hutchens's certainty that the ban was, in the first place, an expression of Christian religious belief, he might have allowed that it was the existing policy that violated the establishment of religion, not the contemplated change. But this was not a line of thought he seemed to pursue. Instead, for emotional effect, he painted a grim picture of a bleeding Christian soldier, wasting away on a battlefield at the hands of a gay chaplain whose ministry would be worse than worthless to him: "Surely the soldier lying on the battlefield with a sucking chest wound and calling for a chaplain has the right to expect the solace, comfort and ministry of a chaplain whose presence and touch is not morally offensive or physically repulsive. A wounded or dying soldier deserves something better than the morally compromised ministry of a homosexual chaplain."[55]

Hutchens left Congress with a list summarizing the Bible's views on homosexuality:

1. The wrath of God is being revealed against it.
2. It is based on a refusal to honor God.
3. It is based on ingratitude toward God.
4. It is based on a willful choice.
5. God has lifted his restraining hand.
6. What starts as a choice becomes all-consuming.
7. Those who practice it know full well God's decree, yet continue to aggressively promote this behavior.
8. Condoning homosexuality is wrong, and is a further step away from God.[56]

The list reflected much about the psychological worldview of Hutchens and, as he had claimed, probably millions of other Americans: First, there is no such thing as a homosexual. Instead, we all have appetites and some of us have strong appetites for aberrant sexual behavior and weak wills for resisting it; so-called homosexuals are really only heterosexuals with a self-control problem. Second, society must make clear that people have the responsibility to make sometimes difficult choices, such as refraining from homosexual behavior, no matter how appealing it may seem. Third, belief in God will help in this endeavor. And finally, the society that condones the wrong choice will suffer at the hands of an angry power.

AS THE HEARINGS made waves across the country, the White House, with input from Defense Secretary Aspin, was privately struggling to hammer out its own policy in classic Clintonian fashion—triangulating in an effort to please all parties. Meanwhile, David Mixner had gotten a string of assurances from White House aides that Clinton would follow through on his promise to lift the ban by executive order after the six-month study period was over. Although skeptical, he took the leap of faith, and made it his job to reassure other gay rights advocates that they had nothing to worry about, a move that further slowed the response of the worried activists. A week before Nunn's hearings even began, Clinton had said publicly that he would consider a proposal to segregate gay troops in job, deployment, and housing assignments. His announcement so angered gay rights activists that Mixner appeared on ABC's *Nightline* to publicly break with the president on the issue of gay service.[57] Clinton, it seemed, was accepting defeat before Nunn's hearings had even begun.

Nunn had been so successful with his hearings that the White House had little hope left that it could beat back a congressional override of an executive order. In March, Barney Frank lent cautious support to a policy compromise being floated around Capitol Hill: It would be a form of "don't ask, don't tell," but it would allow private homosexual conduct off base. Frank was known as a brilliant lawmaker and a powerful public champion of the dignity of gays and lesbians. But he was also a consummate insider in Washington who prided himself on his hard-headed approach to the real world of how things get done in politics. Frank's support for this plan infuriated some gay and lesbian advocates, as it gave opponents of full repeal the political cover to support a halfway measure. And as with Aspin's position in January, Frank's public admission that there was insufficient support in Congress to end the gay ban seemed to sap momentum for the fight; some argued that it became a self-fulfilling prophecy.

Clinton, too, seemed to have lost the stomach for the battle. Despite the work of his transition team in the weeks after being elected, he had largely punted the issue to Aspin at the Defense Department, who was more concerned with reshaping the military for peacetime than devoting political capital to ending the ban. The president did not assign experienced aides to manage the gay service issue. His wish to please a military leadership he was reportedly in awe of further weakened his will to fight the Joint Chiefs. And the slow start and continued disadvantages of gay rights lobbyists meant there was insufficient support on the ground to turn public opinion in their favor. While Vice President Gore argued with Clinton in July that he ought to lift the ban by executive order as a matter of principle, *even if* Congress threatened to write the ban into law, Clinton was through spending political capital on the issue.[58]

THERE WOULD BE no executive order. On July 19, Clinton announced the new policy at a carefully choreographed speech at the National Defense University at Fort McNair in Washington. Flanked by Les Aspin, Colin Powell, and the entire Joint Chiefs of Staff, with a backdrop of fifteen giant flags, Clinton spoke to a military audience. There were no representatives from gay and lesbian groups. He described the policy debate in great detail, acknowledging that it was "not a perfect solution," that it was "not identical with some of my own goals," and that it "certainly will not please everyone, perhaps not anyone." But he cast the policy as a triumph, calling it a "major step forward" and an "honorable compromise." It was, he said "the right thing to do and the best way to do it." Citing the expertise of Charles Moskos, the president said the issue of gay service was probably harder to resolve in the United States than abroad because of the strong emotions of both sides, particularly of religious people. Clinton also accepted the presumed tradeoff between gay service and military effectiveness, saying the compromise "provides a sensible balance between the rights of the individual and the needs of our military to remain the world's number one fighting force."

On the same day, Aspin signed a policy memo. This was the document that actually ordered the military to implement the policy Clinton announced at Fort McNair, though further details of the final policy—its "implementing regulations" and the individual service branch memos designed to ensure servicewide compliance—would await the masterful hands of government lawyers later that year. Thus the "policy" refers to the Pentagon requirement, developed by order of the president, that known gays be discharged, as contained in Aspin's written July memo and subsequent legal regulations directing how it should be implemented. White House officials and, soon, Les Aspin—though not President Clinton himself—described the policy as "don't ask, don't tell, don't pursue," referring to the omission of asking by recruiters, the ban on telling by gays and lesbians, and the promise that gay people would not be proactively sought out for discharge, but would only be separated when their sexuality came to the attention of commanders.[59] It would come to be known as "don't ask, don't tell" for short.

The policy largely implemented the June recommendations of the Military Working Group. Clinton gave scarcely a nod to the five-hundred-page Rand report, released in July, that found sexual orientation "not germane" to military service. Paying lip service to the privacy zone promised for gay and lesbian troops, the policy said that "sexual orientation is a personal and private matter, and homosexual orientation is not a bar to service entry or continued service." In the biggest change from previous regulations, the policy directed that applicants would "not be asked or required to reveal their sexual orientation." But, as in the past, it called for the "separation" of service members "for homosexual conduct," which was defined to include "a statement by a service member that demonstrates a propensity or intent to engage" in homosexual acts. These acts were defined as "any bodily contact" between members of the same sex undertaken "for the purpose of satisfying sexual desires," or which a "reasonable person would understand to demonstrate a propensity or intent to engage in homosexual acts." The policy explained that a "statement by a service member that he or she is a homosexual" would create a "presumption that the service member is engaging in homosexual acts or has the propensity or intent to do so." To make matters more confusing, the policy stated that, despite that presumption, the accused could try to argue that the statement did not indicate a likelihood that homosexual conduct would take place. Otherwise, any statement of sexual orientation would result in separation, as would evidence of homosexual conduct.[60]

ON SEPTEMBER 14, 1993, two months after the final Senate hearings in which Powell and Aspin showed up to defend the Clinton policy, the full Senate voted to codify this impossibly convoluted policy into law; this more restrictive version of the Clinton-Aspin ban looked to some more like a continuation of the old, outright ban on gays. For the first time in history, the policy on gay service was a matter of federal law, and not just Defense Department regulations, thereby making it much harder to change in the future. The final vote in the Senate was 92 to 7, although since the measure on gay service was part of a much larger defense authorization bill, the tally does not directly reflect the actual positions of senators on this issue. A better indication of this came from the Senate's rejection, 63 to 33, of an amendment offered by Senator Barbara Boxer to drop the ban and give the president the final authority in the matter.

Both the policy and the law required gays to conceal their identity and remain celibate both on and off base. The minor differences between the two primarily reflected legal concerns of the senators who were worried about

courts striking down the policy. But the differences also reflected the successful efforts of conservatives in Congress to use the statute to send a message
that gays and lesbians were unwelcome in the military. Unlike the policy, for
instance, the statute did not say that sexual orientation was a private matter,
and in fact did not even mention orientation at all. Instead, it called homosexuality "an unacceptable risk" to morale, order, and discipline and, in a
"sense of Congress," left open the option for the secretary of defense to reinstate the questioning of recruits, which would effectively wipe out the "don't
ask" half of the policy. In this sense, the law was more restrictive than the
Pentagon policy, but this does not mean, as some have argued, that the policy
actually contradicts the law. At bottom, the differences were symbolic. Both
stipulated that gays would be fired if their homosexuality became known, just
as they always had been. And by stating the intention to cease asking recruits
if they were gay at induction, both created a world where gays and lesbians
were formally invited to lie throughout their service. Hence the overall
policy—including the statute—quickly became known as "don't ask, don't
tell." What Nunn's law did was to strip Clinton's policy of even its minimal
references to respecting the privacy of homosexual orientation. This was not
only a slap in the face to gay service members; it also had a damning impact
on how the policy was actually carried out.[61]

Once the Senate weighed in, Clinton again sought to save face, just as he
had done in July when he announced his policy as an "honorable compromise." The White House moved to declare victory, saying through press secretary Dee Dee Myers that the legislation was no defeat but simply "puts back
into play legislation we said we could live with." The Nunn bill was meant as
a repudiation of Clinton's policy; the administration insisted it was "consistent" with the White House policy issued in July, a statement that was technically true.[62]

Two weeks later, the House followed suit, passing an identical bill by a
vote of 301 to 134 as part of that year's defense spending bill. A majority of
Democrats voted for the bill, and only twelve Republicans voted against it.
But 121 Democrats opposed the bill. The House also soundly rejected efforts
by both sides to water down the legislation. By a vote of 291 to 144, lawmakers
defeated a Republican amendment seeking to reinstate the asking of recruits
whether they were gay, and they similarly rejected, 264 to 169, an effort by
Representative Marty Meehan to cancel the ban and leave the matter in the
hands of the president, as Senator Boxer's amendment had sought.[63]

The House bill was sponsored by Representative Skelton, of Missouri, who
said he sought to "close the door on this painful issue." Saying that "enough is

enough," he assured Americans that the law punished only conduct, not status. Skelton said this even though he had personally worked hard to follow in the House what Nunn had done in the Senate: strip the Clinton policy of a provision specifying that sexual orientation was not a "bar to service," and adding language calling gays and lesbians an "unacceptable risk" to the military. On November 30, President Clinton signed the bill into law, and by December, the Pentagon had drafted regulations stating how the policy would be implemented in all branches of the armed forces. "Don't ask, don't tell" went into effect on March 1, 1994.[64]

5

The Evidence

AMERICANS LIKE TO BELIEVE they live in a rational, pragmatic country, a place where laws are fair and justice makes sense. But as we have seen throughout our country's history, the realities of American life are often far less grand than the ideals. So we must ask: How rational is a ban on openly gay troops? How fair is it? And for that matter, does it even make sense? Is this ban truly necessary to preserve the integrity and effectiveness of the U.S. Armed Forces?

And as we look more closely at the ban and its effects, we must consider how we have come to our current situation. What role have public opinion and beliefs played in shaping this policy—and what role should they play? Likewise, what is the proper—or perhaps we should say necessary—role of emotion, fear, prejudice, animus, ignorance? And what is the proper—or desirable—role of facts, research, evidence, scholarship, knowledge?

There are many ways to begin answering these questions. While none of the evidence on gay service is perfect—it is difficult to gather data on something whose very existence is repressed by law—there is actually a vast body of data on homosexuality in the military. And it is worthwhile to pause briefly from our historical narrative in order to fully grasp what is known about gays in the military. This minor detour will look first at research conducted primarily in the United States, and then at the experiences of other militaries around the world that have allowed gays to serve openly over the past generation.

The government's conclusion that banning open gays from the military is necessary to preserve privacy, cohesion, and effectiveness is wholly unsupported by the research. In fact, existing data show clearly that open gays can and do serve in the military without undermining cohesion, and that the gay ban itself causes more problems in the military than the presence of open gays in a unit. The evidence for this is transparent, uniform, and undeniable. It comes from a vast range of sources: studies, statistics, interviews, opinion surveys, military data, government reports, academic experts, independent assessments, internal reviews, press accounts, and more. The sheer volume of this data is surprising. Unfortunately, in our history of the debate over gay service, such evidence has played only a sporadic role. And this is because the evidence has been consistently and tragically ignored every time the government has confronted the issue of homosexuality and the military.

The Rand study, commissioned by Les Aspin, provided invaluable data that was largely ignored. As one Pentagon official explained, the Rand study provided a "methodological approach," while the military itself offered an "independent judgment."[1] And in the contest between the generals and the professors, there was never any question of who would win—a chest full of metals carried far more weight than a Ph.D.

Nevertheless, Rand sent a team of seventy-five credentialed, multidisciplinary social scientists from its National Defense Research Institute across the globe to research the issue. Sociologists, psychologists, anthropologists, historians, economists, doctors, lawyers, and national security experts exhaustively studied the scientific literature on a broad range of related topics: group cohesion, the experiences of foreign militaries, the theory and history of institutional change, public and military opinion, patterns of sexual behavior in the United States, sexual harassment, leadership theory, public health concerns, the history of racial integration in the military, policies on sexuality in police and fire departments, and legal considerations regarding access to military service. The result was a five-hundred-page study, completed in July 1993. The Rand researchers concluded that sexual orientation alone was "not germane" in determining who should serve. The authors stated that Clinton's proposal to lift the ban could be implemented without major problems if senior leaders got behind the change and clear guidelines were disseminated throughout the chain of command. They also suggested that the UCMJ's ban on consensual sodomy should be consigned to the dustbin of history.[2]

The Rand report, produced at a taxpayer cost of $1.3 million, barely made it out of the firm's Santa Monica headquarters. According to *The New York Times,* Pentagon officials tried to keep the study from going public and refused to talk about it. But summaries were leaked to the *Times,* making some military men apoplectic. Senior officers complained bitterly that the report exceeded its mandate by challenging the rationale for gay exclusion rather than simply suggesting a method for implementing a plan that was closer to the compromise policy being bandied about in Washington. Rand's recommendations, said one senior military officer, are "unacceptable to the military," and "unacceptable practically and politically to Congress." According to the *Times,* Pentagon officials admitted that they never actually considered the Rand report when shaping the final policy, because of the resistance of the Joint Chiefs of Staff.[3]

"I think they had their heads up their asses," said Moskos later of the Rand report. Though an academic himself, Moskos had little patience for scholarship that seemed to him to place the aspirations of liberal social reform above the military's right to preserve the culture and self-image to which it was accustomed. Fortunately for Moskos, his own "don't ask, don't tell" plan carried the day instead of Rand's comprehensive study. It was his plan that shaped the Military Working Group's official recommendation for how to preserve the military's anti-gay "core values" in federal law. As promised, the MWG did, indeed, issue the military's "independent judgment"— independent of genuine research or inquiry. Like the Rand commission and the study groups in each of the service branches, the MWG was supposed to advise the Pentagon how—not whether—to end discrimination. But the generals stonewalled. "The military would love to fight this," admitted an army official anonymously, "but we can't fight it openly." Only when press reports embarrassed them with accounts of continued military resistance in heeding Clinton's order did the group even meet to discuss the policy.[4]

When the MWG finally met, they opened an office on Pennsylvania Avenue, not far from the White House. The group was initially headed by Lieutenant General Minter Alexander, a command pilot in the air force with three decades of service. Alexander was serving as deputy assistant secretary of defense when he was asked to chair the MWG, and he was responsible for the regulations that governed separation from military service. While the large staff supplied research materials, the panel of five generals and admirals under Alexander's command took testimony from military members and other interested parties, including gay rights groups.

The flag officers were not exactly experts on the topic at hand. "We didn't really understand entirely what all was meant by 'sexual orientation,'" recalled Alexander, referring to the president's orders to end discrimination based upon sexual orientation. "We had to define in the first few sessions what we figured they were talking about." Like the other officers, Alexander was concerned that a sudden change in policy could jolt the military and strain efforts to bolster morale and discipline during a time of anxiety over force reduction and other changes. But the more he studied the issue of gay service, the less concerned he became; the more he knew, the less he feared change.[5]

Unfortunately, the rest of the group was not as open. Les Aspin and his staff at the Office of the Secretary of Defense were fully aware of this. "They didn't expect a whole lot out of the Military Working Group," said Alexander. "They thought they knew the results of what was going to happen there. It was going to be very difficult to get an objective, rational review of this policy." Part of the reason for this, said Alexander, was the political leadership. The White House had given the military vague direction and little in the way of preparation or research. The Clinton team did not appear to understand how fierce resistance was in the military and how slowly military culture changes. But ultimately the military is subordinate to the civilian leadership, and the resistance of the MWG to ending anti-gay discrimination was a product of the beliefs and feelings of those who comprised it. "Passion leads, and rationale follows," said Alexander. "We didn't have any empirical data." So the conclusions the MWG drew were "subjective, based on the interviews with people" who testified. In tense, private sessions with emotions running high, senior representatives from each service branch rolled out the doomsday scenarios they were bred by instinct and culture to dread. "You just wouldn't believe the litany of" fears that came up in those meetings, Alexander recalled. "Barracks, bathrooms, roommates, hot bedding on submarines, readiness, all this was coming out." The general remembered that conversations were "very strident at that time," and reflected a "different attitude than we have today."[6]

While Alexander was chairing the MWG, Charles Moskos came to see him. The general was, by this time, leaning toward a policy that would allow gays and lesbians to serve, let them tell the truth about their sexual orientation, but prohibit homosexual acts while in the service. Moskos, who was simultaneously selling his policy to Nunn and Aspin, both in direct talks and as a star witness in the congressional hearings that spring, tried to convince Alexander that "don't ask, don't tell" was the best solution.

Alexander never got the chance to lead the MWG toward a somewhat more liberal policy. In May, Senator Nunn's office abruptly assigned him to testify at a set of budget hearings that made it impossible for him to continue leading the MWG. In Alexander's absence, Moskos's policy carried the day. "He won," said Alexander. "He basically got that adopted." It might have gone that direction anyway, as the general was beginning to come under the sway of Moskos's ideas even before he was removed from the MWG. "It was the least worst alternative," said Alexander, echoing Moskos's Churchill quote on democracy. But as Alexander understood it, Moskos's plan was to be temporary, a transitional step to allow people to get used to serving with gays. "But fifteen years is too damned long," said Alexander when sharing his current thoughts. "I think 'don't ask, don't tell' was a good interim solution as a first step to addressing this problem," he said. But the policy "is not necessarily improving readiness," and in fact "we know it has hurt readiness and morale in some cases." Alexander now believes the law "impedes further progress" and should be repealed.

Vincent Patton, the master chief petty officer of the U.S. Coast Guard, was a staff member of the Military Working Group. The highest-ranking enlisted person in the Coast Guard, Patton had two decades of experience in the armed forces and took his appointment to the MWG seriously. But when he got there, he found others did not: "People were still complaining this had to be done." Patton provided a wealth of research to the flag officers in charge, but he never heard a thing in response—no requests for clarification, no follow-up questions, nothing indicating they had even read what he provided. "They had already made a decision about what they were going to do," he said, "and they weren't about to take anything I had to give them." Patton said the policy recommendation was hammered out by a small circle of people "behind closed doors" who had no genuine interest in an honest discussion of whether gay service would be good or bad for the military. Instead, anti-gay stereotypes and resistance to any outside forces that challenged military tradition were the ruling sentiments of the Military Working Group.[7]

The MWG's fifteen-page report was made public in June 1993. According to the group's findings, "the introduction of individuals identified as homosexuals into the military would severely undermine good order and discipline. Moral and ethical beliefs of individuals would be brought into open conflict. Leadership priorities would, of necessity, be reoriented from training for combat to preventing internal discord." Given the president's order to formulate a policy that did not discriminate against homosexual people, the panel begrudgingly endorsed a plan where sexual orientation alone would not be a bar to entry—as long as it never became known. But the report made the officers' views clear: "All homosexuality is incompatible with military service," it said, a direct rejoinder to suggestions that discreet homosexuality might be acceptable. Damage to combat effectiveness "is not limited to known homosexuals." Again and again, the report stated, with no proof, that the presence of gays—known and unknown—would "have a significantly adverse effect on both unit cohesion and the readiness of the force."[8]

TO SOME, BURYING the Rand study and opting for the MWG report came as no surprise. The Pentagon, it turns out, has a long history of denying, destroying, and suppressing studies that undercut the rationale for discriminating against gays. As early as 1957, the secretary of the navy appointed a panel to investigate its homosexual exclusion policy; the outcome, known as the Crittenden report, found that homosexuals posed no greater security risk than heterosexuals. It said security risks were based not on sexual orientation but on "indiscretion." Certain relations among heterosexuals were considered more threatening than homosexual conduct or the simple fact of being gay. It concluded that the notion that gays were a security risk persisted without any evidence. "The number of cases of blackmail as a result of past investigations of homosexuals is negligible," it said. "No factual data exist to support the contention that homosexuals are a greater risk than heterosexuals." The navy refused to release the report, and it was only made public by court order two decades later.[9]

A generation later, the pattern was repeated, with scarcely an update in the playbook. In 1988 and 1989, a Defense Department research center wrote a series of reports about gays in the military as a security risk. These were the studies that Bill Clinton had mentioned as he made the case to lift the ban in 1992, studies that were commissioned by the Personnel Security Research and Education Center (PERSEREC), a research wing of the Pentagon established in 1987. They were authored by Theodore Sarbin, professor emeritus in psychology and criminology at Berkeley; Captain Kenneth Karols, a psychiatrist and navy flight surgeon; and Michael McDaniel, a PERSEREC researcher. The men had no links to gay and lesbian advocacy, no agenda to forward, no chip on their shoulder. Their ideological leanings, if any, as researchers hired by the military were in the direction of supporting existing policy.[10]

Like the Rand study, the PERSEREC reports found no evidence showing that gays were unsuitable for military service and suggested that the policy was unnecessary and even damaging. In fact, they noted, the risk of blackmail was actually worsened by the taboo against homosexuality. Examining 130 cases of possible espionage, researchers found that only 6 of the subjects were suspected of being gay.[11]

The first report directly addressed the unit cohesion rationale for the gay ban and found that it was based on fear rather than facts. "Buried deep in the supporting conceptual structure" of the ban's defense, said the report, "is the fearful imagery of homosexuals polluting the social environment with unrestrained and wanton expressions of deviant sexuality." Yet "all the studies conducted on the psychological adjustment of homosexuals that we have seen lead to contrary inferences." Using heuristic models of shifting social attitudes, the report pointed to growing tolerance of homosexuality and concluded that "the military cannot indefinitely isolate itself from the changes occurring in the wider society, of which it is an integral part." In the final analysis, it found, "having a same-gender or an opposite-gender orientation is unrelated to job performance in the same way as is being left- or right-handed."[12]

The second PERSEREC report actually found something few people have suggested: that gays and lesbians are *better* suited to the military than straights. Using social adjustment surveys, the researchers compared data from gay discharges with that of other discharges in areas such as school behavior and cognitive ability. Their summary found that "the preponderance of the evidence presented indicates that homosexuals show preservice suitability-related adjustment that is as good [as] or better than the average heterosexual," a result that appeared to "conflict with conceptions of homosexuals as unstable, maladjusted persons."[13]

When military brass got word of PERSEREC's findings, they balked. For months, they denied that the studies existed. According to Lawrence Korb, assistant secretary of defense under President Ronald Reagan, the Defense Department ordered the reports destroyed. When presented with salvaged copies that had been leaked to the press and the congressional offices of Gerry Studds and Patricia Schroeder, military officials said the reports were "drafts" that had never been accepted by the Pentagon and therefore they did not have to be released because, as studies, they still did not exist. At one point, the Pentagon even claimed that PERSEREC was not part of the Defense Department, a fact belied by the giant DOD seal on all its official documents. In reality, the research center was established, underwritten, and administered by the U.S. military.[14]

The PERSEREC reports might never have surfaced if they had not been forced out in 1989, during the discovery period of the Joseph Steffan case. Gerry Studds and Patricia Schroeder wrote to Defense Secretary Dick Cheney and demanded the release of the information for the benefit of the Steffan lawyers. The deputy undersecretary of defense, Craig Alderman, Jr., was forced to attack the reports to justify their suppression. The PERSEREC study, he said, "missed the target." In two angrily worded memos to the authors, Alderman wrote that the researchers had "exceeded your authority." They were supposed to assess whether gays in the military were reliable, but they ended up also assessing their "suitability." Apparently two-for-ones are not popular at the Pentagon, particularly when the product conflicts with a treasured policy that's considered essential to long-standing military culture. The "unfortunate" study "has expended considerable government resources, and has not assisted us one whit in our personnel security program," complained

Alderman, further griping that the whole sorry episode would "cause us in Washington to expend even more time and effort satisfying concerns in this whole issue." He directed PERSEREC to "develop a positive response" to the guidelines of his office, coordinate closely with his staff for all further investigations in this area, and await approval before embarking on any more "questionable" research.[15]

PERSEREC replied that the Pentagon would have embraced the report if it had come to the opposite conclusion, suggesting that the rejection was purely ideological and political. The question of suitability, argued its director, Carson Eoyang, was a necessary part of determining whether gays could be given security clearances. "The nature of research," he wrote, "is such that the answers to the focal question are not known in advance. The underlying purpose for asking the question should not be invalidated because the results turn out to be problematic from a policy perspective." Studds, for one, appreciated the humor of the situation: "The Pentagon said, 'We didn't ask you that question; don't answer questions that we didn't ask you.'"[16]

In January 1991, the Steffan case turned up another Pentagon document, this time an army memo echoing PERSEREC's findings. The Pentagon only released it under a federal court order. "Current research has not identified that homosexual personnel are any greater security risk than their heterosexual counterparts," it read. Absent any evidence that gays compromise the mission, "the Army has no basis on which to justify such continued discrimination." Amazingly, it also noted that attitudes toward gays had recently "undergone significant evolution"—and that was in 1991. It would make later debates over whether tolerance of homosexuality has progressed enough seem like a bizarre replay of an earlier era.[17]

In 1992, one of Congress's research arms, the Government Accountability Office (GAO; then called the General Accounting Office), pointed out that the military "has not conducted specific research to develop empirical evidence supporting the overall validity of the premises and rationale underlying its current policy on homosexuality." The Defense Department concurred, saying its policy was a matter of "professional Military judgment, not scientific or sociological analysis." This judgment, admitted the department, is "inherently subjective in nature, and scientific or sociological analyses are unlikely to ever be dispositive."[18]

So the GAO conducted its own extensive study of the gay exclusion policy. Its researchers looked at seventeen different countries and eight police and fire departments in four U.S. cities and reviewed military and nonmilitary polls, studies, legal decisions, and scholarly research on homosexual service.

The GAO study noted the Crittenden report, the PERSEREC studies, the liberal policies in foreign countries and police and fire departments, the discrediting of the security risk rationale, and the evolution of public attitudes toward homosexuality—another reminder that even in the early 1990s, policy makers had evidence that tolerance had grown dramatically. As a result of all these data points, the GAO recommended in an early draft that Congress "may wish to direct the Secretary of Defense to reconsider the basis" for gay exclusion. Oddly, the final GAO report deleted this suggestion, allegedly because Patricia Schroeder's bill to end the ban—which had no real chance of passing—had been introduced.[19]

In a remarkable replay of the response to the PERSEREC report, the Defense Department slammed the GAO report. The assistant secretary of defense called the report "misleading" and said it "minimizes the importance of years of litigation" in which courts had upheld the policy. The courts, it said, "have not required scientific evidence to support the Defense Department policy because the Military constitutes a specialized community, governed by a separate discipline from that of the civilian community." The Defense Department dragged out its dishonest complaints about the PERSEREC report: It wasn't a report at all, merely a draft.

Ultimately, the military commissioned a study, didn't like what it found, refused to accept it, and then rejected its findings based on the fact that it had . . . rejected its findings. It had literally sought to deny the truth out of existence, exactly what "don't ask, don't tell" was designed to do to gays themselves. The PERSEREC "report," said the Defense Department, borrowing a favored tactic of the religious right—mocking scholarship by putting it in quotations—"addressed only civilian security clearance policy and had nothing to do with the Military homosexual exclusion policy." The truth? It had addressed precisely the exclusion policy until Defense officials buried those findings in a "draft" so they could say the Pentagon never addressed the policy. But the Pentagon continued to insist there was no such study. "The opinions expressed in the draft document," it said, "were solely those of the authors, and did not and do not reflect those of the Department of Defense. It is, therefore, not accurate to refer to the PERSEREC 1988 drafts as a Defense Department report, or to consider its tentative findings, as they relate to the Military homosexual exclusion policy, to be authoritative."[20]

For Lawrence Korb, this was the last straw. "After I saw those PERSEREC studies in the 1980s," recalled Korb, "I was convinced that we were really stupid because now, we had data that said there was no real threat posed by gays in uniform." Instead of heeding the data, the military invented a new justification for the ban—the unit cohesion rationale.[21] Though many tried, Korb was im-possible to ignore or vilify. A retired naval flight officer, Korb had a Ph.D. in political science and had worked as a professor of management at the Naval War College, the director of national security studies at the Council on Foreign Rela-tions, a senior fellow at the Brookings Institution, and the dean of the Graduate School of Public and International Affairs at the University of Pittsburgh.

Most important, Korb was no liberal hack and had not always opposed the gay exclusion rule. To the contrary, under Ronald Reagan, he was respon-sible for implementing the 1981 directive deeming homosexuality "incompat-ible with military service." In 1993, in a stunning public reversal, Korb explained to Congress that he was appalled that his policy had led to "an unprecedented era of witch hunts to flush out . . . 'undesirables.'" Korb had watched for over a dozen years as military officials ignored, denied, and sup-pressed their own studies concluding that gays did not pose a threat to readi-ness. In 1994, Korb wrote a very personal essay explaining his radical change of heart. "As a social scientist trained to let research impact policy, I found it unthinkable that Pentagon leaders would try to shoot the messenger," he wrote. He was left to conclude that "empirical evidence or systematic research and analysis has very little impact on such controversial and emotional issues as gays in the military."[22]

Rear Admiral John Hutson knows what Korb was talking about. His front-row seat at the conversations in the navy JAG's office about how to deal with the question of gay service provided an object lesson for him in how good people can let fear, ignorance, and emotion override rational inquiry.

As an assistant, Hutson had to tend to details when his superiors couldn't be bothered. "None of them had much of a sense of what was going on," he recalled. "We were all a bunch of white guys who were born in the 1940s. And the decisions were based on nothing. It wasn't empirical, it wasn't studied, it was completely visceral, intuitive." Hutson said there were "lots of horribles": What about the showers, what about the subs, how are we going to deal with all this? "It was ridiculous, it was all by the seat of our pants."[23]

"So we hung everything on the question of unit cohesion," said Hutson. "That was the catch phrase." Casting their position in terms of unit cohesion had far-reaching consequences. "The leadership of the military was essen-tially telling the young people that we really don't trust you to deal with this, we think you're all pretty bigoted, and you're not very open-minded and we're going to end up with blood in the streets and the units are all going to fall apart." The message that sent down through the ranks, said Hutson, "to boots on the ground, was a very, very negative message." They did not tell the young people under their command that they were capable, mature, and well-disciplined; instead they welcomed their homophobia and used it as an excuse for inaction.[24]

In fact, said Hutson, "I don't think we ever seriously considered the fact that it might not be a problem" to lift the ban, "that it might be a good thing. It was always a question of how little can we compromise and still get away with it. It was all a knee-jerk reaction: not only 'No,' but 'Hell, no.' "[25]

"I think, too, honestly it was our own prejudices and our own fears," said Hutson. The senior officers went through the motions of a dialogue, but at the end of the day, they never seemed to seriously consider lifting the ban. "The feeling was, 'we were all opposed to it because we're all opposed to it.' No one had the moral courage to stand up and say, let's step back, think it through, do the analysis and do the studies; this may be okay, this may not be a problem at all. In fact, we may be a better military because of it."[26]

THE MILITARY, IT is often said, is unique, a world apart. The ordinary standards and rules of civilian society do not apply in the military. But does this mean that ordinary facts don't apply as well? When the 1992 presidential campaign put gay service back on the map, researchers found the Defense Department actually had a servicewide ban on conducting research on the issue. Moskos testified that research "only on gay issues" had been shut down.[27] And why not? No one has held the Pentagon to account. Instead, the federal courts have repeatedly held that the military is exempt from the use of facts in forming policy on gay service. Judges tend to be satisfied by their own assumption that it is common sense that allowing homosexuality in the military would impair combat readiness.

In 1984, a Washington, D.C., circuit court upheld the gay ban in the navy, stating that "the effects of homosexual conduct within a naval or military unit are almost certain to be harmful to morale and discipline." The burden of proof, added the court, does not lie with the military: "The Navy is not required to produce social science data or the results of controlled experiments to prove what common sense and common experience demonstrate." When Judge Oliver Gasch ruled seven years later in the Steffan case that it was perfectly constitutional to ban gay troops because of the "quite rational assumption" that there were no homosexuals in the navy, and that keeping it that way would spare straights undue fear and embarrassment, he cited the 1984 case, in which the arch-conservative Judge Robert Bork, joined by Antonin Scalia, had relied on their own "common sense" to uphold the assertion that gays obviously undercut military discipline and morale.[28]

As Melissa Wells-Petry had written in her 1993 book, *Exclusion,* "Based on the reasonableness of [various] assumptions, presumptions, and common sense propositions—though not proof proper," the Supreme Court upholds laws when they are deemed to have "obvious" justification. The gay ban, she concluded "does not require proof of the factual merits." What Americans sometimes forget, explains Richard Posner, a federal judge and renowned legal theorist, is that sex and sexuality "are emotional topics even to middle-aged and elderly judges," and, as a consequence, "the dominant judicial, and I would say legal, attitude toward the study of sex is that 'I know what I like' and therefore research is superfluous."[29]

Nor, argued Supreme Court Justice Antonin Scalia, in an angry dissent to the 2003 decision striking down sodomy bans, did the government have to show any compelling reason beyond expressing public morality to pass laws trampling on gay rights or sexual freedom. His dissenting opinion quoted earlier cases that found that "legislatures are permitted to legislate with regard to morality . . . rather than confined to preventing demonstrable harm." Scalia approved of the "countless judicial decisions and legislative enactments" that had "relied on the ancient proposition" that society could legitimately ban behavior simply because "a governing majority" believed it was "immoral and unacceptable."[30] He approved, in other words, of writing the reflexive morality of the majority into law, without requiring either a rational basis for the law or the most basic of constitutional tests to ensure that the law did not run roughshod over the fundamental rights of a minority.

Accordingly, it's no secret, both inside and outside the military, that the policy on gay service is not based on factual evidence. In his congressional testimony, David Burrelli acknowledged the obvious when he said that no one knew whether gays undermined the military because current policy prevented evidence from being gathered. Twice he said, "The extent to which open homosexuality in the ranks would prove sufficiently disruptive to justify continued exclusion of homosexuals is not known." Indeed, "the very existence of the policy itself prevents empirical research from discovering whether or not open homosexuals would, in fact, prove to be disruptive." Though pro-ban military leaders used their authority to spread scare stories that recruitment numbers would plunge if the ban were lifted, actual recruiters said there was no evidence to that effect. "We don't know what impact, if any, there'll be on recruiting," said a spokesman for the Army Recruiting Command at Fort Knox early in 1993.[31]

The same had been true of women in combat. In 1991, General Merrill McPeak, the air force chief of staff, had unabashedly announced that "personal prejudices" shaped his opposition to expanding combat roles for women, "even though logic tells us" that women can conduct combat operations just as well as men. McPeak cited "data" and "evidence" showing that women even had some advantages, on average, over men in flying combat planes. But, saying he took "solace in thinking that not all human problems yield to strict logic," he admitted he would choose an inferior male flight instructor over a superior female one even if it made for a "militarily less effective situation." For Mc-Peak, it wasn't about evidence but emotions. "I admit it doesn't make much sense," he said, "but that's the way I feel about it."[32] Readiness, combat effectiveness, military necessity—they were all important, but only until they conflicted with the cultural and moral biases of the leadership, who would sacrifice what's best for the military in order to serve the higher goal of preserving a traditional social order.

Moskos acknowledged as much in Nunn's hearings in an unguarded moment under questioning from Senator Levin. The senator wanted to know why the 1992 Presidential Commission on the Assignment of Women in the Armed Forces, on which Moskos served, had voted not to allow women on combat aircraft. Was it because of a judgment that they would be disruptive to cohesion? "Yes," answered Moskos at first. "Well, if you really want to know the truth," he continued, "it was because the Air Force wanted it that way. That is the real reason." Wasn't it "based on a cohesion argument?" asked Levin. "No," replied Moskos, "it was based on the Air Force's arguments." But it was also Moskos's own argument—one based on cultural and even biological beliefs about sex differences that were highly contested. Female soldiers, he wrote in a 1998 newspaper article, "display a compassion found less frequently among men." Such qualities, while well suited to peace-keeping missions, could be a "hindrance in combat, where the worst instincts in soldiers must be aroused."[33]

IN DEFENDING ITS gay ban, the military said it relied not on actual evidence but on "professional military judgment." So on what did the Pentagon base its vaunted professional judgment that gay exclusion "promotes overall combat effectiveness"?[34] Mostly, just that: judgment, good or bad, right or wrong, grounded or unmoored. But to respond to the 1992 GAO report and to make their case during the 1993 hearings, the military and other supporters of the ban were compelled to bring to the debate some explanation rooted in facts. When pressed, supporters of the gay ban offered two forms of evidence for the need to exclude gays from service. The first was opinion polls showing that lots of military men did not want to serve with gays. And the second was anecdotes, sometimes conveyed in letters from service members or their families, about units with gays and lesbians in which problems arose.

Two main surveys were cited during Sam Nunn's hearings. One was a 1993 *Los Angeles Times* poll, which found that 76 percent of servicemen and 55 percent of servicewomen disapproved of lifting the gay ban. The other was conducted in 1992 and 1993 by Moskos and his Northwestern University research team. It interviewed hundreds of army soldiers and distributed surveys to thousands, investigating a cross section of race, rank, and occupational specialties. Their survey found that 75 percent of army men, but only 43 percent of women, agreed with the gay ban. The air force administered a third poll, by telephone early in 1993, finding that 67 percent of men and, again, 43 percent of women supported the ban. (Women, it turns out, uniformly show greater tolerance of homosexuality and of gay service on surveys across the board; given that the single most important piece of data that ban defenders cite in making their case is the intolerance of military members themselves, one might think that lesbians would be allowed to serve by now.) In February 1993, the Republican Research Committee commissioned confidential surveys of active-duty officers in the military. Of more than six hundred admirals and generals who responded, a whopping 97 percent opposed lifting the ban.[35]

THESE ARE IMPRESSIVE numbers. But they do not, by themselves, address what impact negative attitudes actually have on discipline, morale, or unit cohesion, to say nothing of their effect on combat performance. Polls express opinions; they don't determine behavior, and they don't even necessarily predict it. What's more, evidence from the real world shows that opinion polls on gay service have often told us zero about behavior; instead they serve as an opportunity for military men to register their moral disapproval of homosexuality or simply to bind people to the larger group by allowing them to express beliefs that they think others share.

Similar polls, taken in other countries and in American police and fire departments, reveal a reality wholly unconnected to what is predicted by these widely cited surveys. In numerous military and paramilitary organizations, survey respondents insisted they would leave if gays were allowed to join, but when gay bans ended, almost no one left. Research also shows that respondents express greater animus toward gays in public than in one-on-one interviews, and that people in the military often believe their peers are more homophobic than they are.

The other piece of evidence supporters of the ban cite is the opinions of military members, including both enlisted personnel and celebrity officers like Colin Powell, whose resistance, as we have seen, was the most frequently cited and the most influential throughout the debate over gay service. General Norman Schwarzkopf, commander of allied operations in the Persian Gulf War, was another. Schwarzkopf joined Powell in toeing the unit cohesion line, arguing that "the introduction of an open homosexual into a small unit immediately polarizes that unit and destroys the very bonding that is so important for survival in time of war," but his tone was sharper than Powell's, as he recounted lurid tales of sexual advances and harassment by gay men in military units.[36]

"Why won't you listen to the mothers and fathers, military leaders like General Schwarzkopf and hundreds of thousands of young Americans in uniform," said Representative Duncan Hunter in a 1993 talk directed at President Clinton, "who are begging you not to force our young Marines, soldiers, sailors and airmen into close living quarters with homosexuals?" In the House hearings, Ike Skelton, the chair of the Armed Services Committee, praised Schwarzkopf along with the Joint Chiefs of Staff, and cited their opposition to gay service in making his own case to retain the ban. Skelton also leaned on the words of Lieutenant General Calvin Waller and General Maxwell R. Thurman, who led the U.S. invasion of Panama in 1989, and who argued in 1993 that openly gay service would be "devastating to unit morale, cohesion and, ultimately, unit effectiveness in combat.[37]

Recall, too, the Senate hearings, with hours of field testimony from enlisted personnel and officers insisting that lifting the ban would destroy the military, threaten national security, and earn the wrath of God. Conservative Christian groups eagerly compiled samples of letters saying the same, published them in organs such as *Lambda Report,* and distributed them to as many military and political leaders as possible. Some described the "fear and intimidation experienced by heterosexual female soldiers" at the hands of "bullying lesbians." But most acknowledged, almost proudly, that it was the behavior of angry straight men that was actually responsible for the disruptions, as they would "avoid, stigmatize and harass soldiers whose 'gayness' is revealed." And the Pentagon in 1992 cited tabulations of letters it had received as evidence of the need for the ban, saying "mail from the public now is running more than 2 to 1 in support of the policy."[38]

The reliance of the pro-ban case on military opinion was suspect from the beginning, for reasons already discussed. As the GAO itself noted, "tabulations of self-initiated letters are not valid" when "stronger evidence is available in the form of more technically sound, public opinion poll evidence."[39] But again, the real question is what is the relevance of opinions to begin with?

Charlie Moskos seemed to believe that opinion polls constituted hard evidence. In his congressional testimony, he announced that the social scientific community had "empirical data" showing that sex integration had "degrade[d] military effectiveness" during the Gulf War. What were his data? "According to a Roper poll taken in Desert Shield," he testified, "45 percent of those who served in mixed-gender units in the Gulf said that there was enough sexual activity to degrade military performance. That is a very high number."

"A Roper poll? An opinion poll?" asked Judith Stiehm incredulously, when presented with Moskos's data in an interview. Opinion polls, she said, "are only opinions." To have empirical evidence on cohesion, "you have to measure cohesion." But Stiehm said that when military officials "constructed studies to systematically measure this, they kept getting studies which found no correlation, and so they stopped doing the studies." It's a criticism echoed by other scholars, many of whom believe that Moskos abused his academic credentials. "It's an incredibly insidious role that Moskos has played in the policy process," complained Aaron Belkin, a political scientist who founded the Palm Center at the University of California, Santa Barbara, which studies gays in the military. "He used his academic credentials to pretend that the policy is based on academic evidence when in fact it's based on homophobia." Belkin said that "when you look at the evidence they use and start to scrutinize it, you realize it's not evidence."[40]

But of course, offering military opinions as empirical evidence is par for the course for this sociology expert. In a 1993 essay, "From Citizens' Army to Social Laboratory," Moskos rejected the comparison of racial integration to allowing gays in the military. But rather than make an argument for how the analogy failed, he opted to simply cite Colin Powell's opinion on the matter. In place of models or measurements to account for his concern over "morale and group cohesion," Moskos offered up a pithy quote from a highly decorated veteran who writes for *Newsweek*: "One doesn't need to be a field marshall to understand that sex between service members undermines those critical factors that produce discipline, military orders, spirit, and combat effectiveness." Never mind that no one was talking about "sex between service members," only about the military service of homosexuals—a group of people many Americans still can't seem to discuss without thinking of sex. Moskos continued to defend the ban years after it was passed using the same nonevidence. In 1997, he suggested that critics of his argument about the privacy rights of straights check into the policies of major universities regarding "what really happens in freshman dorm assignments when open gays and straights are assigned the same room and someone objects." Moskos claimed that, at Northwestern, where he taught at the time of his remark, straight students were permitted to change room assignments for this reason alone. But a spokesperson for Northwestern denies that the university ever had such a policy. Either way, should the policies of private American universities dictate—or even help explain—the laws governing U.S. military personnel? Then, when asked in a 1999 radio debate if he could provide actual evidence showing that gay service undermined military effectiveness, he said, "If you want data, we have survey data on this question and there is . . . a vehement opposition by the majority of the men. If that isn't data, I don't know what is."[41]

But as we have discussed, that is not evidence, at least not the kind that should be convincing to honest, rational people. As it turns out, however, an enormous amount of research has been conducted on the connection between cohesion and performance, research that offers overwhelming evidence about whether the gay ban hurts or helps the military mission. What does this research say? Does it bear out the vivid images that ban defenders painted of a nation's military undermined by gays serving openly and cohesive fighting forces torn asunder? What exactly is the connection between homosexuality, unit cohesion, and combat performance?

Unit cohesion is, like love, not an easy concept to pin down. Loosely associated with what sociologists call "primary group solidarity," it refers to a kind of mystical association that ties soldiers together through a shared identification with a leader. The most famous research on military bonding comes from the era after World War II, when American thinkers turned to Freudian insight hoping to understand Nazi soldiers' compliance with Hitler. In 1948, Edward Shils and Morris Janowitz launched the field of military sociology when they published their pioneering study, "Cohesion and Disintegration in the Wehrmacht in World War II." The article argued that camaraderie and leadership, not ideology or cause, motivated the German soldier. Enlisted men form emotional ties with their peers through joint idealization of a leader, the authors explained. The relationship to the leader that the troops share develops into comradeship, inspiring empathy, self-sacrifice, and ultimately a willingness to die for the group.[42]

A generation later, U.S. involvement in Vietnam spawned new inquiries into the social and psychological sources of combat motivation, which largely reiterated the central role of group loyalty as the only force strong enough to compel individuals to risk death. By the time Congress held its hearings in the spring of 1993, a consensus seemed to be emerging around the idea that cohesion was the "essence" of a fighting force, the glue that binds soldiers together in "coordinated action."[43]

Such conclusions were absorbed and echoed by the military brass. The Joint Chiefs' MWG report had written in its findings that "military operations are team operations—units win wars, not individuals. The rights and needs of the group are emphasized while individual rights and needs are often set aside or sacrificed for military necessity." General Powell asserted that, "to win wars, we create cohesive teams of warriors who will bond so tightly that they're prepared to go into battle and give their lives." Together, the reports and testimony of the national security community helped to enshrine an interdisciplinary orthodoxy in military and civilian circles alike which assumed a causal relationship between unit cohesion and effective militaries: Strong cohesion made a fighting force effective, while weak cohesion made it ineffective.[44]

Yet the actual impact of unit cohesion on combat effectiveness is not nearly so simple. The Shils and Janowitz scholarship was heavily critiqued in the years since its publication. Of particular note was a broad reassessment in the 1980s that suggested that their work gave "disproportionate attention" to the issue of primary group solidarity. For instance, one 1989 study argued that, contrary to Shils and Janowitz, primary group cohesion cannot explain the combat motivation in Hitler's army because close-knit groups never existed: German soldiers continued to fight despite staggering personnel losses, which meant human turnover was far too high for them to have ever maintained close cohesive ties. The 1980s research on group behavior, which came mostly from military sociology and psychology, made a crucial distinction between two different kinds of unit cohesion. "Social cohesion" refers to bonds of friendship and affinity among group members. When individuals enjoy spending time together, when they feel emotional ties of loyalty and companionship, they form a socially cohesive group. "Task cohesion," by contrast, refers to the group solidarity that results from the collective efforts of individuals dedicated to achieving a common goal. Members of a legal firm, a theater group, or an assembly line may have no desire to socialize together before or after their work is done, but their mutual devotion to winning a case, producing a play, or building a car can generate superb task cohesion for the purpose of completing their respective missions.[45]

Moskos said in a 2000 interview that he has "never understood the significance of the distinction between task and social cohesion. It is immaterial to my policy prescription of don't ask don't tell." He later said, "To me it's all psychobabble. 'We're going to take this hill even though we all hate each other'? I can't conceive of achieving a task when you all hate each other."[46]

But as usual, his folk wisdom does not stand up to actual research. By almost all accounts, any positive correlation between unit cohesion and military performance relates to task, not social, cohesion. In institutional settings, the relevant question is not whether group members like each other, but whether they are mutually committed to the task at hand. As Judith Stiehm pointed out in a 1992 article, "trust and confidence develop not from homogeneity, but shared experience." When members of different backgrounds come together in the armed forces, "the military assumes the job of training them to behave as a team. It has many powerful tools to develop desired responses." In 1994, Brian Mullen and Carolyn Copper, of Syracuse University, conducted the most complete meta-analysis to date on the cohesion-performance relationship. Their research indicated that, after controlling for task cohesion, social cohesion had no connection to performance.[47]

In 1996, Robert J. MacCoun, a Berkeley psychologist and contributor to the 1993 Rand study on gay service, published his results of an extensive review of fifty years of research, covering nearly two hundred publications. MacCoun concluded that "it is *task cohesion*, not social cohesion or group pride, that drives group performance. This conclusion is consistent with the results of hundreds of studies in the industrial-organizational psychology literature."[48]

Finally, military psychologists have made a distinction between comradeship and friendship, categories which roughly parallel task cohesion and social cohesion, respectively. While comradeship develops by subordinating individual needs to those of the group, friendship is all about individuality and close affective ties, which pose a danger in combat environments no matter if you're gay or straight. As a result, leaders have always maintained a rule of "don't get too close." The question is, under what conditions is comradeship likely to become friendship? For soldiers in combat, the intensity and duration of battle make emotional intimacy a constant threat, "a burden of love," as an American bomber pilot poignantly expressed it, "that couldn't flourish." By this reasoning, the goal of military training is to build group cohesiveness at the expense of individuality, "through a regime that makes prior identities irrelevant." This is the reason for basic training. In other words, the very essence of military training is designed to manage the very problems that critics of gay service claim is a gay problem alone.[49]

Not only does social cohesion fail to augment performance; it can frequently impair it. According to many studies, including some conducted or cited by Charles Moskos himself, social bonding and combat performance are *inversely* correlated: The more soldiers bond with each other, the more combat performance suffers. Fraternizing, desertion, fraggings (the killing or

maiming of a unit leader), sexual harassment—these collective acts of insubordination are not products of lax social ties but of ties that bind too much. It
is not, then, the *presence* of gay soldiers that threatens military effectiveness
but the invitation they represent to get too close. Some advocates of the gay
ban, it seems, fear that service members in units with open gays will get along
too poorly, while others feel they'll get along just a little bit too well.[50]

This reassessment of the unit cohesion theory, and the more subtle appreciation of the difference between social and task cohesion, was also absorbed
by the U.S. military. In fact, despite the military's endless invocation of unit
cohesion, the Pentagon has a long history of trying to minimize social cohesion and encourage individualism in its personnel. In 1985, a Rand report
prepared for the Pentagon warned against "too much affective cohesion," because it "might interfere with the critical appraisal of performance that is
needed to maintain quality output, as members become concerned with supporting each other and raising group morale instead of concentrating on the
task at hand." Between the 1950s and the 1980s, the army experimented with
a buddy system in which units were trained together and then sent into combat. Evaluations by the Walter Reed Army Institute of Research of the unit
manning system, called COHORT, concluded that "military cohesion has not
been valued as a combat multiplier in the U.S. Army." They found that cohesion is "a byproduct, not a core goal leaders need be trained to create and
maintain," and that "there is as yet no commitment in the Army to building
and maintaining group cohesion."[51]

This may be why Moskos's real reasons for opposing an end to the gay ban
had nothing to do with unit cohesion—whether task or social. While his public voice continued to emphasize the centrality of unit cohesion to combat
performance, his private focus was quite different. "Fuck unit cohesion," he
said in a 2000 interview. "I don't care about that." In Moskos's view, the rationale for the double standard was about a discomfort with thinking about
sexuality, which, for him, boiled down to the rights of straight soldiers not to
be watched with eyes of desire. "I've offered all kinds of arguments against
the policy," he said, "but the privacy one is where it breaks down." Indeed,
Moskos felt so strongly about the privacy issue that he viewed mandatory
gay-straight cohabitation as tantamount to Nazism: "I would not want to
fight for a country in which privacy issues are so trampled upon," he said.
"Those are the conditions of concentration camps."[52]

One has to wonder why Moskos took the charge he was given as a social
scientist and used it to give cover to the assertion by generals and politicians
that unit cohesion—not sexual discomfort—was the central basis of the gay

ban, if that is not what he believed. But the concentration camp analogy is not wholly irrelevant, as the ghosts of Nazi Germany have maintained a strange and persistent presence in the dialogue on homosexuality and the military. A little-discussed section of Shils and Janowitz's famous study on Wehrmacht soldiers sheds unwelcome, but inescapable, light on the need to maintain a regime of sexual repression in the armed forces. Revealing the "dark side of cohesion," this research highlights not only the homosocial bonds of enlisted men but the homoerotic tendencies of military culture.[53]

According to the scholarship, it is the unacknowledged erotic bonds of military men that actually underlay the primary group cohesion achieved in the German army during World War II. In 1948, the noted psychiatrist William Menninger characterized the wartime soldier's bond as one of "disguised and sublimated homosexuality." Some scholars suggested that the popular war song "My Buddy" ("I miss your voice and the touch of your hand, my buddy") helped neutralize fears of unexpected longings, making the military a safe place for same-sex intimacy. As long as there were no homosexuals present, soldiers could have intense same-sex relationships and not worry about being gay.[54]

At the 1993 Senate hearings, the sociologist David Segal, who studied under both Shils and Janowitz, described the World War II research to the frequently befuddled assemblage of silver-haired senators. Cohesion in the Wehrmacht, he explained, was based in part on a "latent homosexual subculture." There was, of course, no sanctioning of actual same-sex sexual activity in the Nazi army. But while the Wehrmacht tolerated no avowed gay soldiers, homoerotic attachments seem to have been quite common. As Segal put it, "there was a hard core of enlisted personnel in the Wehrmacht who were attracted to the company of other men. They did not necessarily behave homosexually; indeed, they probably did not. But they preferred the company of men."[55]

Segal reported to Congress that he had never seen this particular piece of Shils and Janowitz research cited before. "I discovered it by accident," he said, "while I was grading some midterm exams." But its implications were clear. "It basically suggests that what we have more recently called 'male bonding' may well have been in the Wehrmacht this propensity to seek other males as erotic objects, although not acting on that." These conclusions, he explained, "throw into question" the assertion that homosexual tendencies undermine unit cohesion. In fact, rather than undermining unit cohesion, the presence of men with quiet same-sex longing appears to have enhanced it by bringing together groups of people with the propensity for intense bonding. The key to successfully cohesive fighting units, it turns out, is that homosexual—or at least homoerotic—affection should be present but repressed: that is, unspoken and, if possible, unacknowledged.[56]

Moskos's testimony before Nunn expanded on this theme: "Precisely because there are homoerotic tendencies in all male groups," he explained, referencing the "sexual insecurities" of straight men, "this is exactly why [we need] the ban. Once these homoerotic tendencies are out, the cat is out of the bag, then you have all kinds of negative effects on unit cohesion." But for Moskos, "the point is that in the Nazi army, you could not be a gay." He struggled to reconcile the presence of latent homosexual desire with what he regarded as "probably the most barbaric system toward gays" in human history. "You have these erotic tendencies operating at one level," he concluded, "but at the same time, the system is the most repressive ever known," an arrangement which has historically "worked for a good fighting army."[57]

In other words, the problem with acknowledging the presence of gays in the military is that it could burden with added meaning the low-level homoerotic behavior that is normally operating among all service members. It would force even men who are effectively straight to come face-to-face with buried strands of their own same-sex desire, feelings that do not make them homosexual but whose very presence is nevertheless a threat to their fragile heterosexual identity.

As Moskos put it in interviews, "in a heterosexual environment, you can do a lot of patting people on the ass, hugging, and all that, which might not be possible among open gays." In many Mediterranean and Middle Eastern cultures, which are homophobic by American standards, men stroll down the street kissing and holding hands without fear that their affection has a sexual meaning. It's the homophobic norms that make this possible. "It might even be that the more homoerotic tendencies there are in a group," said Moskos, "the more homophobic they will be." Does this mean the military must ensure that certain emotions are kept repressed? It must ensure, says Moskos, that they "remain subdued."[58]

DURING THE SENATE hearings, talk of the latent homosexual subculture of the Wehrmacht army passed far over the head of Senator Sam Nunn. "How in the world," he asked, "is that applicable to what we are talking about here? It does not seem to me to apply or have any application to America." But the Wehrmacht research was one of the most directly applicable pieces of research to address the relationship between sexuality, cohesion, and military performance. There was "a strong male homoerotic tendency among these combat groups," Moskos confirmed. And yet, as Senator William Cohen pointed out, they were not barred from military service. In fact, Cohen said, "The one piece of research I am aware of that addresses this issue, a piece of research that has previously been brought to the attention of this committee, throws into question the assertion that homosexual tendencies will necessarily undermine unit cohesion."[59]

Could the Wehrmacht research apply in the United States? No one has replicated the Shils and Janowitz research, and the differences between the U.S. military today and the German army of more than a half century ago are enormous. Yet, though the homoerotic thesis emerged from the specific context of a World War II authoritarian regime, it is surely significant that the reigning study on social cohesion and military performance theorized an erotic foundation for same-sex bonding and combat effectiveness. Cohen's thesis remains sound: The empirical research that was directly responsive to the question of same-sex love and cohesion said the opposite of what the ban's champions were saying: Same-sex desire did not undermine cohesion but strengthened it.

This is not to say that an influx of gay people into the military will increase our chances of winning the war in Iraq. As Moskos and Segal explained, it is repressed homoerotic tendencies that were shown to have helped cohesion in Wehrmacht Germany, not a gaggle of actual homosexuals. But Shils and Janowitz make clear what the real threat is of acknowledging a gay presence in the military: that it could somehow chip away at these repressed feelings and arouse in straight people the kinds of homoerotic tendencies that are typically kept at bay. This means the distinction between conduct and status is immaterial. It is not gay people doing their thing in private that threatens morale, discipline, or cohesion; rather, it is the knowledge by a straight man that a pat on the ass, long considered an expression of innocent bonding, might now be fraught with same-sex desire.

This is why military doctors, during and after World War II, were so concerned with effeminate and showy traits, rather than whether recruits were actually gay or engaging in homosexual conduct. The knowledge that there are gay people in the military could bring straight people face-to-face with same-sex desire, which could trigger insecurities about their own desires.

In the end, one of the few pieces of data that actually spoke to the issue of same-sex love in the military was, like actual gays in the military, acknowledged before Congress but then thoroughly ignored. As strange as it may sound, the Shils and Janowitz literature could have helped focus national attention on what was—and remains—needed to solve the problem of homosexuality in American culture. It is really a problem that straight people must solve (even if, as is most likely, it will come only at the prodding of gays and lesbians). What's needed is for straight people to challenge their reflexive moral opposition to same-sex desire, in others and in themselves. What's so bad about men loving men or women loving women? What would be so horrible about discovering that maybe even you have some love for a same-sex friend that's a bit stronger than friendship? The perspective offered by research into the complex and even discomfiting corners of human psychology was just what the United States needed at the height of the gay service debate. Instead, policy makers and much of the nation dismissed evidence that was difficult and relevant and embraced evidence that was misleading, false, or irrelevant.

WRAPPED IN THE language of individual sacrifice, national security, and the unique conditions of military service, defenders of the military's ban were able to ward off serious scrutiny of the need for reform. They were able to substitute the personal judgment of military leaders for persuasive evidence and cast that judgment as rooted in professional experience rather than personal animus. The courts and the Congress played along willingly, accepting hook, line, and sinker that the risk of flouting military judgment on gay service was too high to brook. And it didn't seem to matter that even trusted military advocates like Charles Moskos acknowledged publicly that the ban was rooted not in genuine concerns over unit cohesion but in "antipathy toward gays"—a "prejudice," the professor added, that has a "rational basis."[60]

6

Gays in Foreign Militaries

THE CLEAREST EVIDENCE that openly gay service does not undermine unit cohesion comes from the experience of foreign militaries. Twenty-four now have no ban on gay service members: Australia, Austria, Bahamas, Belgium, Britain, Canada, the Czech Republic, Denmark, Estonia, Finland, France, Ireland, Israel, Italy, Lithuania, Luxembourg, the Netherlands, New Zealand, Norway, Slovenia, South Africa, Spain, Sweden, and Switzerland. The United States, with its ban on open gays, stands in the company of Argentina, Belarus, Brazil, Croatia, Greece, Poland, Peru, Portugal, Russia, Turkey, and Venezuela. The list does not include those countries in which homosexuality is banned outright, such as Iran, Saudi Arabia, and several other nations in the Middle East. These countries generally have no stated policy on gays in the military because they do not allow or acknowledge the presence of gays at all.

In the fall of 1992, just as Bill Clinton was clinching the U.S. presidency, Canada and Australia lifted their bans on gay service members. And in 1993, as the religious right and Sam Nunn were wooing the nation with their pro-ban messages, Israel followed suit. At the dawn of the twenty-first century, our staunchest ally and cultural compatriot, Great Britain, joined a growing tide of militaries allowing openly gay service. The cumulative picture is striking. The American military was certainly not alone in its opposition to gay service; indeed, much of the world has had formal or informal bans against gays in the armed forces (or, in the case of many countries with no written policy on gay service, collective illusions that gays don't exist). But as the late twentieth century saw an inexorable shift toward recognizing the rights of gays and other minority groups, the U.S. military distinguished itself through its willful resistance to change. Throughout the 1990s, as the American government dug in its heels despite mounting evidence that "don't ask, don't tell" wasn't working, other countries around the globe were taking the opposite tack.

The effects of allowing gays to serve openly were, to the surprise of these militaries themselves, stunningly anticlimatic. It is perhaps one of the reasons why so few people knew about the changes—the media is not wild about stories in which, quite simply, nothing happens. But the lessons from other nations, despite efforts by pro-ban Americans to ignore and dismiss their relevance to the United States, are profound, and make a closer look at the experiences of foreign militaries a worthwhile trip.

UNTIL 1988, THE Canadian Forces had in place a policy nearly identical to the American ban: Gays and lesbians were barred from service and anyone who believed a peer was gay was required to report the suspicion to a superior. The Canadian ban was relaxed in 1988, as pressure mounted to bring the policy in line with the 1978 Canadian Human Rights Act and the 1985 Canadian Charter of Rights and Freedoms. The initial changes involved removing the reporting requirement and loosening enforcement, but unequal treatment of heterosexual and gay troops remained: Known gays and lesbians were routinely denied promotions, security clearances, and awards. The Department of National Defence continued to argue that a formal ban was necessary to protect "cohesion and morale, discipline, leadership, recruiting, medical fitness, and the rights to privacy of other members."[1]

Yet momentum was growing in favor of change. Inspired by other court decisions, five service members sued the Canadian Forces and won an initial ruling that the gay ban violated the Charter of Rights and Freedoms. Ultimately the Canadian military agreed to settle its case in 1992, acknowledging that it was unlikely to win the case on its merits.

It is commonly thought that progressive reform in Canada went over without a whit of resistance. In fact, opposition was intense. Surveys showed that majorities of those in the military would not share sleeping and bathing quarters with known gays, and many said they would refuse to work with gays or accept a gay supervisor. A military task force was formed during the debate; it recommended that gay exclusion remain, as "the effect of the presence of homosexuals would [lead to] a serious decrease in operational effectiveness." Even when the military determined it would lose its case in court, the government delayed the change because of the vociferous opposition of Conservatives in Parliament. The similarities to opposition in the United States were striking.[2]

The Australian Defence Forces did not see quite the same fight. Until 1986 commanders were given wide discretion to decide when to boot gays, and leaders were able to rely on civilian laws against sodomy and homosexual relations to root them out. Ironically, in 1986, at the very moment when the rest of society was liberalizing its limitations on homosexual behavior, the Australian military tightened its own regulations. State and federal laws banning sodomy fell during this decade as the country brought its laws into conformity with new international human rights accords. Unable to continue to draw on civilian laws against homosexual behavior, the ADF banned homosexual service outright in 1986.[3]

The short-lived Australian gay ban was always weaker than the policies in many of its ally nations. While there were reports of witch hunts and unequal treatment, the policy was often enforced unevenly and the tolerance and inconsistent enforcement extended to commanders throughout the services, who were often aware of gays and lesbians under their command and took no steps to kick them out. In the years leading up to the ban's formal end, the ADF had been pressed to respond to several cultural trends toward liberalization and to specific complaints that the military was not doing enough to recruit, retain, and respect women and racial and ethnic minorities. Such criticism could not be ignored, as the armed forces were finding it difficult to fill their ranks.[4]

It was in this context—one that highlighted the needs of the military as much as the social and cultural pressures for greater tolerance—that the Australian military began to consider formally ending its restrictions on gays and lesbians. Legal considerations also held sway: In 1980, the Commonwealth had adopted the International Covenant on Civil and Political Rights, and while homosexuality was not mentioned, political leaders interpreted the covenant to ban discrimination on the basis of sexual orientation. When a lesbian soldier complained to the Australian Human Rights and Equal Opportunities Commission that her sexual orientation was the partial basis of her discharge, the ADA agreed to review its policy but chose to retain its formal ban.

Political pressure, however, was mounting and the government created a study group to look into the policy and make a formal recommendation. During the study period, those who opposed gay service made the familiar arguments: The presence of known gays and lesbians would compromise effectiveness by impairing cohesion and driving down morale. Nevertheless, the study group recommended in 1992 that the gay ban be replaced with a policy of nondiscrimination, and the liberal government of Prime Minister Paul Keating, helped by the health minister's argument that keeping homosexuality secret exacerbated efforts to fight AIDS, ordered the new policy implemented immediately.[5]

As was the case elsewhere, the changes were vehemently opposed. The major veterans group in Australia insisted that tolerating known gays would undermine cohesion and break the bonds of trust that were essential to an effective military. Some claimed that the presence of gays would increase the spread of HIV through battlefield blood transfers. It didn't seem to occur to them that the best way to fight this prospect was to identify gays with AIDS rather than require them to remain in the closet.

Like Australia, Israel did not have a long-standing, explicit ban on homosexual service members, but used discretion to determine when commanders believed gay or lesbian troops were problematic and worthy of exclusion. For most of the country's short history, not surprisingly, routine prejudice meant that the Israel Defense Forces dismissed known gays because leaders assumed their sexuality made them unsuitable. A 1983 regulation made clear that service members were not to be discharged simply because they were gay, but required them to undergo a mental health evaluation and banned them from top-secret positions.[6]

A decade later, while the United States was embroiled in an agonizing discussion about gay service, Israel began its own, more tempered debate. Ironically, given how American policy ended up, Israeli officials acknowledged that President Clinton's support for gay service had been influential in driving debate in Israel, where the issue of gay rights had never been discussed at such high levels of government. The discussion was also prompted by an unusual hearing at the Knesset, when Uzi Even, the chairman of the Chemistry Department at Tel Aviv University and a senior weapons development researcher, told the nation he had been stripped of his security clearance when his homosexuality was revealed. Even had supplied the government with top-notch security research for fifteen years. He was deemed a security threat even though he had just come out of the closet, thus neutralizing any possibility of blackmail.[7]

With the vocal support of Prime Minister Yitzhak Rabin, who stated, "I don't see any reason to discriminate against homosexuals," and the military chief of staff, Lieutenant General Ehud Barak, a military committee was created to review the policy and make recommendations for change. With no military officials testifying against reform,[8] the review committee recommended new regulations that officially "recognized that homosexuals are entitled to serve in the military as are others." In response, the Israeli military banned any restrictions or differential treatment based on sexual orientation and ordered that decisions about placement, promotion, and security clearances be based on individual aptitude and behavior without regard to orientation.

The absence of official resistance did not mean that Israel had ceased to be a homophobic culture—founded, as it was, on biblical precepts, with a government heavily influenced by religious Jews and a society enamored of macho men. A study conducted in the 1980s found that Israeli attitudes toward homosexuals were more negative than American attitudes. Even in the 1990s, Israel's organized gay rights lobby was miniscule compared to its American counterpart, thus limiting the strength of voices pressing for reform. And the military was, as in the United States, a particularly conservative institution within the larger society. During induction, gays were referred to a psychologist for an evaluation. "Based on the assumption, correct or incorrect, that sometimes along with homosexuality come other behavioral disturbances, we conduct a more in-depth clinical interview," said Dr. Reuven Gal, who was chief psychologist for the IDF.[9]

In the early 1990s, Ron Paran, a psychologist working with gays and lesbians in Israel, found marked homophobia in Israeli society, particularly in the military. "I think there are still a lot of people in the psychiatric profession and in the army who still see homosexuality as a problem," he said, "and this policy is their way of expressing that." Paran said Israel was a "paradox" in which the laws are "much more liberal than the general society." As in society generally, he said the military was instinctually uncomfortable with homosexuality. "I work with a lot of teachers and parents who may cognitively understand homosexuality, but in their emotional response to it are still very backward. The army is the same way."[10]

Yet as a nation with compulsory service, which recognized the formative role of that service in creating a sense of citizenship, Israel determined by 1993 that it was unfair, unwise, and unnecessary to bar an entire group of people from the military. Its new regulations said that "there is no limit on the induction of homosexuals to the army and their induction is according to the criteria that apply to all candidates to the army."[11]

That spring, Congress sent researchers from the General Accounting Office to Israel and three other countries to learn from the reforms implemented there. But because the IDF was a conscription military, in which service was mandatory for most Israeli citizens,[12] some opponents of gay service in the United States dismissed the notion that any lessons could be learned from Israel. Lifting the remaining ban in Israel, they pointed out, was less perilous than in other nations, which relied on volunteers to staff their armed forces (the term more properly should be "voluntary recruits" since "volunteer" implies someone who is unpaid, but the language employed here is the traditional usage). Recruitment and retention were therefore not at risk in Israel, where citizens had no choice about whether to join the armed forces and could not be scared off by the presence of open gays.

But the same could not be said of Great Britain, a powerful western European nation that shares cultural roots with the United States, and whose military is strong, voluntary, and combat-tested. Indeed, British troops routinely fight alongside American troops, sharing everything from logistical support to personnel, including commanders. What happened, then, when Great Britain lifted its ban?

Like the United States, Britain banned gay service throughout the twentieth century, just as its civilian laws initially criminalized sexual relations between men. (Because Queen Elizabeth purportedly refused to believe that lesbianism existed, there were no laws against female same-sex relationships.) Depending on the service branch, the military dealt with homosexuals either by banning them outright or by charging them with "disgraceful conduct of an indecent kind," "conduct prejudicial to good order or discipline," or "scandalous conduct by officers."[13]

Reflecting the similarities of American and British culture, the same rationales were invoked to justify the exclusion rules in Britain as in the United States. Only the spelling was different. "Homosexual behaviour can cause offence, polarize relationships, induce ill-discipline, and as a consequence damage morale and unit effectiveness," argued the British Ministry of Defence. One retired general told the BBC that letting gays serve meant "striking at the root of discipline and morale" since service members had to "live huggermugger at most times." The general summarized his opposition on behalf of straight troops by arguing that "the great majority do not want to be brought into contact with homosexual practices." Another retired officer who commanded UN forces in Bosnia recalled that when he had two gay soldiers in his battalion, he "had extreme difficulty in controlling the remainder of the soldiers because they fundamentally wanted to lynch them."[14] In neither country did ban defenders ever explain how denying the presence of gay people who everyone knew were there actually helped preserve privacy, nor why service members who had signed up precisely to leave behind their privacy and risk their very lives should be expected to wither, wilt, and crumble when knowingly exposed to the gaze of gays.

The British rationale for gay exclusion also shared much of its history with the United States. Its language spoke of "sexual deviancy" and "feminine gestures," of mental illness and sexually transmitted diseases. The same distinctions between identity and behavior were made, followed by the same collapsing of those distinctions: Like the American policy, the British rules specified that the admission of homosexuality was grounds for dismissal even if no behavior was involved. The history of gays in the British military is replete with surveillance, informants, blackmail, stakeouts, investigations, and psychological exams.[15]

By the time the British High Court heard a major challenge to the gay ban in 1995, most of the above rationales had been annihilated. Although the court rebuffed the service members' challenge and allowed the military to continue its ban, the Ministry of Defence created the Homosexual Policy Assessment Team to evaluate its policy. The move was a response to a warning by the court that, despite its current ruling in favor of the military, the gay ban was unlikely to survive a direct challenge in the European Convention on Human Rights, which, unlike the British High Court, had the authority to force the military's hand.

The assessment team consulted the experiences of other countries, including Canada, Australia, and Israel. In their visits, they were told by official after official that gay service had not undermined military performance. In response, British researchers acknowledged that the ban could be lifted, but that such a change would be unlikely not because of a military rationale but because of political resistance. The team also took extensive, but flawed, surveys indicating that large majorities of British troops opposed gay service. Questions were stacked ("Do you agree that all homosexual acts are perverted?") and anonymity was compromised by the requirement that respondents disclose numerous personal details, including their service branch, unit, rank, and birthplace.[16]

Ultimately, the team recommended that the military retain its ban. But the rationale it focused on revealed the collapse of all but one of the justifications for gay exclusion. The assumption that gays were a threat to security and a predatory menace to young troops, said the report, was unfounded.[17] Rather, the problem was that straight soldiers disliked gays; letting known gays serve would therefore undermine cohesion and threaten recruitment. Prejudice had become a justification, once again, for continuing itself. Lifting the ban, said the report, "would be an affront to service people" and lead to "heterosexual resentment and hostility." Reform at the urging of civilian society would be viewed by military members as "coercive interference in their way of life."

And there you had it. The self-image of the British military, its members' sense of entitlement to preserve a way of life they saw as besieged, and to carry things out in the way they saw fit—these were the currency of the debate. That "way of life" was a polite way of describing heterosexual supremacy or prejudice against gays. The report made clear that there was no evidence that gays were unsuited to military service. But, as in the American debate, the moral opposition of straights was cleverly tied to military needs, allowing senior leaders to argue that military effectiveness justified gay exclusion.

Leaders of the British forces were not stupid, however, and they were not blind to the changes in society taking shape around them throughout the 1990s. Bracing for a heftier challenge in the European Court of Human Rights, which threatened to cost the government billions in wrongful dismissal claims, the military ordered a relaxation of enforcement of the ban, telling commanders only to investigate suspected homosexuals if an unavoidable problem arose. For gays, the change was minimal: They continued to lose their jobs, receive unequal treatment, and operate in a climate of discrimination, fear, and uncertainty.

It was not until the European Court of Human Rights issued its ruling, in the fall of 1999, that the British government agreed it would have to lift the ban. The court in Strasbourg, France, whose decisions are binding on all member nations, was composed of judges from Britain, France, Cyprus, Lithuania, Austria, Norway, and Albania. The unanimous ruling found that the British Defence Ministry had violated the European Convention's guarantee of an "equal respect" to "private and family life" and that the policy and the investigations it prompted were "exceptionally intrusive."[18] The court soundly rejected the military's claim that the unique circumstances of life in the armed forces justified anti-gay discrimination and ruled that heterosexual bias against gays was no more compelling a reason to ban them than would be animus against groups with a different race or ethnic or national origin. It swiftly dismissed the military's contention that gay service would endanger morale, saying the foundation of such arguments in opinion polls made them unconvincing. A better way to address these worries, said the court, would be with a uniform code of conduct, not a blanket ban on individuals with a particular orientation.

The Ministry of Defence immediately announced that it accepted the ruling and it ordered a halt to all discharges while it studied how to abide by the court's decision. The chief of defence staff general, despite expecting some tough scenarios for commanding officers, expressed confidence in the military's ability to make the changes, saying that "times have changed" since the gay ban was first formulated. "I don't believe that the operational efficiency of the Services will be affected," he said, "although I'm not saying we won't have some difficult incidents." Ultimately, he concluded, "We think we can make it work."[19]

In trying to figure out how to "make it work," the British military considered the American "don't ask, don't tell" policy. What they found was that it was a "disaster," which "hadn't worked," was "unworkable," and was "hypocritical." Instead, the British military opted for full repeal and based its new regulations on the Australian model, which simply banned public displays of affection, harassment, and inappropriate relationships. The Ministry of Defence formally lifted its gay ban on January 12, 2000, inviting ousted troops to reapply for service and squirreling away millions of dollars for anticipated legal complaints for unfair dismissal.

AFTER RUNNING OUT of rationales for gay exclusion, the British military, like the U.S. military, had justified discrimination on the basis of discrimination. The European Court of Human Rights was unconvinced that this reasoning showed a compelling need to ban gays from service. Still, if the prejudice of young straight troops and potential recruits truly meant that forced tolerance would undermine military performance and the capacity of the British government to keep its people safe, and if no leadership or management skills were capable of mitigating this harm, shouldn't this reality have justified continuing discrimination against gays?

Answering this question is necessarily, in part, an ethical question, subject to a cost-benefit analysis. It requires assessing the value of equal treatment and comparing it with the damage that would be wrought—if any—by the ensuing impairment to military performance. But the link itself—between equal treatment and damage to cohesion—remains totally unproven. Worse still, the evidence from country after country shows the link to be false. In the real world, the hypothesis is testable—and it has been tested. So, after all the caution, after all the anxiety and the doomsday warnings about what would happen when open gays were officially allowed to serve, what happened when Britain, Israel, Canada, Australia, and numerous other militaries lifted their bans?

Nothing. Well, almost nothing. The only effects of lifting gay exclusion rules have been positive ones. Militaries in Great Britain, Australia, Canada, and Israel have seen reductions in harassment, less anxiety about sexual orientation in the ranks, greater openness in relations between gays and straights, and less restricted access to recruitment pools as schools and universities welcomed the military back onto campus for dropping their discriminatory practices. Above all, none of the crises in recruitment, retention, resignations, morale, cohesion, readiness, or "operational effectiveness" came to pass.

One of the strongest pieces of evidence came from the British military itself. Six months after lifting its ban, the Ministry of Defence turned to study the consequences. The report was intended for internal use only and not for public release—which suggests that it represented an accurate, comprehensive assessment of the policy change, without risk of being swayed by the requisites of politics or public relations. And it had the benefit of full access to all available data.

The conclusions were definitive. The report, dated October 31, 2000, and eventually leaked to the press, said the lifting of the ban was "hailed as a solid achievement" that was "introduced smoothly with fewer problems than might have been expected." The changes had "no discernible impact" on recruitment. There was "widespread acceptance of the new policy," and military members generally "demonstrated a mature and pragmatic approach" to the change. There were no reported problems with homosexuals harassing heterosexuals, and there were "no reported difficulties of note concerning homophobic behavior amongst Service Personnel." The report concluded that "there has been a marked lack of reaction" to the change.[20]

Independent assessments by senior government and military officials in Britain consistently confirmed the military's findings that lifting the gay ban in Britain had no negative impact on performance. "At the end of the day, operational effectiveness is the critical matter, and there has been no effect at all," reported a high-level official. Just nine months after the new policy was instituted, this official said that "homosexuality doesn't even come up anymore—it's no longer an issue." One lieutenant colonel reported that "there has been absolutely no reaction to the change in policy regarding homosexuals within the military. It's just been accepted." He said that emphasis on fair treatment and personal responsibility meant people had ceased to focus on sexual orientation and cared far more about individual performance and responsibility to the team. Even the very vocal worries about privacy and sharing showers and berths with gays—a perpetual focus of resistance in the United States—turned out to be a dud. A press official at the Ministry of Defence said that "the media likes scare stories—about showers and what have you. A lot of people were worried that they would have to share body heat in close quarters or see two men being affectionate, and they would feel uncomfortable. But it has proved at first look that it's not an issue."[21]

Again and again, experts expressed surprise at how little the change had meant, and how much easier the transition had been than what they expected, given the vocal resistance before the ban ended. The military's director of personnel said, "We've had very few real problems that have emerged, and people seem to have, slightly surprisingly, settled down and accepted the current arrangements. And we don't really have the problems that we thought we'd have." An official of the Personnel Management Agency said, "The anticipated tide of criticism from some quarters within the Service was completely unfounded." One commander attributed the smoother-than-anticipated transition to a generation gap, finding that "our youngsters have just taken it in stride." He concluded that "it's a major nonissue, which has come as a considerable surprise."[22]

What's surprising, really, is that the results in Britain should have surprised so many people. The finding of "no impact" there was simply an echo of what had happened (or hadn't happened, to be more precise) in Canada, Australia, and Israel the decade before. Perhaps people had put too much stock in the 1996 Ministry of Defence opinion survey of 13,500 British service members, which showed that two-thirds would refuse to serve with gays. Instead of the tens of thousands of resignations this poll predicted, officials estimated the actual number as between one and three, and two of those were reportedly planning to leave the service anyway.

But even this contrast between anticipated doom and yawning reality was a replay of the scenario in Canada. Before the Canadian Forces lifted the gay ban, a survey of 6,500 male service members found that 62 percent would refuse to share quarters with gay soldiers and 45 percent would not work with gays. But more than two years after gay exclusion ended, there was no mass exodus and no indication of any impact on cohesion, morale, readiness, recruitment, or retention. An assessment by a bureau of the Canadian military found that, "despite all the anxiety that existed through the late 80s into the early 90s about the change in policy, here's what the indicators show—no effect."[23]

What was true for Britain and Canada was also true for Israel and Australia. Indeed, the results of ending gay exclusion rules in every nation studied have been so uniform, so uneventful, so tediously boring and repetitive that they are almost too dull to describe. A small sampling will have to suffice, so as not to grind book sales to a halt. The Rand report, released in the United States and effectively ignored in the spring of 1993, included an exhaustive assessment of homosexual policies in Canada, Israel, and Britain, as well as Norway, the Netherlands, France, and Germany. At the time, Britain was the only nation to have a full ban on gay service. Of those that allowed gays to serve, Rand found that "none of the militaries studied for this report believe their effectiveness as an organization has been impaired or reduced as a result of the inclusion of homosexuals." In Canada, where the ban had just ended, Rand found "no resignations (despite previous threats to quit), no problems with recruitment, and no diminution of cohesion, morale, or organizational effectiveness." Ditto Israel. The U.S. Army Research Institute for the Behavioral and Social Sciences also studied the situation in Canada and concluded that anticipated damage to readiness never materialized after the ban was lifted: "Negative consequences predicted in the areas of recruitment, employment, attrition, retention, and cohesion and morale have not occurred" since the policy was changed, the report stated.[24]

Also in 1993, the GAO reported its findings from its study of twenty-five foreign militaries. In Australia, the GAO found, "Effects on unit cohesiveness have not yet been fully determined. However, early indications are that the new policy has had little or no adverse impact." Research over time, however, confirmed that openly gay service there caused no trouble. In 1996, when Britain was considering lifting its ban, government researchers issued a report on the situation in Australia, which concluded that, despite an early outcry, homosexuality quickly became a nonissue: Any challenges in integrating open gays were regarded as "just another legitimate management problem." The GAO found precisely the same results for Israel.[25]

In 2000, after Britain lifted its ban, the Palm Center at the University of California, Santa Barbara, conducted exhaustive studies to assess the effects of openly gay service in Britain, Israel, Canada, and Australia. Researchers there reviewed over six hundred documents and contacted every identifiable professional with expertise on the policy change, including military officers, government leaders, academic researchers, journalists who covered the issue, veterans, and nongovernmental observers. Palm found that not one person had observed any impact or any effect at all that "undermined military performance, readiness, or cohesion, led to increased difficulties in recruiting or retention, or increased the rate of HIV infection among the troops." Those interviewed—including generals, civilian defense leaders, field commanders, and many officials who had predicted major problems if gays were permitted to serve openly—uniformly reported there had been "no impact." Again and again, researchers heard the same thing: Lifting the ban was "an absolute nonevent." Openly gay service was "not that big a deal for us." Open gays "do not constitute an issue [with respect to] unit cohesion" and the whole subject "is very marginal indeed as far as this military is concerned." Whether gays serve openly or not "has not impaired the morale, cohesion, readiness, or security of any unit." The policy change has "not caused any degree of difficulty."[26]

The results did not mean that everybody was happy with openly gay service. Nor did researchers conclude that such resistance and resentment were entirely without consequence. Many, many people were upset about the idea.

Male service members, in particular, continued to express concern that the presence of known gays in a unit might damage morale, and the anti-gay sentiment sometimes manifested itself in harassment or abuse. But the evidence has been consistent that these reactions to the policy change did not translate into overall impairment of morale, readiness, or cohesion.

The British military was so convinced by these findings that, in 2006, the Royal Air Force announced it would hire Stonewall, the largest gay rights group in Britain, to help it attract gay and lesbian recruits. The deal meant the RAF would be placed on Stonewall's Workplace Equality Index, a list of Britain's one hundred top employers for gays and lesbians, and that Stonewall would provide intensive training about how to create an inclusive workplace environment with greater appeal to gays and lesbians. The RAF also agreed to provide equal survivor benefits to same-sex partners and to become a sponsor of the gay pride festival. "The Armed Forces are committed to establishing a culture and climate where those who choose to disclose their sexual orientation can do so without risk of abuse or intimidation," said the Ministry of Defence.[27]

The RAF action was prompted in part by recruitment shortfalls. But the move also makes clear that the British Forces believe that a climate of inclusivity and equal treatment makes for a superior military, further evidence that the only impact of gay inclusion is a positive one. At the 2007 British gay pride parade, a Royal Navy commander made this point, stressing that what mattered to military effectiveness was teamwork. "If the team is functioning properly, then we're a professional fighting force," he said. "We want individuals to be themselves 100 percent, so they can give 100 percent and we value them 100 percent." Background, "lifestyle," and sexuality were not a part of the equation, he said, adding that the British military recruits "purely on merit and ability" and new members become a "member of the team and are valued as such."[28] As the year 2000 British Ministry of Defence internal assessment had suggested, the replacement of a group-specific ban with a policy of equal treatment had helped to shift focus away from sexual identity, precisely the aim of the new policy and, incidentally, the opposite of the effect that the American policy of "don't ask, don't tell" has had. Because the new Code of Social Conduct in the British Forces emphasized good behavior and fair treatment for all, sexuality was now regarded as a private matter and service members were freed to concentrate on the duty of each member to behave in ways that were beneficial to the group. The report indicated that the policy change had produced "a marked lack of reaction. Discussion has rather been concerned with freedom of individual choice and exercising personal responsibility across the board, rather than a focus just on sexual orientation."

The Ministry of Defence report also indicated that, because colleges no longer banned the military from campus, recruitment prospects were brightened by greater access to potential recruits: "Some areas that had previously closed to the Forces, such as Student Union 'Freshers' Fairs,' are now allowing access to the Services because of what is seen to be a more enlightened approach." Indeed, the Ministry of Defence called recruitment "quite buoyant" in the year after the ban was lifted. After several years of shortfalls, the year both before and after the policy change finally saw recruiting targets filled.[29]

Reports from many countries now suggest that ending gay exclusion policies may be the best way to move beyond the worrisome focus on sexual identity and its effects on military cohesion. This is certainly true for the gay and lesbian service members themselves, who generally "breathed a sigh of relief"[30] when they learned they no longer had to lie to serve their countries. But the effects of liberalization go beyond just the obvious impact on gays to impact straight people, too. These effects reach to the heart of heterosexual's anxiety about their own role in the military, about how they should behave with respect to homosexuality and how they should interact with those they suspect or know to be gay. And whether such concerns are conscious or not, anyone who serves in a modern Western military must at some point confront the issue of sexuality. The only question is whether they will do so in a way that is healthy or unhealthy for the group.

Chief Petty Officer Rob Nunn, who had been discharged from the Royal Navy in 1992 for being gay, rejoined the British Forces after the ban was lifted in 2000. The response from his comrades was overwhelmingly positive when he returned, and he was even asked casually if his partner would be accompanying him to the Christmas ball. But what's most instructive about Nunn's experience is the impact of the new transparency not on him but on his straight comrades. Immediately after his reinstatement, Nunn found his colleagues were unsure how to respond to him. "It's the old, 'I don't know quite what to say,'" he explained in an interview. With one other service member, in particular, Nunn decided to guide him to a place of greater comfort, now that he could take advantage of the option to speak freely. This "one guy that I talked to who couldn't sort of talk to me, I said, 'Right, I'm going to ask the questions that you want to ask, and answer them.' So I did." Nunn reported that the greater openness, whether it came from him or from others, allowed any remaining discomfort to evaporate and gave him the chance to counter stereotypes, expose friends to greater understanding, and put people at ease. After Nunn helped his reticent comrade out of his shell, the person became "nice as pie."[31]

Having the choice to speak out when it's necessary or desirable yields another highly important fruit: It allows those who are threatened by anti-gay harassment to confront their perpetrator or inform authorities without fear of coming under investigation themselves and facing discharge. Fear of reprisal has been a serious problem in the American military, particularly for women, who are all too often the victims of lesbian-baiting. The term describes a scenario when women who rebuff the advances of men are tarred as lesbian, whether they are straight or not. The phenomenon helps explain why women are discharged at higher rates than men: Many may come out to take control of a situation that otherwise threatens to end in a discharge that's out of their control. Stark evidence of the positive impact of ending gay exclusion is found in the case of Canada, where the number of women who experienced sexual harassment dropped by a whopping 46 percent after the ban was lifted. The drop may not have been exclusively caused by reforming the gay policy, but the statistic can't be ignored. Given the heavily documented evidence for lesbian-baiting as a cause of harassment against women, the decrease in Canada clearly shows the positive, rather than negative, effects of gay inclusion on military cohesion.[32]

Even when harassment statistics are not this clear, though, there is no doubt that the pressure generated by gay exclusion rules to fixate on the private lives of service members is itself a threat to cohesion and morale. This is why Australia's human rights commissioner said he believed his country's termination of the ban had positive effects on the military. "It's bad for morale to have your guys snooping on other of your guys," he concluded. This conclusion is borne out by evidence from gay service members, who reported after the ban ended that the liberalized policy allowed them to spend less energy monitoring what they and others said and more focusing on their work. One army captain, Squadron Leader Chris Renshaw, said that under Australia's new policy, "you can be more honest. That's one of the key things about being in the military—honesty and integrity. Because you haven't got to worry about if someone's saying something behind your back, or is someone gossiping or something, because if they gossip, I don't care. So I'm more focused on my job, I'm more focused on what I'm achieving here, and less worried about [rumors] and what people think. In terms of productivity, I'm far more productive now. . . . Everything's out in the open, no fear, no nothing, no potential of blackmail, no security implications . . . nothing." Renshaw spoke of the positive impact of the new opportunity for casual banter, so much a part of the military bonding experience. Planning to take his male partner to the Christmas party, he told his superior as a courtesy. "He just looked at me with a bit of a pained expression and said, 'I expect you to be-have.' And I just sort of looked at him and said, 'Look, knowing the other people that work on this floor and how they behave with booze, you're wor-ried about me?' "[33]

An enlisted member of the Royal Australian Navy echoed the importance of teasing as a form of bonding and the positive role of joking even about sexual orientation: "I'm quite open about my sexuality. Sometimes the boys decide to give me a bit of a ding-up with a joke or something like that, but that doesn't bother me. We work really well together, and I'm sure it's the same for other gay and lesbian soldiers and sailors who are out, and they're accepted by their peers. O.K.—they're the object of ridicule sometimes, but everybody is." Military experts must surely understand how central it is for young people in the armed forces to navigate their relationships, in part, through playful insults and oneupmanship, at times becoming caustic or even aggressive. It's no secret that the military functions as a proving ground, both as part of the training process and apart from it. Yet many of these ex-perts have cherry-picked instances of gay-straight tension and cast them as dangerous examples of social strife, when in fact it is part and parcel of the military bonding experience.[34]

The Palm Center study on the Australian Defence Forces in 2000 reported that working environments had improved significantly for gay service mem-bers following the end of the ban. But yet again, the most telling lesson from that experience is the impact of reform on the rest of the military. In conjunc-tion with lifting the ban, the ADF issued new instructions on sexual conduct and equal treatment, and leaders made a visible commitment to taking these seriously. As a result, service members saw a marked improvement in a mili-tary climate that had failed in the past to adequately respect the promise of equal opportunity not just for gays but for women, for blacks, and for ethnic minorities. The climate of fear and instances of betrayal that had accompa-nied life for gays in the Australian military carried over to affect the lives of straights, too. In one case, a service member who was reportedly heterosexual committed suicide after coming under investigation for his association with a gay sailor.[35] Suicide is obviously the product of a complex array of personal and social issues. But there's no question that living in a repressive climate of unnecessary, unspoken taboos is an aggravating factor in yielding such a tragic result.

IT IS POSSIBLE, in theory, that all the nations of the world could integrate open gays seamlessly and the United States of America could still be incapable of doing the same. The world's superpower is unique culturally, historically, and militarily—so goes the argument. It cannot afford to take its cues from other, weaker nations, and a traditional streak running through its society bodes ill for imposing liberal norms of sexuality onto the more conservative military population. As more and more countries lifted their bans in the 1990s, conservatives in the United States rushed to make the "irrelevance" case, not long after ban defenders had used those very same countries (before they lifted their bans) as models of appropriate policy on gays.

Bill O'Reilly summed up this case succinctly: "Just remember the different cultures in Britain, Israel, Australia, and the United States," O'Reilly said on his immensely popular television program, *The O'Reilly Factor*. "Different cultures."[36] O'Reilly's point was that eighteen- and nineteen-year-olds from middle America were not the gay-loving, French wine—swilling soldiers of progressive Europe, and whatever went over well there would not necessarily go over well here.

As retired colonel David Hackworth put it, "I don't think gays will ever be openly accepted in the military . . . [by] corn-fed guys from Iowa." Hackworth, who served four tours in Vietnam and ratcheted up over a hundred medals, played the typical "it's not me, it's them" card, saying, "In the views of thousands of soldiers I've spoken to, it won't work." But his own position was hiding in plain sight. When questioned by a group of newspaper editors at the U.S. Naval Academy, Hackworth said he believed gays would make sexual advances if allowed in the military because "it's their nature," and cited an army captain from his Vietnam days who had propositioned another man while drinking at a party. Asked if straight army men ever drank and made passes at women, he said that in airborne units, "we never did anything like that."[37] Hackworth seemed to be trying to prove that the United States was far more boorish than our allied countries, a point for which he was all too happy to sell gays down the river—while, of course, drawing the line when it came to the vaunted behavior of his fellow straight troops.

How different, though, was the United States from other cultures, in actual fact? As previously discussed, evidence suggests that Israel was slightly more homophobic than the United States in the 1990s. In Britain, a law was passed in 1987 banning any discussion in schools that promoted the acceptability of homosexuality. Even in the 1990s, a majority of the British, according to polls, believed sex between members of the same sex was always wrong. In Canada, in the years preceding the admission of open gays, polls showed strong moral disapproval of homosexuality. Military researchers at the U.S. Army Research Institute for the Behavioral and Social Sciences regard the

Anglo-American nations (the UK, Canada, Australia, New Zealand, and Ireland) as sharing "a more-or-less common cultural heritage" with the United States. The researchers pointed to a 1992 study in Germany that found that respondents viewed homosexuals as less acceptable neighbors than foreigners, Hindus, racial minorities, and Jews, and equated gays and lesbians with criminals, AIDS patients, and the mentally handicapped. In France, "deviant behavior" was tolerated because, as it was a Catholic country, the possibility of forgiveness for sin was always available.[38] Not exactly a ringing endorsement for homosexuals. Corn-fed Iowans, it turns out, may not be all that different from their military brethren in the rest of the world.

IN ANY CASE, the U.S. military has never found it irrelevant to learn from other countries, big and small. In 1986, it created the Foreign Military Studies Office in order to research and learn "about the military establishments, doctrine and operational and tactical practices of" foreign armed forces. The FMSO, which expanded its work after the fall of the Soviet Union, studies not only technological, strategic, and tactical operations of foreign militaries, but those relating to cultural aspects of service, such as housing, health care, and personnel policy.[39]

The FMSO was apparently meaningless to Calvin Waller, who had referred in his congressional testimony to "China men" and lumped gays and lesbians in with liars and thieves. Waller's confused testimony both compared the U.S. military to foreign armed forces and simultaneously rejected doing so. The general said he was "dismayed" that so many would compare the U.S. military—the world's sole superpower—to that of other countries. "When we allow comparisons of smaller countries to this great nation of ours, the comparison between these countries with their policies regarding known homosexuals serving their country, it is my belief that we do a grave disservice to our fellow American citizens." Other militaries, he said, have unionized forces, seldom deploy abroad, and let their troops return home at night.[40]

Given his indignant repudiation of the relevance of foreign militaries, it was bizarre that in the very same testimony, he cited the small nation of Korea as a model for the United States: "Now . . . my experience in Korea leads me to understand that their policy is 'no toleration of known homosexuals in their ranks.'" He didn't stop there. "In all my dealing with the many nations who provided military forces to Operations Desert Shield and Desert Storm," he continued, "the vast majority of those nations, as you have heard here today, did not allow known homosexuals to serve in their military units, who were part of the Persian Gulf forces. This is something that was not lost on this old soldier."[41]

Like Waller, Charlie Moskos had testified at Nunn's hearings about the limited relevance of foreign militaries. "No neat and tidy lessons can be drawn from one country to another," he said. Moskos told the senators that studying foreign militaries could yield some insight into the matter of gay service. But ultimately, he said, "inasmuch as the United States has the most formidable military force in the world, it could be argued that such countries might draw lessons from the United States."[42] The remark seemed snide. Did he really believe that if the famously tolerant Dutch armed forces reinstated their ban on gay troops so they looked more like the U.S. Army, then the Netherlands might finally become a true world power? Put the other way around, was he suggesting that the Dutch armed forces were small potatoes largely because they tolerated gays? The thrust of Moskos's congressional testimony, along with his public remarks elsewhere, was that no matter what gay activists and media hacks said about foreign militaries, he knew the truth, and it wasn't gay-friendly.

Moskos acknowledged that many foreign militaries allowed gays to serve, on paper. But he disputed their relevance to the United States, saying other militaries had different cultures or lesser combat obligations or that their practices regarding gay troops were actually less tolerant than their formal policies would suggest. Of the Dutch and Scandinavian militaries, Moskos said, "These aren't real fighting armies like the Brits, the Israelis and us. If a country has a security threat," he argued, that country would then implement "a policy that makes it very tough for gays."[43] But he was wrong. Britain's ban was lifted in 2000 and its powerful military became the chief partner to the United States in its wars in Afghanistan and Iraq beginning the next year. No one ever mentioned the idea of rolling back the clock to start rooting out gays again, in hopes of keeping its military strong enough to do the job. But Moskos had perfected the roving rationale, allowing him to defend his policy, to mutate his answers in order to evade whatever evidence might be put before him.

His discussion of Israel makes this crystal clear. In his effort to dismiss the relevance of foreign militaries to the United States, Moskos told Congress that gay troops in the Israeli military did not fight in elite combat units, did not serve in intelligence units or hold command positions, and did not serve openly in high positions. About this last point, he was adamant. "I can categorically state that no declared gay holds a command position in a combat arm anywhere in the IDF," he stated. Open gays, he said, "are treated much in the manner of women soldiers," in that they are excluded from real fighting and serve primarily in support roles from "open bases" where they can go home at night. He repeated these assertions in a companion essay and op-ed, and in radio broadcasts as late as 2000, saying there were no open gays in combat or intelligence positions in the Israeli military.[44]

But his argument was virtually impossible to defend, given the famous difficulty of "proving a negative," suggesting that Moskos cared more for rhetorical flourish than sound argument. After all, it only takes one person to come out of the woodwork and point out a single example of what is alleged not to exist to undermine the assertion that it doesn't exist. But more than one stepped forward. Dr. Reuven Gal, former chief psychologist for the IDF and later director of the Israeli Institute for Military Studies, wrote that even before Israel liberalized its policy in 1993, gay soldiers in the IDF did serve in "highly classified intelligence units" and that, even when their sexuality was revealed to their commanders, they were allowed to keep serving.[45]

The Palm Center's study on the IDF found repeated instances of openly gay service in combat and intelligence positions, while noting that cultural norms continue to encourage most gays and lesbians to keep their sexual orientation private. According to Palm, "some IDF combat and intelligence units have developed a reputation as particularly welcoming to gay and lesbian soldiers and some have developed a gay culture." One tank corps soldier said his base had "a large gay contingent" and that it was sometimes "even easier" to come out of the closet in the military "because you are protected from society. You don't have friends from the same town, so you can be more open in the Army." The Palm study also reported interviewing over twenty gay IDF soldiers who served in combat units, several of whom said their sexual identity was known by others in their unit. A related study, published in 2003 in *Parameters*, the professional journal of the U.S. Army War College, found that at least one-fifth of IDF combat soldiers knew of a gay peer in their unit, with roughly another fifth saying they "might" have known a gay peer. This suggests that hundreds of Israeli service members were serving openly.[46]

The Palm study concluded that the Israeli case is, indeed, relevant to the situation in the United States, even though many Israelis choose to keep their sexual identity private. In fact, such voluntary discretion is a reminder that the prospect of gay pride floats drifting onto U.S. military bases, replete with scantily clad men in pink boas, is largely the concocted fear of pro-ban champions. "The fact that many gay Israeli soldiers choose not to reveal their orientation does not indicate that the Israeli experience is irrelevant for determining what would happen if the U.S. lifted its gay ban," concluded the Palm study.

"On the contrary, the evidence shows that both Israelis and Americans come out of the closet only when it is safe to do so." The 2003 article in *Parameters* discussed the oft-cited fear among ban defenders that ending discrimination would result in a mass coming out in the military. Until his dying day, Charles Moskos answered questions about why the ban should remain by throwing back rhetorical questions about whether gay pride parades in the military are going to be next. Senator John McCain wondered during Nunn's Senate hearings if lifting the ban might lead to gay service members marching in parades with "bizarre" or "transvestite" clothing. But the fear was not based in fact. "This belief is premised on the flawed assumption that culture and identity politics are the driving forces behind gay soldiers' decisions to disclose their homosexuality," says the article. "What the evidence shows is that personal safety plays a much more powerful role than culture in the decision of whether or not to reveal sexual orientation."[47]

Still, important differences between the Israeli and U.S. militaries remain and have provided defenders of the American gay ban with reasons to continue to dismiss its relevance. Israel is a conscription force, which means recruitment and retention cannot be jeopardized by the presence of gay troops. Owing to the small size of the country and the long periods of mandatory military service, Israeli soldiers spend less time in military quarters than their American counterparts, and more time at home, potentially alleviating concerns about privacy and unit cohesion.[48]

Not so the British. Discharged from the Royal Navy in 1997 for homosexuality, Lieutenant Rolf Kurth was invited to reenlist after the UK lifted its ban in 2000. During the war in Iraq, Kurth was deployed to the Persian Gulf aboard the Royal Navy's largest amphibious ship. As it happened, American sailors also served on his ship, and Kurth worked closely with them, serving as a principal liaison for the American team. Kurth served as an openly gay man in this multinational force, and said it was "fairly well-known around the entire ship" that he was gay. His sexual orientation was "common knowledge," a fact he confirmed by the banter of his colleagues, who playfully told him, when several men convened to discuss an attractive woman, that Kurth was clearly "not the best person to judge!" He characterized his relationship with the American sailors as "great," saying he "got along very well with them." He added that the Americans "didn't behave any differently from British colleagues" toward him, even though he was known as a gay sailor.[49]

AFTER SEPTEMBER 11, 2001, it became far harder to take Moskos seriously when he dismissed foreign militaries as irrelevant. In addition to the UK's forty-five thousand troops that were stationed mostly in southern Iraq since the invasion began, thirty other countries joined the coalition, many of which allowed open gay service. The coalition included two thousand troops provided by Australia, along with submarines and other naval support from Denmark.[50] In Afghanistan, the number of countries contributing troops or support was even higher, numbering nearly fifty at one time. As NATO forces took over the occupation, troops from these countries took on greater combat roles.

In 2006, American, Canadian, British, and Afghan troops led the charge against a resurgent Taliban in Operation Mountain Thrust, the largest offensive to root out Islamic radicals since 2001. Insufficient water meant some troops had to give each other IVs to survive. Enduring heavy mortar attacks, suicide bombings, regular ambushes, and scorching desert temperatures, over ten thousand troops worked together to lug more than seven thousand pounds of supplies from the bottom of a rocky mountain range to its peak, where they had their greatest chance to best the Taliban. The powerful artillery and targeted airstrikes of the coalition took their toll on enemy forces, and by the end of the offensive, over fifteen hundred Taliban fighters had been killed or captured.[51]

Afterward, a NATO International Security Assistance Force, consisting of troops from nearly forty countries, took over operations in some of the most dangerous regions of southern Afghanistan, with Britain, Australia, Canada, Denmark, and the Netherlands doing the heavy lifting. That fall, Canadian forces led American, British, Dutch, and Danish troops in a bloody battle in which five hundred suspected Taliban fighters were surrounded and killed. The defeat prompted complaints by the Taliban that so many of its forces had been wiped out that it was having trouble finding sufficient leadership.[52]

The Canadian "experiment" with open gays was now fourteen years old, its start a distant memory for most. But the proof was in the pudding. Canada, Australia, even the Netherlands, were hardly "irrelevant." Their combat-tested fighting forces, replete with gays and lesbians serving openly, were critical partners in the American national defense strategy, and the United States was all too happy to enlist their indispensable fire power in the wars in the Middle East. The truly irrelevant argument was Moskos's—that these countries were not "real fighting armies." Perhaps in 1992 they hadn't seen much combat; by 2006, the world was a far different place. And nothing was heard from President George Bush, or Colin Powell, or Sam Nunn about cracking down on gays to preserve the fighting spirit of the "coalition of the willing."

The presence of gay service members in multinational military units is another nail in the coffin of the crumbling rationale for gay exclusion. Since the end of the cold war, multinational forces have mushroomed. The United States has participated in at least forty joint military operations, with half involving direct deployment with foreign service members. Many of these participating countries allow open gay service, from Canada to Britain and beyond.[53] Lieutenant Rolf Kurth's service in a multinational force in the Iraq War is only one example of documented evidence that openly gay foreign troops are actually serving right alongside Americans—without causing the kinds of disruptions that naysayers predicted would result from gay service.

Others come from training operations on foreign ships deployed in the Middle East, NATO and UN peacekeeping missions around the world, joint operations at the North American Aerospace Defense Command in Canada and the United States, the Multinational Force and Observers in Sinai, the Multinational Force in Lebanon, U.S. and foreign war colleges, training grounds, and military and diplomatic centers of operations, including NATO headquarters in Belgium. In some cases, U.S. troops are directly under the command of foreign military personnel, some known to be gay. And these cases suggest that coming out of the closet can help improve the working climate in the armed forces. In one example, Colonel René Holtel of the Royal Netherlands Army commanded American service members, including a U.S. tank battalion, in NATO and UN missions. In 2001, he served as chief military observer and chief liaison officer at the headquarters of the UN Mission in Ethiopia and Eritrea. UNMEE was tasked with monitoring the cease-fire between the two nations in the demilitarized security zone running along their mutual border. Six American service members served with him as military observers. Holtel found that when others in his unit knew he was gay, it caused "some relaxation in the unit," reducing the guesswork and allowing people to focus on their jobs. "They are not having questions anymore about who or what their commander is," he said. By telling them who you are, "you pose a clear guideline and that is, 'don't fuck around with gays, because I'm not going to accept that.' "[54]

If the presence of known gays violates the privacy and undermines the morale and cohesion of American troops, then shouldn't foreign gays present the same threat? Shouldn't everyone from Sam Nunn and Colin Powell to Charles Moskos and Gary Bauer be up in arms about the U.S. role in international coalitions where heterosexual troops are exposed to open gays and lesbians? The continued insistence on barring known gays from the U.S. military while inviting foreign militaries, with their open gays, to join us in military operations around the globe raises suspicions that opponents of gay service care more about the image of the U.S. military than about what works for a good fighting force. The loud silence from policy makers in the face of joint operations that bring U.S. service members into fighting teams with declared gays from other countries also shows how the pragmatic need for troop strength has finally outweighed moral qualms about the sexual purity of the American force, with no one complaining it's been a detriment to the operation.

The use of multinational forces is also a reminder that armed services worldwide are trending toward what experts call "the postmodern military." In an age of terrorist threats, where guerilla attacks are more likely than traditional acts of war, the term refers to the blurring of several kinds of boundaries, including national borders, as well as fading distinctions between the different branches of the military and even between the military and civilian society.[55] Nothing has demonstrated this evolution more grimly than the Iraq War. Rocket-propelled grenades (RPGs), snipers, and suicide bombers do not distinguish between civilians and designated fighters, between combat Marines and female supply clerks riding in the rear of a convoy, between uniformed military personnel and field intelligence agents. As it becomes harder and harder to tell who is a civilian and who is a combatant, and to distinguish which jobs fall into the intelligence sphere and which are uniformed, it becomes less and less rational to maintain a policy that draws lines around groups that simply don't exist in the same ways as they did in the past. This is a fact about not only the postmodern military but the postmodern world—it's hard to contain people and restrict behavior by resorting to familiar lines of exclusion when these old categories have a totally different meaning, or none at all.

WHAT, THEN, ARE the lessons that can be learned by studying the evidence from foreign militaries and other analogous institutions where gays serve openly?

First, twenty-four nations now allow gays and lesbians to serve in their armed forces; none has seen any impairment to cohesion, recruitment, or fighting capability.

Second, in closely allied nations such as Britain and Israel, gays actually do serve openly in the highest positions, despite claims that gay tolerance is much more limited in practice than in policy. Even in those situations where gays received unequal treatment in practice, the differences were rare and inconsequential. Based on their review of extensive evidence and their own additional interviews, Palm researchers found that unequal treatment mostly consisted of "local attempts to resolve problems flexibly" and were ultimately no different from countless other, varied responses to managing a large, diverse fighting force. There was no evidence that these infrequent and minor cases of differential treatment undermined performance, cohesion, or morale.[56] The cumulative weight of the evidence from the two dozen countries that permit openly gay service makes for highly relevant, if also imperfect, analogies, which strongly suggest that the U.S. military would be no more crippled by removing gay exclusion than any of these other nations.

Third, the nations that allow open gays to serve have a wide range of different cultures and deployment obligations, which run the gamut from the conservative culture of Israel with its world-renowned, combat-tested military to the relatively liberal Dutch society with its limited combat engagements. Thus some of the countries are more socially liberal than the United States, but some, like Israel, are not.

In either case, a fourth lesson is that social tolerance, while it may be an advantage in making the transition from gay exclusion to gay inclusion, is not required for such a change to work effectively. Anti-gay sentiment, it seems, does not translate into impairment of military performance. Inevitably, there have been scattered, high-profile cases of hostility that cause management problems for commanders—cases that are frequently exploited by defenders of the ban, as happened when Keith Meinhold's reinstatement occasionally generated tension and headlines. But just as social conflict born of a thousand other causes must be managed by effective leaders, dealing with these instances of homophobia is a part of the job; they simply are not, as some would have it, a compelling rationale to exclude an entire group from the U.S. military. Many of the nations that ended their gay bans since the early 1990s faced enormous resistance beforehand, reflecting widespread homophobia, but none of the doomsday scenarios that were bandied about came true after the bans were lifted. The Rand study reported that even in those countries where gays were allowed to serve, "in none of these societies is homosexuality widely accepted by a majority of the population."[57]

This point is strengthened by looking at the historical example of racial integration. In 1943, when the military began talking about integrating black troops, the Surveys Division of the Office of War Information conducted opinion surveys and found that 96 percent of Southerners and 85 percent of Northerners opposed it. When President Truman ordered the military integrated in 1948, opposition had softened, but remained a majority, at 63 percent.[58] On this issue, the military was out in front of society, and the military subculture itself was by no means gung-ho over integration. But as Charles

Moskos had eloquently explained, its hierarchical, bureaucratic organizational structure makes it the ideal institution to implement this controversial policy, despite great intolerance around it. While racial integration of the military was a long and difficult process, political and military leaders did not change course because of opinion polls, and history now holds these champions of integration in high esteem for doing the right thing, both morally and militarily.

The fifth, and related, lesson is that the attitudes people express about homosexuality frequently do not predict how they will actually behave. Recall the thousands in Britain and Canada who said they simply would refuse to serve if open gays were allowed in, and the massive nonevent that resulted when they were. This discrepancy is consistent with social science data that show a poor correlation between stated intentions and actual behavior in paramilitary organizations. The 1993 Rand study examined police and fire departments in several U.S. cities, which it regarded as "the closest possible domestic analog" to the military setting. Rand found that the integration of open gays and lesbians—the status of most departments in the United States—actually enhanced cohesion and improved the police department's community standing and organizational effectiveness. A Palm Center study of the San Diego Police Department in 2001 echoed the finding, adding that nondiscrimination policies in police and fire departments did not impair effectiveness even though many departments were characterized as highly homophobic. Research also shows that heterosexual responses to gay service in police and fire departments were more likely to be positive when expressed privately than in front of their peers. Other polls on attitudes toward gays in the military show that most respondents believe their peers are less tolerant of gay service than they, themselves, are.[59] These data are revealing: They show there is a widespread belief that homosexuality is viewed negatively, but when individuals are asked their own views in private, they express a more tolerant attitude.

An article in *Armed Forces and Society* concludes from this data that there is a "cultural-organizational pressure within the armed forces to appear as though one is either uncomfortable or intolerant of homosexuality" and indeed to "pretend to be uncomfortable" with gays, but which belies greater actual comfort than what is stated. It means that when polls say 59 percent of military men would resign if the ban is lifted,[60] careful observers must recall the differences between stated opinions and actual behavior. Opinion polls sometimes say more about perceived norms than about likely behavior, and they often serve primarily as opportunities to register approval or disapproval. Biased attitudes may not translate into discriminatory behavior. More to the point, the biases may not be nearly as strong as out-of-touch politicians and other cultural leaders believe, especially if they base these beliefs on limited surveys or anecdotes.

A sixth lesson is that, despite fears that gays could turn fighting forces into gay pride floats, the majority of gays serving in foreign militaries and American police and fire departments conform to expected norms of their organization. This means either they do not come out, or they come out to selected peers or supervisors but succeed at fitting in with their units in dress, appearance, and comportment. A lesbian who was a lieutenant in the Canadian Forces, for instance, said that "gay people have never screamed to be really, really out. They just want to be really safe from not being fired." Rand researchers found the same was true with police and fire departments.[61]

Rand found no basis for worries that stereotypical behavior and mannerisms, particularly of effeminate men, would "compromise the image of their force." Gays and lesbians, said the report, "were virtually indistinguishable from their heterosexual peers." Gays were reported and observed to be "sufficiently innocuous in their behavior and appearance to have been able to pass as heterosexual members of the force." Some may question the implication here that "acting gay" would somehow not be "innocuous." But conformity to the mainstream is widely considered a necessity for military and paramilitary organizations. As a gay police officer said, "You can't be flamboyant. Most gay men who are police officers are probably on the 'butch' side. You have to look like a police officer."[62]

The fact that many gay people remain discreet even when they're permitted to disclose their identity has been used by some to argue that "don't ask, don't tell" doesn't need to be repealed—after all, why fuss over a policy that requires gays to do what they're already doing anyway? But it could just as easily be used to argue that the policy is not needed. If social norms and expectations keep gays in check (just like most everybody else), why should a law force people to do what they're going to do anyway? It's an argument conservatives should love: The federal government is a lousy regulator of individual identity; no one is better than individuals at choosing when an open discussion about who they are is going to help form bonds of trust in a unit and when discretion is the better part of valor. Even more important, a blanket policy against honest discussion ends up blocking gay troops from seeking out military chaplains, doctors, and psychologists, the support structures that are essential to preserving morale and readiness, and who are not remotely threatened by knowing a service member is gay. But more on this to come.

Lesson number seven is what makes gay inclusion work: clear, consistent rules governing behavior. In many cases, the countries that lifted their bans on gay troops issued strict guidelines holding gay and straight service members to the same standards of conduct. The rules prohibited sexual behavior that undermined the group or involved the abuse of power, rather than summarily excluding an entire group of people. They also made clear that harassment would not be tolerated. In the militaries they studied, Palm researchers found that, "in each case, although many heterosexual soldiers continue[d] to object to homosexuality, the military's emphasis on conduct and equal standards was sufficient for encouraging service members to work together as a team" without undermining cohesion. In Australia, an official noted that "our focus is on the work people do, and the way they do the work, and that applies to heterosexuals, bisexuals and homosexuals." In the case of Great Britain, the Ministry of Defence issued guidelines and speaking notes that emphasized that sexual orientation was to be considered a private matter, that harassment would not be tolerated, and that the new policy "makes no moral judgments about an individual's behavior. Palm researchers concluded that if people are seen as working hard and contributing to the team effort, "individual differences in opinion or in their personal lives are not considered relevant." As a lieutenant colonel in the Royal Army's public relations office put it: "Our great strength as an Army is that we treat everyone [as] an individual who contributes to the team. We've won three recent wars—Sierra Leone, Kosovo and East Timor—because we place a lot of importance on personal responsibility."[63]

The focus on individual responsibility and behavior—instead of either what homosexual troops say or how they act, or the beliefs or attitudes of heterosexual troops—is an essential part of this lesson. Much of the opposition to gay service, particularly from religious conservatives, remains grounded in the objection that the government should not force people to accept homosexuality (never mind that the current ban is, among other things, precisely an expression of public beliefs about homosexuality). Lifting the ban, it is argued, would be tantamount to a government endorsement of something that traditional religious belief considers anathema. But service members do not need to be pro-gay in order for gay inclusion to work effectively.

We have learned this lesson again and again, from a large body of research that includes the military's early efforts to address racial tension. The assumption of the first advocates for integration was that discriminatory behavior against blacks could best be reduced by changing whites' attitudes and beliefs about minorities. But researchers found that the sensitivity training and educational programs designed to achieve that goal caused resentment and even hostility and so failed to resolve the problems. Instead, better results were achieved when outward behavior was the focus. Over time, the requirement to treat African Americans respectfully did effect attitude changes, as whites internalized equal treatment as being consistent with the values of the institution. But even these attitude changes, which followed rather than preceded changes in policy and behavior, did not always translate into pronounced "pro-black" beliefs; rather, they amounted to an endorsement of fair and equal treatment as a principle embraced by the larger group.[64]

Lesson eight—perhaps the single most important lesson to be learned from the research on foreign militaries and analogous institutions—is the centrality of leadership. In the British case, the chiefs of staff were highly involved in creating the new policy and supported it both privately and publicly. Michael Codner, the assistant director for military sciences at the Royal United Services Institute, noted that one reason for the British military's success was that those at the very top lined up behind the policy change. "If you look at the thinking of senior personnel, they have invested a great deal of credibility and authority into this policy shift," he said. "They want to see it fully implemented." Chief Petty Officer Rob Nunn felt this clearly when he reenlisted: "To a person, everybody I've talked to, commander downwards, has said—if you've got problems, come and see me."[65]

Scholars who observed the lifting of the gay ban in Britain reported that fundamental attitudes did not change as a result of the ban being lifted—and they didn't need to. It is, however, crucial for controversial new policies to be perceived as coming from inside the institution, and from strong leaders within the group, as anything that emanates from external pressures can be seen as a threat to the organization's culture and survival. This perception of outside meddling—from gay rights groups to liberal politicians—formed a large part of the resistance to lifting the gay ban in the United States. In Britain, one of the only officials who reportedly resigned over the lifting of the ban specified that his departure was not prompted by anti-gay beliefs or even opposition to gay service per se, but by his belief that the policy change was spurred by outside political forces rather than sound considerations for the military's interests.[66]

Patrick Lyster-Todd agreed that strong military leadership was essential to the success of Britain's policy reform. An officer in the Royal Navy before the ban was lifted, Lyster-Todd later became head of Rank Outsiders, a group dedicated to lifting the ban. "Our MoD and serving chiefs take equality and diversity issues—including the rights of serving gay personnel, whether out or not—incredibly seriously," he said. "Their approach is that if you want to be a capable force for good in the 21st century, then you need to be of that century and its people." Again, this observation is corroborated by mounds of research showing that controversial new rules are most effective when top leaders make their genuine support absolutely clear so that the next layer of leaders, those who actually must implement the new rules, come to identify their enforcement of the new policy with their own self-interest as leaders of the institution.[67] This is why it is no exaggeration to say that the individual actions of a tiny handful of top military and political leaders—from the determination of Colin Powell and Sam Nunn to the indecisiveness of Bill Clinton—were ultimately responsible for the ongoing policy of gay exclusion. And that policy, which we are still reckoning with today, has been from the beginning an unmitigated disaster.

7

"Don't Ask, Don't Tell" Don't Work

D ON'T ASK, DON'T TELL, don't pursue" took effect on March 1, 1994.[1] It aimed to preserve indispensable talent in the armed forces; to protect privacy, morale, and unit cohesion; and, at Bill Clinton's insistence, it aimed to let gays serve their country discreetly without undue hardship. In short, it was supposed to make sexuality a nonissue in the U.S. military.

But the result has been quite different. Far from protecting military readiness, the policy has resulted in skyrocketing discharges, causing wasteful losses in critical talent. It has struck at the heart of unit cohesion by breaking apart integrated fighting teams and undermining trust and honesty between soldiers. It has hamstrung tens of thousands of gay and lesbian troops from doing their best and deterred countless others from ever joining. It has cost hundreds of millions of taxpayer dollars, with nothing to show for the money spent. And, increasingly, its hypocrisy has embarrassed the military, widening the "civil-military gap" and hampering recruitment efforts by alienating Americans who view the military as out of touch.

The price tag has been far higher than the ruined careers and wasted service of skilled gay linguists, doctors, pilots, and engineers. "Don't ask, don't tell" has invaded the privacy of all service members—gay, straight, and everything in between—by casting a cloud of suspicion and uncertainty over the intimate lives of everyone in the armed forces. Straight service members have been investigated, threatened, and even discharged. Some have been turned into informants against their friends and coworkers and been made into unwitting and unwilling objects of deception by gay peers forced to lie or keep their distance to survive. Reports of anti-gay harassment have mushroomed—not only from gays but straights—often women who did not conform to male expectations of proper gender behavior or who rebuffed or complained about unwanted male attention. The resulting atmosphere was, at times, akin to a witch hunt, accompanied by inevitable fear and uncertainty borne by soldiers, sailors, airmen, Marines, and Coast Guardsmen dedicated to serving their country, but required to do so with always a glance backward.

In other words, the policy has failed. Yet some continue to insist it is "working." The question is: Working to do what? A fair assessment is complicated by the maze of political statements, presidential orders, legal memos, military directives, and implementing regulations that surrounded the passage of the law. "Don't ask, don't tell" bred massive confusion about how service members—gay and straight alike—were expected to behave, what their rights and constraints were, and what military commanders were allowed and expected to do to enforce the rules. The policy was poorly understood and poorly enforced—sometimes due to ignorance and sometimes to animus. Indeed, as we shall see, the mixture of bad policy (vague, unrealistic, rooted in deception, and immoral in any but the narrowest, most sectarian sense) with uneven enforcement (weak-willed, neglectful, and all too often purposely ignored) proved toxic to the lives of troops and the mission of the armed forces.

This toxicity manifested itself in a variety of ways. Each prong of "don't ask, don't tell, don't pursue" was misunderstood, ignored, and abused by the military. Commanders routinely asked service members about their sexual identity, directly or through surrogate questions. Gay and lesbian men and women were hauled before discharge boards not only when they chose to "tell" but when they were outed by coworkers, ex-lovers, psychologists, chaplains, Internet chat rooms, and even their own parents. Pursuits remained rampant, with flimsy evidence used as the basis of discharge proceedings. Mass witch hunts continued and threats and intimidation were all too routine. Gays and lesbians were still thrown in prison for private, consensual sex; their education and retirement benefits were vengefully snatched from them once they were discharged; their mental health suffered as they were denied access to support services that all other troops could use. Finally, "don't harass," which was formally added to the policy's name in 2000 after a young soldier was murdered by a fellow soldier in an anti-gay attack, also went unenforced, with reports of abuse, humiliation, bullying, and violence piling up. The incidents of harassment were invited and exacerbated by the policy itself: Victims were reluctant to report abuse for fear they would come under suspicion, and the language of "don't ask, don't tell"—which says gays and lesbians are an "unacceptable risk to the armed forces' high standards of morale, good order and discipline"—sent a loud message that gays were unwelcome and even dangerous, virtually greenlighting harassment against them.

Despite the needless devastation wrought by the policy over the past fifteen years, a strange but predictable counterdevelopment also occurred, especially in the years since the terrorist attacks of September 11, 2001. On the one hand, not much changed for gay and lesbian troops after the United States became a nation at war, showing the stubbornness of the military and Congress, which clung to homophobia even as evidence mounted that it was hurting national security. On the other hand, the discharge run-up of the 1990s did an about-face, as commanders looked the other way, growing tolerance among young recruits replaced the homophobia of the old guard, the military closet—like its civilian counterpart—began to crack and crumble, and openly gay service became more and more the norm. The contrast was the mark of a policy whose guiding assumptions had become totally at odds with the reality of the boots on the ground.

UNDER THE POLICY, when a commander is faced with evidence of homosexual conduct that he or she deems "credible," the service member is notified and given the opportunity to accept the charge or go before a hearing. The hearings are held before an administrative discharge board or, for officers, a board of inquiry, presided over by a three-member panel of appointed officers. The panel makes a recommendation to the service secretary, who decides whether to separate or retain the service member. Most such discharges are characterized as honorable; the phrase (depending on the circumstances and service branch) "homosexual conduct," "homosexual act," "homosexual statement," or "homosexual admission" is stamped on the service member's discharge papers. If the violation was conducted in certain circumstances, such as by force, with a subordinate, on a ship, or in public, the discharge can be characterized as "less than" or "other than" honorable.

The policy became law in November 1993. From the moment it took effect, on March 1, 1994, homosexual discharges began to increase. In 1994, 617 service members were discharged for "homosexual conduct." The next year, 772. In 1996, 870 got the boot, 1,007 in 1997, 1,163 in 1998, 1,046 in 1999, and 1,241 in 2000. In 2001, a record 1,273 service members were discharged under the policy, a figure nearly double the discharge rate of 1992, the year before the law was passed. Since 2002, the first full year the United States was at war, discharge figures have dropped nearly every year. From their peak in 2001, the number slid to 906 in 2002, 787 in 2003, and 668 in 2004; it swelled to 742 in 2005, dropped again to 623 in 2006, and reached 627 in 2007. Despite the overall plunge in discharges, a total of 4,353 troops have been ousted under the policy just since 9/11. Since 1994, that number has passed 12,342. The cost to taxpayers of discharging and replacing these troops has been at least $364 million, enough to supply about 2,500 uparmored Humvees.[2]

The discharges covered 161 different occupational categories, including intelligence personnel, engineers, medical professionals, administrative specialists, transportation workers, and military police. Over 300 of those lost were language specialists, and more than 750 of the casualties had "critical occupations," according to the GAO. In the summer of 2004, the Pentagon announced it would issue involuntary recalls to thousands of civilians with these same occupational specialties as the ones just wasted by firing gay and lesbian troops. It was one among countless indications of just how the anti-gay policy directly affects the capacity of the military to retain the expertise and troop strength it needs to fight in the Middle East.[3]

HOW DID A policy that was supposed to make sexuality less germane result in such ongoing—and increasing—damage? Why did the talent loss increase despite hopes that it would subside? After all, Clinton had repeatedly proclaimed that the country did not have a person to waste. One answer is that the policy was watered down from the start. In a series of directives, regulations, and instructions written after the policy became law, the Defense Department and the individual service branches were tasked with implementing the federal statute in a way that was consistent with the Clinton-Aspin policy. But in doing so, government lawyers and military leaders issued starkly contradictory instructions to commanders and service members, writing regulations that conflicted not only with one another but also with the original Pentagon policy as outlined by Clinton and Aspin in July 1993.

When Clinton and the military brass announced that policy in the summer of 1993, they closed ranks and displayed what was clearly a politically choreographed, united front. At the July 19 press conference, each of the six members of the Joint Chiefs of Staff, as well as the commandant of the Coast Guard, took a turn at the microphone and read from the same script. The policy "is a workable solution," said Admiral David Jeremiah, and a "good answer" to a "difficult problem." General Gordon Sullivan was "fully supportive of the policy," one that he said the troops will understand and the "commanders will be able to handle." Admiral Frank Kelso: "I fully support this policy. I'm sure we can implement it and it will work." General Carl Mundy: "This is a good policy. It's a policy that can be implemented and it is a courageous policy." General Merrill McPeak: "The Air Force supports the policy," and "will not have a problem implementing this new policy, so I look forward to no problem whatsoever." Admiral J. William Kime rounded out the chorus by saying, "This, too, is a policy that the Coast Guard can support."[4]

For his part, Colin Powell agreed with Clinton that what they had crafted was "an honorable compromise" that "protects the privacy rights of all of those serving in the force, and yet moves in the direction of those who wanted to have a more liberal policy with respect to homosexuals." He said he was "very, very pleased with this decisions of the President, and it's one we can fully support." Most important, Powell said that the policy meant "We will not ask, we will not witch hunt, we will not seek to learn orientation," adding, "this is a significant change on the part of the military." Clinton echoed the promise: "This is an end to witch hunts that spend millions of taxpayer dollars to ferret out individuals who have served their country well."[5]

To that end, the policy announced in July stated: "No investigations or inquiries will be conducted solely to determine a service member's sexual orientation." It promised that "associational" activities such as going to gay bars, having gay friends, marching in a gay parade, or reading gay books or magazines would not be considered "credible information that would provide a basis" for investigation and discharge. Nor would listing someone of the same sex as a beneficiary or emergency contact. It explicitly protected discussions with priests and lawyers, as well as "husband-wife" communications. Finally, in security clearance interviews, troops would not be asked about their sexual orientation, and if the matter came up, according to a Pentagon press release, "information about homosexual orientation or conduct obtained during a security clearance investigation will not be used by the military departments in separation proceedings."[6]

By December, the Pentagon had drafted implementing regulations detailing how to carry out the law and directing the individual service branches how to update their own regulations to be in compliance. In addition to no longer asking recruits about their sexual orientation at induction, the main change, which was announced by Les Aspin on December 21, 1993, updated Department of Defense Directive 1332.14, Enlisted Administrative Separations. The directive now stated that DOD policy was to "judge the suitability of persons to serve in the Armed Forces on the basis of their conduct and their ability to meet required standards of duty performance and discipline." The attached guidelines for inquiries into sexual conduct assured service members that they could only be investigated if commanders received "credible information that there is a basis for discharge." These were the details spelling out the most complicated part of the new policy, "don't pursue." Unit leaders were not supposed to seek out a member's *orientation*. They could ask questions about homosexual *conduct*, but only if they were first met with "articulable facts, not just a belief or suspicion," and even then, orientation itself was not to be the target of the investigation or the reason for discharge, only conduct. "Credible information" did not exist if it was based simply on "the opinions of others that a member is homosexual," or on "rumor, suspicion or capricious claims concerning a member's sexual orientation."[7]

In announcing the directives of the new policy, Les Aspin was joined by the Pentagon's general counsel, Jamie Gorelick. As the military's top lawyer, Gorelick had the unenviable task of overseeing the actual implementation of the new policy, and of ensuring that the Clinton policy was consistent with the congressional statute. In explaining what she had come up with, Gorelick said inquiries would be "limited to the facts involved in the allegation." A service member would not be "interrogated about his or her partners," she added, saying that was the Pentagon's effort to "deal with the concern about witch hunts." Seeking to end the targeting of sexual orientation alone, the new policy eliminated the regulation of "desire." Instead, statements would only prompt a discharge if they were deemed to indicate "a likelihood" that while you were in the service, you would engage in homosexual acts. In other words, simply being gay would not be cause for losing your job, so long as you refrain from indicating that you were likely to engage in homosexual acts.[8]

These were the promises. But as the policy stewed and simmered and slowly congealed into law, directives from the different service branches, anemic enforcement throughout the military, and politically motivated interference made a mockery of these carefully laid-out promises. The trouble started with a loud lament from Senators Strom Thurmond and Dan Coats. The two were so angered by a phrase in the new implementing regulations that, in February 1994, they threatened to hold up confirmation of Clinton's new defense secretary, William Perry. The phrase? "Homosexual orientation is not a bar to service entry or continued service." For Thurmond and Coats, as with Sam Nunn, the main reason to write the policy into law was to scuttle Clinton's effort to let gays serve. The senators did not want to acknowledge that gay people would be serving in the military, so they insisted that "homosexual orientation" be deleted, leaving the comically inane phrase: "Sexual orientation is considered a personal and private matter, and is not a bar to continued service." Which, when you think about it, is a good thing: Since everyone has a sexual orientation, making one's orientation a barrier to service entry would have resulted in a quick end to the U.S. military.[9]

The wording change was pure political theater, and effectively meaningless. But not so the implementing documents of the individual services. While the gay troop policy was Pentagon-wide, each service branch had leeway in determining how it carried out and enforced the rules. In June, a navy memo instructed officers and administrators to pursue investigations based on exactly the "associational" activities that the policy expressly permitted. Merely criticizing the policy in public, read the memo, "may be inconsistent with good military character." It was a chilling threat that has made research on service member opinion extremely difficult. "The wearing of one's uniform," it continued, "or identifying oneself as a member of USN while visibly supporting homosexual interests may violate Uniform Regulations and the Standards of Conduct." Incredibly, the memo also instructed those responsible for enforcing the policy to "be creative" when trying to build a case against suspected gay sailors. "Where the case is premised on a statement alone, the recorder should attempt to find evidence to corroborate the statement and to sustain the presumption flowing logically from the statement," it said. Seek out "additional evidence," it urged, that shows the "unequivocal desire of the respondent to commit criminal acts." The exhortation was a direct violation of "don't pursue." Bracing for a defense that appealed baldly to sentiment, the memo ended with its own plea to stay strong in pursuit of rooting out gays: "Do not easily accept the characterization of respondent as a model sailor."[10]

Another navy memo brazenly flouted the terms of "don't pursue," urging psychologists and other medical professionals to turn in anyone who came to them for counseling if they revealed in the professionals' offices that they might be gay. The memo suggested that many homosexuals were "over-stimulated by members of the same sex" and said that the only way gays and lesbians could successfully adapt to military life was if they remain "invisible and do not seek to disclose their homosexuality. The nonadapters realize they made a mistake in joining the military, and they need to get out. When a nonadapter goes to the physician, the physician will be most helpful by facilitating the legal process" of separation.[11]

A 1994 air force JAG memo had a similar effect, directing commanders to interrogate service members' families, school officials, and friends in an effort to learn if they were gay. It also expanded the sway of intrusive investigations by permitting inquiries into the activities of "other military members" who did not come out but were "discovered" during an investigation of someone else. This was a direct violation of the Pentagon policy, which stated that "inquiries shall be limited to the factual circumstances directly relevant to the specific allegations." They will be limited, that is, to credible evidence that surfaces about a particular individual, not anyone else whose name might come up when the original accused was investigated.[12]

The major selling point of "don't ask, don't tell" was that it claimed to allow discreet homosexuals to serve as long as they did not engage in homosexual conduct. Yet this value-added part was wiped out by the notorious Miller memo that was issued in 1995 as a response to the Dunning case. Lieutenant Commander Maria Zoe Dunning came out publicly early in 1993 as Bill Clinton was insisting he would keep his promise to lift the ban. Dunning was a supply officer who graduated from the U.S. Naval Academy and had served for twelve years, earning a Navy Commendation Medal for her service during the Persian Gulf War. A week after she came out, the navy initiated discharge proceedings and placed her on unpaid reserve status pending the outcome. But in July 1993, when "don't ask, don't tell" was announced, Clinton ordered that anyone whose status was still pending be given a new hearing, using the rules of the new policy—not the pre-1993 rule—as the basis for deciding her fate.

Her second hearing was not held until November 1994. Dunning's executive officer eagerly testified on her behalf, saying he did not want to lose her and describing her performance as "outstanding." He was asked about the reaction of the unit to Dunning's sexual orientation and the effect of her initial removal (pending the hearings) on morale and cohesion. "I think we've already suffered a loss in the unit," he said, "because everybody worked very well with Zoe. Everybody liked her. And we've already basically noticed the loss." He said that while some were surprised by Dunning's announcement, there were no complaints, no insults, no impairment of unit performance, and no one insisting they be reassigned so they didn't have to work or live with a lesbian. If she were retained, he concluded, "we'd welcome her back." Another officer who worked with Dunning agreed, saying Dunning was "getting kind of a raw deal." The feeling in the unit, he said, "was like, 'That's just too bad that they're having to worry about this, because this is a good officer.'"[13]

Dunning's lawyers argued that, under the terms of the new policy, Dunning must be retained because her declaration of her identity as a lesbian did not, in fact, reveal a propensity to engage in homosexual conduct; it was merely a statement of fact about who she was.[14] Recall what the policy says: Declaring you are gay or lesbian creates a "presumption" that you are likely to engage in homosexual acts, which are grounds for dismissal; however, you are invited to "rebut" this presumption at a military hearing. The question is this: How can you rebut a presumption that you are likely to engage in homosexual acts if you've just said you're a homosexual? It's an especially tall order given that the policy actually defines a homosexual as someone who *is* likely to engage in homosexual acts. Ergo, to the Pentagon, if you've said you're a homosexual, you've said you're likely to engage in forbidden conduct.

Dunning's case was one of the first to be heard under the new rules. In a surprising move, her board recommended she be retained, saying they were convinced that her statement did not indicate a "propensity" to engage in homosexual acts. In the meantime, Dunning—fully out and known to the world as a lesbian officer—was promoted to lieutenant commander. She went on to serve openly for thirteen more years, earning a Navy and Marine Corps Medal before her retirement in 2007.[15]

The military was not pleased with the Dunning decision. The idea that a service member could reveal that she was a homosexual and continue to serve defeated the purpose of "don't ask, don't tell"—which was, after all, to protect heterosexual privacy by shielding them from the knowledge of which coworkers might fancy them. So the general counsel of the Defense Department, Judith Miller, issued a memo on August 18, 1995, directing officials never again to accept as a defense against discharge a simple statement from an avowed homosexual denying he or she was likely to engage in homosexual acts. "A member may not avoid the burden," said the memo, "of rebutting the presumption" that he or she is likely to engage in homosexual conduct "merely by asserting that his or her statement of homosexuality was intended to convey only a message about sexual orientation."[16] That is, just as saying you're a drug user is an admission of doing drugs, saying you're gay is an admission that you had (or would likely have) gay sex, and therefore should be fired. The military was saying, in effect, that a member who just said he was gay (or, for that matter was revealed to be gay by a third party, a vengeful lover, an errant e-mail, or a letter left out on a table) could only avoid discharge if he proved that he was not what he just said he was. And no fair just saying so—he had to *prove* it.

The Miller memo has bedeviled attempts of service members, journalists, lawyers, and regular people to fully understand the policy: Does "don't ask, don't tell" ban gay people based on who they are or based only on what they do? Does it make all gays—if they're caught—ineligible for service, or only those who engage in prohibited conduct? Which does it target: identity or behavior? Status or conduct?

The confusion stems from both political and legal calculations that shaped the law. Bill Clinton had repeatedly insisted that people should only be booted from the military "based on something they do, not based on who they are." Meritocracy and equal opportunity were major doctrines of Clinton's campaign and his governing philosophy. By all accounts he believed in these principles, even though in the end, his efforts to abide by them were watered down by his opponents and he chose to stop spending further political capital to defend meritocracy in the military.[17]

Legal challenges played perhaps an even more central role. As Clinton and the Pentagon battled to formulate an acceptable compromise throughout

1993, the very notion of a ban on gays looked increasingly like it would not pass constitutional muster, given court decisions in the cases of Joseph Steffan, Keith Meinhold, Margarethe Cammermeyer, Zoe Dunning, and others. Top lawyers responsible for developing the policy were well aware of this, and took into account the prospect of inevitable legal challenges. For these reasons, it was essential for architects of the policy to present the policy as one that targeted only behavior, and didn't punish people for who they were.

What the lawyers came up with was a legal maneuver that has insulated the Pentagon from constitutional challenges while continuing to oust thousands of gay people from military service, even if they have not engaged in what ordinary Americans—read: nonlawyers—might regard as homosexual conduct. That legal maneuver is the two-pronged clause known as the "propensity clause" and the "rebuttable presumption," and it is enshrined in both Clinton's policy and the congressional statute. The clause was not actually new to "don't ask, don't tell" but was made, in the words of Pentagon general counsel Jamie Gorelick, more "robust" so that "a court might view this policy differently than the old policy."[18]

What the two-part clause says is that service members who state they are gay are "presumed" to have a "propensity" to engage in homosexual acts, but that they would be invited to "rebut" that presumption by showing they do not have such a propensity. Propensity is defined as not just a desire to engage in gay sex but a "likelihood." This is the section of the policy that turns simple statements or facts about one's homosexual orientation—who one is—into "proof" of homosexual behavior: conduct that is grounds for discharge. And the supposed option to "rebut" that propensity was a way to allow lawyers to argue that the policy is not targeting a person's identity or expression, since people have the option to argue that their statement of identity did not indicate behavior.

Yet in reality, despite Dunning's unprecedented (and rarely repeated) success, it was virtually impossible to rebut the presumption. The law's authors admitted that the rebuttable-presumption clause was only inserted as a way to ward off legal challenges, and it created a threshold that would be nearly impossible for anyone to actually meet. Speaking in the final days of Nunn's Senate hearings in July 1993, Secretary of Defense Les Aspin said that it was a "tough standard" to rebut the presumption that a statement of homosexual identity indicated a likelihood of engaging in prohibited conduct, so much so that he thought "it has not been done in the past." The next day, Jamie Gorelick echoed the point even more forcefully: "I would reiterate what the Secretary said yesterday, that" rebutting the presumption "is a very high burden and no one has ever done it." It was expected that the only way to show that a service member did not have a propensity was to prove the statement was a joke or that he or she was drunk or had "lost his or her mind."[19]

In a memo to President Clinton that same fateful week in July, Attorney General Janet Reno explained the legal purpose of the rebuttable-presumption clause. "First Amendment problems would arise," wrote Reno, "if the policy proscribed certain speech, in and of itself." But the "meaningful opportunity to rebut the presumption flowing from statements of homosexuality," wrote Reno, meant the government would be "better able to argue that the policy is not directed at speech or expressions itself," only conduct. "Meaningful opportunity"? It was never meaningful to begin with, and whatever opportunity might have existed was just killed by the Miller memo. Now, a declaration (or revelation) of homosexuality would leave a person no way to rebut the presumption that he was likely to engage in gay sex short of some form of unidentifiable, intangible, perhaps miraculous assurance to a discharge board that the definition of a homosexual somehow did not apply to him. Over the next twelve years, lawyers defending gay service members said they could count on one hand the number of times someone had been able to avoid a discharge based on rebutting the presumption, and they theorized that the only thing explaining the success of those few cases was an effort by the military to show the world (and the courts) that the rebuttable presumption was not the total farce that it was.[20]

If a federal regulation can lie, this one does. While lawyers can argue that "don't ask, don't tell" targets only conduct, it clearly targets status. In fact, with the help of the rebuttable presumption and the propensity clause, the policy defines conduct so broadly that it makes a mockery of the distinction between conduct and status. And this was the point. After all, the fundamental rationale for "don't ask, don't tell" was that many heterosexuals become uncomfortable once they *know* that a coworker is gay, as they don't wish to be the object of homosexual desire. As explained by Charles Moskos and echoed by Colin Powell, it was "the presence of homosexuals in the force" (i.e., not what they did but their very existence) that invaded the privacy of straight troops and thereby impaired unit cohesion.[21] Hence it is the presence of same-sex desire itself—not conduct, but the mere possibility of feelings—that military leaders have said is a danger to the armed forces. This is why the law bars "persons who demonstrate a propensity or intent to engage" in homosexual conduct: No matter how the lawyers spin it, at heart "don't ask, don't tell" bans gay people for who they are, not what they do.

Given this concern, the only sensible policy response would have been to ban gay people, not just gay conduct. And despite the efforts of Clinton, Powell, Aspin, and innumerable lawyers to suggest otherwise, that's effectively what the policy has done. As we'll see in a string of sordid tales of dubious discharges, gay soldiers have routinely been booted not for anything they did but simply because it was impossible, at one time or another, for them to conceal the fact that they were gay—either for deeply personal reasons that prompted a "statement" or because those around them knew, guessed, or suspected their sexuality and threatened them or turned them in. For those eternal optimists who still insisted—or wanted to believe—that the policy only punished conduct, not orientation, the 1995 Miller memo finally squashed the phony distinction between status and conduct.

This sad truth is further revealed by a curious exemption for straight people, known colloquially as "Queen for a Day." It stipulates that a service member "shall be separated" if he or she engages in homosexual conduct "unless . . . such conduct is a departure from the member's usual and customary behavior" and it is "unlikely to recur." This can only be interpreted in one way: On occasion, it is okay for straight people to engage in same-sex behavior. Homosexual "conduct" is not banned for heterosexual people, because when heterosexuals engage in homosexual conduct, it's not a threat. At the same time, gay people are fired for even mentioning to a psychologist that they've experienced same-sex desire, whether or not they've ever engaged in actual homosexual conduct. A gay virgin, who's never had sex with so much as a worm, can be fired merely for saying he is gay; meanwhile the ship's Romeo who downs a bottle of Jack Daniel's at sea and stumbles in a one-night "homosexual lapse" can go right on serving.

The tangle of legal maneuvers, memos, and regulations effectively sabotaged what was already a bad policy and worsened the consequences for gay and lesbian service members. Between complaints by watchdog organizations and defenses by the Pentagon, there lies continued uncertainty about whether these invasive techniques are actually violations of the policy or exactly what the policy allows. Legal challenges have, by and large, defended the military's actions as consistent with the law and have upheld the law as consistent with the Constitution. But by all accounts the witch hunts, seizures of private possessions, security clearance denials and delays, and outings by counselors, doctors, and clergy were not what the politicians promised, and not what a military leader such as Colin Powell publicly supported when he signed onto the policy, saying, "We will not ask, we will not witch hunt, we will not seek to learn orientation."[22] As byzantine as the policy is, some things are quite clear: Commanders are not allowed to ask, and no one is allowed to harass.

Yet hundreds of indisputable violations of the policy's strictures against asking, pursuing, and harassing have been documented each year since 1994. The Servicemembers Legal Defense Network (SLDN), a watchdog and legal aid organization that has monitored the effects of the policy since its inception, reported 340 command violations (perpetrated by the military) in the first year alone, including 15 actual or attempted witch hunts and 10 death threats to service members for perceived homosexuality. For the first three years, SLDN documented 1,146 violations, with the number increasing each year. The abuses have ranged from the purposeful to the neglectful to the vicious. Examples documented by SLDN include the continued use of outdated documents asking recruits if they were gay (as late as 2002, the air force was found to be using a fifteen-year-old form that asked recruits, "Are you homosexual or bisexual?"); routine flouting of the "don't ask" principle by simply asking service members, "Are you gay?" or substitute questions such as, for men, "Do you find men attractive?"; violating the prohibition on asking about sexual identity in security clearance inquiries by asking if applicants are in "a physical relationship" with a roommate of the same sex; and mocking "don't ask" with questions such as, "I'm not going to ask you if you're homosexual, but if I did ask, how would you respond?"[23]

Sometimes the questions were hostile. A chief of boat shouted to a sailor, "You [sic] not going to tell me you're a fucking faggot, are you?" A Marine Corps recruiter said, "Because of President Clinton's new policy, I can't ask you if you're a fag. So I'll just ask if you suck cock." Other times the hostility was less overt but with the same effect, as when an officer told a woman under his command, "I know you're a lesbian," leaving her tongue-tied and unsure of the consequence of his statement. Still other times, the sheer repetition of infractions wore troops down and out. At Lackland Air Force Base in San Antonio, where some of the worst and highest number of violations took place, unit members asked an airman if he was gay so many times that he simply acknowledged the truth—and lost his job. A sailor was asked if she had "ever told anyone on the ship that you are gay." Despite the blatant violation the question constituted, her captain threatened her with criminal prosecution if she did not answer the question or if she made false statements. The threat itself was also completely forbidden under the policy, but the pressure was too much for the sailor, who admitted she was a lesbian and was quickly thrown out.[24]

The limits on pursuits have been even more flagrantly ignored. Investigators have seized letters, diaries, books, magazines, computers, even posters of lesbian singers, including Melissa Etheridge and k.d. lang, in an effort to determine service members' sexuality and past history. In 1996, an air force major was investigated on criminal charges of sodomy after the clerk at the local MotoPhoto store saw fit to make an extra copy of his pictures—nothing sexual, just the major with his arm around another man—and sent them to the Office of Special Investigations. In the navy, a commander read through the medical records of one sailor and started discharge proceedings after noticing treatment of a medical condition associated with gay men. For the discharge investigation of a Marine Corps corporal, inquiry officers counted among admissible evidence attendance at the Dinah Shore golf tournament and buying Anne Rice novels. Such unfounded extrapolations from the slimmest bits of "evidence," such wild and groundless speculation based on nothing but stereotypes, were clearly violations of "don't pursue."[25]

When Airman Sonya Harden was investigated, the "credible evidence" that began the process was the charge of a third-party accuser who was in an ongoing quarrel with Harden over money. Harden insisted she was straight and brought ex-boyfriends to testify on her behalf. Eventually, her accuser admitted she was lying. Harden was discharged anyway, despite the recanted charge and the testimony of ex-boyfriends.[26]

The misuse, abuse, and neglect of evidence in discharge proceedings should come as no surprise given the makeup of many of the discharge boards. In reviews of colonels who were up for board of inquiry spots, one said, "I think homosexuals are immoral." Another said he thought they "have either a physiological or psychological problem as deviant from society." A third said, "My religious beliefs are against homosexuality." The three colonels were placed on the board. "I think it would be hard to find three board members that would have an opinion different from those already expressed," commented the lieutenant colonel responsible for choosing the board.[27]

With such attitudes rampant throughout the military leadership, suspected and accused service members rarely stood a chance. But if violations of "don't pursue" referred to overzealous investigations of friends and family on flimsy evidence, full-scale witch hunts were used to describe expanding webs of inquiry that sought to pressure military members to turn one another in by naming names. The notorious witch hunts were rampant in the years prior to the "don't ask" policy and were a major impetus behind reform, with its promises of a "zone of privacy." But throughout the 1990s, little changed, and in some ways, things got worse: The venomous rhetoric of the

cultural and political debate around gay service, together with the bitterness
felt by many in the military who resented what they perceived as the imposition of social change by military outsiders, raised temperatures on this issue
and injected a new fear into the situation: Who among us might be gay?

The U.S. Military Academy at West Point is the elite training ground for
army officers. Like all military commands, West Point has extensive counseling available to ensure the well-being of service members. So when Cadet
Nikki Galvan's mother died, an academy counselor was available to help her
deal with her grief and suggested she keep a journal as part of her mourning
process. In it, Galvan confided, or so she thought, about a number of very
private emotions she was facing, and one of these was her sexuality. Not long
after she started her journal, she was asked by her lieutenant colonel point-
blank—in front of four other cadets—if she was a lesbian. Instead of answering, Galvan submitted a complaint. But rather than taking action against the
improper questioning of Galvan, the army seized her personal diary and private e-mails under a pretext that officials were investigating a reported "dis-
turbance in the ranks." An investigation ensued; the report states that Galvan
violated regulations "by making various statements in her diary indicating a
propensity or intent to engage in homosexual acts or conduct." Galvan said
she felt "violated and humiliated," and that her friends stopped talking to her
out of fear they would be suspected of being gay. "My cadet life became un-
bearable," she remembered. Facing a discharge, Galvin resigned. West Point
tried to recoup $100,000 in tuition funds, based on failing to honor the ser-
vice obligation that cadets incur by attending for free. Her departure ended
an excruciating ordeal for her, but marked just the beginning for West Point,
where officials expanded the investigation into an outright witch hunt that
took aim at thirty other women at the academy.[28]

The West Point witch hunt was more the rule than the exception. In the
spring of 1994, military investigators interrogated over twenty Marines about
their sexual orientation. One was thrown in a military jail for over a month.
Another had his bed turned on its side, his private possessions ransacked,
and his personal computer confiscated. The navy admitted the next year that
it had engaged in a witch hunt, but—with no punishment for wrongful
investigations—no one in the military was held accountable or suffered any
consequences, besides the Marine who languished in the brig for a month of
his life and the rest of the troops who were terrified into a state of permanent
insecurity.[29]

Later that same year, a young soldier serving in South Korea endured a
horrendous ordeal when she was assaulted by a group of male soldiers who

also threatened to rape her. Her resistance prompted her attackers to spread lies that she was a lesbian. This lesbian-baiting is one of the most troubling abuses of the gay ban (some men, no doubt, have convinced themselves that any woman who refuses their charms must not be straight). Again and again, female service members who report harassment, even rape, end up the target of threatened and actual investigations into their sexuality. And several of these victims, like the soldier in South Korea, were straight. When she reported the incident, her commanding officer turned on her, accusing her of being gay and threatening her with prison if she did not admit it and identify other service members suspected of being gay. A military judge dismissed the charges for lack of evidence, but her commander would not let up, starting administrative discharge proceedings against her. Only after enormous legal intervention by SLDN and great financial cost to the soldier's family did the army relent, allowing the harrowing experience to end with a delayed transfer to a new command.[30]

One of the largest witch hunts unfolded in Sardinia, Italy, early in 1996, aboard the USS *Simon Lake.* Prompted by questions directed at Seaman Amy Barnes, navy personnel expanded their inquiry to encompass a shocking sixty women on the ship. In sworn affidavits, sailors alleged that the navy intimidated, threatened, and harassed them in an effort to force them to out themselves or others. "If you do not tell the truth, you will go to jail for ten to fifteen years," one investigator told Heather Hilbun, before she was grilled on her own sexuality and that of six other named women. "Command Investigators threatened and intimidated me into giving involuntary statements," testified another, "by telling me I would be violating Article 78 of the Uniform Code of Military Justice and would go to jail if I did not answer their questions." The sailor commented that "being forced into giving statements which had the potential to be used against RMSN Barnes, who is my friend, was extremely upsetting." Unchastened, the navy argued in court that service members had "no legal basis upon which to challenge" the extraordinary scope of the investigation, as the current rules "create no enforceable rights" for those who get caught in the military's intrusive net.[31]

During the same period in early 1996, the air force showed exactly what their priorities were in the age of "don't ask, don't tell." Airman Bryan Harris faced life in prison, accused of rape of another man and other charges. Because Harris was gay, his sex life was seen as an invitation for investigators to catch other gays in the military—even if it meant reducing his punishment for a real crime in exchange for learning the names of men who simply happened to be gay. Late in January, air force lawyers struck a deal with Harris: a twenty-month sentence if he named all the men he had had sex with in the military. Of the seventeen men he named, five were in the air force and each was promptly rounded up and charged with homosexual conduct. (The rest were in other service branches.) Questions in the air force investigations into Harris's peers included asking coworkers if they would be "surprised to find out that" the airmen were gay, if the airmen ever talked about women, "you know, the way men talk about women," where and with whom the airmen hung out, and if it would seem "unusual" for the airmen not to have girl-friends—all bald violations of guidelines restricting questions about orienta-tion or about events outside the circumstances in question. Four were fired. The fifth was court-martialed in a criminal trial and threatened by officials that he could get thirty years in prison—for consensual sex with another man. Eventually he was allowed to leave the military without serving jail time.[32]

THE CULTURE OF the military throughout the 1990s—largely unchanged from previous decades—was one that lazily exploited anti-gay and anti-female sentiment to bolster feelings of male vigor and machismo that were, for cen-turies, felt to be central to warrior success. Yet it is the demeaning behavior encouraged by these beliefs—not the private lives of gays and lesbians—that, in the modern age, is damaging to morale and unit cohesion. Under "don't ask, don't tell" such behavior meant not only neglecting promises to end pro-active pursuits and harassment of any kind, but avoiding the hard work of properly enforcing a bad policy. Instead a climate of fear was allowed to run rampant, chasing women and gays away or keeping them quiet and compli-ant.

One chief warrant officer put it this way: "To be the victim of sexual harassment is, in its own right, one of the most degrading and emotionally injurious positions one can be placed in, especially in the military. But to be blackmailed for supposedly being a lesbian so that sexual harassment can continue goes beyond the pale." Another warrant officer agreed: "The ever-present threat of an investigation into our private lives that is designed to keep us quiet is doing just that. Very few women will publicly address these issues for fear of the repercussions. I regret that I am unable to identity my-self, for fear of setting off a new round of rumors and speculations that I am a lesbian," and facing discharge.[33]

But men and women alike suffered these consequences, victims of a unique and unprecedented statute that targeted a particular minority group for unequal treatment and then wrote into law that members of that group—and that group alone—would be barred from speaking up to fight for their own rights and needs. "I feel unable to defend myself from these attacks without raising even more suspicion," wrote a nine-year career officer, after his master chief began to verbally harass him with vulgar insinuations of his homosexuality. His master chief suggested the sailor might be turned on by seeing his penile implant. Similarly, by pointing to the word "homosexual" in a navy document, he gestured to the sailor as a way of calling him gay without saying the words. The behavior continued unabated. Fully aware of what happened to his gay and lesbian peers when they complained of anti-gay harassment, the sailor concluded he could have no control over his career and his life if something didn't change. He wrote a letter to his commander stating the truth, saying, "The only means I see" to "avoid becoming a victim of harassment is by making this disclosure to you."[34]

Some view the persistence of anti-gay harassment in the military as evidence that the institution is too intolerant of homosexuality for the ban to end. They view calls for stronger leadership as naïve, unrealistic, or unfair to commanders, who, they say, are busy with other, more pressing leadership tasks. It is true that much of American military culture remains cool to gays and lesbians, although this is changing dramatically. But whatever the attitudes add up to on the ground, the policy is not helping, and is actually inviting anti-gay abuse. It does so in two ways. It sends a strong, clear message that homosexuals are, as the law puts it, "an unacceptable risk to the armed forces." In other words, U.S. law tells every last member of the military that gays and lesbians—an undeniable presence in all parts of the military—are trouble. And by keeping heterosexuals in the dark about their gay and lesbian coworkers, the policy denies them the opportunity to challenge their own stereotypes; familiarity can and does breed tolerance.

Plenty of research shows that when institutions make it official policy to denigrate the contributions of a particular subgroup, members develop or maintain negative attitudes toward that group, which are often expressed through disrespectful and destructive behavior. A perfect example of this occurred in 1996, when a Marine Corps major expressed an apparently popular sentiment at a conference at the elite Naval War College. "I can't imagine a more basic violation of the natural law than homosexuality," he said. "They are not worthy of our trust. It's intolerable." The room broke out in applause.[35]

Melissa Sheridan Embser-Herbert, a sociologist and retired U.S. Army captain, has studied the link between the rules of an institution and the behavior of its members. Embser-Herbert says that the gay ban casts such an air of suspicion and uncertainty over everyone's sexuality that it encourages "hypermasculinity" as a way of proving one is not gay. By mandating that all soldiers appear as straight, the policy requires both gays and straights to "go out of their way to be read as heterosexual," which often entails making or engaging in homophobic or sexist comments and behaviors.[36]

These findings were borne out by service members' experiences serving in the Middle East wars. "I almost had to create some sort of macho thing," said an infantryman who fought in Iraq. "That's how I'm perceived now in my unit, that I'm a player and that I get women all the time and have these sex parties. Little do they know . . ." One petty officer first class in the navy revealed how the gay ban's forced performance of heterosexuality results in antisocial and disruptive behavior. "On a daily basis, I'm an asshole," he said. In order to avoid giving the impression that he was a stereotypical gay man, he acted out in ways that he thought projected heterosexuality, which, in his case, meant being "an asshole." He learned that several members of his unit thought he was gay "because I have nice white straight teeth and I trim my eyebrows and comb my hair and I wear gold." He said the implication was that "if I come to work with bad breath and I'm messy, then I'd be straight." He also said he thought his peers suspected his homosexuality due to his silence on certain occasions, such as "when I don't take part in conversations about demoralizing women."[37] His experience is also a reminder that it is impossible in many cases to successfully conceal one's homosexuality.

By discouraging people from coming out, the policy prevents what would be the single most important ingredient to generating tolerance of gays and lesbians: knowing someone who is gay or lesbian. Polls show clearly that when people personally know a gay or lesbian, they are more accepting of them. But if rumors and innuendo are left to fester, that's when problems arise. A prime example comes from Brian Muller, a former army staff sergeant. Muller found that many young straight people he encountered had little exposure to open gays and lesbians, and when he did discuss his sexuality, "I think some of them changed their views." He concluded that "the best thing the military can do if they lift this ban is to educate people. . . . Once they see that we have the same relationships, the same fears, go to the same restaurants [as straights do], they come around." Regarding his sexuality, he said, "Some say, look, I don't really like it, but as long as you can carry the same pack, I don't care."[38]

"If they allowed homosexuals to be gay in the military, then a result of that would be teaching acceptance of another part of their family," said Muller, who served in both single-sex and co-ed units and noticed a sharp difference in attitudes between the two. The co-ed units "were always the best units because you don't have as much machismo floating around and you get people who are more tolerant and people realize they have to be more careful with their words." In all-male units, he heard some of the most discriminatory language, largely against women. "So to me, the more diverse the unit, the more tolerant." He saw an explicit analogy between gays and women: "When they mixed females with males, they taught acceptance, so they could do the same with gays."[39]

A petty officer first class drew the very same conclusion from his experience in the navy. The sailor was deployed twice to the Persian Gulf since 2001, having joined the service in 1990. As a nuclear operator with a top security clearance, he spent time in both all-male units and mixed-sex units. "As the navy changes and allows women on combat ships," he said, "I have found that conversations have changed over the years. They're not quite as trashy toward women." Straight men, in particular, he reported, "are not as demoralizing toward women as they used to be because we work with them."[40]

Other service members echoed the importance of allowing gays and straights to get to know one another and speak freely. "I've had people come up to me who were dead set against [letting gays serve openly]," recalled one, "and then they found out I was gay and they changed their minds." Thus the policy, by keeping people in the dark about sexual orientation, breeds a culture of ignorance and prejudice, which perpetuates the anti-gay sentiment, which is then used to justify "don't ask, don't tell." Many people wrongly believe they are not even allowed to discuss the issue of homosexuality. This perceived gag rule on ordinary conversation and political expression erodes the opportunity to hear, contemplate, and weigh information about gay service. By contrast, in those situations where people knew they were allowed to discuss the policy, open debate prevailed. In a Marine Corps training office of six people, for instance, a service member reported that after a discussion of gay service, one person's opposition to letting gays serve evolved into support. "People in the office convinced him otherwise," he said.[41]

As these examples remind us, and as the study of foreign militaries reveals, the tone in the military is set by clear signals from the leadership and simple policies effectively communicated. "In the military," said an army JAG officer who deployed to Afghanistan while serving in the navy, "we learn to follow rules, and we promote what we're told to promote." She said that laws and policies send clear messages about what is and is not acceptable in the service. "The best thing you can do as a soldier or sailor is to stand up for what the military says is right." If the military said that gays and lesbians were welcome, it would have an enormous impact on attitudes toward them in the service. But "when the military is giving the message that there's something wrong and shameful about being gay, then we're also giving the message that to hate gays is acceptable." She also pointed out that the policy deprived people in the armed services of the opportunity to understand and come to accept all the people they're serving with. "If you're in the military, then you'll never be exposed to anyone who's gay unless they out themselves and you choose not to turn them in."[42]

Part of leadership is carrying out the prescribed training on existing rules, including the "don't harass" component of the policy. But leaders charged with training their subordinates on what the law says and how to enforce it have been missing in action, and their lackluster performance when they did go through the motions was the mark of those with a vested interest in the policy's failure. A gay senior noncommissioned officer in the air force said commanders ignored training on the policy, and, as a result, few people understood what the law said and required. "The first time young troops hear about 'don't ask, don't tell,' it's in basic training," he said. "And there's no refresher training at all." He noticed it was in the lesson plan but recalled that his instructor at Lackland Air Force Base said they would skip right over it. An army staff sergeant had much the same experience: "They're supposed to have annual training on the policy, but in eight years I had one. They don't follow their own policies." He said that, although the training is supposed to be a part of the policy, "because of the personal beliefs of some commanders, it doesn't happen. It's not something they like to talk about."[43]

Training does not have to be this hard. In fact, the Pentagon already has an office in place that would be a natural source of training and oversight to ensure that anti-gay harassment is taken seriously: the Defense Equal Opportunity Management Institute. Established in 1971 by the military to teach and enforce racial tolerance and cultural diversity, DEOMI's mission is to optimize "combat readiness by promoting human dignity through equity education, diversity, cultural competency, research, and consultation worldwide." The Pentagon could rather easily extend the sway of DEOMI to include tolerance of sexuality, an effort that would simply work to implement a policy—"don't harass"—that's already on the books, using an existing mechanism designed for this very purpose. But a representative from the institute has said they "do not teach courses relating to gayism."[44]

Indeed, the very leadership and training that turns a socially diverse population into a unified, cohesive fighting force centered around the task at hand is the same leadership and training that could be used to stigmatize and minimize anti-gay harassment. And it's not a one-way street, but a compromise. Starting in basic training, gays—like everybody else—learn they must not stand out; and at the same time, heterosexuals who might prefer not to serve with gays can learn that part of military service is enduring minimal privacy and even less choice over the people who live and work with them.

This, after all, is the purpose of basic training: to strip the prior identities of all recruits—Christians, Jews, and Muslims, Republicans, Democrats, and independents, urbanites and country folks, coastal ones and plains ones, older and younger, liberal and conservative, male and female, black, white, and other, and yes, gay and straight—and resocialize them by way of molding them into one effective fighting force. "A cadet training a basic cadet can be shorter, smaller, and of a different gender, but the basic is required to respect rank, no matter what," writes Reichen Lehmkuhl, an actor and model who publicized his experience as a gay air force cadet in a 2006 book. The point is to reduce individuals to nothing, break their identities, deprive them of sleep, frighten them, shatter them—until the only way they feel they can survive is to seek one another's help and support. Cadets quickly learn not to stand out; the only way to make it is to stand with the others.[45]

During Nunn's Senate hearings, William Henderson, a retired colonel who taught military psychology at West Point, had explained the crucial role of resocialization in boot camp, a process that is further evidence that combat readiness depends not on uniformity of prior cultural values but on the effective creation of task cohesion during intense military training. Referring to the core values of the soldier, he said that "when recruits come into the service, they do not come into the service with those values," but are put through an "intense resocialization" program to achieve those values and build loyalty to the group and its mission.[46] The idea of boot camp is to isolate and stress new recruits to such an extent that they yearn for the support of the group. This is the purpose, in part, of the intense schedule, lack of sleep, demanding physical requirements, and various other endurance tests that greet new members of the military. Anyone who has been through it understands its effect on the process by which a new group identity is formed with a sense of shared values that sets the group apart from anything outside or previously known.

And yet, somehow, champions of the gay ban want us to believe that tough young Marines will be able to endure every last slight, months of sleep deprivation, hazing so fierce it's caused litigation, and even the prospect of making the ultimate sacrifice, but they will wilt at the sight of a gay coworker?

These scant few minutes of passing through group showers to rid yourself of a day's or a week's grime, sweat, and worries are the site of all this drama, the source of U.S. senators' endless consternation that America's sons and daughters will not be able to survive if they know there are gays in their midst? The military can successfully eradicate the individual identities of these young people and create for them from the ground up a new persona as a Marine, a soldier, a sailor, an airman—but not if it includes standing in the same room with a known gay?

THE SILENCE REQUIRED by "don't ask, don't tell" has created untenable situations throughout the ranks, often made worse by abuses and violations of the policy. In 1998, Midshipman Robert Gaige, a member of Cornell University's Reserve Officer Training Corps (ROTC), wore a red ribbon in solidarity with AIDS victims, a gesture that is supposed to be entirely protected under the policy. When his instructor asked him about the ribbon, Gaige told him what it signified, prompting the response, "What are you, some kind of fucking homo?" His instructor, Major Richard Stickel, began to harangue Gaige, asking him about his sexuality in front of others and suggesting he was sexually involved with another cadet. These two are always working out together, said Stickel of Gaige and his workout partner, Mark Navin. "I don't know what else they do together," he sneered, "but we're not allowed to talk about it anyway."[47]

Having stoked rumors that Gaige was gay, Stickel encouraged others to join in the harassment. The perfect opportunity arose during summer training cruises when the ship was in port and it was time for sailors to pay a visit to the local brothel. Gaige, not surprisingly, opted out, spawning more suspicions and more questions. "Don't tell me you play for the other team, kid," said one shipmate, creating a moment when Gaige might have sought to end the raucous, divisive speculation once and for all if the rules hadn't barred him from saying, "Yes, I'm gay, what of it?" Instead, Gaige reluctantly agreed to visit the brothel, stepping into a room with a prostitute but refraining from sex. The experience was more than he thought he should have to take. Soon after, he acknowledged his sexual orientation and was fired.[48] His story, unfortunately, is common.

The fear created by a climate of threats, harassment, and insecurity could lead service members to behave in ways that ended their careers. During advanced training, Private First Class Gabrielle Butler was asked by a noncommissioned officer if she planned on "marrying a female." Shocked and unsure what to do, Butler took an unauthorized absence, worried that the sergeant

had learned of her homosexuality. Butler recalled that she "dreaded the possibility of an intrusive investigation, it getting back to my peers, or having
punitive actions taken against me." The experience was a wake-up call that
she would have to "live in constant fear of being 'found out' no matter how
discreet my private behavior." Though Butler returned to face the consequences of her unauthorized absence, her defense of her actions required her
to explain what caused her fear, which meant disclosing her sexuality. She
was subsequently discharged.[49]

The rules on security clearances, whether they were followed or flouted—
put service members in a double bind. SLDN found that security clearance
investigators both denied clearance to some people whose homosexuality was
revealed in the inquiry and threatened denial if they did *not* reveal their homosexuality.[50] These were clear violations of the policy. But even when no
abuse was taking place, gay and lesbian troops were damned if they did and
damned if they didn't: They were told to be honest about their sexual
orientation—after all, national security was at stake in these investigations—
they were also told to be honest with those close to them outside the military,
so as not to create a situation where they could be blackmailed. Yet if they
were honest with those at home, they risked discharge. Friends or family with
a score to settle could actually turn them in and prompt a discharge. Even
when they didn't, friends and family could be contacted by investigators
seeking wider evidence of homosexual conduct.

Sure enough, with no protection against the questioning of family members, troops have faced embarrassing, dangerous, and humiliating invasions
of family privacy. Those under investigation learned that their parents, sib-
lings, and partners were sought out for detailed questions about sexual orientation and past history. In an air force criminal investigation, investigators
even questioned a young child to find out if her father was gay. The mother of
a Marine Corps helicopter pilot was questioned about whether her daughter
had "a propensity to engage in homosexual behavior in the future." The pilot's chaplain was also contacted, despite promises of confidentiality for conversations with religious leaders. Trusting another chaplain for counseling
during the discharge process, the pilot was met with judgment and disdain.
She was called a "sinner" and told she needed to get help for her "un-Christian
tendencies."[51]

The rise of the Internet created new opportunities for the military to
needlessly and improperly invade the privacy of its members. Creating a profile on AOL to help meet other gay people could not, in a million years, harm
the morale or compromise the privacy of straight troops—unless they were

trolling the Internet to, well, meet gay people. Still, in late 1997, the navy decided it was fair game to ferret out Senior Chief Officer Timothy McVeigh (no relation to the Oklahoma City bomber), a seventeen-year career sailor and the senior enlisted member of a nuclear submarine, the USS *Chicago*. McVeigh had sent an e-mail to a shipmate's wife who, unsure of the sender's identity, looked up his profile on America Online. There she learned that one of his hobbies was "boy-watching." The woman showed her husband, who showed others in the navy, and eventually the news worked its way up the chain of command.

At this point, investigators sought and obtained private information from AOL, which later made a statement that it should not have provided the material but that the navy had "deliberately violated federal law" in seeking it out, a conclusion seconded by a federal judge, who stopped McVeigh's discharge and ruled that the "Navy went too far" and "violated the very essence of 'don't ask, don't pursue' [*sic*] by launching a search and destroy mission." McVeigh was allowed to retire with benefits intact and reached a financial settlement with America Online.[52]

Others were forced out through means never contemplated by the architects of "don't ask, don't tell." Alex Nicholson, who, as a kid watched his army father go off to duty in Saudi Arabia and Kuwait, already spoke four languages when he began his own army training as a human intelligence collector just days after the attacks of 9/11. One of Nicholson's languages was Portuguese, buffed from a recent relationship with a Brazilian man. Still in touch, he wrote a letter to his ex-boyfriend in Portuguese that he never thought would see the light of day. Unfortunately it spent a short time on his desk while awaiting completion and was seen by a friend of Nicholson's who knew enough Portuguese to decipher the letter and absorb its meaning. Nicholson thought little of it, unsure if his friend had had time and expertise enough to translate the letter. More important, he had little reason to expect she would care, much less spread the news around the base. He was wrong. A few weeks later he was called into a superior's office and notified that there was information that Nicholson was gay. The details mentioned by his commander came right out of the letter.[53]

Nicholson was told he could "go the easy way or go the hard way." If he didn't acknowledge he was gay and accept a discharge, he would be investigated. The climate at his training base in Arizona was generally tolerant, but a few people had problems with homosexuality and made it known. Nicholson worried that, even though discharges for homosexuality are normally honorable, if he contested the charges, vengeful superiors might seek to give him less than an honorable discharge. He decided not to contest, and was discharged on March 22, 2002.[54]

Nicholson loved his time in the army. But the policy, he said, is a monumental waste. "It's a very lonely existence to have to live in the closet like that and be in constant fear of someone finding out," he said. Because of that, many talented people leave early. And all for what? The people who are adamant against homosexuals in the military, he said, "are a minority." Those with the problems, those who engage in harassment, "are not usually the brightest in the bunch. They are usually troublemakers anyway. So you're choosing the rejects and outcasts and troublemakers over the gays and lesbians."[55]

DESPITE THE BLATANT violations of "don't ask," "don't pursue," and "don't harass," military spokespeople and champions of the ban frequently defend the policy by charging that most discharges result from people choosing to out themselves. If only they would abide by the regulations and keep quiet, ban supporters say, they could continue to serve without incident. This, after all, is precisely the point of the policy. Even many otherwise sympathetic Americans, people who don't like to think they discriminate and who don't consider themselves anti-gay, often feel it is fair to ask gays to conceal their homosexuality. The belief is widespread that, since sexuality is a private issue that should not be discussed in public, anyone who announces his or her homosexuality in the military is "just trying to get out of service."[56]

But the question is, what does it mean to tell? What drives a service member to tell? What kind of choice is involved in a "voluntary" statement?

Jennifer Dorsey offers one answer to these questions. In the summer of 1996, the airman came under suspicion that she was a lesbian by two women in her dorm who began to harass her. The ordeal climaxed when the bullies assaulted her in the bathroom, punching her repeatedly in the stomach, all the while yelling, "You sick fucking dyke." Dorsey had no choice but to report the incident, first to her master sergeant and then to her commander, Major Richard Roche. Instead of disciplining the two attackers, Major Roche told Dorsey that "if that's your lifestyle, you need to cease and desist." He threatened to launch an investigation if she didn't make the problem go away. So she went away: She made a "voluntary" statement that she was gay and left under a "don't ask, don't tell" discharge.[57]

This pattern has been repeated endlessly. A member of the Coast Guard was routinely accused of being gay; his coworkers called him "faggot" and "cocksucker," pasted pictures of male models to his rack, and vandalized his car. "If I ever find out for sure you're a fag," said one member of his unit, "I'll kick your ass." The victim had little recourse to end the torment besides leaving the Coast Guard. An inquiry officer in an air force investigation reported that an officer announced his sexuality "after he could not tolerate derogatory comments concerning homosexuals." A nineteen-year-old private first class in the army was called "faggot" by his drill sergeant, which prompted other unit members to tell him they'd "pound your face" and he should not "go to sleep tonight." They were no empty threats. "I have some bad news for you," the soldier found himself writing to his parents not long after. "I got beat up last night. Someone came to my bed—a group of someones—and they were hitting me with blankets and soap. I am aching all over my body. My whole body hurts. I can't tell anyone because they left no marks. Who'll believe me? I can't believe this all has happened. Who did I hurt?" He eventually told his command he was gay and was fired.[58]

On the same base, Fort Meade, Maryland, Airman Sean Fucci became the target of gossip that he was gay. One morning, he awoke to find a sheet of paper on his desk on which someone had scribbled, DIE FAG. Terrified, Fucci wondered whether he would face a discharge investigation if he reported the threat. With trepidation, he decided his safety was more important than his job and he told his commander what had happened without coming out as gay. It was, said his commander, "an issue of anonymous intimidation for which there is not much that can be done." Sure enough, Fucci was questioned by a superior about his sexual orientation, although no formal investigation followed. Fucci dug into his own pocket to pay for an apartment off base, where he felt his safety would be better assured.

But soon after, Fucci found another note, this one saying YOU CAN'T HIDE, FAG. After continued harassment, Fucci reported the events to higher-ups, who eventually opened an investigation into the threats. But to no avail; with Fucci still in the closet, he had to carefully watch what he said, and he ended up providing insufficient information for the search to go anywhere. The airman left the air force at the end of his enlistment. Fucci's decision to leave was voluntary, but was certainly not free from coercion—and his is a whole category of losses for the military that cannot be accounted for in the raw statistics that measure homosexual discharges.[59]

Fucci, at least, escaped with his life. Private First Class Barry Winchell was not so lucky. In 1999, an eighteen-year-old private named Calvin Glover, suspecting that Winchell was gay and encouraged by a permissive culture of homophobic harassment in the barracks, goaded Winchell into a fist fight.

Winchell (who was dating a transsexual at the time) won the duel, and the vanquished Glover suffered derision from peers for having "his ass kicked by a faggot."

What does it mean to lose a fist fight to a queer? Often, it means utter humiliation and quick emasculation. And in the aggressively masculine culture of the U.S. Army, it can mean shame deep enough to retaliate with the brutal murder of your victor. Aided by a friend who handed him the weapon and shared his outspoken hatred of homosexuals, Glover sought to avenge his shaken manhood. On July 5, 1999, Glover took a baseball bat to the bed of Winchell, twenty-one, and bludgeoned him to death as he slept. When Winchell was pronounced dead, his skull had been cracked open, his eyes swollen shut, and his face beaten beyond recognition. Glover was convicted of premeditated murder and sentenced to life in prison with the possibility of parole.

Winchell's murder was probably preventable. He had been the target of daily anti-gay taunting for months leading up to his murder. He was denounced as a "queer," a "faggot," and a "homo," and was repeatedly threatened with violence. Just two days before his murder, Winchell received a death threat in the presence of at least one noncommissioned officer.

Because of "don't ask, don't tell," Winchell feared expulsion if he complained about abuse, yet following the rules did him no good. Even as Winchell remained silent in accordance with the law, soldiers and officers flagrantly violated the policy by harassing and threatening Winchell, investigating his sexuality, and failing to enforce prohibitions against anti-gay abuse.

His own platoon sergeant, Michael Kleifgen, acknowledged in court testimony that he had asked Winchell directly if he was gay after hearing gossip that he might have attended a gay nightclub in Nashville. Kleifgen and others also testified that other superiors participated in the harassment on a regular basis and did nothing to stop the abuse. Kleifgen, perhaps remorseful over his own violations, later filed a complaint about a superior who called Winchell a "faggot." Kleifgen said he was told that "basically, there was nothing we could do because of the 'don't ask, don't tell' policy." Despite Kleifgen's taking his complaint all the way up to the inspector general's office, no action was taken.[60]

It is tempting to think of the Winchell case as a tragedy that can only be blamed on the young monsters who perpetrated the deadly violence. Crying "failure of leadership" can seem like a stab in the dark, an effort to blame something and someone official instead of accepting the unavoidable presence of bad apples in our midst. But the climate at Fort Campbell is actually an object lesson in how leadership fails and how politics and moralizing can turn deadly.

The leader responsible for the command climate at Fort Campbell was Major General Robert Clark. An army inspector general report released in July 2000 found that leadership at Fort Campbell under Clark was anemic. The base suffered low morale commandwide; its soldiers received inadequate health-care delivery; and leaders routinely allowed underage soldiers to drink to the point of intoxication while on base. The report noted rampant anti-gay harassment at Fort Campbell, homophobic graffiti, and a complete absence of training about the "don't ask, don't tell" policy. Soldiers reported that the platoon's daily run included the chant, "Faggot, Faggot, down the street, shoot him, shoot him, till he retreats." When the reports surfaced, Clark responded as though he were living in a different world: "There is not, nor has there ever been, during my time here, a climate of homophobia on post. The climate here is one that promotes just the opposite, respect for all."[61]

In the months following Winchell's murder, as hordes of gay soldiers bolted from Fort Campbell, often announcing their homosexuality just to avoid having to continue living on the base in fear, Clark remained indifferent to the command problems that led to the attack. He made no public indication of his distaste for what had happened to Winchell and no public directive discouraging such behavior among his soldiers. He did not attend the memorial service and he even refused to meet with Winchell's parents or offer them condolences, or discuss with them the plea bargain he cut, reducing one attacker's sentence from a possible life in prison to a twelve-and-a-half-year term. Winchell's parents received their son's personal effects in a cardboard box through the mail months after his death.[62]

Under Clark's leadership vacuum, anti-gay language and graffiti continued to be welcome on base. One soldier heard a peer threaten to beat perceived gays with a baseball bat while in the presence of a superior, who did nothing to correct the misconduct. Confronted with evidence of continuing anti-gay harassment under his command, Clark not only continued to remain silent, but refused to permit publication of an advertisement in the base newspaper instructing soldiers how they could anonymously report anti-gay abuse. Gay discharges tripled at Fort Campbell, reaching 120 in the first year after Winchell's murder, the highest number ever from an army base.[63]

Clark's story—that he himself was never aware of any problems with anti-gay harassment before Winchell's murder—was compelling to President George W. Bush, who felt the major general was doing a heckuva job. In 2002, President Bush nominated him to the Senate for promotion to lieutenant general, the army's third-highest rank. Over the objections of several senators—who caused a highly unusual delay in his nominating process—the Senate confirmed Clark's promotion in 2003.

We will never know what a true leader might have done to save Barry Winchell's life. But it is clear that Major General Clark's lack of leadership allowed a fatally anti-gay climate to fester at Fort Campbell. Clark not only failed to provide moral leadership; he refused to enforce federal law and provide a safe environment for all soldiers.

Winchell's murder was sandwiched in between the issuance of two Pentagon reports on the policy. In April 1998, the Defense Department issued its report. One finding of note focused on women, saying it was "critical that military women feel free to report sexual harassment or threats without fear of reprisal or inappropriate governmental response." It recommended that the department (i.e., itself) issue guidelines to make clear that complaints of harassment must not prompt an inquiry into the sexuality or behavior of the victim. But the Pentagon did not take its own recommendation—departmentwide guidelines were never sent to the field. This, even though guidelines had actually been written up years before; they were apparently gathering dust on the desk of the undersecretary of defense.[64]

Five months after Winchell's murder (and three months after Britain announced it would lift its ban on gay troops entirely), Secretary of Defense William Cohen ordered an inspector general report to evaluate anti-gay harassment in the service. The report, released in March 2000, finally acknowledged what some knew for years: that the military had an anti-gay harassment problem. Of seventy-five thousand service members surveyed, 80 percent said they had heard anti-gay comments in the past year; 37 percent said they'd witnessed or experienced anti-gay harassment; 85 percent said their superiors tolerated anti-gay harassment; and 57 percent said they were never trained on the "don't ask, don't tell" policy.[65]

In the wake of the report, the Pentagon formed a working group to devise an anti-harassment action plan (AHAP), which the Pentagon quickly adopted. The AHAP was promising. It acknowledged that the harassment and abuse found in the inspector general report undermined "good order and discipline." It offered guidelines for what constituted harassment and it provided for holding command violators (instead of only gay people) accountable for asking, pursing, and harassing.[66]

But there was a small problem: By the next year, the Pentagon, having adopted the plan, and dutifully drafted implementing directives, never issued them. Though the individual services took some steps to enact the plan, the Pentagon itself failed to do what its own plan required. Why the plan sat in a filing cabinet is unclear, but there it remained for four years. In response to a congressional inquiry, Undersecretary of Defense David Chu said a servicewide directive was "not necessary" because existing programs were "sufficient to address" the problem.[67] It was a remarkable punt from a Pentagon that made great inroads into the related problem of sexual harassment against women.

When the military brass decide to support a policy, they throw their weight behind it and ensure it is carried out to the best of their ability. This is what happened in the 1990s following the Tailhook fiasco, when the Pentagon decided it had no choice but to crack down on sexual harassment against women. With new tracking in place and increased accountability, episodes of sexual harassment plummeted from 1,599 in 1993 to 319 in the year 2000. Military leaders helped make sure of that by turning sexual harassment into "a career killer," as David Chu put it. At the Pentagon, said Chu, "we make sure that we enforce those standards."[68] When they want to.

8

A Flawed Policy at Its Core

S OME CHAMPIONS OF THE ANTI-GAY ban have tried to defend the "don't ask, don't tell" policy itself as fair and workable while chalking up its grave social, psychological, and military costs to poor enforcement and implementation.[1] Yet this perspective is woefully narrow, requiring nearly as much blindness as the policy itself. The unanticipated, often hidden costs of "don't ask, don't tell" are simply exorbitant, creating untenable situations for service members that reveal the utter incompatibility of silence and survival in the military. Heterosexuals are never asked to go through life concealing their sexual orientation, much less refrain from sex altogether, so they don't spend much time contemplating the astounding difficulty of doing either. But listen to the voices of gay and lesbian Americans who have served and fought under the ban. A picture begins to emerge of what this policy—even when properly enforced—requires of its troops and what effect these burdens have not only on gay troops but on heterosexuals and the entire armed forces.

A simple glance at the contents of the Servicemembers Legal Defense Network (SLDN) survival guide published for gay and lesbian service members is a powerful reminder of the string of unforeseen burdens the policy imposes on our troops: extra caution during room inspections, during phone calls, in online profiles, when receiving letters or magazines, during security clearance interviews and visits to doctors and psychologists, while filing insurance paperwork, and in any unexpected encounter with the law, civilian police, or during family or personal crises.[2]

When asked, gay and lesbian service members tell. They tell about the absurdity of trying to abide by the "don't ask" and "don't tell" clauses in the real world where subtle cues, cultural norms, and reading between the lines can make it literally impossible to refrain from asking or telling; they tell about being forced to lie to their peers; about isolating themselves from coworkers to avoid awkward moments and coming off as aloof and distant as a result; about enduring harassment against which they are unable to defend themselves; about shunning the support of clergy, mental health counselors, and doctors that all other troops are encouraged to use, especially during deployment to hostile territory; about choosing to end their tours early or decline additional tours because of the hostile climate created in "friendly" territory by this flawed policy. They tell how the policy affects their morale, their preparedness, their commitment to the military, and their overall ability to do their jobs. They tell what it's like to risk their lives alongside other soldiers in their unit while not being able to speak to these comrades about the most basic aspects of their personal lives. They recount the dramatic steps they sometimes take to avoid revealing information that everyone else spills without a second thought. And they tell what impact the ban has on the rest of the military—what it's like for heterosexuals to be forced to live, fight, and work alongside peers who are forbidden to be truthful with them.

As scores of these voices will show, it is not poor implementation but the policy itself that invites nonenforcement and abuse. Nowhere does the policy or its implementing regulations provide for the punishment of military members who *do* ask, *do* pursue, *do* harass. The policy does not even bar individual service members from asking others if they are gay. While the rules sharply limit investigations and the collection of evidence, evidence obtained improperly is nowhere disallowed.[3] That means commanders are, *by the terms of the policy,* free to ignore these limits and launch discharge procedures even if they've run roughshod over the privacy of service members. The policy is not only a failure because of poor enforcement; it is a failure because it is flawed at its very core.

THE COSTS OF "don't ask, don't tell"—even when it's running as designed—are everywhere apparent. While Aspin's policy memo had promised that religious conversations would be held in confidence, visits with psychologists and doctors are not protected by the letter of the law, a fact which Kevin Blaesing learned the hard way. The Marine corporal had some questions about sexuality that he wanted to discuss with a professional. Trusting a naval psychologist, he arranged a session for consultation. Fully aware of the rules, Corporal Blaesing was careful not to say anything that indicated he was, or even might be, gay. He simply asked questions. "I sat down and we discussed homosexuality in general—if you are gay, do you stay gay, how does that go along with being in the military," he explained. "I never made a statement of what my sexual orientation was." But even that was apparently too much. The naval psychologist turned him in and his commander ordered a discharge investigation, against the advice of military lawyers. Blaesing had been named Marine of the Quarter. "From my experience, I can tell you that this policy is a failure," he said. "It's like a mine field, and you're just wandering in this mine field because they don't advise you what the rules are. The military is basically waiting for you to step on that mine."[4]

Blaesing's ordeal is a reminder of the uncertainty and insecurity under which gay and lesbian troops must live, ever under the whim of their commanders. Blaesing's first commander, Ronald Rueger, chose not to pursue the allegations against him. The corporal had revealed "no inkling of homosexual conduct," and Rueger "felt the young fella gave us really good service." Since his contract would expire in a year, he "deserved to go all the way through." Blaesing thought he was safe. But suddenly Rueger retired and was replaced by Lieutenant Colonel M. J. Martinson, who said homosexuality brought shame to the Marines. He warned Blaesing that if he returned to the barracks, "I don't know what would happen." The military, said Rueger after he retired in 1994, is "five to 10 years behind" civilian society. "We need to catch up."[5]

The Blaesing case is also a dramatic illustration of one of the more hidden costs of the ban: restricted access to support services. Because there is no guarantee of confidentiality, many avoid seeking out these services even though they're considered vital during deployment. This pattern has been repeated countless times. Psychiatrists in the air force even reported that military physicians contributed to a hostile, anti-gay climate by their use of homophobic remarks, and that they had been directed by superiors not to provide mental health counseling on any matter related to sexual orientation—a shocking dereliction of duty in a nation that professes to do all it can to support its troops. As a result, the pursuit of gay soldiers in the air force has been particularly rampant. One psychologist forced an airman to choose between tending to his mental health and keeping his career, telling him that any revelation of homosexuality would be fair game for a discharge. For choosing his well-being, he was subjected to discharge proceedings. Astonishingly, an airman who spoke to his *civilian* psychologist about his private sex life faced discharge; a letter from the air force stated: "The evidence suggests you made statements to a civilian clinical psychologist that you had engaged in homosexual acts, had enjoyed a homosexual relationship, and had a 'basic' homosexual attraction."[6] While professional psychologists are supposed to be bound by ethical limitations on revealing information told to them in confidence, many are easily cowed when military officials appear at their doors or at the other end of a phone line asking questions about their patients. Too many, apparently, believe they have no choice but to turn their patients in.

The consequences of this reality can be disastrous. Fred Fox was an enlisted infantry soldier deployed to combat in Somalia during the infamous battle of Mogadishu that prompted President Clinton to withdraw troops following heavy U.S. casualties. Ten years later, Fox became an officer supporting Operation Iraqi Freedom and Operation Enduring Freedom. His time in the army was a valuable part of his life, but, for much of it, he struggled mightily with anxiety around trust and relationships, particularly feelings of anger and fear of violence—his own and that of others. By the end of his service in 2003, Fox was diagnosed with post-traumatic stress disorder (PTSD) by the Veterans Administration during out-processing. The tragedy was that he had been unable to speak openly with army counselors during his service. He had occasionally sought such help, but each time he was asked pressing questions about his inner life, he hesitated, and ended up lying about all the things that he really needed to say to address his vulnerable mental health. "I was asked if I was having problems with relationships," he said, which he was. "But it was easier just to say I'm not having any relationships rather than open up a whole avenue of other questions you can't respond to." Worst of all, it was impossible for Fox to parse whether his relationship problems were due to unresolved issues about his sexuality, the strictures of the policy, or some form of traumatic stress disorder, which in the military continues to be a source of shame, just like homosexuality. "Having spent twelve years in the Army denying my homosexuality, this was just one more thing that's easy for me to bury," he said of what he eventually learned was PTSD. "And this isn't something you want to bury, because then it becomes a bomb you've sort of hidden somewhere." "Don't ask, don't tell" just helped him repress his feelings further, which was not, Fox concluded, a recipe for mental health.[7]

The military provides substantial support services for its troops both stateside and during deployment: legal assistance, paid time off, life insurance, health care, death and burial benefits. There is also a large array of family support services, including chaplains, counseling, crisis assistance, personal finance management, spouse employment assistance, adoption expenses, and more. In addition, individual branches offer their own networks of support. For example, the navy's Morale, Welfare and Recreation (MWR) offers child development and youth recreation programs, educational benefits, medical care, housing, legal assistance, and an array of insurance options for sailors, spouses, and children. The army has long attracted recruits with its popular scholarships, loans, and other educational opportunities, and it also offers its own employment assistance, health care, civilian transition and relocation support, retirement benefits, and a variety of religious and psychological consultation services.[8]

These services are designed to make living, training, and combat conditions as appealing and stress-free as possible so as to maximize recruitment, retention, readiness, and combat effectiveness. Support services are also offered to families of service members both as added incentives for recruitment and to help relieve troop stress during deployment. The logic is that if troops can rest assured that things at home are taken care of, they will be less concerned with matters outside their training and combat missions and more able to focus on their military objectives.[9]

But gays and lesbians are routinely cut out of these support networks. When you don't feel at liberty to seek help, a central premise of readiness—troop support—is torn. And it's a burden that's dramatically worsened for troops who are deployed overseas, where they have no outside recourse to obtain support that they can't get from the military itself. There is a certain absurdity to this cost; it buys the military nothing but grief. The "don't ask, don't tell" policy is meant to shield the rank and file from gay service. But in reality, gay troops can effectively assess which peers to confide in and when to remain discreet. Instead, it's the military bureaucracy that soldiers must hide from: commanders, administrators, physicians, clergy—in short, those whose knowledge of a soldier's sexuality is least likely to be disruptive, and whose familiarity with his personal life is most essential to helping him prepare for the demands of war. The rationale for the gay ban was that it was needed to protect the comfort and privacy of young, enlisted men—not the administrative and professional support staff. What could the military possibly gain by keeping its service members from speaking candidly with the professionals who are there to ensure troop readiness?

In one of the most troubling cases to come to light, Captain Monica Hill, who joined the military in 1994 after winning an air force scholarship to medical school, learned in 2001 that her partner of fourteen years had developed lung cancer that had spread to the brain. Her prognosis was grim, and Hill requested a deferred report date so she could care for her dying partner. Hill explained the minimal details of her predicament that she deemed necessary to make her case a compelling one. When her request was received, it was met instead with an investigation into Hill's sexual orientation. The inquiry was hostile. Hill faced demeaning and invasive questioning about her sex life, and investigators' insinuation that she had sought the deferment only to get out of her service. After her partner died—on September 11, 2001—Hill was required to produce a death certificate to prove she had not made the story up. She was discharged on October 2, 2002, and the air force subsequently sought to force her to pay back the cost of her medical school scholarship.[10]

A related cost is the impact on morale and readiness of gay troops who cannot access the family support programs and networks that are offered to all other service members. Because it is a violation of policy to reveal that a service member's spouse or partner is a member of the same sex, gay and lesbian troops are banned from designating members of their family as beneficiaries of support, access, or even information. The statute also prohibits marrying or "attempting to marry" a member of the same sex, further precluding gay and lesbian service members from forming and designating recognized family units with access to support and services. Since phone calls and e-mails are often monitored for operational security, gay and lesbian service members report that they are not free to contact their partners without resorting to extraordinary means, including changing names and pronouns, writing or speaking in codes, or leaving the base to make phone calls. As the military well knows, family ties and communication with loved ones at home are the first line of recourse to ease the stresses borne by those deployed to combat. Not all service members enjoy such ties, but to have them and be barred from using them seems to be the height of senselessness.

Service members deployed to Iraq and Afghanistan have unfailingly cited these constraints as sources of stress. "We always had to be ready," explained a senior noncommissioned officer in the air force in 2004. "Before you hop on a plane" for a deployment, he said, "you hope you'll have peace of mind. That means having your personal affairs ready, such as a will, power of attorney, etc." But the officer said he could not put his partner's name in the will he had on file without risking raising a flag and prompting an investigation. And so he departed to the Middle East with the worry that if something happened to him, his partner would have no way of knowing about it because he could not be listed on the next-of-kin form. "This guy would have pretty much been left in the dark; he would have probably found out on the news," he said. For his second deployment, the two worked out a plan where they added an *e* onto the partner's name to make it look female while still remaining legally valid (in court, it could be chalked up to an error). "It was almost impossible to remain in the service and still be gay," the officer concluded, especially once he was deployed for war. "The DOD is cutting their own throats with this policy."[11]

As more gays and lesbians seek to have their relationships recognized in state marriages or civil partnerships, the situation for gay military families becomes even more strained. Any record of a marriage or civil partnership (which vary in name and form by state, among those that offer them) is publicly available and constitutes evidence of "homosexual conduct" under "don't ask, don't tell." Service members with dependents are actually required to inform the military, compelling the creation of paperwork that automatically puts their jobs at risk, particularly because adoption paperwork will list the second parent if there is joint custody.[12]

Service members are beginning to leave the military to avoid this double bind. This is just what Army Staff Sergeant Jeffrey Schmalz did in 2004 when Massachusetts legalized same-sex marriage. The problem is compounded as civilian society continues to speed past military policy. After Massachusetts legalized marriage, many companies eliminated the ad hoc benefits that had been offered under civil partnership laws, because they deemed them no longer necessary. This was an added incentive to get married. When Lieutenant Colonel Peggy Laneri took that step, she remained in the army and listed her new wife as a beneficiary of her military life insurance plan, putting at risk her job and future retirement benefits.[13]

Every time her paperwork surfaced, her heart skipped a beat. Ultimately, her decision to take an early retirement was prompted by the adoption of her daughter. Enrolling the child in the Defense Enrollment Eligibility Reporting System, the database that manages family benefit eligibility, would essentially out Laneri. Ditto Tricare, the military's vast health-care benefit program that offers everything from dental care to emergency medicine to service members, retirees, and dependents. Much of this care was offered on military base facilities. Just imagine the questions and risks that would attend walking your small daughter to a military medical facility on base. Meanwhile, if anything happened to Laneri in the military, her family would not be notified and would not get survival benefits. Faced with choosing between continuing her twenty-two-year military career and looking after the needs of her family, she retired in the summer of 2005 and became an executive coach. The cumulative package of benefits and protections that most military members take for granted is simply not available to gay military families. If children are involved, the scenario is even worse, as it not only forces military members to provide evidence of their homosexuality, but it can make the economics of having a family prohibitive.[14]

The army JAG officer who served in Afghanistan faced the same set of problems. Her command "made it a point" to encourage personnel to use support services that were available for significant others. But she and her partner could do no such thing. She could not designate her partner's name on the list that the ombudsman used to convey certain information to family members of deployed troops, such as their whereabouts, condition, and points of contact. "There was this whole network at home designed to help with significant others, and [my partner] couldn't do that because that would have outed me," she said. "Just to be on a mailing list would have raised eyebrows and could have gotten me kicked out."[15]

Captain Austin Rooke said he would not have considered availing himself of many of the support services available to straight troops in the army. "I never would have gone to clergy, to discuss anything about my particular issues with my sexuality," he said. "I might have, if I could have been open, but it was so far removed from anything that would have been an intelligent thing to do." He said he never would have brought up anything having to do with sexual health to a military physician, and instead had to use outside clinics.[16]

Rooke said that for any gay person who leaves the military, the policy is definitely part of their decision. "If the ban weren't there, it's quite possible that I could still be on active duty to this day," he said, adding that it was difficult to measure the true costs of the policy because many gay people leave prematurely because of the ban. Rooke's sentiment echoed remarks by many other service members. Wendy Biehl, a former army specialist who served in the Middle East, opted for a discharge when her tour ended, having decided that the policy did not allow her to be herself. "It's one of the reasons I got out of the military, because I wanted to be gay, I wanted to be openly gay," she said. "It became a big issue because the person I am now and the person I was in the military are two completely different people. I really wasn't happy and that became a problem for me."[17]

Brian Hughes agreed. Hughes was part of the U.S. Army Ranger team that rescued Jessica Lynch in 2003. The Ranger regiment is an elite infantry unit that is part of the Special Operations Command. Hughes took time off from Yale University to join the army in August 2000 and became a sergeant. In the fall of 2002, he was deployed to Afghanistan, where he did search patrols for personnel and weapons. He then cycled into Iraq for the start of Operation Iraqi Freedom, where he participated in the Lynch rescue. For Hughes, the policy meant he was not allowed to "bring your partner to events" and it precluded his partner from being able to "plug into support networks" that others took for granted. "When people ask me why I don't want to reenlist, I say because of the family life," he said.[18]

One service member reported that many gays grow to resent the military when they realize what they're being asked to do in order to serve. In preparing to go to war, he said, "some people have the sense: 'Why should I face that situation if I'm being dealt such a hard hand by the military?' Frankly a lot of gay people are driven to take advantage of the policy and to come out because of this. If the military is not going to let me form normal, happy, healthy relationships," he asked rhetorically, "if they're going to discriminate against me, why should I fight for this institution and risk death?" This conclusion was seconded by a sailor who deployed to Iraq, and reported that "a lot of people are getting out" by exploiting the policy. "They don't want to be there." An officer with an air force expeditionary unit in the Middle East echoed this report, saying "a lot of the people who were voluntarily identifying as gay were [doing so] with the full knowledge that they were going to be discharged."[19]

After nearly eight years of service and a deployment to Bosnia and Afghanistan, in which he slept in the same safe houses as British troops who are allowed to serve openly if they are gay, Brian Muller knew he had done his best to conform to the policy. The army staff sergeant was trained in counterterrorism and bomb assessment. He had celebrated his eighteenth birthday in Bosnia. He had been to war, and had twenty-one medals to show for it. His commander knew he was gay—he'd guessed as much and there had been some third-party disclosures to that effect over the years. This seemed not to be a problem. But Muller had heard other commanders say, "All fags should get AIDS and die," and, as he strove to continue service while maintaining a forbidden relationship, he felt the burden grow. So he came out. "I'd done everything I could do in the military," he recalled. "People couldn't say I was trying to get out of war because I had gone to war, so for me, it was a principle." He was also tired of not being able to be with his partner. But equally important, he was driven to leave by fear and uncertainty about the policy. "My fear was that they'd discover it and I'd be dishonorably discharged," he said.[20]

Despite successfully serving as an out gay man, Robert Stout, like too many soldiers fighting in Iraq, had a life-altering experience during his tour that made him think twice about the institution to which he gave so much. A twenty-three-year-old army combat engineer from Utica, Ohio, Stout was out to most of his twenty-six-member platoon, which served in Iraq as part of the 1st Infantry Division's 9th Engineer Battalion, based in Schweinfurt, Germany. "Almost everyone I know is supportive and handled it just fine," he said. "I have never seen someone refuse to work with a soldier based on his or her being gay or straight. People forget that we are a family in the Army. We stick by each other no matter what. You can really see that after a long deployment."[21]

The platoon's job was to sweep roads and forward operating bases in order to locate IEDs and roadside bombs. The task was vital to securing the battleground for fellow soldiers. The idea of route clearance is to scan the area for attacks on fuel and supply convoys. Soldiers look for dead vegetation, which can indicate the presence of chemicals used in an IED, or for fresh mounds of dirt that suggest the recent burial of an explosive device. Once such devices are located, soldiers either destroy the explosives themselves or cordon off the area and call in the Explosives Ordnance Disposal (EOD) team. The EOD teams had no room to mount machine guns on their trucks, so they had to be escorted and protected by the 9th Engineers.[22]

In early May 2004, Stout was made a gunner, the soldier mounted atop a Humvee with a .50-caliber machine gun. It's one of the most dangerous spots in all of Iraq. Within his first week, his platoon got a call from the squadron. A suspicious truck had been found in the rebel stronghold of Ad Duluiyah, less than an hour north of Baghdad, and troops were needed to determine if it contained explosives. Stout strapped on his night vision goggles, mounted his M1114 uparmored Humvee, and drove through the town of Ad Duluiyah to assess the threat. The truck was abandoned and no bombs were found. All sighed with relief.[23]

But they weren't out of danger yet. Stout was in a rear vehicle, doing security patrols, scanning out to his right, when suddenly, from his left, someone began firing. Before anyone had time to fire back, a rocket-propelled grenade slammed into the Humvee, just above the left rear tire. The RPG detonated and went through two plates of armor and the steel piping that attaches the weapons mount to the top of the vehicle. "It shot through it like butter," Stout recalled.[24]

The blast blew his night vision goggles off. Suddenly, Stout couldn't see or hear. His face felt completely wet. He managed to squeeze himself out of the vehicle. It was then he noticed a large wedge of shrapnel lodged in his arm and bits peppered in his legs and neck. His vision and most of his hearing came back in a matter of hours, but his ears continued to ring. Stout was sent to Germany for surgery to remove the biggest chunks of metal from his arm, but his injuries were superficial enough to allow for his return to duty by July of that year. In fact, while he was in recovery, his tour was extended by stop-loss.[25]

Stout's injury changed him. "I'm a lot more assertive now and no longer see the need to stand idly by and let the world go by," he said the year after his ordeal. "It has changed me to the point where I am no longer scared of day-to-day life. There is nothing the army can do to me that is worse than what happened that night, and I now know what it is like to be truly afraid." Emboldened, fearless, with three combat tours under his belt, three Army Achievement Medals, a Good Conduct Medal, and now a Purple Heart for the shrapnel shards still lodged in his limbs, Stout decided it was no longer his duty to serve

his country in silence. If he could expose himself to the enemy and take incoming fire in order to secure the battleground for his fellow soldiers, then he
would insist on being at least as open to the fellow soldiers whose recognition
he had earned in his service to them and the country. What sense did it make
for him to remain silent when most of his platoon already knew he was gay?
"We can't keep hiding the fact that there's gay people in the military and they
aren't causing any harm," Stout thought.[26]

Stout made headlines in April 2005 as the first gay wounded soldier to
come forward during the Iraq War. He announced that he would reenlist, but
only if he could be honest. His story quickly spread throughout the Internet
and landed on the editorial pages of major papers, including *The Washington
Post*. When a photographer from *The Advocate* called his base in Germany
for permission to take photos on post, Stout's battalion commander called
him in and asked him to sign a letter stating he would stop speaking with the
media. But by then it was too late. His story was already public. Eventually, an
agreement was reached for Stout to sign a form saying he would not (further)
violate the "don't ask, don't tell" policy, which meant he must stop talking
about his sexuality, not have sex, and not marry or attempt to marry a man as
long as he remained in the military. By signing the agreement, Stout was allowed to serve out the remaining weeks of his contract until his tour expired.
Stout said gays and lesbians routinely leave early because of the policy. "I
know a ton of gay men that would be more than willing to stay in the Army if
they could just be open," he told reporters. "But if we have to stay here and
hide our lives all the time, it's just not worth it."[27]

What is particularly damaging about the talent loss is that the older and
more senior a service member becomes, the more difficult it is to serve without explaining the details of one's personal life. It is often expected that officers and other senior personnel will be married and will attend social events
designed to encourage comradery and identification with the force. The gay
policy's gag rule and its ban on homosexual relationships make it uniquely
difficult for people with senior positions to attend such events and maintain
normal ties with their peers, since they face increased scrutiny about whether
they have a spouse or why they have not shown up with a date. And the more
time a soldier has invested in a military career, the more she has to lose if
she's suddenly rooted out. The result is that the most experienced, highly
trained, and skilled gay service members have a greater incentive to leave the
military because of the risks and requirements of serving silently.

"I'm getting up in age there," said a senior noncommissioned officer in the
air force, "and they're asking me, 'Hey, where's your girlfriend? Where's your

wife?' and I say, 'She's away, she has a very prestigious job, she couldn't be here.'" He said the policy stifles innovative thinking by discouraging experienced personnel from building a career in the military. Plum jobs, he said, would prompt close scrutiny of his files and many detailed questions, and being an apparent bachelor would count against him in promotions, as it might seem to suggest instability. And when people take visible jobs that put them in charge of many subordinates, others routinely try to fix them up with dates. "You can only duck a blind date so many times," he said, and "lies are very hard to juggle; it's hard to keep the story straight." Often, it just didn't seem worth it.[28]

A captain in the air force reserves said that at age thirty-five people are expected to have a "traditional" family. Seemingly harmless questions, which reflect a "genuine interest in getting to know" one another, follow accordingly. "Don't tell" disqualifies him from participating in these forms of socializing: "When I find myself in a discussion regarding personal experiences," he said, "I often stay silent or don't add much to the conversation in order to avoid those uncomfortable moments. If I have to think very carefully about each word I say, then I'd rather say nothing at all." As a result, "I've earned a reputation for being all business, hard-nosed and very difficult to get close to. This is an accurate description; however, it's not by choice. The military has forced me to become this person."[29]

Rear Admiral Alan Steinman served in the Coast Guard for twenty-five years, retiring in 1997 at the age of fifty-two. In 2003, he became one of the three highest-ranking military officers to reveal he was gay, in an article in *The New York Times*. Steinman had graduated from Stanford University School of Medicine and served the Coast Guard as a flight surgeon. Eventually, he became the top doctor of the Coast Guard, overseeing the entire medical establishment of the force. The position earned him the prestigious Coast Guard Distinguished Service Medal. But to land where he did, he had to close off an enormous part of himself. "I was denied the opportunity to share my life with a loved one, to have a family, to do all the things that heterosexual Americans take for granted," Steinman said. "That's the sacrifice I made to serve my country." Steinman knew that if he wanted to make admiral in the Coast Guard, he would surely need to have a companion—but of course that person would have to be a woman. So he placed an advertisement in the personals section of the *Washingtonian*, an upscale magazine. The ad caught the eye of Mureille Key, a widow who used to look through the personals section because she found them amusing. "Gay businessman looking for social partner," it read. She called, they met and hit it off, beginning a long friendship of many years, in which the two appeared at Coast Guard functions together. They didn't have to lie; generally, no one asked and they didn't tell. But it was a mark of the extraordinary lengths to which gay service members often have to go to have a career in the armed forces. Steinman was willing to make this enormous sacrifice for a career serving his country. "I loved the Coast Guard," he said, "and I loved what I was doing. But the price for that was I could not be who I knew I was." Not everyone is willing to bear that burden. Giving up a family, living a life of secrecy, suppressing the human desire that lies in us all, these are what Steinman called "the tragedies of 'don't ask, don't tell.'" And he added that "a lot of our younger generation doesn't want to pay that price."[30]

This was especially true in the years after September 11, 2001, when the military needed them the most. It wasn't that younger people were less willing to sacrifice. They simply had less and less experience living in the closet and they increasingly believed—correctly so—that crawling inside one to appease some three-star general from a bygone era was utterly unnecessary. They also saw firsthand the damage this policy was doing not only to careers but to the military itself. In Afghanistan and Iraq, gay troops described long hours of down time, even in combat zones. People would talk informally and discuss friends, family, and other personal matters. During these moments of social bonding, some gay troops had to censor themselves, remain silent, or opt out of conversations altogether. The result was that these troops were seen as uncaring or uninterested. They were compelled to shut down in an environment in which forming close bonds was encouraged.[31]

"It can't be all business all the time," said the army JAG officer. "You have to be able to talk about your life, you have to be able to bond with the people, and I could never do that." An enlisted man said that in some units, he felt comfortable enough to come out to most of his coworkers. But when he was in a unit where people did not know his sexuality, "it makes it harder to form interpersonal relationships to the point where people can go to war together."[32]

One petty officer first class in the navy explained the added strains created by "don't tell," the gag rule of the policy. "If I have to sit there and hide my life," he said, "that is stressful. Because people talk: When you're at work, do you sit there and talk about work all the time? When I can't sit there and talk about my life and my family, it does get stressful." The sailor recounted a rumor that circulated after he was spotted in a Starbucks with his civilian boyfriend. The next day at work on the ship, it was reported that they had been holding hands, which was untrue. Wishing to confront people and correct the record, the sailor opted instead to lay low so as not to draw attention to himself in a matter relating to sexuality. The silence took a toll. "Their closed minds just make me into a very impersonable person here at work," he said.[33]

A senior noncommissioned officer in the air force who has served for eighteen years said the squadron is like a family, which serves as a support group away from home. "If you can't be yourself or reveal too much about yourself, you're still going to be odd man out," he said. A senior airman said she avoided get-togethers with coworkers for fear of battling awkward moments in conversation: "That's like your family when you're [deployed], so if you can't be open with them and trust them, it's kind of like you're out there by yourself." Because of the gag rule, "you don't really have anybody to talk to."[34]

An enlisted service member elaborated on how the policy can compromise the development of trust between people in a unit. "A great deal of military service is being able to trust people around you," he said, "being able to be comfortable enough around them that you can trust someone with your life. Having to conceal something like this can make you doubt the personal bonds and professional bonds that you have with people."[35]

A navy lieutenant studying aeronautical engineering at the Air Force Institute of Technology observed a similar problem. He said the ban "ends up driving more of a wedge [between gays and straights] than really helping." The policy, in his view, "makes very sharp distinctions . . . but if everyone were able to be out, there wouldn't be such sharp distinctions." As a result of the policy, "I don't socialize as much with the people I work with because I can't be out to them, and that's not good for cohesion." If he were able to be out, he said, he would probably socialize more with his peers, which is especially important among officers in the squadron, who function "like your little social group." He called the ban "detrimental" and said it was exhausting to keep up appearances and pretend to be interested in women on a regular basis. The lieutenant was out to over a dozen other gay sailors, but was never sure whom he could trust, and worked and lived with the daily fear of being revealed. "It makes it a little bit more sane for my state of mind that there are a few people who know and you don't have to be secret from everyone," he said.[36]

The policy's damage is not restricted to gays and lesbians. By requiring that gay people conceal basic information about themselves, it institutionalizes the presence of dishonest troops; service members know that people in their midst are misleading them. Imagine trying to build a cohesive fighting force while effectively announcing to recruits that they are serving with people they cannot trust. "It's a forced lack of integrity on your part," said a lower enlisted service member. "If you're living a lie," your comrades "are not trusting you, they're trusting a picture of you that you put in their head."[37]

A surgical technician in the navy said it was more important to be "true to [people] at the origins," so they would not find out later and feel deceived. "I think it would bother them more if you say you're straight and they find out you're gay and feel like you should have let them know before," he said. He explained that some people who remain intolerant of homosexuality prefer to know who is gay so they can feel better able to protect their privacy. He added that the requirement to conceal sexual orientation can distract gays and lesbians from their mission: "I think it hurts the unit itself if you don't tell who you really are because if you can't focus on what you need to focus on because you have other things in your head, then you're wasting time because you're not putting 100 percent into it."[38]

The army JAG officer explained how "don't tell" shortchanged not only gays and lesbians, but her straight coworkers. "One of the ways I concealed was to become more detached, more cold, which is not a good thing in the military because we're supposed to be laying our lives down for one another," she said. "It's so ingrained in military culture to bond on a social level that it takes away a fundamental stress release and a fundamental bonding experience to have to hide who you really are. Either you become a cold, detached person or you're a liar. It's such a disservice to do that to other service members."[39]

Austin Rooke, who was trained in counterintelligence, echoed that the policy burdens not only gay troops but members of the force at large. Rooke came out to a few coworkers to a very positive response. But when friends of gay troops know of a soldier's homosexuality, either through a direct acknowledgment or through informal signs, statements, and innuendo, the straight service members become accomplices. "When you come out to someone," Rooke said, "you put them in an uncomfortable position, you burden them, because they now have knowledge that you are serving illegally." This means gay troops are forced to choose between bonding effectively at the cost of burdening their comrades and shutting down as the cost of effective bonding. Rooke said that when he was stationed in Qatar, the gag rule "definitely prevented me from feeling like I could make a connection with the people I was working with." He struggled with whether or not to come out to his roommate, who he thought might be accepting but who had apparently not been exposed to many gays before. He decided not to tell him he was gay, but recalled a need to have "that kind of human connection when I was away from my support network."[40]

Many people do not initially appreciate what the policy will require them to do throughout the duration of their service. As one soldier explained, the policy prohibits gays from revealing or discussing their sexuality even to one another, depriving them of one of the essential sources of support—which other members of minority groups enjoy. He went further, saying the ban effectively hampers all kinds of bonding among members of the same sex. "We're not allowed to experience any sort of relationship with people of the same gender," he said, including nonsexual intimacy, which could raise suspicions. "It requires a conscious effort to avoid the situation where that [sexual orientation] would come up," said another, "or it requires outright deception."[41]

But in addition to the misguided rationale for the "don't ask" and "don't tell" clauses of the policy, the very concepts are, upon careful thought, nonsensical. "There is no such thing as 'don't ask,'" said the army JAG officer, or "don't tell" for that matter, because the most basic conversations entail questions about friends, lovers, spouses, and family that, if answered fully and honestly, could reveal one's sexual orientation. Another soldier pointed out that "don't tell" is never a genuine option. "Using the policy in defense to not answer the question is basically the same as admitting guilt."[42] And even when soldiers faithfully follow the law, it is rarely fully under one's control to totally conceal one's sexual orientation, since unconscious codes, signals, and mannerisms frequently mark a person or raise suspicions, thus giving a form of knowledge to straight soldiers who do not know what to do with it.

This difficulty of defining what it truly means to "ask" or "tell" lies at the root of endless problems with the policy. The law requires a discharge (subject to the notorious rebuttable presumption) when a service member "has stated that he or she is a homosexual or bisexual, or words to that effect," leaving a gray area in the definition of "tell." As we've seen from the string of earlier examples, such action need not be verbal or explicit. One sailor in the Pacific Fleet, for instance, had a female friend in the navy who saw him looking at an attractive guy and said, "I saw you looking." He blushed and said, "Please don't tell him." From that point on, the two interacted honestly as friends, sharing their attractions to men. Did she ask? Did he tell? Another sailor explained the difficulty of concealing sexual orientation even if one conforms to the silence provision: "Some people can just figure things out, especially if they're from the more liberal states like California, places where they may have been around gay people before." A senior noncommissioned officer recounted one individual who "didn't really have any choice but to be openly gay, because he was very effeminate." The officer said, however, that he was "treated with dignity and respect," a result he attributed to the service member's effort to "always go above and beyond and do the best job possible."[43]

Of course, you don't have to be a liberal from California to be able to figure out which of your coworkers might be gay. Senator John McCain, who aggressively grilled gay soldiers and sailors from his seat on the Senate Committee on Armed Services at Nunn's hearings, said controversially during his 2000 presidential run that he served in the navy with gay men, but he was never told they were gay. How did he know? "Well, I think we know by behavior and by attitudes. I think that it's clear to some of us when some people have that lifestyle."[44]

"DON'T ASK, DON'T tell" is a farce. It is a policy based on ignorance, denial, and deception. Even if it had been properly understood and enforced throughout the ranks, this policy and the spirit behind it would have caused heightened confusion, harassment, deception, mistrust, unit unrest, impaired bonding, and wasted talent. But the reality is that it was not properly enforced. Leaders at all levels (although certainly not all leaders) simply refused to cooperate with the spirit of the Clinton policy: to allow gays and lesbians who kept their identities private to enter and continue to serve in the military. For years, this policy has gone shamelessly unenforced. But it is also unenforceable at its core, relying as it does, on artificial and superficial lines between knowledge and ignorance, conduct and status, utterance and silence. And to the extent that the policy has been run as planned, the damage to service members and the military has been immense. The policy increases stress, lowers morale, impairs the capacity of both gay and straight troops to form trusting bonds with one another, restricts access to support services, and creates a culture of indiscipline by mandating behavior that is virtually impossible to enforce.

9

Brain Drain: Arabic Linguists

ON SEPTEMBER 10, 2001, the U.S. government intercepted two phone calls placed from Afghanistan between Al Qaeda operatives. "Tomorrow is zero hour," said one of the voices. "The match is about to begin," came another ominous line. The National Security Agency intercepts millions of messages every hour, but these calls came from sources deemed to be high priority. They were, of course, spoken in Arabic, so they made their way to a translator's queue, waiting to be interpreted. Unfortunately, in the fall of 2001 our government did not have enough Arabic linguists to translate the messages quickly. The phone calls were not translated until two days later, on September 12, 2001. It was two days too late.[1]

The terrorist attacks of September 11, 2001, changed everything. Almost immediately, a national consensus emerged, if only briefly, that nothing should stand in the way of true reform of the nation's broken intelligence apparatus. Nothing should stop a thorough and efficient reorientation of our national security perspective, which must immediately be geared toward fending off future terrorist attacks. Nothing, that is, except letting gays in uniform take part in the fight. The story of the ongoing purges of gay soldiers, sailors, airmen, and Marines with language skills critical to waging the war on terrorism pits political expediency and moral dogma against national security, social scientific research, and common sense. It is a story that shines a spotlight on certain truisms that Americans seem to grasp only when it's too late, and then to promptly forget until the next time it's too late: that prejudice is generally self-defeating rather than productive, and that it nearly always has unexpected consequences. But it's a story that should also be told with the hope—perhaps against our better judgment—that maybe this time we will learn from our mistakes, reorder our priorities, and face significant truths before we further compromise the security of our citizens and the safety of our troops.

THE SHORTAGE OF language specialists in the intelligence and military forces has been hobbling national defense since the days of the cold war. But between the fall of the Berlin Wall and the fall of the World Trade Center, the focus of the armed forces and the intelligence agencies was mainly on Russian language fluency as the essential skill for keeping the country safe from its enemies. Some students had begun to grasp the significance of the Arab world. The number of enrollees in Arabic language courses in colleges and universities nearly doubled between 1998 and 2002, but it wasn't nearly enough. The month before the 9/11 attacks, the University of Maryland's National Foreign Language Center warned that the country "faces a critical shortage of linguistically competent professionals across federal agencies and departments responsible for national security."[2]

Less than a month after the attacks, a House Intelligence Committee report criticized the nation's three intelligence agencies—the FBI, the CIA, and the National Security Agency (NSA)—for relying on "intelligence generalists" rather than linguists with expertise in a specific foreign language, culture, and geographical area. The report concluded that "at the NSA and CIA, thousands of pieces of data are never analyzed, or are analyzed 'after the fact' because there are too few analysts; even fewer with the necessary language skills. Written materials can sit for months, and sometimes years, before a linguist with proper security clearances and skills can begin a translation." Meanwhile, the intelligence agencies poured funds into advertisements, including Internet marketing overseas, to try to lure linguists into the fight against terrorism.[3]

By the fall of 2002, one year after the attacks, CIA director George Tenet warned that the United States faced a terrorist threat every bit as grave as it did before 9/11. A week later, the Council on Foreign Relations issued an even more sobering report. Despite bipartisan support for intelligence reform, backed by overwhelming public demand for addressing unpreparedness, the study found that "America remains dangerously unprepared to prevent and respond to a catastrophic terrorist attack. In all likelihood, the next attack will result in even greater casualties and widespread disruption to American lives and the economy" than those wrought by 9/11. During the first year of the war in Afghanistan, the United States had sixty-nine intelligence teams on the ground but had a 75 percent shortfall of daily intelligence reports. This meant that no matter the number of troops sent into foreign territory, and despite the billions of dollars being thrown into our military campaigns, a full three-quarters of the data collected about the looming threats from our enemies was not getting processed. A major obstacle to producing the reports, according to an assessment by the Center for Army Lessons Learned at Fort Leavenworth, was the shortage of Arabic speakers.[4]

The problem was not confined to intelligence agencies, but was felt in the armed forces, too. In 2002, the army reported, it could only find forty-two of the eighty-four Arabic linguists it was seeking to hire. In addition to this 50 percent shortage of Arabic experts, it faced a 68 percent shortage of Farsi translators and a 37 percent shortage of Korean experts. According to a GAO study released the same year, the army, along with the FBI, the State Department, and the Commerce Department, failed in 2001 to fill all their jobs that required expertise in Arabic, Chinese, Korean, Farsi, or Russian. The army reported that the "linguist shortfalls affect its readiness to conduct current and anticipated military and other missions." It said, for instance, that it lacked the linguistic capacity to support the prosecution of two major wars at one time, the baseline requirement of American military planners since the end of the cold war. The GAO study concluded that staff shortages at these agencies "have adversely affected agency operations and compromised U.S. military, law enforcement, intelligence, counterterrorism and diplomatic efforts." And it stated that shortages in language expertise resulted in "less timely interpretation and translation of intercepted materials possibly related to terrorism or national security threats."[5]

Two years after 9/11, the situation had not improved. The shortage of Arabic speakers had become so desperate by 2003 that one of the top Arabic speakers in the Iraqi theater was being used to translate a common housekeeping exchange, taking him away from the critical duties needed to keep U.S. troops safe, mine the Iraqi desert for intelligence, and win over Iraqi civilians. On several occasions, the impact of the shortage was downright treacherous. In the summer of 2003, the Wedding Island Bridge in Baghdad was the site of an explosion targeting U.S. troops. The soldiers, part of the 40th Engineer Battalion of the 2nd Brigade of the army's 1st Armored Division, had crossed the bridge repeatedly in search of their translator. If the army had been able to hire and retain enough of its own translators, it would have made unnecessary these perilous trips, which ended this time with a land mine explosion that sent shrapnel and bits of road into the windshield and body of the engineers' Humvee. It also might have prevented tragedies before they occurred. An Arabic document was reportedly found in Kabul before the murder of journalist Daniel Pearl, describing a kidnapping plot strikingly similar to the one that ended in his disappearance and murder. It was never translated because of the shortage of Arabic speakers.[6]

An army report released that year by the Center for Army Lessons Learned at Fort Leavenworth, Kansas, found that "the lack of competent interpreters throughout the theater impeded operations" in Iraq and Afghanistan. "The US Army does not have a fraction of the linguists required." The report of the 9/11 Commission concluded that the government "lacked sufficient translators proficient in Arabic and other key languages, resulting in significant backlog of untranslated intercepts." The secretary of Homeland Security, Tom Ridge, pleaded that "we need more Arabic-speaking analysts." A Pentagon advisory panel reported in 2004 that the United States "is without a working channel of communications to the world of Muslims and Islam." A Justice Department inspector general report that same year found that the government "cannot translate all the foreign language counterterrorism and counterintelligence material it collects," largely because of inadequate translation capabilities in "languages primarily related to counterterrorism activities" such as Arabic and Farsi.[7]

In response, President Bush ordered a 50 percent increase in intelligence officers trained in "mission-critical" languages such as Arabic. But the shortage was a problem that could not be cleared up overnight—precisely the reason that preparedness was so important. Despite tens of thousands of responses to post-9/11 calls for more Arabic speakers to join the government's intelligence efforts, actual hires take time, especially for those positions that require security clearances. Background checks can take six months to a year. By the spring of 2005, Senator Pat Roberts, the Kansas Republican who chaired the Senate Intelligence Committee, said the United States still had a "broken system."[8]

THE U.S. MILITARY is the most powerful fighting force in the history of the world. Its troops are trained to crush the enemy with the sheer strength of superior technological might. Yet the success of these missions relies on one prime ingredient: intelligence. On the tense streets of Baghdad; in the Sunni strongholds of Ramadi and Falluja, still seething with anti-Western resentment from the errant bomb dropped by a British plane during the first Gulf War; and in the restive outposts of Mosul, where insurgents have mastered the use of car bombs, roadside bombs, and rocket-propelled grenades against American forces, nothing is more vital to staving off casualties and ultimately winning the war than information culled from Arabic-speaking natives. Without it, commanders and their troops are crippled in their efforts to protect American forces, plan attacks against the enemy, and earn the trust and aid of Iraqi citizens. Poor, faulty, or inadequate intelligence plays straight into the hands of guerrilla tactics, as the ignorant behemoth staggers about in the shadows, sets up camp in oblivion, or accidentally strikes civilian targets, further alienating the people whose assistance is critical to winning the war. The astounding amount of money the United States invests in its campaigns and the volume of soldiers risking their lives mean little without knowing when and where and how to deploy.

IN THE MIDST of this confusion, what the nation needed more than anything was Ian Finkenbinder. In 2003, Finkenbinder served an eight-month combat tour with the army's 3rd Infantry Division, which spearheaded the invasion of Iraq with its "thunder run" to Baghdad. He was tasked with human intelligence gathering, one of the most critical ingredients in the effort to battle the deadly Iraqi insurgency. His job was to translate radio transmissions, interview Iraqi citizens who had information to volunteer, and screen native speakers for possible employment in translation units. His efforts were essential to keeping U.S. soldiers safe and winning support from civilians on the streets of Iraq.[9]

Finkenbinder was a rare and coveted commodity. Having attended the army's elite Defense Language Institute at the Presidio of Monterey, he graduated in the fall of 2002 with proficiency in Arabic just as the United States was scrambling to fill dire shortfalls of linguists. After receiving the Army Commendation Medal while in Iraq, as well as the Good Conduct Medal and the Army Achievement Medal, Finkenbinder finished his tour and returned to his unit's base at Fort Stewart, Georgia. There he was confronted with a "moral and personal question," as he put it, and a practical one as well: Could he continue to serve an institution that discriminated against him? Finkenbinder was gay; and though he had done all he could to follow the rules, his life under "don't ask, don't tell" was becoming untenable. He loved the army, but as a linguist training in the intelligence community, he had become accustomed to serving amid educated, tolerant people. The atmosphere at Fort Stewart was different. He got wind of people gossiping about his sexuality. Because of "don't ask, don't tell," he knew he could not confront them and had no recourse with the chain of command. It was a paralyzing, demeaning, and worrisome experience. "I reached the point where I couldn't live under fear of retribution," he recalled. So in 2004, he wrote a letter to his commander stating that he would continue serving so long as he could be openly gay.[10]

In January 2005, the 3rd Infantry became the first army unit to cycle back into Iraq since the war began in March 2003. Finkenbinder stayed behind, having received an honorable discharge for Christmas. His commander was distraught, but his hands were tied by "don't ask, don't tell"; he was required to initiate discharge proceedings once Finkenbinder had announced he was gay. "There was definitely a feeling of, 'we could really use you,'" Finkenbinder recalled of the moment when his commander learned he would not be staying with the unit. "I was an Arabic linguist, and those are pretty valuable over there."[11]

More damning than Finkenbinder's particular story is the number of similar stories that have piled up since the policy took effect. And they were not stories that the military wanted to share. The firing of gay Arabic language specialists during the war on terrorism is a particularly stark illustration of the gay ban's costs to national security, so it's no surprise that the Pentagon has not been forthcoming about the number of linguists fired. In 2004, when Palm Center researchers asked the Pentagon for the total discharge figures of gay linguists (including all foreign language specialties), they were told that figures only existed since 1998. It took a Freedom of Information Act request and pressure from members of the House Armed Services Committee to force the Pentagon to release even these incomplete figures. There were seventy-three discharges of language specialists from the Defense Language Institute between 1998 and 2004. Of these, seventeen were Arabic speakers, eleven spoke Russian, eighteen studied Korean, six were training in Farsi, and the rest studied other languages.[12]

Then in February 2005, a GAO report was released that included figures dating back to 1994, the period when data was not supposed to have existed. Those figures were even more troubling. According to the GAO report, 757 troops with "critical occupations" were fired under the policy. These included voice interceptors, interrogators, translators, explosive ordnance disposal specialists, signal intelligence analysts, and missile and cryptologic technicians. Three hundred and twenty-two fired service members had skills in what the military deemed "an important foreign language." Fifty-four of them spoke Arabic.[13] Ian Finkenbinder made fifty-five. And counting.

These loses have torn a hole in the nation's defenses against Arab insurgents in the Middle East, as the thousands of fellow soldiers who relied on these linguists were forced to drift through Iraq and elsewhere with one fewer conduit to the Arabic-speaking world. It has also meant that, eventually, some other infantryman who had dutifully served out his initial obligation with the army would have to add an additional tour to fill the vacancy, taxing his morale and compromising the readiness of the entire force.[14]

THERE IS NO magic bullet for the nation's lack of preparedness in the fight against radical Islamic violence. But one tactic seems pretty obvious: beefing up the security forces and the intelligence teams needed the most on the front lines of the war against terrorism. As we struggle against an enemy whose world most Americans can scarcely begin to comprehend, the few men and women in the military conversant in that world would seem an invaluable asset. Instead, more than fifty-five Arabic language specialists are no longer working for the U.S. military because they are gay. In the two years following 9/11 alone, thirty-seven language experts were discharged under the policy, with skills in Arabic, Korean, Farsi, Chinese, and Russian.[15] The purging of gay language specialists has seen no respite in the years after 9/11, despite ongoing pleas by military and political leaders to increase the numbers of Arabic translators.

The bulk of these men and women came from the Defense Language Institute, an elite training school for military linguists. DLI is a "joint service installation," run by the army but training service members from all military branches. Its campus sits on a hill in Monterey, California, peering over the rocky cliffs that tumble down to the Pacific Ocean. The school teaches 80 percent of the government's foreign language classes, with 1,000 faculty members serving 3,800 students. Because of the battery of entrance tests and the intensity of its courses, it is known to attract students who are older and more skilled than most enlisted personnel.[16]

DLI also seems to attract a large share of gay students. "There were way too many gay people at DLI for anybody to fear the 'don't ask, don't tell' policy," said Alastair Gamble, a gay student who arrived at DLI in 2001. While there, he was out to all his gay peers and to any enlisted personnel who seemed gay-friendly. "Nobody cared," he explained. "I knew someone who was a flaming queen in a uniform, and nobody cared. Sometimes we lived on halls that were more than 50 percent homosexual. I never even got a sideways glance."[17]

To complete a course in a traditional Romance language—Spanish, French, Italian, Portuguese—requires a twenty-five-week training regimen. But Arabic is what DLI calls a "category 4" language. Along with Chinese, Japanese, and Korean, Arabic is the hardest for English speakers to learn, and the course lasts sixty-three weeks for basic knowledge. Because it's not a "cognate" language for English speakers—not one that shares the roots of the Germanic or Romance family language trees—most American students hit the books for several hours each night, after taking up to seven hours of class every day. Arabic reads from right to left; it has no capital letters and its characters run together like cursive, making it difficult for the untrained to distinguish them without months of practice. The year after 9/11, the number of students graduating from all American colleges and universities with an undergraduate degree in Arabic was a whopping six. Six.[18]

Because of its difficulty for native English speakers, and because of how long and challenging the course is, only the strongest students at DLI are selected to take Arabic. Most students make their language choices under the considerable sway of their teachers. Many are told to take an easier course of study.

But Patricia Ramirez was up to the challenge. "It's always a matter of what the military needs from you," she said, expressing a common sentiment among those who look forward to military service. Ramirez was hoping to use her language skills to serve the army. She saw it as an opportunity to thrive in a realm that could build self-confidence while also giving back to her community. She entered the army in October 2000 and completed basic training at Fort Jackson, South Carolina. The following January, she entered DLI.[19]

Ramirez was only nineteen. She knew she was a lesbian, but at that age, she didn't believe she was going to meet someone who would "turn my world upside-down." After she enlisted, two things changed. She met Julie Evans. And she found it harder than she had imagined to deny her identity. And then came 9/11. Her first reaction to the terrorist attacks was that now she would be useful.

But thoughts of war—the values and ethics behind it, the usefulness she felt in being part of it—coincided with a reevaluation of what it meant to serve that cause under a false identity. "Great soldiers are honest and have integrity," she thought. "It was a terrible way to live," to be forced to violate the code of ethical conduct in order to remain a soldier. It was, in fact, a logical impossibility: To remain a soldier, you had to lie; but to truly be a soldier, you had to tell the truth. In February 2002, Ramirez and Evans, also a soldier at DLI, decided to tell their commander that they were lesbians.[20]

Why did they tell? Why did a pair of lesbians—who knew full well what the policy on gays dictated, who understood the likely consequences of announcing their sexuality to their commanders—choose to come out?

"It was a decision we made about what mattered and how much we felt like hypocrites," said Ramirez. But there were other reasons. The military is an environment that affords few protections to gays and lesbians, not just from harassment but from violence. If you hear derogatory terms aimed at gays, the urge is to protect yourself, and yet you have to go out of your way to appear unconcerned, lest someone suspect you're gay. The mandate of silence is a double bind because if you say anything, you immediately become suspect, and once you're suspect, you have even less room to say anything.[21]

At DLI, Ramirez remarked, the students were well-educated and open-minded. But she wasn't confident that everywhere in the military would be like that. Facing war meant enduring a dread all too familiar to gays approaching a high school locker room: Defending yourself in a potentially hostile and unsupervised climate meant calling attention to your sexual difference, which meant risking further revelation and indictment.[22]

Then there was a practical matter: When the Arabic course ended, Ramirez and Evans would be placed at the military's discretion. A married couple might be placed together, but a gay couple earned no such consideration. The two were simply not willing to tolerate a separation that would not befall an equivalent heterosexual couple. "If you would like us to continue to serve in the military," they wrote to their commander, "we would like nothing more. Our sexual orientation has nothing to do with our capacity to serve."[23]

Their announcement was a disaster. To Ramirez's dismay, after she had mustered the courage to face the consequences of revealing her true identity, her commander wrote a blunt reply, deeming her statement "not credible." In rejecting her statement, he claimed there were no other signs of homosexuality on her record. He also argued that the time frame, two weeks before completing her studies in Arabic, looked suspicious. The implication was that since she had completed her government-subsidized training, she sought to skip out on her obligations and use her skills elsewhere. Finally, her commander noted that many people at DLI have trouble adjusting to military life and some try to get out of service before making the transition out of school.[24]

Ramirez was incensed. How could there be any other evidence of her homosexuality when it was prohibited by law? Any such "signs"—including, as we have seen, things as ridiculous as posters of Melissa Etheridge—are mandated to be carefully kept from coming to the attention of commanders. And the idea that she would exploit government training only to bail out and take her skills to the private sector was similarly ludicrous. She would need much more training to work for a high-paying company, and her skills were nowhere as needed as they were in the military, where Americans had no idea what Arab terrorists and Arab housewives alike were saying. Most absurd of all, Ramirez had risked everything in deciding to come out. She went from speaking to her family every day to barely speaking with them at all. "I was willing to lose them, and for a while I thought I had," she said. "I had to make a choice and this was my choice."[25]

For the first time, Ramirez was actually telling the truth about her life, and she didn't like being called a liar. She considered ignoring the situation and letting it pass, but that would not resolve the likely separation that would be imposed on her and Evans. Ramirez began putting statements together from peers and family who were willing to say she was gay. She also had lawyers write letters indicating violations that may have been committed by the investigators, making clear that the investigations might be investigated. Her efforts are a remarkable testimony to the inane situations created by "don't ask, don't tell": She had to hire a lawyer to help her "prove" her sexual identity, while other soldiers got the boot for merely mentioning that they had desirous thoughts about the same sex.[26]

Her labor began to pay off. She soon got word that, finally, investigators were pursuing a discharge. But she also got word that they were pursuing something else: dirt for a smear campaign. A friend alerted her that investigators had asked her whether Ramirez and Evans had ever been seen kissing. They were also trying to determine if Ramirez had violated visitation policies. Investigators, it turned out, were threatening other soldiers at DLI with courts-martial if they did not disclose material about Ramirez and Evans, including details about their sex lives. The word "jail" was even mentioned.[27]

Soon after, Ramirez learned that her commanding officer was leaving the military. On his last day, he took her aside. He told her he felt strongly that, by choosing to come out, she was being selfish and putting herself above the ideal of selfless service to the group. He said that if every soldier he had was like her, there wouldn't be an army.[28]

That same day, Ramirez's commander gave a parting speech. In it, he said how grateful he was for having a wife, and what an important difference she made in making him a better commander. "It was so hypocritical that he stood up there in front of all those people to say how grateful he was for having her and chided me for wanting the exact same thing," remarked Ramirez. Many service members, she suggested, wouldn't tolerate this. "How many fewer soldiers would we have if everyone came in thinking they could not fall in love?"[29]

With her commander gone, the smear campaign against Ramirez evaporated. She and Evans were both honorably discharged for "homosexual conduct" in October 2002. Even after her whole ordeal, Ramirez was not bitter. "I love it even now," she said of the army, in an interview a month after her discharge. Then she changed her verb to the past tense: "I loved my life there." When she first joined, she believed that "don't ask, don't tell" made sense. She understood that there had to be limitations placed on all soldiers, and she didn't think it would be too hard to abide by the regulations placed on lesbians and gays. She thought, "Basic training, taking community showers, I felt, they're probably better off not knowing. But that was the last time I felt that way." And this is precisely the point: If the law hadn't meddled in her personal life, she would have had the freedom to navigate her interpersonal relationships as necessary, just as straight soldiers do. If she felt some people should not know, she could remain silent. If concealing her identity became awkward, conspicuous, or detrimental to her ability to be a good soldier, she could tell. Having lived under the thumb of the law, the policy made no sense to her at all. "Now for the life of me I don't understand it," she said, "being in the military I saw how unbelievably ridiculous it is and how it is hurting the military more than it is benefiting it."[30]

Ramirez's case was typical. Hers was one of the large majority of "tell" discharges. That is, it resulted not from a witch hunt or a surprise inspection or a covert investigation, but from a "voluntary" admission that she was homosexual. But as we've seen, "voluntary" has a funny kind of meaning when you're living under "don't ask, don't tell."

There were those at DLI, however, who never volunteered to disclose their sexuality at all. Like Alastair Gamble. Gamble was always drawn to languages. His mother was an English professor, and by the time he entered Emory University, he had already studied German for seven years. In college, he continued German and took up Latin. He knew he wanted to do something "functional" with his knack for language, but he hadn't yet realized the army would offer that opportunity, even after he had joined. "I tried to enter as a navy officer," he recalled, "and was told my eyesight was too bad." Then someone suggested Arabic. Or Korean. Though Gamble still envisioned himself entering the service as an officer, perhaps an army officer, he was quickly convinced that if he began as enlisted personnel, with a specialty in languages, the army would pay off his student loans, and he could finally make his skills functional. "I was sold on the language issue," he said.[31]

Gamble started out as a human intelligence collector, a position the GAO report cited as one of the army's "greatest foreign language needs." Once in the army, he completed interrogation training, a nine-week intelligence course that trains a small number of soldiers to collect information through direct-questioning techniques. He then spent six weeks working for the Foreign Area Officer program, which trains officers to recruit U.S. allies, where his performance won him a Certificate of Commendation from his commander. He entered DLI in June 2001 to study Arabic and earned a perfect 300 on his physical fitness test. His grades placed him at the top of his class, and several teachers told him they thought he was the strongest student they had.[32]

On April 20, 2002, Gamble was finishing his second semester of basic Arabic at DLI when he awoke to a pounding on his bedroom door. "This is a health and welfare inspection," came a rousing voice from the hallway. It was 3:30 A.M. These routine barracks sweeps were designed to enforce discipline for matters such as drugs, drinking, and curfew. But any legitimately discovered material that might indicate a "propensity to engage in homosexual conduct," as Gamble knew, could launch an investigation into someone's sexuality.[33]

On this evening, after eight long months of scrupulously avoiding late-night contact, Gamble and his boyfriend, Rob Hicks, a twenty-seven-year-old Korean linguist from Colorado, had decided to spend the evening together. Hicks was nearing the end of his course and preparing to relocate to Goodfellow Air Force Base in Texas. As their separation approached, they decided they could risk one night of sleeping side by side. The move violated curfew regulations, and meant risking exposure. But who knew this would also be the night for a "health and welfare"?[34]

Hicks climbed out the window, and was literally scaling the wall of the dorm building when a dozen noncommissioned officers shoved open the door. The men rummaged through photographs, letters, and videotapes while Gamble was shipped off to his first sergeant's office. The search turned up a gay-themed, nonpornographic film, photographs showing affectionate, but not sexual, behavior between Gamble and his boyfriend, and several gift cards expressing romantic sentiments. Two weeks later, Gamble was officially notified that his unit was initiating an investigation into his sexual orientation. He was pulled from class and honorably discharged on August 2. About eight weeks later, Hicks was discharged as well.[35]

When Charlie Moskos heard what happened, he said of Gamble and Hicks that they brought their punishment on themselves, and that gays should abide by the policy and remain celibate and silent. "It's disgraceful," he told the Associated Press. "These guys betrayed the gay cause. They put their own self-interest above fighting al-Qaeda."[36]

Gamble remembers the episode as one of the most humiliating moments of his life. "I was just absolutely embarrassed," he recalled in an interview. "There's really nothing like having someone who's your age, but a slight rank above you, discussing whether or not lube is sufficient evidence to prove homosexuality. It's like getting felt up; it's horrible." After his discharge, Gamble took a job with a government contractor, a job where his sexuality didn't matter, but neither did his valuable skills as a linguist.[37]

THE ARMY CAST the DLI firings as routine enforcement of military regulations. Harvey Perritt, a spokesman for U.S. Army Training and Doctrine Command, said late in 2002 that the expulsions of Arabic linguists were "not relevant" to the nation's war against Arabic-speaking terrorists. He insisted that discharges resulting from "don't ask, don't tell" were consistent with those for other violations of army regulations. "If someone is enrolled somewhere and they don't pass the P.T. [physical training] standards," he said, by way of comparison, "they'll be discharged. There are policies and they are always in effect."[38]

Actually, not always. The week after the twin towers fell, the Pentagon looked around and noticed it would need as many soldiers as it could get its hands on for the wars it was about to wage. Under the authority of President George W. Bush, the Defense Department issued an order giving each military service the authority to suspend administrative discharges (called "stop-loss" in military speak). In explaining the decision, the folks in the Pentagon's public affairs office showed that no one was more confused than they were about how to retain badly needed gay troops while reassuring the public that the military was abiding by the law that required their discharge. "Stop-loss has been authorized," spokesperson Major James P. Cassella told the *San Francisco Chronicle,* referring to the status of the gay discharge policy. "However, consistent with past practices, administrative discharges could continue under stop-loss." To clarify what the military really intended to do, Cassella said that "commanders would be given enough latitude in this area to apply good judgment and balance the best interests of the service, the unit and the individual involved."[39]

Just in case that didn't make it clear, a Pentagon spokesperson told *The Advocate* soon after that there had been no shift at all in the status of gay troops: "There is no policy that would generate a change in the standards or in the administrative due process for [Pentagon] programs," he said, "including the department's management of homosexual conduct policies as prescribed in law."[40] Though officially there was no change with regard to the implementation of "don't ask, don't tell," the authorization of stop-loss implied an obvious concern about losing troops just as U.S. forces were preparing to land in Afghanistan.

In September 2005, the Palm Center obtained an army commander's handbook for reserve soldiers, which left no room for ambiguity about whether gay troops would be mobilized when they were needed. Under the section entitled "Personnel Actions During the Mobilization Process," it said that in cases of homosexuality, "if discharge isn't requested prior to the unit's receipt of alert notification, discharge isn't authorized. Member will enter AD [active duty] with the unit."[41]

The handbook was from 1999, but was still in effect in the years following

9/11. When the media confronted the army with the document, the Defense Department admitted that it knowingly sent gays to war in the Middle East. Kim Waldron, a spokesperson at the U.S. Army Forces Command at Fort McPherson, told the *Washington Blade* that the reason was to deny soldiers a "get out of jail free" card. "The bottom line," she said, "is some people are using sexual orientation to avoid deployment. So in this case, with the Reserve and Guard forces, if a soldier 'tells,' they still have to go to war and the homosexual issue is postponed until they return to the U.S. and the unit is demobilized." True to form, the Pentagon then tried to take it back. Lieutenant Colonel Ellen Krenke, a Department of Defense spokesperson, said that the "don't ask, don't tell" policy remained in effect. "Our policy has not changed," she said.[42]

Two weeks later, a worried public affairs official from the headquarters of the U.S. Army Forces Command contacted the Palm Center to say that media reports had been "somewhat in error" and he wished to "clarify and amplify the story." He explained that if a soldier is activated and says he is gay, it can take several months to corroborate the claim. During that inquiry, the soldier can indeed be mobilized. However, while the initial spokesperson "may have been accurately quoted" in saying that gay soldiers "still have to go to war and the homosexual issue is postponed until they return to the U.S.," that spokesperson was wrong. In fact, the soldier's case "is not postponed until the unit returns. The review process continues while the unit is deployed and there is no delay in resolving the matter or discharging the soldier if that is the resolution."[43]

The honesty of this clarification was perhaps admirable. Here was a top army spokesperson admitting that a gay soldier is not so threatening to cohesion that he can't be deployed with his unit; however, when the bureaucrats back home finally "resolve" that the soldier is gay, they'll immediately pull him from the front lines. What we are left with is this: Gays were indeed sent to war, and were removed not because they threatened cohesion but because they disappointed officials in Virginia and Washington. Even David Burrelli, who had testified at Nunn's hearings about the "causes" of homosexuality along with "asexuality, fetishes, and other paraphilias," admitted the military sent known gays to war: "The situation that arises during a time of deployment place[s] homosexuals in a no-win situation. They are allowed or ordered to serve at the risk of their own lives with the probability of forced discharge when hostilities end if their sexuality becomes an issue. By deploying suspected homosexuals with their units, the services bring into question their own argument that the presence of homosexuals seriously impairs the accomplishment of the military mission."[44]

In fact, there is no question that the military delays and neglects gay discharges during the current wars in the Middle East. In 2006 and 2007, the navy twice deployed a gay Hebrew linguist, Jason Knight, to duty despite his public acknowledgment that he was gay. His dismissal form was marked "completion of service" rather than homosexual conduct, thus allowing the navy to redeploy him in the future. Only after the sailor became the subject of an article in *Stars and Stripes,* a military newspaper, did the navy finally and swiftly discharge him.[45]

There could be no clearer proof than the story of Jason Knight, along with the discovery of the army commander's handbook, that when it comes to real life, the military has no trouble sending gays to war. According to *The Boston Globe,* following 9/11 the military allowed an increasing number of service members identified as gay to remain in uniform—twelve gays and lesbians to continue to serve in 2003, twenty-two in 2004, thirty-six in 2005.[46] And these were only the reported ones. The pattern raises serious questions about the elaborate rationale that the presence of open homosexuals would undermine unit cohesion. After all, if gays impair cohesion, and if cohesion is most critical during wartime, then the years following 9/11 would be the last time you would want to relax the ban.

And yet, wartime is exactly when the ban has long been relaxed and sometimes totally ignored or officially suspended. In every war this country has fought over the last century gays have been knowingly retained. During World War II, the army ordered commanders to "salvage" soldiers who were facing the boot for sodomy, to review pending cases with the aim of "conserving all available manpower," and to cancel discharges and make convicted "sodomists" eligible for reassignment after prison. Indeed, a psychiatric study during the war found that it was unofficial policy in the army and navy to permit virtually all gay troops to serve.[47]

In the peacetime years between World War II and 1950, the ousting of gays more than tripled. Yet during the Korean War, discharges in the navy fell by half. In 1953, the year the truce was signed at Panmunjom, they more than doubled again. Ditto Vietnam, when discharges plummeted during the biggest buildups of troop strength in the second half of the 1960s.[48]

During the first Gulf War, the Pentagon resumed its pattern. Even before the air assault began to drive Saddam's forces out of Kuwait, a Defense Department spokesperson said that in case of a war, gay discharges could be "deferred" based on "operational needs" and indicated they could resume when the soldiers were no longer needed. "Any administrative procedure is dependent on operational considerations of the unit that would administer such proceedings," the spokesperson said. "Just because a person says they're gay, that doesn't mean they can stop packing their bags." He added that the action "doesn't abdicate the rules," but that in war, "you just have to establish priorities."[49]

Despite the clear indications that gays would be knowingly sent to war, on the eve of the invasion of Iraq, a Defense Department spokesman, Bill Caldwell, somehow managed to stammer that "the policy on gays continues that homosexuality is incompatible with military service." Lest this particular round of doublespeak leave you unclear on exactly what the policy or practice was during the Persian Gulf War, a similar directive to the 1999 army commander's handbook revealed that commanders were being instructed to mobilize known gays during this conflict, too. Lawyers and gay rights advocates cited at least seventeen cases of service members during this period who told their superiors they were gay but were informed they would still have to deploy. One lesbian reservist was even told she would have to provide documentation that she tried to marry another woman if she was to prove she was gay, a particularly tough trick to pull off given that same-sex marriage was not legal anywhere in the world. In the six months after the war, over a thousand gays were discharged, many of whom were known to be gay at the time they were sent to fight.[50]

One almost feels sorry for the Pentagon, or at least the poor creatures who staff the public affairs office and have to defend the indefensible. But instead of ignoring the law, military leaders had another option: They could have tried to change it. After all, the military leadership routinely presses the legislature to enact laws it deems essential to military readiness. In November 2002, for instance, the office of the undersecretary of defense ordered a comprehensive review of the military's language programs—requirements, training, personnel—with an eye toward radically revamping how the government provided language expertise for the war on terrorism. The result was a "Defense Language Transformation Team," which ultimately produced a "road map" to identify appropriate actions needed to create a new "global footprint" for the Defense Department and a "new approach to warfighting in the 21st century."

The road map instructed that language personnel policy be updated, "given the lessons of current operations and the Global War on Terrorism." The objective was to "reinvigorate the Defense Language Program" and "maximize the accession, development, and employment of individuals with language skills." It also provided for the creation of a database with the names of former military personnel who had been separated so they could be tracked for possible "recall or voluntary return." The objective was to be able to trace the accession and separation of military linguists so that they could be "developed and managed as critical strategic assets." This would include tracking trends in the "accession and retention of individuals" with critical language skills and "explor[ing] innovative concepts to expand capabilities."[51]

Here's one: Stop firing gay linguists! In none of the dozens of recommendations included in the road map's extensive appendix did there appear any reconsideration of the gay policy. If ever there were a time to recommend revisiting a personnel policy that was ill-suited to our nation's defense, surely this was it. Could the silence be a factor of the Pentagon's inability to lift the ban without congressional action? Not judging by its other recommendations. The road map did not shy away from counseling several other actions that would require approval by lawmakers, such as its support for a Civilian Linguist Reserve Corps, which, said the road map, would be "subject to legislative enactment."[52]

Nor did the Pentagon's February 2005 white paper, entitled, "A Call to Action for National Foreign Language Capabilities." The paper "urgently recommended" that the president appoint a National Language Authority to oversee a new foreign language strategy coordinated by the federal government. Like the Defense Language Transformation Team's road map, "A Call to Action" stressed the need to "move the Nation toward a 21st century vision" of cultural insight and strategic effectiveness.[53]

The white paper was explicit about calling for congressional action. It recommended the formation of a National Foreign Language Coordination Council, which would "advocate maximum use of resources" and "recommend policy and legislation to build the national capacity in language ability and cultural understanding." The Coordination Council, it said, should have its work "enabled and funded through legislation proposed by the Administration and approved by Congress." Elsewhere in the report appeared a hearty endorsement of proposed legislation in Congress to address the need to increase American language expertise. The pending laws, it said, "are welcome signs of the emergence of [national-level] leadership."[54]

The need for legislative action was clearly no cause for pause in taking strong stands for radical change. Beyond calls for legal change, both papers sought, to their credit, to change those cultural components in the national security and educational communities that served to hamstring real progress in American language expertise. And they gestured toward policies and practices that could have incorporated revisiting the wisdom of kicking out gay linguists. "Government agencies," said "A Call to Action," "should review current personnel positions to ensure that foreign language, cultural under-standing, and crisis preparedness needs have been identified" and addressed.[55]

Could these calls for reform prompt a revisit of the gay ban? Perhaps, if prejudice and inertia were not standing in the way. But what about the senti-ments of the civilian leaders in charge of the military? It sometimes seems they're getting the picture. "We must identify the critical nodes in our culture that can be influenced most effectively, and we must identify the means to influence them—to cause a shift, now," said Undersecretary of Defense David Chu, in announcing the release of the white paper. "We must find where and how we can best concentrate our effort in order to produce significant change." Donald Rumsfeld also weighed in. "We simply must develop a greater capacity for languages that reflect the demands of this century," he said. "No technol-ogy delivers this capability; it is a truly human skill that our forces must have to win, and that we must have to keep the peace."[56] Indeed, as Rumsfeld had been saying whenever anyone would listen, the twenty-first century is differ-ent from the one before it, and it brings with it a different culture. But when asked if the gay ban should survive the end of the twentieth century, Rums-feld said there were no plans to reexamine the policy.

Given the enormous energy spent over the last several years addressing how to stem a recruitment and retention crisis that is undermining the war on terrorism, the general unwillingness to revisit the gay ban can seem like a comical misunderstanding of the policy's title. It's as if officials believe that "don't ask, don't tell" means they're not allowed to even raise the issue. More probable is that the same sentiment that lay behind the initial policy contin-ues to characterize the outlook of those who might otherwise have the moral authority to ask the hard questions; most people simply wish the issue would never come up. The question now is whether the military—and the nation—can afford to remain silent about a policy that is needlessly undermining the readiness of the armed forces.

WITH NO ACTION to review the policy, unable to keep up with a backlog of Arabic documents, and understaffed in its interrogations of Middle Eastern detainees, the government turned increasingly to private contracting compa-nies at much greater financial cost and far lower oversight. As a result, quality suffered. One company, the San Diego–based Titan Corporation, was or-dered in 2005 to pay $28.5 million for violating the Foreign Corrupt Practices Act, barring bribery of foreign leaders. Another, Worldwide Language Re-sources, hastily hired a former army intelligence specialist to translate Arabic responses from detainees at Guantánamo Bay Naval Base. The translator,

William Tierney, had used his translations skills as a chief warrant officer in the army, but had left the service in 2000 amid tensions with superiors. His tenure at Guantánamo met a similar fate. Just six weeks after he began, Worldwide relieved him of his duties there because of complaints from military officials who worked with him. They said he was insubordinate, "divisive," and a "burden to the mission."[57]

When Arabic speakers like Tierney didn't work out, the pool of replacements looked grim indeed. In October 2003, Pentagon officials acknowledged to Congress that the military had relaxed its security standards due to a need to fill linguist positions, even hiring people without conducting proper background checks. A Defense Department official admitted that "in our rush to meet the requirements . . . folks were brought on with sort of interim level checks," since there wasn't time to worry about all the details until after they were hired. The results, said Charles Abell, undersecretary of defense for personnel and readiness, in testimony before Congress, included cutting corners at Guantánamo, where U.S. military translators serve as essential intermediaries to facilitate communication, logistics, and counterintelligence between interrogators and prisoners. "We found a couple who were not as trustworthy as we had hoped initially," said Abell. Three translators that year faced espionage charges.[58]

WHILE OVERALL DISCHARGE numbers have fallen since 9/11, the firing of Arabic language specialists has not stopped. In January 2006, the army booted an Arabic linguist who graduated from DLI and was outed by a string of anonymous e-mails. The decorated sergeant, Bleu Copas, who was serving in the 82nd Airborne Division, was not open about his sexual orientation, but believes he was targeted by vengeful acquaintances that he confided in unwisely. Inquiry officials wrote in their investigation notes that Copas was "dealing with at least two jealous lovers," and they theorized that one was behind the e-mails. The e-mail author threatened to "inform your entire battalion of the information I gave you" if commanders did not take action against Copas. They launched an investigation in December and Copas was discharged shortly thereafter.[59]

Then, in the spring of 2007, three more Arabic linguists were fired after military officials listened in on conversations conducted on a government computer system that allows intelligence personnel to communicate with troops on the front lines. The total number of Arabic linguists fired under "don't ask, don't tell" now stood at fifty-nine.[60]

Stephen Benjamin was one of the three. Graduating at the top of his class at DLI, he became a cryptologic interpreter, responsible for collecting and analyzing signals and assigned targets to support combatant commanders and other tactical units. In October 2006, the army inspector general conducted an audit of a government communications system and investigated seventy service members for abusing the system—primarily using it for personal communications. Benjamin was called in for questioning and was asked about a comment he made: "That was so gay—the good gay, not the bad one." Out of the seventy people, a handful of gays, including Benjamin, were eventually investigated for violations of the "don't ask, don't tell" policy. The worst abuses of the computer system involved straight people using it to have cybersex, but those violators retained their jobs.[61]

Benjamin was already out to nearly everyone he worked with. "The only harm to unit cohesion that was caused was because I was leaving," he said. "That's where the real harm is, when they pull valuable members out of a team." His commanding officers were sorry to lose him. His JAG officer told him the policy was "politically unpopular," and that military attorneys didn't like enforcing it. His captain's evaluation read: "EXCEPTIONAL LEADER. Extremely focused on mission accomplishment. Dedicated to his personal development and that of his sailors. takes pride in his work and promotes professionalism in his subordinates."[62]

When he was discharged, Benjamin was preparing to reenlist for another six years. He volunteered to deploy, hoping to serve in Iraq so he could work in the environment—and with the soldiers—he had directly assisted as an Arabic translator at Fort Gordon, Georgia. "I wanted to go to Iraq so I could be in the environment with the soldiers I was protecting," he said. Though he could not discuss the details of his intelligence work, he said it involved sending reports with critical information out to the front lines, and he knew that in his work, he "made a difference."[63]

In response to his ouster, Benjamin created a blog, on which he posted a navy administrative memo. It read:

> Diversity is critical to mission accomplishment. Everyone in our navy contributes to mission success and everyone brings to that collective effort unique capabilities and individual talent. How we harness those capabilities and foster that talent bears considerable effect on our ability to successfully accomplish the mission.[64]

There were also talented linguists who escaped the clutches of the homosexual discharge machine, but who took themselves out of the picture because the added burdens that gays alone had to bear were too much. Jarrod Chlapowski was so proud of finishing the army's basic training just months before 9/11 that he had the Chinese character for "honor" tattooed on his shoulder. "That's the main army value," he says in the documentary film *Ask Not*. Chlapowski studied Korean at DLI and graduated as a cryptologic voice interceptor, finishing second in his class. He served in Korea as an interpreter for the 3rd Military Intelligence Battalion on sensitive reconnaissance missions. Eventually he earned the Army Achievement Medal and an Army Commendation Medal for leadership and training.[65]

Chlapowski was out to nearly everyone in his unit. Because he didn't fit stereotypes, he said people were often shocked when he mentioned it, "but I never got a negative response." He estimated that 80 percent of his unit knew he was gay by the end of his time at DLI. "And no one cared," he added. On the few occasions he heard crass comments, he recognized that it mostly amounted to people "just kind of ribbing each other." Still, as time wore on, Chlapowski watched friends and other soldiers get caught up in the jaws of the gay ban, and it led to deepening anxiety. "You're always going to be paranoid," he said, adding that someone who knows your open secret could "take issue with it." When he transferred to a new unit at Fort Lewis, Washington, to train soldiers, he didn't know anyone there and was unsure of the climate. "I opted to put myself back in the closet and I was miserable," he said. "Within a few months I knew this was something I couldn't continue." Chlapowski chose not to reenlist and left the army in November 2005.[66]

The loss of critical talent that results from "don't ask, don't tell" is undeniable. It is damaging to the mission and integrity of the armed forces, and by extension, it weakens our security as a nation. But perhaps most maddening of all, it is unnecessary. Why, then, do we let it continue? Unlike world poverty, ethnic conflict in the Middle East, or brain cancer, all of which lack a simple, straightforward solution, the ban on openly gay troops in the military could be ended if a few hundred men and women in the U.S. Congress decided to heed both a growing body of evidence and public opinion polls and vote for its demise. In fact, a few public statements by just a tiny handful of men who have the ear and respect of the military and political establishment could virtually seal the deal, greatly aiding those men and women in Congress to cast the vote that most know is right but are too timid to cast. Yet they don't speak out and Congress doesn't overturn the policy. Why? Many simply don't care. Others worry they would face criticism from colleagues or backlash at the polls. Still others genuinely believe that, despite overwhelming evidence that military readiness does not require closeting gay and lesbian soldiers, letting them serve openly would needlessly saddle military commanders with dangerous new burdens.

Running through all these reasons is a commitment not to face the truth. And this, every bit as much as the wasted Arabic linguists, counterintelligence officers, artillery operators, pilots, and surgeons, is the insidious nature of "don't ask, don't tell." There is something deeply embarrassing about the most powerful nation in the world imposing a gag rule on itself; we have voluntarily shackled ourselves in order to deny what we know to be true, all in the name of protecting our supposedly fragile soldiers from a phantom gay menace. The gay ban is no less than the stalling of the march toward Enlightenment. The last three centuries of Western civilization have celebrated the ideals of freedom, truth, reason, and self-understanding. In the United States we often consider ourselves to be a world beacon for these efforts. We hallow our Constitution for its use and protection of these traits; we broadcast and praise our commitment to liberty and free speech; and we have framed our war on terrorism as a struggle against sectarian, anti-intellectual, and illiberal forces who are trying to overturn all we hold sacred. Yet "don't ask, don't tell" demonstrates that the U.S. government is helping these forces along, to our own detriment. Americans should be asking themselves: What is gained and what is lost by sticking our collective head in the sand?

10

Gays Out, Ex-convicts In

W HILE THE PENTAGON WAS BUSY kicking out gay troops who were willing to serve, those it considered qualified were finding other ways to spend their time. Arabic linguists were not the only people that the U.S. military could not find enough of. All four major service branches were plagued throughout the years preceding and following 9/11 with recruitment and retention shortfalls. The problem achieved crisis proportions about two years into the Iraq War. In 2004, Congress approved increasing the size of the army by twenty thousand recruits,[1] greatly expanding the challenge of filling all its ranks. And in 2007, President Bush sent twenty thousand additional troops to Iraq in the so-called surge.

The military had trouble filling and maintaining its ranks for several reasons. One was economic. Whenever the economy is humming along at a brisk pace, potential military recruits are more likely to find jobs in the private sector; during a recession, joining the military may seem more appealing. As a simple cost-benefit analysis, most people will choose higher pay and lower risk of death over the other way around. Despite the lull in the economy following September 11, consistent growth from the late 1990s through 2006 diminished the appeal of the military. Also, the growing opposition to wars in Iraq and Afghanistan has increased reluctance to enlist or stay beyond an initial tour. The sheer number of people needed to fight these wars, which came at a time when leaders like Defense Secretary Donald Rumsfeld had been planning for a leaner, more agile force, raised the number of slots that needed to be filled, making shortfalls virtually inevitable.

The gay ban added to the shortfall crisis in several ways: By the end of 2007 there had been more than twelve thousand expulsions. Thousands more never enlisted or left early because of the hostility engendered by the gay ban. And perhaps least acknowledged is the role the gay ban has played in widening the gap between civilian and military culture, alienating a significant chunk of Americans from interest in, or support for, the military simply by virtue of its image as a lumbering bureaucracy that's out of touch with the modern world.

Under grilling from Senator John McCain during Sam Nunn's hearings, Colonel Margarethe Cammermeyer said that children of her coworkers were writing off the military after hearing about her expulsion. "Because of my separation and the regulation that discriminates against homosexuals serving in the military," she said "they choose not to think about the military as a career." Thomas Paniccia, a gay staff sergeant in the air force who testified beside Cammermeyer, echoed the point. He cited supportive people from gay groups around the world who would not tell their heterosexual children to join the military "while this ban is in place."[2] The gay ban has exacerbated the military's recruitment troubles, and it did so both indirectly and directly. Not only did it turn potential recruits—gay and straight—away for reasons of principle, but it hampered recruiters' access to schools and universities that sought to keep them at bay as long as they continued their discriminatory policy.

Apologists for the ban point out that the more than twelve thousand "don't ask, don't tell" discharges represent a minute percentage of both the entire force and total early discharges each year.[3] But the devil is in the details—in the particular jobs that were lost, not the raw figures. The military was canning troops in the very occupational specialties it most desperately needed to fill, and it had to press civilian reservists, ex-convicts, drug abusers, and other underqualified individuals into service in the war on terrorism. The consequences were dire. Rather than preserving unit cohesion by protecting fragile straight men from knowing which coworkers were gay, the "don't ask, don't tell" policy was reducing combat readiness of the overall force. Due in part to the expulsions of thousands of competent and highly trained gay service members, the military relied ever more on untrained, overburdened, and unwilling troops, serving under terms they had not expected, in units with compromised cohesion, and on tours that outlasted the contracts they had signed.

In 1998 and 1999, all branches fell short of their recruiting goals. They were able to turn the situation around only after delivering substantial pay increases and enlistment bonuses, hiring hundreds of new recruiters, and pumping hundreds of millions of dollars into new advertising and marketing. The air force introduced television commercials for the first time, more than tripling its advertising budget. Among the reserves, only the Marine Corps met its goals in 1997, 1998, and 1999; the Air Force Reserves fell short by 40 percent. Those who did enlist in the reserves during this period came with less active-duty experience, on average, raising training costs and prompting concern among military officials about a negative "impact on units." All the reserves raised enlistment bonuses, paying enormous sums for specialists. The army offered $40,000 in educational benefits to doctors who agreed to sign up for duty.[4]

In 1999, the air force increased its advertising spending from $12 million to over $56 million, and subsequently announced it would feature air force Thunderbirds on Frosted Flakes cereal boxes in a continuing effort to attract recruits. The navy doubled its recruitment staff and intensified its local television advertising, hiring Spike Lee to direct a glossy new campaign. The navy met its recruitment goals in 1999 only after agreeing to double the number of high school dropouts it would accept. And in 2001, the army met its goals only after spending $150 million on its Army of One television and Internet campaign, and through the unexpected help of a slowing economy.[5]

By early 2001, the Marine Corps had fully acknowledged the extent of the problem, and it had a solution. It hired Captain Shawn Haney as a liaison officer to Hollywood and began working with Fox Television on a survival reality show that used Marine sergeants to run a "boot camp." The hope, Captain Haney said, was to help "give the public a glimpse into the Marine Corps." Meanwhile, President Bush requested a $5.7 billion increase in the 2002 budget specifically for pay raises, better housing, and greater benefits, all designed to respond to recruitment shortfalls.[6]

In the wake of the terrorist attacks of 2001, a surge in patriotism among ordinary Americans helped recruitment bounce back in the active-duty branches. But the gains turned out to be temporary, as the wars in Iraq and Afghanistan took a toll on young Americans' willingness to sign up or stay in. At the end of 2004, the National Guard said it would triple signing bonuses for certain new recruits and reenlistments after suffering two consecutive months of recruitment shortfalls. In October, the Guard had missed its goals by 30 percent. By year's end, it was supposed to have 350,000 soldiers but had only 340,000. And because of the war on terrorism and the war in Iraq, the Guard, which is responsible for homeland security as well as serving abroad when called, had to increase its overall rolls. The Army Reserve approved identical bonus increases after its top general, Lieutenant General James Helmly, acknowledged that its recruiting was in "precipitous decline" that could prompt a return to a draft if not reversed.[7]

The situation became so dire that Major General Michael Rochelle, head of army recruiting, called 2005 the "toughest recruiting climate ever faced by the all-volunteer army." In January, the Marine Corps missed its recruitment goal for the first time in nearly ten years. The army made only 73 percent of its target goal in February, 68 percent in March, and 57 percent in April. In some regions, new enlistments were down 20 percent since 2000. In 2005, applications to the three U.S. military academies dropped. Eventually, the Department of Defense simply withheld new figures, raising fears that the numbers were too far off even to announce. In an effort to boost recruits, the army replayed its strategy from 1999: It hired hundreds of new recruiters, devoted $100 million for new ads, raised bonuses for some job categories by $2000, and added $20,000 to its college fund. It also raised the maximum age for National Guard and reserve recruits by five years. The Pentagon announced $150,000 bonuses to certain highly trained, badly needed specialists who would agree to remain in the service for another term, the largest amount ever offered. It announced it would double enlistment bonuses for certain high-demand jobs, including linguists. In July, the army announced it would likely miss its recruiting goal for the year, including for the reserve and National Guard. By some estimates, the army was projected to fall short by seven thousand enlistees. These failures came despite the fact that in 2005 the army allotted a record $400 million to bonuses.[8]

In July 2005, just as the army announced it would not be able to fill its ranks, a new data analysis of 2000 census figures from the Williams Institute, at the UCLA School of Law, suggested that lifting the gay ban could increase the number of active-duty personnel by 41,000 troops. If gays were allowed to serve openly, concluded the study, the number of gay enlistees would likely rise to approach the service rates of straights, resulting in a significant net gain of new recruits. Another study from the Williams Institute found that the number of losses resulting from "don't ask don't tell" is far higher than what the actual discharge figures show. When combined with an estimate of the number of gays and lesbians who leave prematurely because of the policy, the annual figure rises from a few hundred to four thousand.[9] These numbers suggested that a large percentage of empty slots in the military would likely be full if the anti-gay policy were ended.

Instead, the army announced it would throw more money at the problem and further lower standards. That summer new recruits were offered the option of earning over $100,000 in incentives. At the same time, the military asked Congress to raise the age limit for new enlistees to forty-two. The previous age limit had been thirty-nine for Army Reserves and National Guard and thirty-five for active-duty.[10]

Even so, General Peter Pace, a former recruiter who had just been selected as the new chairman of the Joint Chiefs of Staff, acknowledged that enlistees could not simply be bought; they had to be enticed with words of respect and approval. "This is not about money and benefits," he told reporters. "This is about message. If we let our young folks and middle-young folks know how much we appreciate their service to their country—there are thousands and thousands of young men and women out there who want to serve this country." Despite the emphasis on "message," the Pentagon continued to project an increasingly unpopular image of intolerance with its support for the gay ban—precisely the kind of image it should have been shedding as it reached further and further into civilian society to attract new recruits. Pace did not help matters when, that same year, he told a Wharton student conference: "The U.S. military mission fundamentally rests on the trust, confidence and cooperation amongst its members, and the homosexual lifestyle does not comport with that kind of trust and confidence." It was an odd way to "let our young folks and middle-young folks know how much we appreciate their service to their country." His initial remarks were little noticed, but in March 2007, he repeated his anti-gay stance to the *Chicago Tribune,* saying homosexuality was "immoral" and likening it to adultery. "I believe homosexual acts between two individuals are immoral," he said, "and that we should not condone immoral acts." Six months later, he was forced to step down, primarily because of these remarks, which were widely seen as a gaff. It was a telling commentary on how American attitudes toward homosexuality were leaving people like Pace behind. (His successor, Admiral Mike Mullen, suggested the American people, through Congress, should decide whether to lift the ban and promised the military would oblige.)[11]

What happens when the military cannot fill its slots with qualified people? It fills them with unqualified people, if it can fill them at all. In 2005, reports emerged of recruiters concealing police and medical records of recruits, doctoring paperwork, helping applicants cheat on tests, and cleaning up evidence of drug use, all in an effort to reach their goals and enlist enough bodies to fill the ranks. Recruiting agents also engaged in threats, coercion, and lies to attract people. According to the army, the number of "recruitment improprieties" shot up by over 50 percent from 2002 to 2004.[12]

While recruiting spokesmen claimed there was no official policy to lower standards, the army that year increased by nearly 50 percent the number of new recruits it granted "moral waivers"—an invitation to enlist despite a prior record of criminal activity or substance abuse that would have normally been a barrier to entry. In general, the story goes, the Pentagon seeks recruits "of good moral character," in order to avoid hiring people whose past behavior would make them more likely "to become disciplinary cases or security risks, or [to] disrupt good order, morale, and discipline." Though "don't ask, don't tell" does not characterize gays as having character defects, it does borrow the language of "good order, morale, and discipline" to argue that gays who don't hide their identity somehow imperil all three, despite a complete absence of evidence for that case. Yet between 2003 and 2006, thanks to the military's moral waivers program, 4,230 convicted felons, 43,977 individuals convicted of serious misdemeanors, including assault, and 58,561 illegal drug abusers were allowed to enlist. Between 2004 and 2007, the number of convicted felons nearly doubled, rising from 824 to 1,605. Allowable offenses under the program include murder, kidnapping, and "making terrorist threats."[13]

In 2008, an army spokesman, Paul Boyce, defended the latest round of moral waivers, which included an 88 percent rise of convicted felons over the previous year in the Army and Marine Corps. Hundreds of waivers were granted for serious crimes, including burglary, aggravated assault, sex crimes, and making bomb threats. "We are a reflection of American society and the changes that affect it," Boyce explained. But the military, it appeared, remained deaf to the revolution in attitudes toward gays and lesbians.[14]

INDEED, WHILE THE military regards gays as dispensable, its drug abusers and underachievers have become prized possessions, warm bodies to be kept at great cost. In the spring of 2005, the army reported it was recruiting higher numbers of ex-convicts, drug addicts, and high school dropouts; it acknowledged that they were being advanced even when they failed basic training and that they had "performed poorly" and become a "liability." "Even if they graduate," said one drill instructor, "they may not have Army values." By March, the army had doubled its share of recruits without a high school diploma from 2004, as well as the number of new members who scored at the lowest level on the aptitude test, bringing that figure to the highest level since 2001. In 2005, the army hired 667 soldiers who fell into Category 4, those who scored in the lowest third of the military aptitude test. That number is fourteen more than the military discharged the previous year under the anti-gay policy.[15]

Part of the reason officials were retaining underqualified members was that rising attrition rates were also cutting into their numbers. Indeed, that summer, the military sent a memo to commanders in all four service branches instructing them to buck high attrition rates by retaining drug addicts, alcoholics, and those who failed to perform adequately or pass physical fitness tests. "We need your concerted effort to reverse the negative trend," said the memo, referring to the slide in personnel. "By reducing attrition 1%, we can save up to 3,000 initial-term soldiers. That's 3,000 more soldiers in our formations."[16]

At the time, this number was less than all the gays discharged since 9/11. Advocates of the gay ban have long dismissed gay discharges as a tiny portion of the overall force, but the numbers here are too obvious to ignore, and quality is, of course, the bottom line. Yet the Pentagon was willing to accept drug addicts, alcoholics, and others—who by definition are more likely to threaten discipline and morale—just to get "3,000 more soldiers in our formations." When it comes to gays, over 12,000 unnecessary discharges is a drop in the bucket; when it comes to those who are truly a risk to military readiness, the Pentagon will sacrifice quality to hold the numbers. As the memo concludes, "Each soldier retained reduces the strain on recruiting command and our retention program, which must replace every soldier who departs the Army early."[17]

The Pentagon, in short, hired less competent recruits to fight our wars rather than hire or retain fully competent gay troops. The risks of this path are far higher than any risks associated with letting gays serve. While no evidence has ever tied gay service members to impairing military operations, plenty of evidence shows that people who have not graduated from high school have higher dropout rates from the service and are more difficult to train. They are also more prone to disciplinary problems and are less likely to serve out their contracts. According to one GAO study of soldiers who leave service early, those who were granted moral waivers were more likely to be discharged for misconduct than those who were not.[18]

Or worse: They're not discharged soon enough. One of the most damaging developments in the American effort to combat terrorism and stabilize the Middle East was the string of war crimes that came to light at Abu Ghraib, Haditha, and other notorious sites of American abuse. On March 11, 2006, four U.S. soldiers from the army's 101st Airborne Division were manning a checkpoint in a residential area of Mahmudiya, a town twenty miles south of Baghdad; these men were liquored up and armed with M4 rifles. According to reports, the soldiers began plotting to rape a civilian in a nearby home. Assigning one man to monitor the radio, the others changed into black clothes and raided the home of Abeer Qasim Hamza, a young Iraqi girl. According to allegations, Private Steven Green shot and killed the girl's parents and sister, raped and murdered the teenager, and then set her body on fire. The nineteen-year-old Green was a high school dropout with three misdemeanor convictions and a history of drug and alcohol abuse.[19]

When Green was arrested, it marked the fifth atrocity the Pentagon investigated just in the spring of 2006. The developments spawned strenuous debate about what causes such war crimes and where responsibility should lie. But the question the military is most loathe to answer is also the most obvious one: What was Steven Green doing in Iraq in the first place? After all, he had enlisted literally days after leaving his jail cell in Texas, where he was serving time for his third misdemeanor conviction, this time for alcohol possession. He had a history of difficulties and disruptions and, not surprisingly, only lasted in the military for eleven months before being booted out in April for a personality disorder, one month after the killings. His arrest came three months later.[20]

The answer is that Green was admitted on a moral waiver. That year, 733 ex-convicts who would not otherwise have been accepted into the armed forces were allowed to wear the uniform and represent their country. The same year, the Pentagon booted 742 troops under "don't ask, don't tell." It might not have had to hire a single ex-convict if it had let gays serve.

In the case of Abu Ghraib, it is not known if any of the alleged perpetrators were hired on moral waivers. It's clear, however, that undertrained and underqualified personnel worked at the prison. It's also clear that the military traded competent gays away and filled their slots with those who perpetrated abuse. Private Lynndie England, a chief perpetrator of the Abu Ghraib abuses, was a file clerk who did not "have any reason to be handling prisoners," according to a military prosecutor. The head of the prison's interrogation center was a civil affairs officer and had no experience with interrogation. He even had to ask military intelligence soldiers to show him the ropes so he could figure out what he was supposed to be doing. In 2004, the Fay Report, a high-level army investigation examining the causes of the Abu Ghraib scandal, identified forty-four instances of abuse committed by military police, military intelligence soldiers, and civilian contractors. (One incident was an alleged rape committed by an American translator.) The report found that "systemic problems," including "an acute shortage of M.P. and M.I. soldiers," contributed to the climate that produced Abu Ghraib.[21] So what does the military do? In the six years before Abu Ghraib, it fires 268 intelligence personnel and 232 military police and security troops because they're gay.

In 2007, a federal government study found that gang members were entering the military at alarming rates. Between 2003 and 2006, incidents of gang-related activity in the armed forces quadrupled. Some experts estimated 2 percent of all new recruits had gang affiliations. "Officials do not want this topic spoken about because it uncovers how the Army, in its rush to recruit more soldiers, has had to lower its security standards, allowing in volunteers with criminal backgrounds," said Gregory Lee, a former supervisor of the national Drug Enforcement Agency. "We don't have enough soldiers and the army has strict orders to increase the number of enlisted troops nationwide, even if that means recruiting criminals."[22]

PERHAPS COMMANDERS SHOULD have thought twice about hounding Derek Sparks out of the navy just after the United States invaded Afghanistan. Sparks, who enlisted in 1987, was a signalman seaman recruit specializing in visual communications. As a command career counselor, Sparks had his own office aboard the USNS *Bridge,* a combat logistics ship, where one night he and two other gay friends were socializing while deployed off the coast of Pakistan. After leaving his two friends behind in his office, he learned the next morning that they had been caught by the command master chief in violation of the homosexual conduct policy.

The first report of the master of arms made no mention of Sparks, but his report statement tried to implicate Sparks in the violation, despite dozens of witnesses who saw him elsewhere at the time of the incident. Rumors began to fly and Sparks heard that his master of arms might try to call him up on more serious charges than homosexual conduct. At this point, he admitted he was gay. "I was tired of playing, I was tired of hiding, I was tired of all the bullshit," he recalled. "The only reason the command master chief tried to implicate me was because he knew I was gay and had something against me." In 2002, four months into Operation Enduring Freedom, Sparks was pulled off his ship in Bahrain, airlifted to Dubai, and deposited in Seattle.[23]

THE AIR FORCE might also have been missing Beth Schissel. Like any stepmom, Schissel worried about the health and safety of her twenty-four-year-old son, James, while he finished his first tour of duty in Iraq. A first lieutenant in the army, James was tasked as a transportation officer, responsible for ferrying supplies through hostile terrain that was often bombarded with RPGs and littered with IEDs. "There's no front line over there," said Schissel. "You're in harm's way no matter what you're doing."[24]

But Schissel was not like most stepmoms. If her instinct to shield James from harm seems familiar, her predicament was not. As a former air force officer and a physician specializing in pediatric emergency medicine, Schissel felt she should have been there with him, helping to ensure that he and anyone else needing medical treatment got the best care possible. And she would have been, if it weren't for one thing: She was gay.[25]

After graduating from the Air Force Academy in 1989, she entered active duty and eventually joined the reserves while she completed medical school, which she hoped would be a route to a military medical career. But during medical school, a male civilian began to stalk and harass her, threatening to out her as a tool of vengeance against someone they both knew well. Terrified, Schissel decided her only recourse was to come out in hopes of blunting the stalker's weapon. She was discharged on September 10, 2001.

In the first ten years under "don't ask, don't tell," the Pentagon fired 244 surgeons, nurses, dentists, ophthalmologists, and other highly trained medical specialists. The consequences of shortfalls in military medical specialists during wartime are grave. According to a Senate report issued in 2003 by Senators Christopher Bond and Patrick Leahy, hundreds of injured National Guard and Army Reserve soldiers received "inadequate medical attention" while housed at Fort Stewart because of a lack of preparedness that included "an insufficient number of medical clinicians and specialists, which has caused excessive delays in the delivery of care." The situation created the perception among soldiers that they were receiving care that was inferior to that received by active-duty personnel, which had a "devastating and negative impact on morale."[26]

The firing of badly needed medical personnel also made things worse for those who stayed. When the military lacks enough specialists to serve, it must increase the rotations of those it has under contract, adding burdens which make service less appealing to new recruits and to those already in uniform. In the years between 2001 and 2006, more than half of the nonstudent population of the Army Medical Department had deployed to the Middle East. Many were rotating back into the theater for the second and even third time in four years.[27] Such frequent rotations compound stress, lower morale, and increase the risk of injury or death. The unexpected extension of military service was a particular burden to the National Guard and reserves, who had on average less training, higher stress levels, and lower morale than full-time soldiers and whose civilian jobs can be difficult to maintain in the face of combat tours with unknown end points.

This was particularly true for doctors. According to 2005 Senate testimony of Lieutenant General Kevin Kiley, surgeon general of the army, the potential for repetitive deployments is a special challenge for physicians, especially reservists, who cannot afford to leave their practices for years at a time. As a result, many are "very reluctant to sign up," further exacerbating the shortage. For homeland defense operations, said Kiley, "we may be stretched very thin" by relying on medical reservists. Vice Admiral Donald Arthur, surgeon general of the navy, echoed Kiley's concern in the same session, citing the "difficulty retaining those specialties who tend to have more deployments than others: the surgeons, the nurse-anesthetists, the periopera-tive nurses, the combat medic equivalents in the Navy."[28]

These difficulties are quantifiable. A November 2005 study released by the GAO on recruitment and reenlistment shortfalls concluded that the military had "failed to fully staff 41 percent of its array of combat and noncombat spe-cialties." One of the specialties is the medical field. Between 2000 and 2005, according to the report, the army fell short of its target for special forces medical sergeants, as did the reserves with their medical logistics and labora-tory specialists. The report warned that "the recruiting environment will become even more challenging in fiscal year 2006." In testimony before Con-gress, Major General Joseph G. Webb, Jr., army deputy surgeon general, told lawmakers that, for the first time since before the attacks of September 11, 2001, the army did not meet its goal for health professions scholarship ap-plicants, the "bedrock" of medical department accessions. Both the army and the air force, he said, were straining to recruit enough physicians, nurses, dentists, and other medical specialists to treat service members who are wounded in combat and to provide adequate ongoing care when they return home.[29]

THE FRIGHTENING COSTS of troop shortages—exacerbated by "don't ask, don't tell"—do not end here. It's not just that the military admits unqualified people while wasting qualified gay ones; the ensuing shortfalls also end up overtaxing the qualified people who have to take up the slack where fired troops left off. The result is an overreliance on the National Guard and the reserves, extended deployments throughout the ranks, stop-loss orders de-laying discharges of thousands of people prepping to return to their families, more frequent rotations, and forced recalls of civilian reservists who thought their contracts had been fulfilled. This last category is particularly troubling. As a result of the military's failure to fill all its slots for the wars in the Middle East, in 2004 the government began what some have called a "backdoor draft," issuing mandatory recalls to thousands of troops for deployment to Iraq and Afghanistan. One of the most controversial and taxing uses of the recalls was to force the return to duty of civilian reservists—not the "week-end warriors" who train together one weekend per month and two weeks per year, but former troops who no longer train at all. The contracts of these unfortunate Individual Ready Reserve (IRR) troops say in small print that they are subject to recall in rare circumstances. IRR soldiers, through no fault of their own, are even less prepared and less cohesive than regular reservists because they have not been training with a unit at all while out of the service.[30]

The 5,674 recalls from the IRR announced in 2004 targeted specialists with needed skills in intelligence, engineering, medicine, administration, transportation, security, and other key support and logistical areas. In certain badly needed specialties, the military could have avoided involuntary recalls altogether if it had not expelled competent gay troops in exactly the same fields. For instance, during the six-year period from 1998 to 2003, the military recalled 72 soldiers in communication and navigation but discharged 115 gay troops in that category; 33 in operational intelligence but expelled 50 gays; 33 in combat operations control but expelled 106. In total, while the army announced it would recall 5,674 troops from the Individual Ready Reserve, 6,416 troops had been discharged for being gay, lesbian, or bisexual in the previous six years. Appallingly, 260 of the recalls were for medical specialists—those in the very same occupational categories as the 244 who were discharged over the first ten years of the anti-gay policy, including Beth Schissel. "If those gay service members were allowed to stay in their trained professions," said Representative Marty Meehan, then a senior member of the House Armed Services Committee who sponsored legislation to repeal the current policy, "forced recalls in those fields would not be an issue."[31]

THERE ARE STILL people out there who argue that it's the right thing to do to kick out gay troops because they undermine privacy and morale. But the larger question is this: Even if the presence of openly gay troops did exact a cost to straight privacy (which is, of course, already compromised in military life), that cost would need to be weighed against the damage that is surely done to cohesion by yanking gays out of the highly cohesive teams in which medical personnel train in order to save soldiers' lives. Among the success stories of modern military medicine is the development of forward surgical teams, which provide "total team training" to doctors, nurses, and medics who will treat acutely injured patients on the battlefield. These predeployment group training methods have now replaced on-the-job training as the most effective approach to treating casualties, and the cohesion of the team is thus critical to the viability of the entire fighting force. Deputy Surgeon General Webb testified that it is this type of "clinical teamwork that makes a tremendously positive difference in the care of the wounded." The special skills of military medical personnel are not easy to attract, retain, or replace. Of the medical corps, Webb concluded that "it is critical that we develop the appropriate programs to ensure that their expertise and experience are not lost."

Beth Schissel agreed. "You can't go out on the street tomorrow and pick out someone to replace me," she said. "You can't just find people with my qualifications who are ready to serve as I did. I was created by [the military training] system and then discarded." Schissel said her mentor, who went on to become air force surgeon general, was grooming her to eventually run military hospitals, the same path that Margarethe Cammermeyer was on. "He recognized what I could become" she said. "So it was a rude awakening for me to find out that I was a decorated junior officer and I couldn't serve my country because of the person I loved."[32]

AS IF IT'S not enough to lose critical talent, compromise quality, and overtax remaining troops, there is another source of damage wrought by this policy: the tarnished image of a military that is seen by millions of Americans—gay and straight alike—as behind the curve. Indeed, it is not only gays who have been turned away from military service under the ban. Countless others are turned off by the prospect of serving in an institution that flies in the face of the principles of nondiscrimination that they hold dear. To them, the military has increasingly come to be seen as a last bastion of discrimination, a lumbering, bureaucratic institution that refuses to change with the changing times. This is not just a question of offended liberals resisting the military because it rejects their pacifist values. According to 2005 polls, nearly 80 percent of the American public believe gays should be allowed to serve openly in the military. The respondents to the poll included majorities of Republicans, regular churchgoers, and people with negative attitudes toward gays.[33]

Since the Vietnam era, a "civil-military gap" has worried strategists and observers who recognize how crucial it is for both military culture and civilian society to enjoy mutual respect. Americans generally hold a high level of esteem for the armed forces; nevertheless, tensions have persisted for over a generation between a society that has grown more and more liberal in its cultural values and a military that often appears to be clinging to a world that has ceased to exist. This gap, along with an unpopular war in Iraq, strains the capacity of military recruiters to appeal to the highest quality and quantity of potential enlistees.

The most obvious roots of resistance to the American military lie in the anti-war movement of the 1960s and the disillusionment bred by the Vietnam War. But the Reagan years rebuilt a good deal of support for the military, and by the 1990s it was discrimination against gays and lesbians that gave many the sense that the military was a bulwark of conservative intolerance in a world whose values and attitudes were quickly changing.

Resentment toward anti-gay exclusion came to a fore following the Persian Gulf War when Americans learned that known gays had been sent into battle and then fired on their return. In 1993 hundreds of graduates and faculty members at Harvard stood and turned their backs on Colin Powell when he delivered the college's commencement address. The military's image remained plagued by ongoing embarrassments throughout the 1990s and beyond, rooted in the perception that it refused to evolve with the times. During the 2000s, revelations of the discharges of critical specialists like Arabic linguists exacerbated the situation, as the stupidity of kicking out the most badly needed personnel became a recurring joke on late-night talk shows.

It also didn't help matters when Americans learned the air force had sought $7 million to develop a "gay bomb" that would turn enemy soldiers into inept homosexual warriors. The idea was to break down the unit cohesion of hostile armies with a chemical aphrodisiac that would make their soldiers more interested in one another than in toppling the United States. Though the gay bomb was never developed, the idea shone a light onto the mentality of military officials who continued to believe both that people could be turned gay and that homosexuality would destroy a fighting force. Nor did it help when the Palm Center revealed that, as late as 2006, military documents still defined homosexuality as a "mental disorder"—along with retardation and impulse control disorder—more than thirty years after the American Psychiatric Association removed homosexuality from its list of mental illnesses.[34]

Resistance to military intolerance was not solely the purview of idealistic, liberal college students. Mainstream commentators and small newspapers throughout the country found the military's ouster of gay troops during the war on terrorism to be utterly confounding. "Military Dumb in Any Language," read the headline of an editorial in *The Charleston Gazette*. "The Pentagon has let prejudice come in the way of the fight against terror," read the editorial. *The Atlanta Journal-Constitution* called the policy "ludicrous" and wrote that it was "utterly inconceivable that our government would compromise the safety of the nation" by firing nearly ten thousand troops just for being gay. "The current policy lacks common sense," editorialized *USA Today*. In May 2005, the neoconservative columnist Max Boot wrote in the *Los Angeles Times* that he had reversed his position on the gay ban. "The fight against gay rights is hurting the fight against our real enemies," he argued. "In the struggle against Islamic fanatics, we can't afford to turn volunteers away."[35]

Such indictments, which reflected broad distaste for the military's intolerance, had real consequences for recruitment. It was not just that people were turning away from the military; in thousands of instances, recruiters themselves have been turned away, deprived of the opportunity to reach the students they needed to fill empty slots in the armed forces—all because the policy on gay troops violates the laws or principles of school districts and colleges across the country. Indeed, there is little greater evidence of the damage to military readiness wrought by "don't ask, don't tell" than the exile of military recruiters from high school and college campuses nationwide.

Undersecretary of Defense Charles Abell told Congress that "part of the challenge we face" in closing recruitment shortfalls is in getting "influencers"— parents, teachers, coaches, and other adults with a direct impact on the choices made by young people—to "understand the nobility and the true nature of" military service.[36] Such high-minded ideals are difficult to maintain when the pall of discrimination hangs over the institution. Of course, some influencers think more highly of the military precisely because it seeks to free its ranks from known homosexuals; but as four-fifths of Americans oppose discrimination in the military, "don't ask, don't tell" has become a drag on the enthusiasm influencers are likely to show in nudging young people toward military service.

Far and away the largest concentrated pool of potential recruits for the military is America's high schools. "Don't ask, don't tell" ripped into this pool and cordoned off countless high school students, putting them out of reach of military recruiters. In many cases, military discrimination directly conflicts with a school's nondiscrimination policy, prompting efforts to restrict recruiters' access to campus. Until they were forced by law to abandon their position, for instance, all San Francisco schools had banned recruiters because of "don't ask, don't tell." Nationwide, more than two thousand high schools have sought to deny military recruiters access to students or student information in the last ten years, and the Pentagon acknowledged that in just one year, high schools barred military officials from recruiting on campus more than nineteen thousand times.[37]

When high schools refuse to cooperate with the armed forces, the consequences for recruiting can be serious. The military's constrained ability to appeal to the nation's young people made it harder to fill its shortfalls and contributed to the reduced standards of incoming troops. The result, as described in a House Armed Services Committee report, was "higher operational risks, reduced readiness, and increased stress on both deployed and nondeployed forces." The services, it said, "are not able to attract sufficient high-quality recruits to maintain the quality force so critical to readiness." The committee concluded that "further reductions to recruit quality standards present a very costly and dangerous risk to military readiness."[38]

The committee's recommendations reflected its understanding that the recruitment ban held by the nation's high schools in protest of the military's discriminatory policy was a major hurdle in meeting its personnel needs. It advised adding up to $200 million in federal funds for recruitment and encouraging localities to "provide military recruiters the same access to high school students that is provided to other prospective employers." It also took pains to note that more money could achieve only limited gains in meeting recruitment goals, and that a "broad range of reforms outside those of military pay and compensation" would be necessary to resolve the shortfalls.[39] The "broad range of reforms," however, was never broad enough to incorporate a reconsideration of the gay ban, whose presence directly contributed to the shortfall and recruitment problems.

Thus the huge recruitment hurdles faced by the military are, in some regard, self-imposed, or at least avoidable. The policy violates both the values and, frequently, the regulations or laws of school districts and colleges across the land, prompting a costly, embarrassing, and needless battle between the military and the schools they are seeking to tap for service. As long as the Pentagon continues to fire gay and lesbian service members, recruitment will suffer because many high schools will refuse to cooperate with the military, or will cooperate only when forced to at the hands of a self-defeating law that further alienates many of the people it seeks to attract.

The situation with colleges is similar to that of high schools. One congressional study found 140 institutions of higher education that denied military recruiters access to campus. Resistance to military recruitment was so strong that Congress decided it had to pass laws to force schools to accept military recruiters on campus. Angered by what many saw as an expression of protest against the military, Congress decided to flex its muscle in response. It passed a law that yanked federal funding from any college that refused to grant recruiters access—even when doing so would violate long-standing antidiscrimination clauses held by the universities. In introducing the legislation, Representative Gerald Solomon of New York, its sponsor, said that if universities did not like the military, that was their prerogative. "But do not expect Federal dollars to support your interference with our military recruiters."[40]

Of course, the universities that barred recruiters did not necessarily dislike the military, nor was their objective to interfere with military recruitment. They were obliged by their own policies, and frequently by external policies such as those set by the American Association of Law Schools (in the case of law schools), to limit employer recruiting to those who signed forms stating they followed nondiscrimination clauses as laid out in university rule books.

In 1996, the so-called Solomon amendment was expanded, revoking Defense Department funds for any college or university with an "anti-ROTC policy." Over the next several years, the law was repeatedly fine-tuned to put more teeth in the arsenal of the federal government. It was expanded to deny funding not only from the Department of Defense but from a host of other agencies, including the Departments of Labor, Health and Human Services, and Education.[41] By 2002, the law's sway had quietly metastasized, growing into a spiteful punishment—as evidenced by the denial not just of Pentagon funds but of grant money from whatever federal sources the Congress could control.

That year, just before school reopened for the fall semester, Harvard Law School announced it would end its long-standing ban on military recruiters. The newly strengthened and enforced Solomon amendment threatened to eliminate hundreds of millions of federal research dollars from the entire university if the law school continued to honor its nondiscrimination policy. Following the attacks of 9/11, well aware that the United States was gearing up for military action and might suffer from restricted recruitment access to American campuses, the air force had reviewed the list of schools deemed to be in compliance with Solomon's demands. Harvard fell short, it decided. The school was told it was no longer in compliance and if it did not reverse course, the air force would recommend to the secretary of defense that it cut off funding to the entire university because of the law school's sins. In a letter to the law school community, Dean Robert Clark wrote that he had struggled mightily with the issue, but that ultimately Harvard stood to lose $328 million each year in federal funds that went to student aid, faculty pay, and scientific research that was earmarked for finding cures and treatments for life-threatening medical conditions.[42] The money took precedence over the principle of nondiscrimination, and the Congress had succeeded in strong-arming Harvard into doing its bidding.

The Solomon amendment has created some of the most asinine situations to come out of the military's gay ban. As the United States became a war nation, government reports began calling for greater cooperation between national defense agencies and the educational system, including universities. One such report, the Pentagon's 2005 white paper, "A Call to Action for National Foreign Language Capabilities," called for government-sponsored research into innovative academic approaches to language specialization—precisely the kind of research that the government threatens to cut off if universities, in accordance with their nondiscrimination policies, refuse to let military officials recruit on campus.[43]

But the absurdities began earlier. In 1996, the Connecticut Supreme Court ruled that "don't ask, don't tell" violated the state's nondiscrimination law protecting gays and lesbians. The result was to let stand a University of Connecticut Law School rule that blocked the military from recruiting on campus. Yet for a different reason entirely, the university had to retain its ROTC unit on campus: Federal law required it, as a land-grant college, to teach military tactics, something accomplished by the ROTC program. Thus a state law required giving the armed forces the boot, which meant the loss of federal funds for the university, while a federal law required bringing them on board, which would be a clear violation of the state law that canned recruiters in the first place.[44]

The next year, the Defense Department published a list of schools that were in violation of the Solomon amendment. Of twenty-two schools, seventeen offenders were in Connecticut, all of which lost federal funding, including the tuition assistance given to ROTC students. Although the ROTC programs remained, because of the land-grant requirement, recruiters were still barred by the state law requiring nondiscrimination. The result was that the students who enjoyed tuition breaks through ROTC would lose this assistance if they attended one of the seventeen offending schools.[45]

The quandary required hours of attention by congressional committees, Pentagon lawyers, the state legislature, and the governor of Connecticut. In the fall of 1997, little could be done to resolve the situation because the Connecticut state legislature would not be meeting again until the next winter. So the congressional committee responsible for drawing up the National Defense Authorization Act got assurance from the state's governor that he would pass a special law, a state version of the Solomon amendment that would dance around the nondiscrimination clause. Then the committee drafted special language to try to freeze the withheld funds before they were redirected to other uses—for just long enough that the Connecticut legislature could meet next winter and find a way around the provisions that were now inadvertently punishing ROTC students who depended on the now-inaccessible tuition aid to attend college and train as reserve officers. For good measure, the committee noted that, even though it was sequestering funds while awaiting future state action, the conferees "insist that military recruiters be afforded access to institutions of higher education or [the schools would] face the consequence of loss of federal funds."[46]

The governor of Connecticut was all too happy to toss aside his state's principled policy of nondiscrimination. On October 29, 1997, he called a special session of the state legislature, which quickly brought the matter to a rest by approving a law forcing recruiters back on campus. Congress then amended the law to exempt student tuition assistance from any funds that would be cut off as punishment for barring recruiters.[47] This particular embarrassing situation would not be allowed to happen again.

In the years following 9/11, as recruitment needs became more dire, Congress became more belligerent. Early in 2005, Congress updated the Solomon amendment to reflect the urgency: "Congress remains committed to the achievement of military personnel readiness through vigorous application of the requirements set forth" in earlier renditions of the law. "It is the sense of Congress that the executive branch should aggressively continue to pursue measures to challenge any decision impeding or prohibiting" the freedom of military recruiters to access the enormous pool of young bodies needed to go off to war. Finally, the updated language recommended that the Bush administration follow a "doctrine of non-acquiescence," which meant that any legal decision affecting one region's freedom to recruit on campus should not be construed to similarly limit all other jurisdictions.[48]

In none of the suggestions for how to "challenge any decision impeding or prohibiting" the access of military recruiters to college campuses did the Congress consider the most obvious decision impeding such access: the decision of Congress itself to leave "don't ask, don't tell" standing. College campuses had not gone out of their way to make trouble for military recruiters. Though some of the resistance to the military was rooted specifically in opposition to the Vietnam War, the universities presently had no policy singling out the military for impeded access to campus. It was simply a matter of enforcing nondiscrimination policies in an evenhanded manner. Despite complaints from the government, the military *did* enjoy "equal access" to campuses—the same access as all other employers who refused to sign a vow of nondiscrimination. Yet nearly all the lumbering instruments of federal and local government that got involved chose to fight a battle of spite and raw muscle; none of these elected officials or bodies ever seemed to consider that lifting the unnecessary ban would wipe away the problem overnight, without incurring the embarrassing costs of appearing to strong-arm academia with threats to cease funding for cancer research. And without, according to all evidence, any detriment to military readiness.

Indeed, when the courts took up the case, a panel in the Third Circuit struck down the law, noting that the policy "generate[s] ill will toward the military" and "actually impedes recruitment." Defenders of discrimination, however, such as a dissenting judge on the same panel, complained that "the court was interfering with congressional powers to raise and support the military." Similarly, the Bush administration argued that the initial ruling against the law would "undermine military recruitment in a time of war."[49] In 2006, the Supreme Court agreed with President Bush, reversing the Third Circuit decision, and allowing Solomon to stand.

Rather than take the simple step, which happened in this case to be the right step—both militarily and morally—for all involved, political leaders and their supporting lawyers have done everything they could to uphold discrimination against gays and lesbians in the military. The result is a crippling policy that is hampering recruitment, and along with it, military readiness at a time when we desperately need every tool at our disposal. Despite ample evidence to the contrary, these men and women refuse to acknowledge that they have created a fundamental problem that shadows the military's every move. That problem is not a gay menace. That problem is discrimination itself.

The badly stretched U.S. military is firing badly needed, capable troops because they're gay and filling slots with ex-convicts, drug abusers, and high school dropouts. And why? Because top military brass, and a handful of their friends in Congress, have their fingers in their ears: They do not want to hear that patriotic gay Americans are serving their country valiantly, because admitting that gay soldiers are good soldiers threatens to upend the self-image of traditional American manhood. Politicians either believe this, too, or are unwilling to say otherwise and risk alienating their political base. That this policy is about politics and prejudice rather than military necessity is made abundantly clear by the line drawn in the sand around gays and lesbians. Again and again, military officials are willing to take major risks and make compromising exceptions in order to fill the ranks with warm bodies—unless those warm bodies prefer warm bodies of the same sex. As put by the father of a mentally ill recruit who was enlisted by desperate recruiters, despite being warned of his unsuitability: "They were willing to put my son and other recruits at risk" just to fill a slot. And yet, to the Pentagon and Congress, letting openly gay patriots serve their country constitutes "an unacceptable risk" that *could* undermine unit cohesion (never mind that, actually, it doesn't).

The army's commander of recruiting, Major General Michael Rochelle, defended his compromising recruitment tactics by describing a "shift in thinking," saying that in the past, "if an individual was accused of doctoring a high-school diploma, it was an open-and-shut case," but that "now, I look at a person's value to the command first." Why not do that with gays, who are surely more valuable to the military than the mentally unfit? In truth, this "whole person" philosophy makes sense when assessing difficult personnel decisions. "The Army has always issued waivers to otherwise qualified applicants who may not meet all our stringent requirements," said another recruiting official, S. Douglas Smith. "Waiver authorities apply the 'whole person' concept when considering waiver applications. This is the right thing to do for those Americans who want to serve."[50] The right thing, indeed.

11

Rainbow Warriors

A s the pentagon's recruiting woes mounted and homosexual discharges continued, though at lower rates than before 2001, a less-reported narrative was emerging that starkly contradicted the very assumptions of "don't ask, don't tell"—that gays couldn't serve openly without causing problems. Reflecting dramatic shifts in American attitudes about homosexuality and a gradual crumbling of the civilian closet, more and more gays and lesbians were refusing to conceal their true selves and were serving in the military without pretense. Judging from the actions of commanders, we can see that the upper echelons of the military are thinking differently than they did even a decade ago. When a service member says to a superior, "I'm gay," the most common response may now be, "That's nice. Now get back to work." But commanders continue to be hamstrung by the law, and enough of the old brass, born in the 1940s and 1950s, still support the law or toe the party line because they believe their colleagues demand no less. What has emerged is a vast population of young people who simply don't care about sexual orientation, a growing number of senior military officers who find the policy wrong and destructive but won't or can't say, and a growing number of top military brass who—once they retire—feel free to say what they really think and condemn the policy. The result is enormous momentum for change, both inside and outside the military, but the ban persists, with its arbitrary enforcement, because of a small group of powerful politicians and military officials.

In this climate, some service members get lucky. They serve openly without any consequences or hostility and they live their lives just like their heterosexual friends and colleagues, serving their country with the necessary focus on their training and mission. Others are not so lucky. They continue to live and serve in fear and uncertainty, face hostility, and even vengeance, sometimes from homophobic superiors and sometimes from colleagues who will simply use whatever tools they can to settle a totally unrelated score.

They serve their country hampered and diminished, and all too often lose their jobs and benefits because of a policy that never should have been created in the first place.

What explains why some gays and lesbians serve openly without problems and others continue to suffer under the weight of "don't ask, don't tell"? In part, nothing. It is simply a testimony to the utterly arbitrary reality of living under a policy that is based on regulating the unregulatable, on deception and denial, and on assumptions about reality that are false. But there are some explanations for the patterns, and many of them echo what the evidence reveals from foreign militaries. As we'll see, many commanders have no problem letting gays continue serving so long as they don't make the commander look bad. That is, they expect discretion from gays and lesbians, though not formal compliance with "don't tell." A second explanation of successful open service is the capacity of service members to use good judgment about when and where to come out. And a third factor is good leadership. Whatever the views of an individual commander about homosexuality, strong leadership means making clear what is expected of the rank and file and the chaotic, unrealistic dictates of "don't ask, don't tell" make this essentially impossible.

The policy relies on the assumption that straight service members are more comfortable and more willing to serve with gays if they do not know about their sexual orientation. It also assumes that formally lifting the ban will cause many more gays to come out than are already out under the existing rules. The argument that has prevailed in retaining a ban linked these factors to military necessity, suggesting that "don't tell" could successfully preserve privacy and that doing so was essential to preserving unit cohesion. Though no evidence ever proved the link, enough people thought it was "common sense" that the argument carried the day. Is it still, though, common sense? As we near the second decade of the twenty-first century, is sentiment in the U.S. military still fiercely opposed to knowing about the presence of gays and lesbians in the barracks? How much has changed since 1993 in attitudes and understandings about gays in the military? And how accurate are the guiding assumptions of "don't ask, don't tell" that a federal law can keep American service members from knowing which of their coworkers are gay?

Since 1993, several remarkable things have happened. More and more gay people have refused to hide their identities when they don their country's uniform; at first they did so out of righteous defiance and then, more and more, they stopped hiding because they simply found they didn't need to. The law was still in place, but their peers, their subordinates, increasingly even their superiors, made it clear they didn't care whether their coworkers loved men or women, so long as they could do their jobs. Over the last decade and a half, poll after poll has confirmed what story after story has told: Adamant opposition to homosexuality is simply less common. With each passing year, it seems, prejudice and fear are the weapons of an increasingly marginalized minority. At the same time, pop culture has made leaps and bounds in expanding tolerance of homosexuality and, for the first time in history, a generation of young people has emerged in which many never knew the inside of a closet. Eventually, military experts—from academic researchers to retired senior officers—followed suit and have acknowledged publicly what others had known for some time: You don't need to be straight to shoot straight.

AS WE'LL SEE, the changes in the experiences of gay and lesbian troops have been most dramatic in recent years. But openly gay service is by no means new. Even in the policy's infancy, many gays and lesbians served openly throughout the ranks. Notably, the kind of harassment that was rampant in some units was significantly less of a problem in units with open gays in their ranks, a finding borne out by the research on foreign militaries. In the first full year the American policy was in effect, Servicemembers Legal Defense Network knew of more than a dozen gays and lesbians that were out to their peers. In their units, harassment had become "almost non-existent," according to a 1996 report. (That figure would explode from a dozen to five hundred by 2008, and that's just the number of openly gay troops of which SLDN was directly aware.)[1]

Many of the service members SLDN documented, such as Zoe Dunning, were serving because highly publicized legal or administrative challenges were pending or had resulted in mandated reinstatement, setting up a situation where the homosexuality of a member was widely known. Consider also Keith Meinhold, the sailor who had made waves when a federal court ordered his reinstatement after he challenged a discharge in 1993. Some navy officials had used the incident to argue that known gays caused disruptions, citing the media racket and the hubbub caused by a small number of sailors who fussed about his return. The claims were utterly disingenuous, however, as the incident had become just one more opportunity for moralizers to vent their anti-gay feelings. In reality, the minor disruptions caused by Meinhold's return were temporary and unique, and largely spurred by the grandstanding of senior officials who were bitter about the exercise of judicial power in their military. And as previously stated, none of this would have occurred if the policy hadn't caused his ouster in the first place. In any event, during Meinhold's three additional years of open service, his unit fully embraced him. His crew was named the most combat-ready in his fleet, and his final evaluation said that his "inspirational leadership has significantly contributed to the efficiency, training and readiness of my squadron." One of his coworkers, a self-described "bigot from hell," said that knowing Meinhold had "totally changed" his feelings about the service of gays.[2]

Another case was the high-profile service of Colonel Margarethe Cammermeyer. In 1994, a Washington state judge ordered her reinstated, prompting joyous phone calls from high-ranking officers welcoming her back. She served openly for three more years, and her story was broadcast to the world in 1995 in a TV movie while she was still serving. There were others. In the mid-1990s, Justin Elzie served four years openly and was named NCO of the Quarter and top marksman for his base at Camp LeJeune. One of his reports touted his "leadership abilities to lead the Marine Corps into the twenty-first century." Coworkers of Petty Officer Mark Phillips celebrated the anniversary of his coming out by giving him a chocolate cake, and a surprise birthday party while he was in the thick of battle—a legal challenge to his discharge for homosexuality.[3]

Steve Clark Hall also served openly in the early years of "don't ask, don't tell." Hall entered the navy as an officer out of the Naval Academy and, after four consecutive sea tours, rose to commanding officer of a nuclear submarine. Before the 1990s, Hall recalls, it was a common understanding that there were plenty of gays in the navy, even open ones. Once while training over one hundred people in the engineering department, he was suggesting bars to visit while in port, and one man known to be gay asked in a high-pitched voice where the bars were for him. Without missing a beat, Hall referred him to several gay bars by name, an indication to all present that there were gays in their midst and that this was not a problem. "So not only was he totally out, I was also pretty open to my department in the early '80s," Hall recalled.[4]

In his own case, Hall said, "everybody else figured it out before I did." Eventually, he bought a house in the Castro, San Francisco's gay district, which was widely known in the navy. He even hosted parties there with other officers, the source of many good-natured jokes referencing his neighborhood and what it suggested about Hall's sexuality. Though he did not announce his sexuality, he was later told by peers that his entire crew knew he was gay.[5]

For Hall, "don't ask, don't tell" was worse than the previous policy because the times were changing around it. When he was promoted to commander, his momentum was toward coming out, toward ceasing any final vestiges of lying, deceiving, or concealing. It had become clear to him by the early 1990s that people did not care about his sexuality—only about how he did his job. He told his men that it was important to respect differences, a thinly veiled reference to his sexuality. But suddenly came a policy that defined certain differences as a threat to cohesion and an "unacceptable risk" to the military.[6]

He had the most trouble explaining the policy to young sailors, who literally didn't get it. "The officers who were significantly senior to me were the ones brought up to think of homosexuality as this deviant behavior that causes loss of morale," he recalled. "Young kids these days grow up with kids who are gay. They know that they're real people. They know that they're not the 'deviant' people who have always been portrayed as being bad for morale. . . . The younger troops didn't have a problem with the gay thing." What really hurts morale, he said, was when you boot someone for being gay and it takes several months to get a replacement. "You have three guys on watch rotation of six hours on, twelve hours off; now you're missing a person so they're on six and off six. Talk about something that's bad for morale. That kills morale to lose one of your team members because they happen to be gay."[7]

THESE CASES OF American service members who were out to their peers, even in the 1990s as "don't ask, don't tell" was first being implemented, are a part of a global body of evidence that an open environment actually breeds tolerance and readiness, not disruptions and disaster. That evidence has only mounted in the twenty-first century. Once the United States mobilized for war, sexual orientation became even less important. Throughout their tours in Iraq and Afghanistan, gay troops were out and about; and for the most part, they were tolerated and even embraced by straights who didn't think twice about their sexuality, or, if they did, thought twice and moved on.

According to interviews with gays and lesbians, coworkers "just don't care" about whether their comrades are gay or lesbian, especially the younger ones. A staff sergeant noted that "enlisted soldiers are generally younger and more willing to accept new things" while "officers tend to look to regulations for guidance in soldiering," and "are generally distanced from their soldiers and are therefore less likely to know that one of their soldiers is gay." Another service member, an army specialist who was deployed to Afghanistan in 2003, said, "People my age, high school through my age, don't care." Her platoon sergeant also found out about her sexuality and fully tolerated it. "He said, 'Well, don't go tell the world, but I don't really care; I'll try to look out for you unless you're a total piece of crap. Just don't make it to where me looking out for you makes me look stupid.'" The specialist said she could "read people a bit and I can tell who it's okay to be open with and who not."[8]

The examples go on and on: "Most of my unit does know I am gay and they don't care one way or the other . . . that's really the last thing on anyone's mind." "There was another gay guy in my squadron who was really good friends with my roommates, and they were really cool with it and so that kind of paved the way for me." "Most of it's accepted . . . it's not a problem." "I came out to a couple of coworkers and that went quite well." "After I developed a strong relationship with my supervisor, we would talk about it [sexual orientation] and would even joke about it." "If I told someone, it never changed our relationships . . . I was never looked at differently for being gay." "Almost every one of my friends said, 'Oh, we all knew that. What's the big deal?'" When in port or off base, it is not uncommon for gays and straights to visit gay bars together. These service members, far from being divided by their differing sexual identities, come together to socialize in genuine and open ways. And more often than not, these men and women observe that form of bodily contact which so riles certain members of the military—that bodily contact that a "reasonable person" would "understand to demonstrate a propensity or intent to engage in" prohibited acts. Perhaps we should add this to the list of reasons why we haven't yet won the war on terrorism?[9]

The rationale for "don't ask, don't tell" rests on the assumption that straight men are intolerant of gay men. Surveys of women's attitudes toward lesbians in the military show much greater willingness to tolerate gay women. In the latest surveys, a majority of military women actually support letting open gays serve. But a ban on gay men and not gay women would be a public relations nightmare. The result is that women are caught up in a ban whose rationale, such as it is, really only applies to men. A related oddity is that the policy can hamper the special bonds that are sometimes made between gay men and straight women, and between gay women and straight men in the military. The privacy and unit cohesion rationales would never apply to these relationships. This is significant because gay people have historically confided in straight members of the opposite sex (think *Will and Grace*), forging important relationships that can be more comforting and less threatening than those among straight members of the same sex. Their shared objects of affection can even become a source of commonality. That means "don't ask, don't tell" deprives service members of the opportunity to forge such relationships. Or rather, it would if people followed it. "Guys loved me," said Wendy Biehl, the army specialist who discussed her sexuality with straight men during deployment to the Middle East. "I had the best of both worlds," she said, enjoying friendships with women, while "shar[ing] sexual secrets" with men. Biehl recounted how straight men asked her for sexual advice and they would bond over the women they found attractive. "They were like my brothers," she said. "They'd stick up for me."[10]

Often it's straight members of the opposite sex who break the ice and facilitate the meeting of gay people who might otherwise be hesitant to identify one another as gay. One sailor in the Pacific Fleet, for instance, said his female friend gave him the lowdown on a shy newcomer to the ship. The sailor had wondered if the new recruit might be gay, but decided it was too risky to ask him directly. According to the woman's report, the shy sailor had "perked up" at hearing mention of the first sailor's name, suggesting they might have something in common. "Looks like we have another rainbow warrior," the sailor said with a grin.[11]

Despite the ubiquity of open gay service, fear, not surprisingly, remains. But once the ice is broken, it often evaporates. An army specialist serving in a combat unit in Iraq was coming out of a gay bar when on leave in the states, and was spotted on the street by another soldier. "Cheapest drinks in the city," said the specialist awkwardly, trying to explain away his presence at the bar. His fellow soldier wasn't convinced. "So I told him," the specialist recalled later, "and he said, 'I don't care.'" His combat unit, he said, was "as intimate as intimate can get," and none of that changed once his sexuality was known. Back in Iraq, he slept in the same three to five cubic feet as his sergeant, surrounded by other men inside their tent. "It didn't matter," he said. "There wasn't much of a question of, 'Okay, this guy does this, would he do it here?'" When his sergeant during another tour learned of his sexuality, he told him he would not mention it to anyone. The specialist also described a gay soldier "who was girlier than any girl I knew. He was extremely flamboyant and nobody gave a shit." A gay surgical technician on board the USS *Abraham Lincoln* said he works with gays who are so flamboyant that "we need an extinguisher." He said one of his JAG officers "sashayed down the hangar bay, hand on the hip and everything," and it did not create problems.[12]

A squadron leader who commanded Bradley fighting vehicles in Iraq, and who also commanded a dismounted unit for the 4th Infantry Division, said he served openly with no problems. "I don't advertise," he said, "but I don't hide anything either." He said all nine of the soldiers who worked under him knew he was gay. "It doesn't affect unit cohesion," he said. "When I was on the ground, I was leading the charges through buildings," he said. "And I've never had people not follow me. I've never heard of that happening at all," referring to insubordination due to a leader's sexual orientation.[13]

ONE OF THE reasons that openly gay service turns out to work so well, it seems, is because of the judgment calls made by individual gay troops, based on the appropriateness of individual situations. Gays and lesbians explain that, while they feel the need to confide in someone about their sexuality, they are careful to establish preliminary bonds of trust with confidantes, or to judge the probability of acceptance before coming out, and they choose to come out privately or quietly in moments that seem appropriate for intimate conversation.

"I see myself as a good instinctive judge of character," said an army captain, "and thankfully for me that's turned out to be the case when I told my friends [that I'm gay]." On one occasion, when a date went longer than expected, the captain's best friend hounded him about his whereabouts. After staving off the questions, he finally said, "I'm not going to lie to you, you're my best friend. I went to meet a guy." The captain's friend nearly choked on his burrito, collected his thoughts, and then said, "That's cool, but don't expect me to be down with it because I'm not. Now let's go get a beer." The friendship has remained strong and the captain now baby-sits for his friend's children.[14] Such is an important illustration of the kind of reaction that could ensue even from those who may have indicated on surveys that they oppose letting gays serve in the military.

Indeed, many service members describe an informal "don't ask, don't tell" norm prevailing among both gay and straight troops. This could be partly a product of the policy's strictures on discussing the matter of sexuality. But the fact that so many gays and lesbians do come out to their peers in certain situations shows that the policy alone is not what governs their behavior; instead, decisions are shaped by individual judgments about when and to whom to reveal their sexual orientation. The same holds true of "asking": One soldier, for instance, said that "many people are just not asking, not because of the ban but because it's none of their business." He said the custom was "don't know, don't want to find out."[15]

A final ingredient in explaining the success of openly gay service is good leadership. A petty officer first class in the navy described working with effeminate men who were known to be gay. He reported that these suspected or known gays worked successfully with their peers, in part, because of a tolerant and dedicated command structure. "Our commanders made it clear that anti-gay harassment would not be accepted," he said. "And that's why those effeminate men were accepted." He said that tolerance was the product of "a climate that's created," just as evidence from foreign militaries suggests. "All they need to do is hear it from a higher-up. If you create a climate at a commanding officer level that [homosexuality] is acceptable, then I think everybody will fall in line."[16]

Unfortunately, the policy itself makes it virtually impossible even for strong leaders to make clear what expected behavior is in the ranks. Many gays and lesbians note that other troops assume or suspect they or other service members are gay. These findings are confirmed in a major poll of troops who served in Iraq and Afghanistan, two-thirds of whom said they knew or suspected there were gays in their unit. Many of these troops said they could simply tell a person's sexual orientation by observing "speech, behavior or appearance," a reminder of the ultimate impossibility of regulating the expression of sexuality. Though such guesswork is an imperfect gauge of actual sexual orientation, the fact is that even when service members abide by "don't tell" entirely, it's often abundantly clear to people that there are gays in their midst, just as John McCain said in 2000, when he claimed he knew he served with gay people by their "behavior and by attitudes."[17] This means, too, that privacy cannot be protected by banning statements about homosexuality, since knowledge or suspicion of a person's sexuality often emerges without actual statements to that effect.

Of course, the best way to protect privacy is to create a climate in which individuals are expected to respect one another. And the reality is that most gays and lesbians, like straights, choose to share certain personal details about their lives with people they trust, but generally don't wish to announce the details of their sex lives publicly, and have no intention of doing so if the policy is changed to technically allow it. A lifting of the ban would not result in a military awash in gay gossip and drag shows. It would simply allow the gays in the service to get on with their jobs, reduce their stress, remove impediments to productive work, and free them from needing to misrepresent and isolate themselves. None of us should be surprised to know that gays care about privacy, too.

The Bradley commander made clear that he used discretion in choosing the people with whom he shared his sexual orientation. "You won't see me walking in the gay pride parade," he said, "but the people who need to know know, and the people that don't, it's none of their business." A Marine said, "I don't think that people should be going to work and announcing [their sexual orientation], but if it does come out I don't think it should [matter]." A petty officer first class said if the ban were lifted, "I wouldn't just tell people I'm gay, but I probably wouldn't go through such measures to hide it." "I wouldn't come out just for the hell of it," said another.[18]

The Bradley commander's experience also shows how attempting to regulate knowledge of sexual orientation is futile. Although he did not announce his sexuality publicly, "the stuff I do, it causes people to wonder." He said when he lived in the barracks, "you can look at the visitor's log and see that no women come in under my name." His vocal opposition to derogatory statements about women, the placement of rainbow stickers in his room, and the lack of female visitors add up to a clear picture that he is gay, he said. "If you look at the whole big picture," he concluded, "eventually people will start to wonder." Those soldiers who didn't know that he was gay "suspect that I am." "People know by deduction," agreed a navy pilot who has served since 1984. "You're not married, you're in your forties, all your friends are male, and you don't talk about any personal or private life."[19]

A gay army captain was confident that changing the policy would not unleash a torrent of homosexual announcements. "Just lifting the ban, there's not going to be a rainbow flag hoisted on the headquarters of the army," he said. "All you're doing by lifting the ban is allowing people not to live in secrecy." If the ban were lifted, said another, "I don't think I'd run and tell everyone at once." He did, however, say the main reason he didn't tell people was the fear that someone could turn him in. "If the law were overturned, I'd probably gradually come out to everyone," he concluded, emphasizing that he would do so in a private manner.[20]

"I'd be truthful as far as filling out documentation," said a senior noncommissioned officer in the air force, about how things would change if the gag rule were lifted. "But as far as sticking a big old rainbow sticker on my car, [I wouldn't do that]." At the same time, some did report that they had rainbow stickers on their belongings in public view, or that they had seen such stickers on base. Such signs are not allowed to be used to initiate an investigation into the sexuality of a service member.[21]

A sailor, who described himself as inconspicuous with regard to his sexuality, said that most gays in the military blended in. "Just because you're gay doesn't mean you have to be really queeny," he said. "I'm not like that and most of the time, people aren't." He added that if people were to see him walking down the street, "they'd be like, who's that boring guy dressed in jeans and a T-shirt?"[22]

Not only do gays serve openly without causing problems; they report that when they can be honest about who they are, things get better. Bonds between gays and straights improved when suspicions and uncertainty were put to rest by a revelation or acknowledgment of their homosexuality. The Bradley commander described this evolution in his relationship to the gunner who served on his crew. "Prior to us being a crew," he recalled, "I wouldn't associate with him at all." The gay squad leader had reason to believe the gunner might not be fully accepting of homosexuality. "Then we became a crew, and we became friends. When he actually found out, when I was actually able to open up to him, things got better in the sense that I'm able to be myself and he accepts me and that's cool and he even asks me about my partner now." The gay soldier concluded that serving openly "brought me and my soldiers closer together because now they know who I am. I'm a little bit more confident about myself because now I don't have to walk around with this big ape on my back and we're just that much closer and I don't have to feel afraid of talking to them about what's going on in my life." A former army staff sergeant agreed, saying that "it became easier to talk to people once I was open with them." A supply specialist who served in Iraq—and whose tour was extended because of stop-loss orders—said his service would have been improved if he had enjoyed the freedom to discuss his personal life. "I mean, these are your best friends," he said. "These are people you live with, you die with. How easy it would have been to say, hey, I'm gay, this is who I sleep with. I think it would have just brought us a hell of a lot closer."[23]

THE RESULT, HOWEVER, of trying to enforce a law that seeks to regulate what cannot, at bottom, be regulated is that the policy, which was routinely violated, came to be seen as a joke. Both the horror stories of abuse and wrecked careers and the lighter stories of rainbow warriors serving openly with no consequences yield the same result: a climate of disrespect for law and procedure. As a result, "don't ask, don't tell" quickly gained a reputation as a "hollow shell of a policy" and a "joke," phrases that were repeatedly heard in a string of separate interviews. Said one soldier in 2004, "'Don't ask, don't tell' became a punch line in the military." The policy became the butt of jokes and increased the frequency with which discussion and jokes about gay issues occurred. "It was almost a daily occurrence," he said, adding that even he had used the name of the policy as shorthand. People would ask simple questions such as, "Where are you going tonight?" and the retort would be, "Don't ask, don't tell." Or two men would appear together and someone would point and say, "Don't ask, don't tell."[24]

Many others also reported that the policy is not taken seriously and ultimately makes a mockery of military law. When a policy is so at odds with reality that it is virtually unenforceable, it undermines respect for all rules and regulations in the institution. "The policy is a joke," said an army national guardsman. "It basically says that I can be gay but I can't *be* gay; a person can only repress himself so long before it starts to have negative effects on his performance and attitude." "The ban's a joke. It's a joke. It's not uniformly enforced," said another, adding that enforcement is, in reality, at the discretion of each commander. "The whole policy literally became a joke," agreed an air force captain who entered the military before the policy was adopted. "It still is to this day."[25]

THE EMERGENCE OF "don't ask, don't tell" as a joke has corresponded with the lighter attitude toward gays and lesbians themselves. As the more virulent anti-gay animus recedes, it seems to be replaced by gentler humor and teasing, which older bureaucrats and politicians often mistake for—or exploit to suggest—dangerous and disruptive anti-gay hostility. Indeed, one sailor in the Pacific Fleet said, "the day we stop cracking jokes about you is the day you should start worrying because that's the day we hate your guts." Even joking that does have a homophobic bent does not necessarily indicate dangerous levels of hostility in the force. In 2004, a Marine commented on how much attitudes had changed since he joined the military in 1987, and how residual homophobia had struck a much lighter tone. Recounting a recent discussion in his unit about a proposed law to ban same-sex marriage, he said only one person backed it. "That, to me, shows how much attitudes have changed," he said, adding that people care less about sexual orientation and more about performance. If a gay person was a "shitbird," as he put it, a slacker or a complainer, he or she might be singled out for criticism. "But if a person performs his job really well, they might make a joke and move on, but they'd not try to beat them up or anything like that." A navy lieutenant who joined the service in 1993, just before "don't ask, don't tell" was implemented, agreed that anti-gay comments were simply part of a larger culture of ribbing. In a revealing characterization, he said that a "high school" culture still prevailed in the military, in which "you have to make anti-gay remarks every once in a while in order to really be a guy, even though the majority of them really don't care."[26] In this sense, homophobic banter is more of a knee-jerk device service members use to fit in with each other and does not reflect deep animosity.

A soldier in the National Guard said the only disruption he had witnessed as a result of someone's sexual orientation involved "the one queeny guy from my home unit. They call him names and . . . make fun of him behind his back." But the soldier concluded that people are not "hateful" because he is gay. In general, he said about suspected gays that "no one seems to care because the persons suspected do not say it one way or the other, they just take a little ribbing from time to time." He said attitudes were improving. "Some people instead of witch hunting us are now just making jokes and letting it go," he said.[27]

Some gay troops attributed privacy concerns to the same kinds of misunderstandings (or misrepresentations) by senior officials about how service members bond. Fred Fox, for instance, the Somalia combat veteran, said that stated concerns over the impact of openly gay service on military privacy "misunderstands what it means to be a soldier." He explained: "I have never loved any man more deeply than some of the men I served with in Somalia, and I never had any sexual feelings for them. It's not some big gay porn movie; it's a brotherhood." As infantrymen, Fox said, "we wrestle and beat each other up a lot." Fox theorized that such rituals stem "from the fact that it's just awkward for anyone to love someone that deeply and you don't know how to express it, so I'm just going to sneak up behind you and throw you on the ground and wrestle for a while." He added, "It's like a big hug."[28]

A psychological operations sergeant who fought in Kirkuk agreed that privacy concerns were overblown, saying that context matters far more than the simple fact of being naked in someone's presence. During both training and fighting conditions, he said, "a separate bond occurs between soldiers. You no longer look at them as 'Joe' or think 'Joe' is cute. You look at them as your brother who just saved your ass while you were fighting, or someone that you can rely on when the shit hits the fan. You don't look at them as a potential sex partner. Once the bond as a military brother is formed, it is extremely hard to break that bond and look at them as a sexual possibility. Whoever thinks that gays join the military to sleep with a bunch of soldiers has obviously never served a day in the shoes of a soldier."[29]

THE SENSE THAT "don't ask, don't tell" has become a joke by the twenty-first century, and that the privacy bogeyman is overblown, reflects just how much the reality for young troops has changed since the policy began. And nothing bears out this reality like hard numbers. Between 1993 and the present, public opinion polls across the board reveal a substantial, and nationwide, transformation in feelings about homosexuality. While polls in late 1992 and early 1993 revealed large fluctuations in opinion, as Americans responded to the heated rhetoric of those months, support for Clinton's pledge to lift the earlier ban on gay service sunk to a low of 35 percent in January 1993, according to a Gallup poll taken for *Newsweek* magazine. Conservatives, no doubt, took comfort in this figure, as it implied that a clear majority of Americans believed that gays should not serve in the armed forces. Throughout this period, polls showed the percentage of Americans supporting gay service as hovering between 35 and 45 percent, with occasional spurts above the 50 percent line. Gallup polls showed that, in 1992, just 48 percent of Americans thought homosexual relations should be legal, and only 38 percent thought homosexuality should be viewed as an "acceptable alternative lifestyle."[30]

Throughout the 1990s, levels of support for gay service remained in roughly the same range—40 to 50 percent. But early in the new century, support began to swell. In 2003, a Fox News poll put the number at 64 percent, while a Gallup poll put it at 79 percent. Each year since then, a wide variety of national polls has found that between 58 percent and 79 percent of Americans favor openly gay service. Between 2003 and 2007 small backlashes emerged in support for gay rights. By all accounts, they came as a reaction to the rapid pace of change in social norms and institutional rules during those years, a phenomenon that is consistent with the unfolding of every civil rights story in American history. In 2003, for example, the Supreme Court struck down state sodomy bans in the landmark *Lawrence v. Texas* case. The ruling reversed the notorious 1986 decision in *Bowers v. Hardwick* that had upheld the statutes. In a closely divided 5-4 decision, *Lawrence* said that "Bowers was not correct when it was decided, is not correct today, and is hereby overruled."[31]

Also in 2003 the Massachusetts Supreme Court ruled that marriage rights could not be denied to same-sex partners, a decision that paved the way for the first legal same-sex marriages in the United States a year later (although they were not recognized by the federal government because of the 1996 Defense of Marriage Act, which denies benefits and recognition to same-sex couples even when lawfully married in their home state). And not surprisingly, in the summer of 2003, Gallup registered the first major reversal of general support for gay rights since talk of gay troops spawned a similar backlash in 1993. In just three months, the percentage of Americans who thought homosexual relations should be legal declined from 60 to 48 percent. More than half of respondents said being gay should not be considered an "acceptable alternative lifestyle," the first time a majority said so in six years; and 57 percent said gays should not enjoy the same rights as married people, the highest number opposed to equality since 2000. Pollsters were so taken aback at the numbers that they did the poll twice, but the same results only confirmed that talk of gay progress had set back support for gay equality.[32]

The backlash, however, proved temporary. A major 2005 poll conducted by the University of New Hampshire Survey Center showed that 79 percent of Americans favored openly gay service in the U.S. military; just as significant was the fact that these supporters included a majority of Republicans, religious people, and even individuals with negative attitudes toward gays. By 2007, Gallup reported that support for gay rights stood "at the high-water mark of attitudes recorded over the past three decades." After several years of sagging tolerance, attitudes were bouncing back toward acceptance of homosexuality, as evidenced, for example, by responses to that perennial question: Should homosexual relations be legal? According to a Gallup report in 2007, "Public tolerance for this aspect of gay rights expanded from 43 percent at the inception of the question in 1977 to 60 percent in May 2003. Then in July 2003, it fell to 50 percent and remained at about that level through 2005. In 2006 it jumped to 56 percent, and in 2007 it reached 59 percent, similar to the 2003 high point." In 2008, a *Washington Post*–ABC News poll found that 75 percent of Americans favored openly gay service, including a majority of white evangelicals, veterans, and Republicans, whose support had doubled since 1993. Nearly two-thirds of conservatives as well as 82 percent of white Catholics supported letting open gays serve.[33]

Acceptance of homosexuality was also strongly reflected in an explosion in pop culture portrayals of gay characters, both real and fictional. In 1996, 32 million television viewers watched two lesbian characters wed on NBC's hit comedy *Friends*. Only two of the station's affiliates, in Texas and Ohio, chose not to air the episode, while the remaining 212 left it alone, perhaps because just weeks earlier, another gay couple got married on ABC's popular *Roseanne*, and the world continued to turn.[34]

The next year, a record thirty gay characters turned up in network shows, a rather sudden 23 percent increase over the previous year. It was also the season when Ellen DeGeneres, the comedian and actor, came out as a lesbian on the cover of *Time* and had her television character, Ellen Morgan, follow suit two weeks later on her show, *Ellen*. A whopping 42 million viewers tuned in, the biggest rating of any network show that year besides the Oscars. Religious conservatives organized a boycott of Disney, ABC's parent company, but it did nothing to stop the momentum of America's closet doors as they flung open. Ellen's coming out was not trouble-free, but the lesson in the long term was telling. Television critics (and gay and lesbian fans) lauded the impact of her newfound candor on the show's humor, making it more open, honest, and natural. But her ratings slowly declined, as her focus became "too gay" for some. Yet Ellen bounced back in the ensuing years, launching in 2003 a successful and critically acclaimed daytime talk show that focused on general issues and was embraced by mainstream audiences. Everyone knew Ellen was a lesbian, but at the end of the day, few cared.[35]

Will and Grace burst onto the entertainment scene in 1998. It rose steadily in popularity and eventually became the third most watched sitcom on network TV, with a weekly audience of nearly 17 million. In 2003, the Bravo network, owned by NBC, launched a reality show called *Queer Eye for the Straight Guy*. The show's 1.6 million viewers represented a startling 435 percent jump for its time slot and put Bravo on the map. In fact, NBC was so delighted by the ratings that it aired a version of the show itself, snagging an average of 7 million viewers.[36] The show has bred product endorsements, book deals, licensing agreements, and spinoffs. Though a relatively small number of Americans actually watched the show, many more knew about it and understood what it represented: a new day in gay-straight relations. Some critics groused about the primping and prancing of the gay lifestyle coaches, too reminiscent for some of the sidelined, stick-figure minority characters of an earlier day. But the fact remained that *Queer Eye* signaled a dramatically different cultural landscape from the one that birthed "don't ask, don't tell' exactly a decade before.

Media critics, gay groups, and ordinary Americans alike marveled at the revolution in attitudes exemplified by the growth of gay characters on TV. "Mainstream Americans welcome out gay men into their homes where once they would have protested to the network until advertisers withdrew their support and the show folded," crowed *The Guardian* of London. The paper said the gay-positive shows were "being hailed by mainstream media as a revolution for American attitudes to homosexuality on TV . . . America is being forced to confront its homophobia." The editor of *Out Magazine* said, "American media can't get enough of homosexuality right now. There is a changed climate and network executives are less afraid than a few years ago." *The New York Times* saw the "growing prime-time roster of gay-themed programming" as signaling "a major shift in attitudes about gay subjects," and said that entertainment executives viewed the *Lawrence* decision as confirmation that "the nation's attitudes toward gays and lesbians are radically changing."[37]

Queer Eye was followed by a gay dating show, *Boy Meets Boy*, and the following year by a lesbian drama, *The L Word*. In 2005, *Brokeback Mountain*, an epic western about two young men who fall in love under the open skies of Wyoming ranchland, garnered critical acclaim, box-office success, and three Oscars. Despite concern about controversy and boycotts, only one theater yanked the film at the last minute, in Utah. The story of *Brokeback*'s release was not that a gay love story was made, but that the sexuality of its characters, while central to the story, was a nonevent. Yet the film's release was a cultural watershed: The rights had been bought nearly a decade earlier, but the project had been rejected by several directors as too risky—would straight audiences pay to see a gay love story? Either it wasn't time yet, or Hollywood was too scared or conservative to take the plunge. They had no idea that, in 2005, the Ang Lee film would become a critical favorite and one of the most successful independent films of all time.

While the embrace of gays and lesbians in pop culture by no means assures full acceptance of homosexuality, television executives are notoriously risk-averse. By the time a controversial issue is confronted on national television, it usually means that commercial entertainment has caught up with, not pushed ahead on, American cultural mores. As we saw with the public opinion backlash around the 2003 court decisions on sodomy and marriage, progress almost always sparks resistance. *Will and Grace* premiered within a month of the savage beating death of twenty-one-year-old Matthew Shepard in Wyoming, an event that both reminded gays and lesbians of the persistent threat to their safety and rights and spurred new momentum and sympathy for gay progress. While critics continued to raise questions about how gays were portrayed in the media, their presence had a far-ranging impact, not only as a reflection of growing acceptance of homosexuality, but also as a venue for Americans to face—often through humor—their conflicting feelings about homosexuality and the gays and lesbians in their own lives. *The Boston Globe* eulogized *Will and Grace* as a show that "worked to liberate homosexuality from centuries of silence by deploying nonstop gay-related jokes that could be self-ironic, silly, and sometimes touching." It offered "a way to laugh about gay, lesbian, bisexual, and straight sexual politics from a place of pure affection, not fear and hatred." Added one social critic, the show was "a signal moment. It brought everyday gayness into American living rooms in a way that made it almost banal."[38]

The embrace of gay culture is not limited to the nation's living rooms; young recruits who enter the military come out of these living rooms, and the programming and culture follow them onto military bases around the world. Beginning in the mid-1990s, gay-straight alliances blossomed in high schools across the country; Fortune 500 companies rushed to offer benefits to same-sex partners; and the once radical act of coming out to a neighbor, friend, or family member became commonplace. The result was a tipping point in the visibility and acceptability of homosexuality that did not escape those in the armed forces. Far from being stuck in the past, the U.S. military is irrevocably shaped by the culture around it. A repeated refrain from interviews with service members fighting in Iraq and Afghanistan was this shift in popular culture. From *Queer Eye* and *Will and Grace* to *Brokeback Mountain,* the landscape seems awash in things gay. The English language itself has shifted, these troops notice, as the term "metrosexual" has invaded even the straight-laced ranks of the armed forces. The result, repeated over and over again, is that troops have discovered not only increased tolerance, but also a new kind of iconic status for gay-straight relations. "The metrosexuals would come to me," said one soldier. And they would say, " 'I'm going out on a first date, what should I wear?' We became very good friends and my sexuality was never an issue." "I think in today's military," said another, "there's certainly not as much concern as there was before. Look what's on TV these days: *Queer Eye, Boy Meets Boy;* the perception of gays has changed so much since the policy was first instituted that no one really cares anymore." He said the people keeping the policy in place were those who wrote it or backed it initially and have supported it since the beginning. "We're talking generals, who have basically fallen out of touch with everyday people. To enlisted personnel, it's a big joke." "I think the most important factor is generational," said an air force captain. "It's the old-school leaders who insist on these types of policies."[39]

IT'S NOT JUST young people and housewives whose attitudes are changing. In fact, in many ways, the story of the gay ban is a story of its professional champions, one by one, abandoning the very policy they once fought for. As these experts weighed new evidence, became embarrassed by the policy, or simply got caught up with the changing world around them, they realized "don't ask, don't tell" was no longer tenable. There was Lawrence Korb, the assistant secretary of defense under Ronald Reagan, who worked with the military to implement the 1981 gay ban. After witnessing the suppression of the PERSEREC studies, Korb concluded "once and for all that this was a clear case of blind prejudice and bigotry rather than a readiness issue, and that I had to do something about it or I could not call myself a social scientist." The year "don't ask, don't tell" was implemented, he wrote that "over the past decade, my own views on this subject have changed considerably and I now feel that the nation and the military would be best served by dropping the ban entirely."[40]

In 1993, Gerald Garvey and John DiIulio, politics professors at Princeton, wrote an article in *The New Republic,* explaining that the reason for the ban was that, "by military cultural definition, a soldier can't be gay and be a part of all that is best or most cherished in military life and lore." To straights, letting gays serve would "change the meaning of who they are."[41] For those who viewed warriors as male conquerors, who penetrate women and enemy lines alike but never their own, gays could not be soldiers. Directing romantic love toward another man is tantamount to turning on your own, a form of treason. DiIulio, who went on to briefly run George W. Bush's office of faith-based and community initiatives, opposed the ban from the start. But Garvey, at the time, supported it for cultural reasons, even though he believed there was no convincing evidence that lifting it would harm morale or cohesion.

But in 1998, Garvey backed away from his position. "My own thinking has become a little more complicated on this issue," he said in an interview that year. His experience with a former student who felt obliged to resign from the air force because he was gay "brought me up very sharply" on the issue. Garvey was also moved by statistics he heard about the suicide rate among gay teens. "If this policy somehow contributes to an ambience which accounts for those statistics," he said, "I think that's a very powerful argument against the ban."[42]

But it was the turn of the new century, spurred initially by the beating death of Barry Winchell, that saw the most rapid-fire change in attitudes toward gay service by key participants and observers. In December 1999, his presidency winding down, Bill Clinton told CBS News that the policy was not working and was "out of whack." The remarks stopped short of indicting the policy in the first place, which he had signed into law six years earlier. But his line had always been that he tried to get more, and settled for "85 percent." Now, he was focusing on its poor implementation, and promised a "reexamination of how this policy is implemented and whether we can do a better job of fulfilling its original intent." The next year, he candidly acknowledged that what he "should have done is issued a clean executive order, let them overturn it and basically let them live with the consequences." He said he "might have actually gotten a better result in the end, more like the one I wanted." Three years later, on the tenth anniversary of his policy, Clinton fully broke with it. "Simply put," he wrote in a letter to SLDN, "there is no evidence to support a ban on gays in the military." The former president explained that the nation had changed since 1993 and moved dramatically "toward recognizing the full citizenship of gay Americans." His policy was unaffordable and "unfairly restricts the talent pool available to the military—and that diminishes our security."[43]

In 2000, Charles Moskos cowrote an op-ed in The Washington Post calling the effects of his own policy "insidious." Entitled "Suffering in Silence," the piece shared a byline with Michelle Benecke, then codirector of SLDN. The two ideological foes had come together in the wake of the Pentagon's

2000 report—itself prompted by the Winchell murder—showing widespread anti-gay harassment in the military. Their piece explained that troops who have been harassed and assaulted too often feel they cannot report the incidents, fearing investigation and discharge. Too many "gay and lesbian service members," they wrote, "fear reporting harassment and assaults because many military doctors, psychologists, inspectors general, and law enforcement officials erroneously believe that 'don't ask, don't tell' requires them to turn in gay people who seek their help." Significantly, the article said that "military members who reveal their sexual orientation during private medical treatment, or in the course of reporting harassment or assaults, are not 'telling' in a manner contemplated by 'don't ask, don't tell, don't pursue.'"[44] Moskos, however, remained a defender of the policy itself; it was only the implementation and the poor enforcement that he denounced.

But the year 2000 was a banner year for changing opinion on gays in the military. Christopher Dandeker, head of the Department of War Studies and professor of military sociology at Kings College London, had favored the gay exclusion rule in both Britain and the United States as recently as 1999. That year, he wrote in the journal *International Security* that if soldiers were allowed to serve openly, "cohesion and military effectiveness would be negatively affected." He called for deferring any change "until circumstances are more propitious."[45]

But in 2000, the British military lifted its ban and gave Dandeker the opportunity to weigh its impact. "In light of evidence, argument and discussion," he said at a conference in December 2000, he had been led to "revise" his position. "I think I underestimated the extent to which integration can proceed," he said the next year. Today, he remains hesitant, wishing to see more research on cohesion in units with open gays before he's ready to pronounce repeal an unqualified success. But Dandeker is one of a growing number of heavyweights whose views have evolved as study after study demonstrates the uselessness of banning gays from military service.[46]

Then there were the changes across the legal landscape. Cass Sunstein, the noted professor of constitutional law at the University of Chicago, testified before Congress in 1993 about the legal viability of the Clinton compromise. Though personally opposed to the ban, Sunstein believed at that time that it would pass constitutional muster and satisfy the courts as a "rational" policy serving a "legitimate government interest." He counseled judicial restraint, saying, "I think the ideal is for this question to be resolved politically rather than judicially." But in 2000, Sunstein reversed course on his legal analysis and argued that the courts should invalidate "don't ask, don't tell." "I thought that then," he said in a 2000 interview, referring back to 1993. "I've kind of changed my mind." The gay ban in the United States, he came to believe, has been so ineffective and is so unnecessary as to warrant a legally "adventure-some" approach. "This policy has been so disastrous in its effects," he said, "and the experience of other nations is so articulate about the ability of fair-minded people to run a military that is not discriminatory, that I guess if the courts struck this down, you should gulp a bit, but smile." Sunstein's change of heart is a reminder of the organic interplay between the law and society. As we've seen in legal battles that rely on what constitutes a "rational basis" and a "reasonable person," these important terms are always shifting as their cultural context evolves. The *Lawrence* decision three years later was only the latest example of this phenomenon, as it declared that U.S. laws and traditions now "show an emerging awareness that liberty gives substantial protection to adult persons in deciding how to conduct their private lives in matters pertaining to sex."[47]

The swell of changing opinions on gay service was not restricted to the academy. As the ban slogged on, even top members of the military grew unable to ignore its startling failure. In 2003, retired Rear Admiral John Hutson, who as judge advocate general of the navy had been responsible for enforcing "don't ask, don't tell," called for the policy's repeal. In an article in *The National Law Journal,* Hutson called the gay ban "odious" and "virtually unworkable in the military." The article argued that the policy was the "quintessential example of a bad compromise," and that the "don't ask, don't tell" regulations are a "cha-rade" that "demeans the military as an honorable institution."[48]

As JAG, Hutson was the senior uniformed attorney in the navy. His job was to oversee all legal issues, supervise the 750 lawyers in the JAG Corps who serve around the world, and provide legal counsel to top commanders, including the secretary of the navy. He never liked the policy, but he sup-ported it as a practical measure, concluding that "a satisfactory resolution was impossible then."[49]

But despite genuine concerns that "the sky could fall" if the ban were lifted, Hutson now believes things are different. "That was then and this is now," he said in recent interviews. "I am now convinced, as I was not then, that the military could survive" lifting the ban. The unit cohesion argument, said Hut-son, has now been "completely reversed." Telling military members that they can't deal with open gays, that they're not mature enough or well disciplined enough, "is divisive." Ending discrimination "will enhance rather than de-tract from unit cohesion. . . . It will make us a stronger force rather than a less strong force, and it's a good thing for the country." In addition, it would remove a "blemish" on the armed forces and increase the public's regard for the military. Hutson's biggest fear is that the military he loves is "falling further and further behind" the American public. "This is what's discouraging to me," he said. "I don't want an institution for which I have great affection to be anti-quated in its ideas. The military is better than that."[50]

Hutson's support for ending the ban was pegged largely to broader changes in American culture. But does this mean the ban was the right thing to do in 1993? "I think we could have made it work" even then, said Hutson about lift-ing the ban entirely. "We probably were not giving enlisted men and women enough credit. They probably would have handled it better than we thought they would." The concern that an influx of gays would cause good straight soldiers to flee turned out to be "completely bogus," he said. And even by 2000, "things had changed so considerably, that I think 18- and 19- and 20-year-olds were just laughing at us because we didn't understand what they were thinking. Young people had so dramatically opened up to the idea of working alongside openly gay people that us crusty old farts protecting them was just a joke."[51]

In 2007, Hutson drafted an op-ed summarizing his feelings about his own involvement in the shaping of "don't ask, don't tell." "While we did our best," he wrote about the efforts of the navy in 1993, "what we came up with was not good enough. Blaming the supposed intolerance of young recruits for a pol-icy of continued intolerance toward patriotic gay Americans was a moral passing of the buck." Hutson concluded that "while our fears of damage to cohesion, morale and recruitment were genuine, we failed to exercise the leadership that, with some difficulty, could nevertheless have guided the mil-itary through this necessary change."[52]

In recent years, even the Pentagon itself has stopped trying to defend the gay ban, instead simply punting questions about it to Congress. Spokespeople deflected press inquiries by saying, "The Department of Defense policy on homosexual conduct in the military implements a federal law enacted in 1993 after extensive hearings and debate. The law would need to be changed to af-fect the Department's policy. We are complying with this statute." It almost sounded as if they were waiting for Congress to repeal the law and end the vice on the military. In 2007, Stephen Herbits, a gay civilian Pentagon insider and close aide to former secretary of defense Donald Rumsfeld, said that both Rumsfeld and Vice President Cheney were against the gay ban. "Both of them would change it in a second if the president changed his mind," Herbits said in an interview that year. "It would be gone in a second—I know that."[53]

Slowly but surely, the reality of the gay ban, and its harmful, unnecessary consequences, have crept up the military chain of command. In January 2007, retired general John Shalikashvili, who succeeded Colin Powell as chairman of the Joint Chiefs of Staff, published an op-ed in *The New York Times* calling for the end of "don't ask, don't tell." The highest-ranking uniformed officer in the nation, Shalikashvili was the most senior general to call for repeal. In 1993, he had supported the compromise as "a useful speed bump that allowed temperatures to cool for a period of time while the culture continued to evolve." But in 2007 he said it was crucial to "consider the evidence that has emerged over the last 14 years."[54]

What changed his mind? Shalikashvili held several meetings in 2006 with service members, including ones with combat experience in Iraq. He wrote that the conversations showed him "just how much the military has changed, and that gays and lesbians can be accepted by their peers." The general called for political caution on changing the policy, mentioning that finding a workable direction on the Iraq War was the first priority. But ultimately, he suggested, a sound national defense required "welcom[ing] the service of any American who is willing and able to do the job." An end to the ban, he wrote, was inevitable. "When that day comes, gay men and lesbians will no longer have to conceal who they are, and the military will no longer need to sacrifice those whose service it cannot afford to lose."[55]

In April 2007, Admiral William Crowe, chairman of the Joint Chiefs of Staff under Ronald Reagan and George H. W. Bush, had a private conversation with Aaron Belkin, director of the Palm Center. Crowe had counseled Clinton strongly against lifting the ban in 1992 but has since changed his view. He told Belkin he knew many good gay sailors, that he had long believed the policy was based more on "emotionalism than fact," and that he thought it was time for the policy to end.[56]

Among the data Shalikashvili cited in his op-ed was a 2006 Zogby poll of 545 troops who served in Afghanistan and Iraq. It found that 72 percent of service members were personally comfortable interacting with gays and lesbians, a key finding, given that the main rationale of "don't ask, don't tell" was that straights would not accept serving with gays. In 1993, just 16 percent of male troops supported letting gays and lesbians serve. One survey from that year found that 97 percent of generals and admirals opposed lifting the ban. But it turns out that this animus toward gay service would never again be as widespread as it was at the dawn of "don't ask, don't tell." Between 1992 and 1998, the percentage of male soldiers who "strongly oppose" gays serving in uniform dropped nearly in half, from 67 to 37 percent. The percentage of army women opposed to gay troops fell from 32 to 16 percent. The trend was not limited to enlisted personnel. A 2000 study conducted at the Naval Postgraduate School found that between 1994 and 1999, the percentage of U.S. Navy officers who "feel uncomfortable in the presence of homosexuals" decreased from 57.8 to 36.4 percent.[57]

By 2006, a tipping point had been reached. The Zogby poll was illuminating on this front in a number of ways. Nearly 80 percent of the respondents said they would have joined the military regardless of whether known gays were serving. Nearly half the respondents reported that they suspected there were gays in their unit, and even more important, that their presence was well known by others. Nearly a quarter said they knew for sure there were gays in their unit. Tellingly, of those who knew of gays in their unit, the overwhelming majority stated that their presence had little or no impact on the unit's morale; those who were not aware of gays in their midst registered a stronger belief that such a presence would—hypothetically, of course—have a negative impact on morale. In other words, consistent with countless other polls, familiarity breeds acceptance—and this repeated demonstration of the capacity for humans to evolve in their beliefs makes the ban on openly gay service even more odious, since by its very nature it blocks the possibility for learning more about different kinds of people. Even more important, these findings show that those who remain ignorant of (or in denial about) the gays in their midst cling to the mistaken belief that their presence would undermine morale and cohesion: The problem, as I have pointed out already, is not the actual reality of gays in the military, but rather the *fear* of gays in the military. Within the military, those serving less than four years, along with veterans already out of the service, were more likely to support the inclusion of open gay troops, while officers and those serving more than fifteen years were less likely. These figures strongly suggest that military culture itself encourages toeing the line that gays must not be allowed to serve.

Polling did not show unanimous or even majority support from within the military for openly gay service. The Zogby poll found that more service members strongly opposed letting open gays serve than strongly supported it, 21 percent to 9 percent, though the largest category was "neutral," at 32 percent. And in a 2008 *Foreign Policy* poll of 3,400 senior and retired officers, a majority said the military was weaker than it was five years ago, when the United States invaded Iraq. Yet only 22 percent thought that the gay ban should be lifted as a way to help fill recruiting shortfalls. The large majority of officers favored instead letting in high school dropouts and noncitizens.[58]

But the persistence of opposition to gay service on opinion polls raises, well, thorny questions. As we've seen, research and reality both upend the assumption that anti-gay sentiment, as registered in opinion polls, has any bearing on what actually happens when a sound policy of equal treatment is put into place and properly enforced. We only need to look at the militaries of Britain, Canada, and others, where fierce resistance to gay service melted away when they lifted their bans. Equally important is the ethical question of how many homophobes have to come around before a nation is allowed to do the right thing. To what extent should public policy languish at the whim of prejudice? Should the question of what is the right or wrong thing to do rely on opinion polls? As Hutson pointed out, part of the calculus was necessarily the practical question of whether widespread opposition to gay service could be overcome. But determining what is true opposition and what its impact would be is nearly impossible, since sometimes good people choose the safety of the practical option over the rectitude of the moral one. All the evidence we do have shows there is no cause for alarm—the practical and moral option are one and the same.

Whatever the judgment of history about the behavior of political, military, and cultural leaders at the dawn of "don't ask, don't tell," the fact remains that the fracas of 1993 was a world away from today. Back then, overwhelming majorities of military members objected stridently to opening up the ranks to known gays. But as retired NATO commander Wesley Clark put it a decade later as he questioned troops on gay service, the "temperature of the issue has changed" since then. "People were much more irate about this issue in the early '90s than I found in the late '90s, for whatever reason, [perhaps because of] younger people coming into the military. It just didn't seem to be the same emotional hot button issue by '98, '99, that it had been in '92, '93." The most dramatic and relevant changes, as Clark mentioned, were in the attitudes of young people. An October 2004 poll by the National Annenberg Election Survey found that 42 percent of service members generally believed that gays and lesbians should be allowed to serve openly. But for the first time, 50 percent, a statistical majority, of junior enlisted service members supported gay service.[59]

Interviews with straight service members bear out the polls. Brett Keen, a former E4 army specialist, served in Afghanistan as an intelligence analyst. He said that people's homosexual orientation was no secret. "When you live in close quarters with someone for months or years, you learn a lot about them," he said. "You're obviously going to learn their sexuality." He added that it's often "obvious" who is gay even when they don't say. "It's just part of who you are," he said. "No one really cared." Of course, there was joking about the matter, perhaps as a way to defuse any discomfort people might have had. "It was just like ribbing on someone for dressing funny," he said. "It wasn't hate-related." Keen even described a new sensitivity to those who clearly don't wish to talk about their homosexuality. If you have a gay co-worker, "you know not to ask him how his girlfriend's doing, because that would be insensitive.[60]

Keen also found that the gay ban, to the extent that it stifled people from being open, caused a strain. "They're asking you to hold back a crucial part of who you are," he said. "I think it's impossible." As for opponents of gay service, Keen said he wouldn't want to serve with someone who is "so wrapped up in their own bigotry and judgment that they don't really have time to focus on the mission." Privacy? In Afghanistan, Keen's unit spent months in primitive barracks where everyone showered together. "It was never an issue," he said, even though it was widely known that at least one of the men in his unit was gay. "No one was ever like, he's in there, I'm not going in."[61]

Sean May is a straight machinist mate in the navy's Pacific Fleet who spent eight months on a forward-deployed ship in support of Operation Iraqi Freedom. "It's becoming more and more common now that you hear about people coming out of the closet," he said. "If civilians can do it, why can't they. If they're comfortable with that, that's who they are. I don't care, just as long as they know where we are." Some of the chiefs, May said, were "straight-up homophobes." But May's view was different. "If a person wants to live the way they want to live, everyone else can eat shit."[62]

Another straight sailor said that there will always be those who oppose gays in the military, but they are increasingly a minority. "You got your homophobes who are up in arms that someone's looking at your wanker," he said, and they try to say that gay people are "lesser." But to him, "it's just a preference. To me, it's look but don't touch. And if they want to say some guy has a nice this or that, fine, and if they come on to me, I just say I'm not into that."[63]

Stephen Jay Vossler joined the army as a nineteen-year-old in 2002, became a Korean linguist, and served as a voice signals interceptor. Vossler came from a small town in southeastern Nebraska where it's still okay to call people "fag." Yet he insists that trust and cohesion only increase when his gay and lesbian coworkers are allowed to be themselves. "Right now," he said, "the policy forces gay people, if they're not open, to lie about their personal life, or to not talk about it." As a result, Vossler said, "you don't get that sort of personal cohesion that is really beneficial in the military. The gay service member always feels at a distance, and that drives a wedge between you and your peers." Vossler spoke of fundamentalist Christian friends who came to the military with cool or even hostile feelings about homosexuality and changed once they met gays in their unit. "The military," he concluded, "would become better" if there were no ban. "It would be more cohesive and would be a really great work environment because it would force people to accept more people."[64]

Straight opinions like these do not just come from young liberals. Some older veterans are also changing their tune. Dan Rossi, a straight fifty-eight-year-old former Marine who belongs to a New York coalition of veterans organizations, says his children would probably call him a "homophobe." He strongly opposes same-sex marriage. But recently, he struggled with the issue of gays in the military in some tough conversations in his veterans groups. And now his position is clear. "If I'm standing next to a Marine and he is a better shot than me, I don't care if he's gay or not," he said. "If a person goes into the service to make a career out of it, as long as they're good at what they do, let them do it." In a moving testimony before New York City Council in January 2008, Rossi shared his thoughts publicly: "I come from the old school," he said, "Italian, macho, all that stuff. But we have to face facts." About "gender and all this stuff," he said, "what the hell's the difference? Let's let these people alone and let's go to work."[65]

EVENTUALLY EVEN CONSERVATIVE political leaders began to get the picture. In 2007, after Shalikashvili made his statement calling for repeal, two prominent former Republican lawmakers came out publicly for repealing "don't ask, don't tell," both citing Shalikashvili's stance. Bob Barr was a staunch conservative Georgia congressman from 1995 to 2003. He still opposes same-sex marriage and efforts to classify gays and lesbians as members of a constitutionally protected minority class. But "service in the armed forces," he wrote in a *Wall Street Journal* piece entitled, "Don't Ask, Who Cares," "is another matter. The bottom line here is that, with nearly a decade and a half of the hybrid 'don't ask, don't tell' policy to guide us, I have become deeply impressed with the growing weight of credible military opinion which concludes that allowing gays to serve openly in the military does not pose insurmountable problems for the good order and discipline of the services." Barr argued that treating gay and lesbian troops equally was actually "about as conservative a position" as there is, because the gay ban was an invasion of individual freedom and privacy; it harmed the military by mocking meritocracy, spurning the talents of skilled individuals and replacing them with unqualified ones; and it wasted taxpayer money with unnecessary government spending. "For all these reasons, many conservatives and other former supporters of the policy have concluded it's time to change," he wrote.[66]

Alan Simpson, an army veteran and former Republican senator from Wyoming, voted for "don't ask, don't tell" in 1993. But in 2007, he reversed course. "My thinking shifted," he wrote that spring in *The Washington Post,* "when I read that the military was firing translators because they are gay." Simpson wondered: "Is there a 'straight' way to translate Arabic? Is there a 'gay' Farsi? My God, we'd better start talking sense before it is too late. We need every able-bodied, smart patriot to help us win this war." For Simpson, so much had changed since his 1993 vote that it had become "critical that we review—and overturn—the ban on gay service in the military." He cited a 2003 Gallup poll showing that 91 percent of Americans between ages eighteen and twenty-nine favored lifting the ban, again a key finding considering these were the people cited as the very reason a ban was needed. "Let us end 'don't ask, don't tell,'" concluded Simpson. "This policy has become a serious detriment to the readiness of America's forces."[67]

And perhaps even more remarkable, especially for Washington, D.C., is that the talk of these politicians has actually been translated into action. In 2005 (and each year thereafter), Congress has introduced the Military Readiness Enhancement Act to repeal "don't ask, don't tell." Initially spearheaded by Marty Meehan of Massachusetts, who has long protested the gay ban, it had little chance of even getting out of committee, but the act soon gained over 140 cosponsors, including several Republicans. In the spring of 2005, a group of eight retired generals and admirals announced their support for the repeal bill, becoming the highest-ranking military members to do so. Then, in 2007, a group of twenty-eight retired flag officers released a statement urging Congress to repeal the ban. The officers said that replacing "don't ask, don't tell" with a policy of equal treatment "would not harm, and would indeed help, our armed forces," and it pointed to foreign militaries as good examples of effective policies of equal treatment. "Our service members are professionals who are able to work together effectively despite differences in race, gender, religion, and sexuality," said the statement. "Such collaboration reflects the strength and the best traditions of our democracy." By the next year, the number of signatories had grown to one hundred.[68]

In July 2008, a bipartisan panel of retired flag officers released a report through the Palm Center that represented what John Shalikashvili called "one of the most comprehensive evaluations of the issue of gays in the military since the Rand study" in 1993. The panel found that lifting the ban is "unlikely to pose any significant risk to morale, good order, discipline, or cohesion." It marked the first time a Marine Corps general ever called publicly for an end to the gay ban. "I believe this should have been done much earlier," said Brigadier General Hugh Aitken, one of the authors. Another was Lieutenant General Minter Alexander, the former chair of the Military Working Group that helped create "don't ask, don't tell."[69]

Later that month, the first hearings since 1993 were held on "don't ask, don't tell" by the House Armed Services Military Personnel Subcommittee. The Pentagon declined to send anyone to defend the policy, and pro-ban forces were only able to supply two witnesses to argue their case. One was retired sergeant major Brian Jones, who, echoing the moral angst of Maginnis and Wells-Petry in the early 1990s, dwelled on the fragile climate of "self-less service" and "esprit decor" [sic] in the military. He argued that the "introduction of homosexual men under these conditions would create unnecessary tension and potential for disruption that would be disastrous in terms of increased risk to individual soldier's [sic] lives as well as mission-accomplishment." Although Jones had volunteered to testify, he found it "surprising that we are here today to talk about this issue of repealing the 1993 law." Using the charged language of special rights, he explained why it was a waste of time for the lawmakers and witnesses to gather together that day: "With all of the important issues that require attention, it is difficult to understand why a minority faction is demanding that their concerns be given priority over more important issues." Jones insisted he was comfortable around gays and lesbians and was not anti-gay even though he resorted to the basest stereotypes of homosexual indulgence. In a subsequent radio interview he asserted—falsely—that the fired Arabic linguists were discharged because they were having orgies and warned that lifting the ban would result in wild parties hosted by gay couples living on bases.[70]

The other anti-gay witness was Elaine Donnelly, a Michigan-based social conservative who runs the Center for Military Readiness, which is dedicated to opposing women and gays in combat. Donnelly's testimony revealed just how morally and intellectually bankrupt opposition to gay service had become by 2008. Her testimony was so confused and shocking that normally staid lawmakers blurted out that it was "dumb," "bonkers," "inappropriate," and an "insult" to the army. Donnelly spoke of "HIV positivity" and "exotic forms of sexual expression," including "passive/aggressive actions" that she claimed were common in the homosexual community. She charged that letting gays serve openly would introduce "erotic factors" into the military and "sexualize the atmosphere." It would amount, she said, to a policy of "relax and enjoy it." Her evidence that gay service would undermine the military was a lurid tale of a band of "black lesbians" who allegedly "gang-assult[ed]" a fellow soldier. The story was thirty-four years old.[71]

The only other evidence Donnelly presented, which she took from a companion article she wrote the previous year, was an assertion that Britain was having more trouble than reported with its eight-year-old policy of allowing openly gay service. "They do have recruiting and retention problems," she said, implying that the presence of gays was the culprit. But the articles she cited as evidence said nothing about gays, stating simply that the Iraq War was straining recruitment. The one article she cited that did discuss a same-sex assault—an incident that, if used to ban gays, would also require banning straights—described an episode that occurred well before Britain lifted its ban. Incredibly, she claimed that Britain had a problem with "homosexual bullying," except that the article she mentioned actually described "homophobic bullying." She had turned gay victims into gay menaces.[72]

Representative Chris Shays, Republican of Connecticut, was appalled. He pointed to Captain Joan Darrah, a lesbian veteran who had given thirty years of service to her country and became chief of staff and deputy commander at the Office of Naval Intelligence. "Would you please tell me, Ms. Donnelly, why I should give one twit about this woman's sexual orientation when it didn't interfere one bit with her service?" Representative Nancy Boyda, Democrat of Kansas, looked at another gay veteran testifying that day, Staff Sergeant Eric Alva, a Marine who lost his leg in Basra and became the first American service member wounded in the Iraq War. Speaking to Jones, she said incredulously: "I know that you were not implying that Staff Sergeant Eric Alva didn't perform selfless service in his line of duty, did you?"[73]

WITH EACH PASSING year, the evidence becomes clearer and further exposes the fault line between the main assumption of "don't ask, don't tell" (that gays cannot serve openly without undermining cohesion) and the reality on the ground—that thousands of gay U.S. troops already serve, including openly on the front lines of the wars in Iraq and Afghanistan. This disconnect is held together by another reality: A policy affecting tens of thousands of American troops is propped up by a small group of removed military and political leaders whose most basic assumptions are totally at odds with what really goes on in the barracks, at training camps, and on the front lines of U.S. military campaigns. While thousands of gays in uniform are probably out to their peers, with no damage to unit cohesion, an old guard is stuck in an earlier era, either unaware of or unwilling to acknowledge this reality, and thus unable to command their troops from a position of understanding and insight.

These defenders of the ban, like intransigent dictators bewildered when their people rise up against them, continue to insist that openly gay service would be detrimental to the military—and remain blind to the existing reality of openly gay service. The story of "don't ask, don't tell," then, is the story of what happens when a gathering flood of evidence and criticism begins to wash over an old guard that is unwilling to respond to a new world: Badly needed Arabic translators are sacrificed to the prejudice of military brass, a vocal minority of social conservatives, and their allies in Congress; reservists are dragged from civilian life to replace them, and stop-loss and forced contract extensions—made necessary by an overstretched force—lower the morale and effectiveness of deployed troops; taxpayers spend over $360 million to replace ousted service members; and our military and our nation are increasingly isolated and embarrassed as our allies lurch past us in liberalizing their policies on gay troops.

Listening to the voices of the troops themselves yields a portrait of a military in transition, in which the fears, discomfort, and dislike reported during the time when "don't ask, don't tell" was formulated are not nearly as pronounced. To be sure, terrible fates still befall gays and lesbians who wear a military uniform, particularly those who dare to be honest about who they are in climates that remain hostile. There are still significant pockets of prejudice and even bigotry in this country, furthering the stain on the U.S. military. But alongside incidents of hostile behavior is a much quieter and far more significant story of integration and compromise. Relations between gays and straights create negligible disruptions, and the rapport between gays and straights—even in the bastion of traditionalism that is the U.S. military—can actually provide a positive source of bonding and social cohesion. When gays are out, they report greater success in bonding and professional advancement, as well as increased levels of commitment, retention, morale, and access to essential support services.[74]

The simple fact is that younger people are substantially more tolerant of gays and lesbians than older people are. The positive responses from younger service members to the presence of open gays and lesbians in the military reflect that the armed forces are no exception, and that, indeed, a marked liberalization of attitudes toward gays and lesbians has been underway for some time. Service members who served both before and after the current policy was adopted say a significant evolution in feelings about homosexuality has occurred since 1993. Nevertheless, many gay service members remain afraid of the consequences of being out or of being outed, as well as the harm that can come from anti-gay harassment in the military. Consequently, many remain closeted, to the detriment of their own well-being and that of their comrades. Though the realities of our world are so very different from the world as seen by the creators and promulgators of "don't ask, don't tell," far too many gay men and women—and along with them, our military as a whole—are hamstrung, trapped, and wasted by this useless and harmful creation of a bygone era.

WHAT OF COLIN Powell, Sam Nunn, and Charles Moskos? In 1991, Powell had written of the role of the military in American life with glowing praise: "The armed forces of the United States," he wrote, "afford the opportunity for advancement" that "regrettably, is not in every part of our society, . . . the kind of opportunity that the armed forces lead the way with, and hopefully will eventually spread to all parts of our society so that only achievement and performance will be the basis for advancement. My generation in the military [is] a generation where almost all barriers have now been dropped." It was a stark contrast to the discriminatory policy he spearheaded and championed for so many years. In 2007, he softened his tone, saying that while the policy "was an appropriate response to the situation back in 1993," the country "certainly has changed" since then, though he wasn't sure if Americans were ready for openly gay service. In December 2008, two months after crossing party lines to endorse the anti-ban Barack Obama, Powell went a step further, saying the nation "definitely should re-evaluate" the policy. "It is time for the Congress," he said, "to have a full review" of the law, "and I'm quite sure that's what President-Elect Obama will want to do."[75]

Around the same time, former senator Alan Simpson, who had recently written his op-ed calling for an end to the ban, asked his friend Sam Nunn what he thought. At long last, Nunn budged. He wrote Simpson a letter saying that public and military opinion have "evolved" and that "no personnel policy should be set in concrete." He said that enough evidence had accumulated to show that "don't ask, don't tell" is "getting in the way" of filling the military's empty slots with talented personnel. And he called for "a thorough review by the Congress" of the "don't ask, don't tell" law.[76] His acknowledgment of the brain drain the policy had wrought was perhaps a tiny step beyond where Powell had landed.

Nunn took the opportunity to ask his friend Moskos what he thought. But Moskos held fast. In a memo to Nunn dated October 6, 2007, Moskos wrote that there would still be problems if the ban were to end, and he worried recruitment would suffer. "Lifting the ban will not be trouble-free," he wrote. Yet he continued, in good form, to focus on the little things that had always driven his interest in this policy. Most of the discharges come from voluntary statements, he wrote. When he was in the army, fifty long years ago, he was teased for buying a girl's bicycle. "Today, they would be punished for such behavior. Is that going too far the other way?" Then there's the law on "homosexual conduct." It "specifically states," he wrote, that "homosexuality is incompatible with military service." But in fact it doesn't. In a 2008 interview, he boiled his defense of the policy down to one of his famous pithy phrases. "Prudes have rights too," he said. Asked if he was perhaps swayed by an emotional attachment to the policy he long claimed as his own, he responded, "Obviously I am. I think some of my friends would be disappointed if I turncoated."[77] Moskos died on May 31, 2008.

EPILOGUE

THIS BOOK HAS made an argument for why "don't ask, don't tell" *must* end if we are to reverse the damage it has caused to military readiness. The damage caused by this insidious policy has been far smaller than the wounds to the military from larger, geopolitical forces, but it has made its mark nevertheless. If the United States continues to ban open gays and lesbians from service, the detriment to our military and our nation will also continue.

Fortunately, it is increasingly clear that "don't ask, don't tell" *will* end. It was designed as a temporary compromise, and political inertia has allowed it to outlive whatever usefulness it may have had. As we have seen, reason, facts, and evidence often have little bearing on public policy, but the sheer weight of the burdens of this policy—the cumulative impact of the vivid stories of lives turned inside out, of ugly animus and pointless logic—seems, at long last, to be having an impact. With every year since 2005, when lawmakers introduced the bipartisan Military Readiness Enhancement Act, support for this latest congressional bill for repeal has increased. It is likely that within a relatively short period of time, the federal government will strike "don't ask, don't tell" from the lawbooks.

It is also crucial to consider why "don't ask, don't tell" *should* end, for the history and impact of this bizarre and convoluted policy raises pressing questions about who we are as Americans. How we answer these questions will help shape what it means to be an American in the twenty-first century—well beyond the rise and fall of "don't ask, don't tell."

What's really at stake in the battle over gay service? Once we have dispatched the chimera of "unit cohesion," what is the real meaning of the outcry over homosexuality in the military? Unlike other exclusionary policies, the central issue here is not status or strength or performance. Instead, underlying our fifteen-year drama are fundamental anxieties over knowledge, expression, and revelation. Fittingly for a postindustrial world, this battle is not over resources but self-understanding.

This is why Professors Garvey and DiIulio wrote in their 1993 *New Repub-lic* article that the real reason gay service is opposed by so many military men is that it would "change the meaning of who they are." The "shared meaning" of military identity that they describe is not trivial. The willingness to put one's life on the line relies heavily on the cultivated desire to participate in the shared meaning of the military. It is their self-image as members of a warrior culture that allows soldiers to carry on in battle despite unthinkable danger. A shared sense of self is also the reason that morality, in the end, does matter. Doing the right thing is essential to mutual survival in war, and to the larger ethos that legitimates warfare. Soldiers and civilians are not likely to support a killing machine if they're not convinced it's battling for a just cause. When patrolmen on the road out of Baghdad Airport spot what they think is a road-side bomb, only their moral compass can ensure they stop their convoy to approach and disarm it rather than leaving it to decimate the next batch of troops.

The question is, how do we define what is moral in the twenty-first cen-tury? It's a question that won't be answered in these pages, but one thing seems clear: How American troops conduct their consensual sex lives in pri-vate should no longer be part of that definition. General Peter Pace found that out the hard way in 2007 when he tried to prop up an outdated rationale for the gay ban by bluntly calling homosexuality "immoral." He didn't remain chairman of the Joint Chiefs of Staff for long. And the issue is not only a mat-ter of "don't ask, don't tell." The fact that consensual sodomy—for gays and straights—remains a jailable offense in the military (while surveys say 80 percent of adults engage in one or more of its varieties) should be prompting insistent demands for change toward a more realistic, humane, and respect-ful code of military justice.

Ultimately, of course, these questions are not solely about the shared mean-ing of warrior culture, but about the meaning of American identity. To accept gays fully into the military, to remove ancient, useless, and damaging taboos from our civilization, Americans must change the shared meaning of who we are. Are we—and should we remain—a culture that relies on ignorance, re-pression, and denial to stay afloat? Charlie Moskos's privacy argument, and its continued usage as a rationale for the gay ban, seemed to suggest that we are. The notion that gays and lesbians must conceal their true selves to preserve the comfort of other troops is based on resistance not to the *presence* of gays in the barracks but to *knowledge* of that presence. And it's a tenuous distinction. If knowledge creates the problem, then does ignorance resolve it? For Moskos, it did, and he was prepared to accept the consequences.

But the gay ban is not really about privacy, either, for "don't ask, don't tell" quite simply does nothing to preserve privacy. Heterosexuals know they are serving with gays, and know that they could be undressing before eyes of desire. If the policy does anything useful for heterosexuals in inviting them to stick their head in the sand, its complicity in their repression is a grave disservice in the long run.

At bottom, the ban on open gays is really about how Americans confront the question of desire—the desire to fight and other desires that some fear might sap it. Moskos's congressional testimony made this clear. By acknowledging the presence of homoerotic desire in military culture, he gave voice to the half-conscious fears of sexual chaos and social breakdown that can accompany the confrontation of our true selves. The frank admission of this policy's foundation in the repression of desire raises pressing questions not only about the appropriate basis for denying equal rights but also about what has happened to a fundamental ideal of Western civilization: the Enlightenment quest for progress through knowledge, liberation through illumination, and democracy through genuine self-command.

The reason gays are denied equal treatment in the military is because our culture remains unequipped to acknowledge the full range of human desires, and the mere presence of gays is a painful reminder of this collective inadequacy. The significance of what might be called the "repressive hypothesis" in the military is not, of course, that all the troops are really gay, but that a variety of messy desires, needs, and fears swirl around in each of us. To manage them well, we must learn to confront them, not pretend they don't exist. The alternative is the persistence of sexual repression, with the kinds of consequences we've seen not only under "don't ask, don't tell" but also in the revelations of the secret and destructive double lives of too many governors, congressmembers, pastors, and—to be sure—millions of ordinary people across the nation.

For many, especially social and religious conservatives, simply acknowledging certain desires means tempting fate. But this fear raises a larger question: Must we pretend that we're angels without impulses in order to ensure we're not reduced to those impulses? Must we deny our sexual underside in order to decline its invitation to sin? Isn't the greatest form of human freedom to know and govern yourself rather than to have to bury part of you to survive?

The military's effort to repress homosexuality embodies this tension between illumination and denial and highlights the failure of American culture to deliver the Enlightenment promise of achieving freedom through self-government. This is where the current debate over sexuality policy in the military should be played out. True, the strongest argument against the policy is one of national security: We simply can't afford to waste good talent. But it is also one of national greatness: We can't afford to treat the men and women of our armed forces like children, to indulge—with the approval of the military leadership—their worst instincts and to write repression and denial into federal policy. American service members are not infants who think that when they close their eyes, the world disappears. Operating as if they are doesn't make our country great; it diminishes us.

Fighting repression is obviously a worthy project for the small minority of people who identify as gay or lesbian and suffer the brunt of homophobia. It may seem less compelling for millions of people who are perfectly comfortable ignoring the full scope of human sexuality. Why should heterosexuals join in this battle?

Gays and lesbians are denied equal treatment in the military not because they threaten national security but because of the unresolved issues of too many straight people. "Don't ask, don't tell" is an expression of collective denial that requires deception in the name of "morale." By creating a climate that is blindly intolerant of difference, by turning itself into a proving ground for fragile masculinity, the military mocks the freedom it is paid to protect. It sends the message that anyone who doesn't fit conventional notions of what it means to be a "real man" or a "real woman" is somehow dangerous, ineffectual, or both. It suggests that only the straightest of arrows—in the narrowest sense—deserve equal treatment and the opportunity to take their place as full American citizens. And it perpetuates the notion that unconventional sexuality is so sinful that it is, literally, unspeakable.

What would it mean to challenge this worldview? In the military, it would mean scrapping a policy that views off-base homosexual activity or on-base acknowledgments of homosexual orientation as threats to Americans' hard-won and well-proven capacity for self-government. It would mean applying a single standard to the expression and conduct of all its members. It would mean retiring the outdated view that homosexuality is incompatible with selfless service and that heterosexuality is the mark of moral superiority. And it would mean reforming the Uniform Code of Military Justice to reflect the way Americans truly—and properly—live their lives today.

For American culture at large, it would mean acknowledging and wrestling with the true range of our deepest impulses and fears, and it would mean continuing to cultivate and celebrate our capacities for self-command and self-authorship as the height of democratic liberty. Reassuring ourselves and our institutions, particularly the Pentagon, of these commitments and capacities will go far toward curbing the fear, hatred, and oppression—directed at one another and often at ourselves—that is currently bred by our collective denial.

The closet walls are crumbling. Modern life has cast enough light on our repression that such studied ignorance has fewer and fewer places left to hide. But if the military closet, and the hatred and fear that fester in its darkness, are ever to be truly eradicated, it will take far more than sound policy or exhortations to tolerance, and certainly more than the shadows and silence of denial. It will take an ongoing democratic conversation that offers multiple visions of what it means to be free. What the story of "don't ask, don't tell" suggests is how far we, as a culture, have yet to go in expressing a vision of freedom that invites us to be fully human. It is not gays and lesbians alone who are silenced by "don't ask, don't tell"—it is all of us.

NOTES

PROLOGUE

1. Author interviews with Charles Moskos, February 17, 2000, subsequent follow-up communications, and March 13, 2008.
2. Charles Moskos, "Has the Army Killed Jim Crow?" *Negro History Bulletin* 21 (November 1957): 27–29; Charles Moskos, "Racial Integration in the Armed Forces," *American Journal of Sociology* 72 (September 1966): 148.
3. Author interviews with Moskos.

1. THE LONG HISTORY OF THE MILITARY CLOSET

1. Randy Shilts, *Conduct Unbecoming: Gays and Lesbians in the U.S. Military* (New York: Ballantine Books, 1994), 11 12; John D'Emilio and Estelle Freedman, *Intimate Matters: A History of Sexuality in America* (Chicago: University of Chicago Press, 1988), 30.
2. David M. Halperin, *One Hundred Years of Homosexuality: And Other Essays on Greek Love* (New York: Routledge, 1990); Wayne Dynes, *Homolexis: A Historical and Cultural Lexicon of Homosexuality* (New York: Gay Academic Union, 1985); John D'Emilio, "Capitalism and Gay Identity," in Henry Abelove et al., eds., *The Lesbian and Gay Studies Reader* (New York: Routledge, 1993), 467–76.
3. Shilts, *Conduct Unbecoming*, 16.
4. D'Emilio and Freedman, *Intimate Matters*.
5. Shilts, *Conduct Unbecoming*, 7–11.
6. Gary Gates, "Gay Men and Lesbians in the U.S. Military: Estimates from Census 2000," Urban Institute, September 28, 2004; U.S. Census Bureau, "Facts for Features: Women's History Month (March)," February 22, 2005, http://www.census.gov/Press-Release/www/releases/archives/facts_for_features_special_editions/003897.html (accessed March 8, 2008). Shilts mentions estimates by "military lesbians" in the 1980s, suggesting that between 25 and 35 percent of women in uniform were lesbian during that decade, and that the percentage dropped over the course of the decade as the stigma against women serving in the military faded. See Shilts, *Conduct Unbecoming*, 561. A 1984 study in the *Journal of Homosexuality* found that gay women were "significantly more likely to have served" in the military than their straight counterparts, and that gay and straight men were "equally likely" to have been in the military: Joseph Harry, "Homosexual Men and Women Who Served Their Country," *Journal of Homosexuality* 10, no. 1/2 (1984): 117–25.
7. Gates, "Gay Men and Lesbians."
8. This account of gays and lesbians in the military during the midtwentieth century draws heavily on Allan Bérubé, *Coming Out Under Fire: The History of Gay Men and Women in World War Two* (New York: Free Press, 1990).

9. Sigmund Freud, "Letter to an American Mother," in Chris Bull, *Come Out Fighting: A Century of Essential Writing on Gay and Lesbian Liberation* (New York: Thunder's Mouth Press/Nation Books, 2001), 18; Shilts, *Conduct Unbecoming*, 15; Gregory Herek and Aaron Belkin, "Sexual Orientation and Military Service: Prospects for Organizational and Individual Change in the United States," in *Military Life: The Psychology of Serving in Peace and Combat*, vol. 4, *Military Culture*, Thomas Britt, Amy Adler, and Carl Andrew Castro, eds. (Westport, CT: Praeger Security International, 2005), 119–42.

10. David Burrelli, "An Overview of the Debate on Homosexuals in the U.S. Military," in Wilbur Scott and Sandra Carson Stanley, eds., *Gays and Lesbians in the Military: Issues, Concerns, and Contrasts* (New York: Aldine de Gruyter, 1994), 17.

11. Lawrence R. Murphy, *Perverts by Official Order: The Campaign Against Homosexuals by the United States Navy* (New York: Haworth Press, 1988).

12. Bérubé, *Coming Out*, 13–14.

13. Ibid., 14, 19.

14. Ibid., 16, 20.

15. Ibid., 15.

16. Shilts, *Conduct Unbecoming*, 17.

17. Bérubé, *Coming Out*, 261; National Defense Research Institute, *Sexual Orientation and U.S. Military Personnel Policy: Options and Assessments* (Santa Monica, CA: Rand Corporation, 1993), hereinafter referred to as Rand, *Sexual Orientation*.

18. The quote is from Rhonda Evans, "U.S. Military Policies Concerning Homosexuals: Development, Implementation and Outcomes," white paper, Palm Center, University of California, Santa Barbara, 2001. The ruling is the effective result of the "judicial deference" principle established by federal courts, which argues that the military is due special leeway in making decisions with a bearing on national security. In *Loomis v. United States*, for instance, the Court ruled that deference to the military had not been weakened by the 2003 Supreme Court decision, *Lawrence v. Texas*, which struck down state sodomy laws. "Plaintiff argues that [previous] cases are not persuasive as they relied upon *Bowers* before it was overruled by *Lawrence*," said the Court. "We are not persuaded." It then said, "We owe Congress a great deal of deference in matters concerning the military," and that the gay ban was "rationally related to the military's interest in promoting unit cohesion, reducing sexual tension, and protecting privacy." *Loomis v. United States*, 68 Fed. Cl. 503 (2005). See also Marc Wolinsky and Kenneth Sherrill, eds., *Gays and the Military: Joseph Steffan Versus the United States* (Princeton, NJ: Princeton University Press, 1993).

19. U.S. Department of Defense, Office of the Assistant Secretary of Defense, Directive No. 1332.14, Enlisted Administrative Separations, January 28, 1982.

20. Shilts, *Conduct Unbecoming*, 532–39.

21. "Defense Force Management: DOD's Policy on Homosexuality," U.S. Government Accountability Office (GAO), June 12, 1992, http://archive.gao.gov/d33t10/146980.pdf (accessed March 8, 2008), 4.

22. Shilts, *Conduct Unbecoming*, 561, 595.

23. Urvashi Vaid, *Virtual Equality: The Mainstreaming of Gay and Lesbian Liberation* (New York: Anchor Books, 1995), 155–56.

24. Charles Moskos, "Why Banning Homosexuals Still Makes Sense," *Navy Times*, March 30 1992; Shilts, *Conduct Unbecoming*, 699, 709.

25. Shilts, *Conduct Unbecoming*, 729, 735–38; Wade Lambert and Stephanie Simon, "U.S. Military Moves to Discharge Some Gay Vets of Gulf War," *Wall Street Journal*, July 20, 1991.

26. Michelangelo Signorile, "The Outing of Assistant Secretary of Defense Pete Williams," *The Advocate*, August 27, 1991; Theodore Sarbin and Kenneth Karols, *Nonconforming Sexual Orientations and Military Suitability*, Defense Personnel Security Research and Education Center, December 1988; Michael Frisby, "Military Seeks Third Study of Policy on Gays," *Boston Globe*, November 2, 1989.

27. Barton Gellman, "Cheney Rejects Idea That Gays Are Security Risk," *Washington Post,* August 1, 1991.
28. "1992 Campaign Nunn Rules Out Seeking Presidency," *St. Louis Post-Dispatch,* March 6, 1991; Sharen Shaw Johnson, "Women in Combat: The Battle Moves to Congress," *USA Today,* January 24, 1990.
29. A. L. May, "Nunn and Miller Endorse Clinton for White House," *Atlanta Journal and Constitution,* December 20, 1991.
30. Author interview with David Mixner, December 27, 2006; David Mixner, *Stranger Among Friends* (New York: Bantam, 1996).
31. Lawrence Korb, "The President, the Congress, and the Pentagon: Obstacles to Implementing the 'Don't Ask, Don't Tell' Policy," in Gregory M. Herek et al., eds., *Out in Force: Sexual Orientation and the Military* (Chicago: University of Chicago Press, 1996), 290–301.
32. John Gallagher and Chris Bull, *Perfect Enemies: The Religious Right, the Gay Movement, and the Politics of the 1990s* (New York: Crown, 1996), 72–77.
33. Author interview with Urvashi Vaid, March 5, 2008; Vaid, *Virtual Equality,* 148–77.
34. Vaid, *Virtual Equality,* 148–77.
35. Marla Williams, Carol Ostrom, and David Schaefer, "Reaching Out at Westlake— Seattle Crowd Cheers Clinton—Democratic Candidate Promises Change in Jobs, Schools, Health Care," *Seattle Times,* July 26, 1992.
36. Author interview with Vaid; Vaid, *Virtual Equality,* 148–77; Mixner, *Stranger Among Friends,* 207.
37. Mixner, *Stranger Among Friends,* 204.
38. Author interview with Mixner.
39. Curtis Wilkie, "Harvard Tosses Warmup Queries to Clinton on Eve of New Hampshire Debate," *Boston Globe,* October 31, 1991; "Remarks Announcing the New Policy on Gays and Lesbians in the Military," National Defense University at Fort McNair (Weekly Compilation of Presidential Documents, vol. 29), July 19, 1993.
40. Joseph Steffan, *Honor Bound: A Gay American Fights for the Right to Serve His Country* (New York: Villard Books, 1992).
41. Department of Justice, "Reply Memorandum in Support of Defendants' Motion for Judgment on the Pleadings or, in the Alternative, for Summary Judgment and in Opposition to Plaintiff's Cross-Motion for Summary Judgment," in Wolinsky and Sherrill, *Gays and the Military,* 150–60.
42. Ibid.
43. Ibid.
44. *Joseph C. Steffan v. Dick Cheney, Secretary of Defense,* 780 F. Supp. 1 (1991).
45. "Judge Criticized for Calling Former Navy Cadet 'a Homo,'" *San Francisco Chronicle,* March 9, 1991; Department of Justice, "Reply Memorandum"; *Steffan v. Cheney;* Wolinsky and Sherrill, *Gays and the Military,* xiv.
46. *Steffan v. Cheney.*
47. "World News Tonight," *ABC News,* transcript, May 19, 1992; Laura Myers, "Navy Board Recommends Honorable Discharge for Gay Sailor," Associated Press, July 1, 1992; "Nightline," *ABC News,* May 19, 1992; Stephen Power, "Bill Would Ban U.S. Military Exclusion of Gays," *Boston Globe,* May 20, 1992; Charles Doe, "Metzenbaum Introduces Bill to Overturn Military Gay Ban," United Press International, July 28, 1992; John Enders, "Gay Sailor Cites 'Openly Hateful' Reaction to Homosexuals in Military," Associated Press, January 28, 1993.
48. Joe Taylor, "Navy Flier Challenges Pentagon Policy of Discharging Gays," Associated Press, July 23, 1992; Robert Stone, "Uncle Sam Doesn't Want You," *New York Review of Books,* September 23, 1993; Melissa Healy, "Military Chiefs Reject Idea of Women in Combat," *The Record* (Ontario), July 31, 1992.
49. Marcy Gordon, "For Thorne, First Day of Navy Discharge Hearing Bittersweet," Associated Press, July 11, 1994.

50. Joe Taylor, "Navy Flier Challenges Pentagon Policy of Discharging Gays," Associated Press, July 23, 1992; Joe Taylor, "Discharge Recommended for Gay Navy Flier," Associated Press, July 24, 1992; Charles Doe, "Metzenbaum Introduces Bill to Overturn Military Gay Ban," United Press International, July 28, 1992.
51. "Lesbian Sues Military in Parting Shot," *Boston Globe,* June 12, 1992; "Lesbian Colonel Removed by Guard," Associated Press, May 28, 1992.
52. Margarethe Cammermeyer, *Serving in Silence* (New York: Viking, 1994).
53. Williams, Ostrom, and Schaefer, "Reaching Out at Westlake"; Cammermeyer, *Serving in Silence.*
54. Senate Committee on Armed Services, *Policy Concerning Homosexuality in the Armed Forces,* 103rd Cong., 2nd sess., 1993, 284; Ed Offley, "Guard Bans Lesbian Colonel," *Seattle Post-Intelligencer,* May 29, 1992.
55. Gallagher and Bull, *Perfect Enemies,* 126–29; Jeffrey Schmalz, "Difficult First Step," *New York Times,* November 15, 1992. Estimates of money raised by gays and lesbians range from $3 to $4 million: See Elizabeth Drew, *On The Edge: The Clinton Presidency* (New York: Simon and Schuster, 1994), 42.

2. CHRISTIAN SOLDIERS: THE MORALITY OF BEING GAY

1. Charles Moskos, "Racial Integration in the Armed Forces," *American Journal of Sociology* 72, no. 2 (1966): 132–48.
2. Charles Moskos, "From Citizens' Army to Social Laboratory," in Wilbur Scott and Sandra Carson Stanley, eds., *Gays and Lesbians in the Military: Issues, Concerns, and Contrasts* (New York: Aldine de Gruyter, 1994), 53–65; Charles Moskos, "Soldiering: It's a Job, Not an Adventure in Social Change," *Washington Post,* January 31, 1993.
3. Ibid.
4. Author interview with Charles Moskos, February 17, 2000.
5. Sharen Shaw Johnson, "Women in Combat: The Battle Moves to Congress," *USA Today,* January 24, 1990.
6. Author interview with Moskos.
7. "Newsweek/Gallup Profile American Voters on Gay Rights," *The Hotline,* September 8, 1992; "61 Percent Seek Delay in Lifting Ban on Gays in Military," Associated Press, November 21, 1992; John Gallagher and Chris Bull, *Perfect Enemies: The Religious Right, the Gay Movement, and the Politics of the 1990s* (New York: Crown Publishers, 1996), 150; David Tuller, "Gays Say Debate Could Be Beneficial," *San Francisco Chronicle,* January 28, 1993; *Morning Edition,* NPR, January 29, 1993; John Bicknell, "Study of Naval Officers' Attitudes Toward Homosexuals in the Military," master's thesis, Naval Postgraduate School, March 2000.
8. Gallagher and Bull, *Perfect Enemies,* 20–31.
9. Ibid., 32–33.
10. The reported reach of Dobson's empire ranges widely, with Dobson's own material claiming that 220 million people hear his radio broadcast daily; other sources put the number at only 5 million: See Focus on the Family, "Press Biography: Dr. James Dobson," http://www.focusonthefamily.com/press/focusvoices/A000000025.cfm (accessed March 8, 2008); *Economist,* "Trouble in the Family," March 3, 2007; Alison Mitchell, "Fretting Over Grip on House, G.O.P. Courts Conservatives," *New York Times,* May 9, 1998. See also "Focus on the Family Head Embroiled in Policy Fights," *Grand Rapid Press,* May 14, 2005; Marc Fisher, "The GOP, Facing a Dobson's Choice," *Washington Post,* July 2, 1996.
11. Fisher, "The GOP"; Laura Maggi, "Perkins; From Pulpit to Politics; U.S. Senate Hopeful Is Comfortable with Both," *Times Picayune,* October 9, 2002; Max Blumenthal, "Justice Sunday Preachers," *The Nation,* April 26, 2005.
12. Peter Applebome, "Homosexual Issue Galvanizes Conservative Foes of Clinton," *New York Times,* February 1, 1993.

13. Ibid.; Gallagher and Bull, *Perfect Enemies*, 84, 150.
14. Michael Weisskopf, "Energized by Pulpit or Passion, the Public Is Calling," *Washington Post*, February 3, 1993; "Clinton Compromises on Lifting Military Ban on Gays," *Facts on File World News Digest*, January 28, 1993; Thomas Ricks and Jill Abramson, "Clinton Agrees to Compromise on Military Ban," *Wall Street Journal*, January 28, 1993.
15. Ibid.; John King, "Religious Right Raising Money Over Gays-in-the-Military Fight," Associated Press, February 1993; Gallagher and Bull, *Perfect Enemies*, 150.
16. Anne Loveland, *American Evangelicals and the U.S. Military, 1942–1993* (Baton Rouge: Louisiana State University Press, 1996), 16–26, 221–25, 247, 250.
17. Robert H. Knight, "How Lifting the Military Homosexual Ban May Affect Families," policy paper, *InFocus*, Family Research Council, November 1992.
18. Ibid.; Robert H. Knight, "Should the Military's Ban on Homosexuals Be Lifted?" policy paper, *Insight*, Family Research Council, November 1992.
19. Knight, "Lifting the Military Homosexual Ban."
20. Ibid.
21. Robert Maginnis, "The Ethical Challenges of Future Strategy," speech, 13th Annual Strategy Conference, U.S. Army War College, Carlisle, PA, April 11, 2002; Robert L. Maginnis, "The Homosexual Subculture," enclosure in House Committee on Armed Services, *Policy Implications of Lifting the Ban on Homosexuals in the Military: Hearings Before the House Committee on Armed Services*, 103rd Cong., 1st sess., 1993 (testimony of Brig. Gen. William Weise).
22. Eric Schmitt, "Months After Order on Gay Ban, Military Is Still Resisting Clinton," *New York Times*, March 23, 1993.
23. Anne Loveland interview with Robert Maginnis, August 10, 1994, Anne Loveland papers; Maginnis, "The Ethical Challenges."
24. Maginnis, "The Homosexual Subculture."
25. Ibid.
26. Ibid.
27. Ibid.
28. Ibid.
29. Andrew Sullivan, "False Bennett," *New Republic*, January 5 and 12, 1998; Gallagher and Bull, *Perfect Enemies*, 27–28, 122.
30. Tony Marco, "The Homosexual Deception: Making Sin a Civil Right," policy paper, Concerned Women for America, 1991–1992.
31. Family Research Council, "First Lady Attacks Readiness by Opposing Ban on Homosexuals in the Military," press release, December 9, 1999; "Forum: Gays in the Military," *Online NewsHour*, PBS, January 2000, http://www.pbs.org/newshour/forum/januaryoo/gays_military.html; Robert Maginnis, "Homosexuals in the Military, 2001 Update," Family Research Council, http://www.frc.org/get/mpo1c1.cfm (site now discontinued); Maginnis, "The Ethical Challenges."
32. Loveland interview with Maginnis; Rowan Scarborough, "Army Investigates Release of Data on Gay Crime," *Washington Times*, June 9, 1993; Cathryn Donohoe, "The Major's March: In Step with Military's Ban on Homosexuals, Army Litigator Makes Her Personal Case," *Washington Times*, June 10, 1993.
33. Melissa Wells-Petry, *Exclusion: Homosexuals and the Right to Serve* (Washington, DC: Regnery Gateway, 1993), 50.
34. Ibid., 76.
35. Ibid., 39, 75, 81, 94; *Lawrence v. Texas*, 539 U.S. 558 (2003).
36. Wells-Petry, *Exclusion*, 90–91.
37. U.S. Department of Defense, Office of the Secretary of Defense, *Summary Report of the Military Working Group*, July 1, 1993; Maginnis, "The Ethical Challenges"; Gallagher and Bull, *Perfect Enemies*, 139, 151, 152.
38. Eric Schmitt, "Pentagon Speeds Plan to Lift Gay Ban," *New York Times*, April 16, 1993;

Peter Copeland, "Don't Tell, Don't Have Sex: Background Report Says Homosexuals Can Serve—Quietly," Scripps Howard News Service, June 19, 1993; Peter Copeland, "Gay-Ban Decision Is Near," *Houston Chronicle,* June 23, 1993.

39. Department of Defense, *Military Working Group.*
40. Maginnis, "The Ethical Challenges."
41. Knight, "Should the Military's Ban on Homosexuals Be Lifted?"
42. Knight, "Should the Military's Ban on Homosexuals Be Lifted?"; Knight, "Lifting the Military Homosexual Ban."
43. Loveland, *American Evangelicals,* 335–37; Loveland interview with Maginnis.
44. Anne Loveland interview with Ron Soderquist, February 26, 1993, Anne Loveland papers.
45. "Defending 'Don't Ask, Don't Tell,'" Yale Law School panel discussion, October 5, 2006.
46. Rowan Scarborough, "Senate Panel OK's Gay-Ban Hearings; Kennedy Dissents, Lambastes Nunn," *Washington Times,* May 4 1993.
47. Rowan Scarborough, "Court-Martials of Gays Usually for Sex Assaults," *Washington Times,* June 4, 1993; House Committee on Armed Services, *Policy Implications of Lifting the Ban on Homosexuals in the Military: Hearings Before the House Committee on Armed Services,* 103rd Cong., 1st sess., 1993.
48. House Committee on Armed Services, *Policy Implications.*
49. Ibid.; also see http://www.dod.mil/pubs/foi/reading_room/633-3.pdf (accessed May 5, 2008).
50. Art Pine, "Issue Explodes into an All-Out Lobbying War," *Los Angeles Times,* January 28, 1993.
51. *Lambda Report,* no. 2, June and July 1993.
52. John Lancaster, "Clinton and the Military: Is Gay Policy Just the Opening Skirmish?" *Washington Post,* February 1, 1993; Anne Loveland interview with Bill Horn, March 2, 1993, Anne Loveland papers.
53. Laurie Goodstein, "For Muslims in the Military, a Chaplain of Their Own," *Washington Post,* December 4, 1993.
54. Eugene Gomulka, untitled position paper.
55. Erick Schmitt, "Chaplain Says Homosexuals Threaten the Military," *New York Times,* August 26, 1992.
56. Gomulka, position paper, emphasis added.
57. House Republican Research Committee, *Testimony of Chaplain (Col.) James A. Edgren, USA (Ret.),* March 24, 1993.
58. Letter from Robert Dugan to Anne Loveland, September 14, 1994, Anne Loveland papers; American Security Council Foundation, press release, April 14, 1993; miscellaneous notes by Anne Loveland, Anne Loveland papers.
59. National Association of Evangelicals, enclosure to Anne Loveland, March 2 1993, Anne Loveland papers.
60. Richard Abel, "Should Homosexuals Serve in the Military," position paper, Anne Loveland papers.
61. Dugan letter to Loveland.
62. Letters reprinted in National Association of Evangelicals (NAE), Commission on Chaplains, *The Centurion* (newsletter), March 1993, emphasis in original.
63. Rand, *Sexual Orientation,* 1993; NAE, Commission on Chaplains, "Homosexual Behavior and Military Service," November 30, 1992.
64. NAE, *Insight* (newsletter), March 1993, June 1993.
65. Ibid., August 1993.
66. House Republican Research Committee, *Edgren Testimony.*
67. NAE, *The Centurion,* March 1993.
68. House Committee on Armed Services, *Policy Implications of Lifting the Ban,* 142–81.
69. David Plummer letter to Anne Loveland, February 19, 1993, Anne Loveland papers;

Chaplaincy Full Gospel Churches, letter to William J. Clinton, January 29, 1993 (in February newsletter), Anne Loveland papers.

70. Chaplaincy Full Gospel Churches letter.
71. Letter from Ted Shadid to Anne Loveland, Anne Loveland papers.
72. Chaplaincy Full Gospel Churches, "Policy Paper on Homosexuality in the U.S. Military," adopted June 23, 1993, Anne Loveland papers; Chaplaincy Full Gospel Churches, newsletter, July 1993, Anne Loveland papers.
73. Chaplaincy Full Gospel Churches, newsletter, April 1993, Anne Loveland papers; Ronald Ray, "Military Necessity and Homosexuality," in Ronald Ray, *Gays: In or Out? The U.S. Military and Homosexuals: A Sourcebook* (Washington, D.C.: Brassley's, 1993), 36–41.
74. Ray, "Military Necessity."
75. Vaid, *Virtual Equality*, 165.
76. Moskos interview, February 17, 2000.

3. THE POWELL-NUNN ALLIANCE

1. Barton Gellman, "Cheney Rejects Idea That Gays Are Security Risk," *Washington Post*, August 1, 1991.
2. "Powell Says Discipline Is Basis of Military Homosexual Ban," Associated Press, February 6, 1992.
3. Morris J. MacGregor, *Integration of the Armed Forces 1940–1965* (Washington, D.C.: Center of Military History, US Army, 1981), 23; Charles Doe, "Metzenbaum Introduces Bill to Overturn Military Gay Ban," United Press International, July 28, 1992.
4. U.S. Department of Defense, Office of the Assistant Secretary of Defense, Directive No. 1332.14, Enlisted Administrative Separations, January 28, 1982; Senate Committee on Armed Services, *Policy Concerning Homosexuality in the Armed Forces*, 103rd Cong., 2nd sess., 1993, 293–95; Charles Moskos, "From Citizens' Army to Social Laboratory," in Wilbur Scott and Sandra Carson Stanley, eds., *Gays and Lesbians in the Military: Issues, Concerns, and Contrasts* (New York: Aldine de Gruyter, 1994), 58; David Ari Bianco, "Echoes of Prejudice: The Debates over Race and Sexuality in the Armed Forces," in Craig Rimmerman, ed., *Gay Rights, Military Wrongs: Political Perspectives on Lesbians and Gays in the Military* (New York: Garland Publishing, 1996), 49.
5. Ibid., 50.
6. Ibid., 51; Eric Schmitt, "Settling In: The Armed Services; Joint Chiefs Fighting Clinton Plan to Allow Homosexuals in Military," *New York Times*, January 23, 1993.
7. Bianco, "Echoes of Prejudice," 51–55.
8. Randy Shilts, *Conduct Unbecoming: Gays and Lesbians in the U.S. Military* (New York: Ballantine Books, 1994), 744; John Gallagher and Chris Bull, *Perfect Enemies: The Religious Right, the Gay Movement, and the Politics of the 1990s* (New York: Crown Publishers, 1996), 136.
9. Jim Wolffe, "Powell Stands by Gay Ban," *Army Times*, May 25, 1992.
10. Ibid.
11. Author interview with John Hutson, February 19, 2008.
12. Jon Meacham, "How Colin Powell Plays the Game," *Washington Monthly*, December 1994; Christopher Hitchens, "The Case Against Powell," *Globe and Mail* (Toronto), December 26, 2000.
13. Susanne Schafer, "Changing Directions: Military Unprepared for Change on Gays," Associated Press, November 11, 1992; John Cushman, "The Transition: Gay Rights; Top Military Officers Object to Lifting the Ban," *New York Times*, November 14, 1992.
14. Schafer, "Changing Directions."
15. Republican Research Committee's Task Force on Military Personnel, *Hearing of the*

Republican Research Committee's Task Force on Military Personnel; Subject: Proposal to End the Ban on Gays in the Military, February 4, 1993.

16. Robert Burns, "Top Navy Official Opposes Lifting Ban on Gays in Military," Associated Press, November 24, 1992.

17. Eric Schmitt, "Military Cites Wide Range of Reasons for Its Gay Ban," *New York Times,* January 27, 1993.

18. Ibid.; Eric Schmitt, "In Tailhook Deal, Top Admiral Says He'll Retire Early," *New York Times,* February 16, 1994.

19. "Joint Chiefs of Staff Chairman Gen. Colin Powell Remarks to the U.S. Naval Academy," Annapolis, MD, January 11, 1993.

20. Author interviews with Charles Moskos, February 17, 2000, and subsequent follow-up communications.

21. Ibid.; Charles Moskos, "Soldiering: It's a Job, Not an Adventure in Social Change," *Washington Post,* January 31, 1993; Charles Moskos, "Don't Ignore Good Reasons for Homosexual Ban," *Army Times,* March 16, 1992; Charles Moskos, "Why Banning Homosexuals Still Makes Sense," *Navy Times,* March 30, 1992.

22. Schafer, "Changing Directions"; W. Dale Nelson, "Clinton: No Timetable on Gays in Military, but He'll Act 'Firmly,'" Associated Press, November 16, 1992.

23. Gallagher and Bull, *Perfect Enemies,* 88–94.

24. Ibid., 129.

25. Leslie Dreyfous, "Gays in the Military? The Rank and File React," Associated Press, November 12, 1992; Debbie Howlett, "Fate of Gays in Military Tests Tradition," *USA Today,* November 12, 1992.

26. John Cushman, "The Transition: Gay Rights; Top Military Officers Object to Lifting the Ban," *New York Times,* November 14, 1992; "How the System Works—Civilians Will Decide About Gays in the Military," *Seattle Times,* November 19, 1992.

27. Cushman, "The Transition."

28. John Lancaster, "Clinton and the Military: Is Gay Policy Just the Opening Skirmish?" *Washington Post,* February 1, 1993; author interview with David Mixner; David Mixner, *Stranger Among Friends* (New York: Bantam, 1996).

29. Greg McDonald, "Clinton Seeks Bipartisan Help in Visit to Congress," *Houston Chronicle,* November 20, 1992.

30. "Capitol Real Estate," *USA Today,* December 1, 1992; "Straightforward Approach to Gays in Military," *St. Louis Post-Dispatch,* December 8, 1992.

31. Tom Morganthau, "Gays and the Military," *Newsweek,* February 1, 1993.

32. Eric Schmitt, "Clinton Aides Study Indirect End to Military Ban on Homosexuals," *New York Times,* January 13, 1993; Rowland Evans and Robert Novak, "Military Chiefs Resist the Admission of Gays," *Chicago Sun-Times,* January 27, 1993.

33. Author interview with John Holum, March 12, 2008.

34. Ibid.

35. "Dole, Nunn Urge Clinton to Go Slow Lifting Ban on Gays," United Press International, November 15, 1992; Cragg Hines, "Two Key Senators Object to Letting Gays in Military," *Houston Chronicle,* November 16, 1992.

36. Michael Binyon, "Nunn's Past Provides New Twist to Tower Debate," *Times* (London), March 1, 1989.

37. Michael Wines, "The Gay Troop Issue; This Time, Nunn Tests a Democrat," *New York Times,* January 30, 1993.

38. Author interview with Urvashi Vaid, March 5, 2008. For an example of Nunn's hostility, see his questioning of Lt. JG Richard Dirk Selland and Lt. JG Tracy Thorne in Senate Committee on Armed Services, *Policy Concerning Homosexuality in the Armed Forces,* 103rd Cong., 2nd sess., 1993; Dan Balz, "Homosexual Rights Stance Praised; Georgia's Sen. Nunn Lauds Glenn, but Stops Short of Endorsing Him," *Washington Post,* January 21, 1984; David Pace, "Nunn Target of Protest for Dismissal of Homosexual Aides in Early 1980s," Associated Press, December 7, 1992.

39. Ron Fournier, "Aspin Says Changes in Military Ban Would Be Made Cautiously," Associated Press, December 22, 1992.
40. David Lauter, "Clash with Nunn Becomes Test of Power for Clinton," *Los Angeles Times,* January 28, 1993; Wines, "The Gay Troop Issue."
41. "Dole, Nunn Urge Clinton to Go Slow."
42. Lauter, "Clash with Nunn Becomes Test"; Michael Gordon, "Man in the News; Pathfinders of the Middle Ground: Leslie Aspin, Jr.," *New York Times,* December 23, 1992.
43. Author interview with Vaid.
44. Shilts, *Conduct Unbecoming,* 743; Vaid, *Virtual Equality,* 165; Gallagher and Bull, *Perfect Enemies,* 132–33; Art Pine, "Issue Explodes into an All-Out Lobbying War," *Los Angeles Times,* January 28, 1993.
45. Author interview with Chai Feldblum, March 11, 2008; Tim McFeeley, "Getting It Straight: A Review of the 'Gays in the Military' Debate," in John D'Emilio et al., eds., *Creating Change: Sexuality, Public Policy, and Civil Rights* (New York: St. Martin's Press, 2000), 236–50; author interview with Vaid.
46. Leonard Larsen, "Clinton Should Listen to His Soldiers," *Cleveland Plain Dealer,* November 25, 1992; Gallagher and Bull, *Perfect Enemies,* 141.
47. *CNN Live,* CNN, January 27, 1993; Ruth Marcus and Helen Dewar, "Clinton Seeks Deal on Gays in Military; Nunn Urges Delay of 'Final' Action," *Washington Post,* January 28, 1993.
48. John Marsh, "Let Congress Decide," *New York Times,* January 14, 1993.
49. Evans and Novak, "Military Chiefs Resist the Admission of Gays," January 27, 1993.
50. Ibid.
51. Melissa Healy and Karen Tumulty, "Aides Say Clinton to End Prosecution of Military's Gays," *Los Angeles Times,* January 28, 1993; Lauter, "Clash with Nunn Becomes Test."
52. Balz, "Homosexual Rights Stance Praised"; Sam Nunn, "This . . . May Even Require His Resignation," *Washington Post,* August 23, 1998.
53. Eric Schmitt, "Settling In."
54. Ibid.; Eric Schmitt, "Pentagon Chief Warns Clinton on Gay Policy," *New York Times,* January 25, 1993.
55. Schmitt, "Pentagon Chief Warns Clinton"; *Face the Nation,* CBS News, January 24, 1993.
56. *Face the Nation,* January 24, 1993; author interview with Tim McFeeley, March 7, 2008.
57. Eric Schmitt, "Joint Chiefs Hear Clinton Again Vow to Ease Gay Policy," *New York Times,* January 26, 1993.
58. Lauter, "Clash with Nunn Becomes Test"; *Nightline,* ABC News, January 29, 1993.
59. Adam Clymer, "Lawmakers Revolt on Lifting Gay Ban in Military Service," *New York Times,* January 27, 1993; Schmitt, "Joint Chiefs Hear Clinton."
60. Clymer, "Lawmakers Revolt on Lifting Gay Ban"; Gwen Ifill, "White House Backs 2-Step Plan to End Military's Gay Ban," *New York Times,* January 28, 1993.
61. Les Aspin, "Policy on Homosexual Conduct in the Armed Forces, Memorandum for the Secretary of the Army, Secretary of the Navy, Secretary of the Air Force, Chairman, Joint Chiefs of Staff," Office of the Secretary of Defense, Weekly Compilation of Presidential Documents, vol. 29, July 19, 1993.
62. Thomas Friedman, "Compromise Near on Military's Ban on Homosexuals," *New York Times,* January 29, 1993.
63. Eric Schmitt, "The Gay Troop Issue; How Rules Will be Altered on Homosexuals in Military," *New York Times,* January 30, 1993; Ifill, "White House Backs 2-Step Plan"; Gwen Ifill, "The Gay Troop Issue; Clinton Accepts Delay in Lifting Military Gay Ban," *New York Times,* January 30, 1993.
64. Thomas Ricks and Jill Abramson, "Clinton Agrees to Compromise on Military Ban," *Wall Street Journal,* January 28, 1993; "The Gay Troop Issue; Excerpts from the News

Conferences by Clinton and Nunn," *New York Times,* January 30, 1993; Ifill, "White House Backs 2-Step Plan"; Ifill, "The Gay Troop Issue."

65. Ifill, "White House Backs 2-Step Plan"; Dan Coats, "Clinton's Big Mistake," *New York Times,* January 30, 1993; Ifill, "The Gay Troop Issue."

66. *Nightline,* January 29, 1993; Healy and Tumulty, "Aides Say Clinton to End Prosecution."

4. LISTENING TO NUNN: THE CONGRESSIONAL HEARINGS ON GAY SERVICE

1. Bill Gertz, "Nunn Defies Clinton on Gays in Military," *Washington Times,* November 16, 1992.

2. Susan Rasky, "Washington at Work; Two Unlikely Voices That Find Harmony on the Military Budget," *New York Times,* May 2, 1990.

3. Author interview with Tim McFeeley, March 7, 2008; author interview with Robert Raben, February 20, 2008.

4. Senate Committee on Armed Services, *Policy Concerning Homosexuality,* 1993, 3–4.

5. Ibid.; David Ari Bianco, "Echoes of Prejudice: The Debates over Race and Sexuality in the Armed Forces," in Craig Rimmerman, ed., *Gay Rights, Military Wrongs: Political Perspectives on Lesbians and Gays in the Military* (New York: Garland Publishing, 1996), 60.

6. *Meet the Press,* NBC News, May 30, 1993.

7. Senate Committee on Armed Services, *Policy Concerning Homosexuality,* 1993, 4, 6, 7, 10, 40, 50, 167, 168.

8. Senate Committee on Armed Services, *Policy Concerning Homosexuality,* 1993, 100–103; House Committee on Armed Services, *Policy Implications of Lifting the Ban,* 1993.

9. Senate Committee on Armed Services, *Policy Concerning Homosexuality,* 1993, 163–68.

10. Ibid., 170.

11. Ibid., 499–512.

12. Ibid., 347, 348, 468.

13. Ibid., 239–40.

14. Ibid.

15. Author interview with Judith Stiehm, March 23, 2000.

16. Senate Committee on Armed Services, *Policy Concerning Homosexuality,* 1993, 400–33.

17. Ibid.

18. Ibid.

19. Ibid., 433–34.

20. Ibid., 452–53.

21. Ibid., 469; on HIV incidence, see Centers for Disease Control at http://www.cdc.gov/mmwr/preview/mmwrhtml/mm5127a2.htm (accessed May 3, 2007).

22. Senate Committee on Armed Services, *Policy Concerning Homosexuality,* 1993, 470.

23. Ibid., 484–85.

24. Ibid., 457–59.

25. Ibid., 458.

26. Ibid., 477–81, 490–92.

27. Ibid., 478.

28. Ibid., 478–79.

29. Ibid., 492.

30. Kari Frederickson, *The Dixiecrat Revolt and the End of the Solid South, 1932–1968* (Chapel Hill: University of North Carolina Press, 2001), 140; *Sixty Minutes,* CBS News, December 17, 2003; Senate Committee on Armed Services, *Policy Concerning Homosexuality,* 1993, 493–94.

31. Senate Committee on Armed Services, *Policy Concerning Homosexuality*, 1993, 493–94.
32. Ibid., 490–95.
33. "News Conference Secretary of Defense Les Aspin, Jamie Gorelick, General Counsel, Department of Defense Regarding the Regulations on Homosexual Conduct in the Military," press conference, December 22, 1993.
34. Senate Committee on Armed Services, *Policy Concerning Homosexuality*, 1993, 483–91.
35. Ibid., 494.
36. Ibid., 534; Jim Drinkard, "Gay-Rights Backers Not That Harsh on McCain," *USA Today*, January 19, 2000.
37. Kent Jenkins, "Into Troubled Waters," *Washington Post*, May 11, 1993.
38. Senate Committee on Armed Services, *Policy Concerning Homosexuality*, 1993, 491, 524–35.
39. Ibid., 526–34, 585.
40. Ibid., 540, 548.
41. Ibid., 540.
42. Ibid., 523, 541–43.
43. Jenkins, "Into Troubled Waters"; Senate Committee on Armed Services, *Policy Concerning Homosexuality*, 1993, 561–62.
44. Senate Committee on Armed Services, *Policy Concerning Homosexuality*, 1993, 564–65.
45. Ibid., 567, 572.
46. Ibid., 567.
47. Ibid., 537, 568–69.
48. Aaron Belkin, "'Don't Ask, Don't Tell': Is the Gay Ban Based on Military Necessity?" *Parameters* (Summer, 2003): 117; John Gallagher and Chris Bull, *Perfect Enemies: The Religious Right, the Gay Movement, and the Politics of the 1990s* (New York: Crown Publishers, 1996), 147; Jenkins, "Into Troubled Waters"; David Mixner, *Stranger Among Friends* (New York: Bantam, 1996), 319.
49. Senate Committee on Armed Services, *Policy Concerning Homosexuality*, 1993, 588–89.
50. *Meet the Press*, NBC News, May 30, 1993.
51. House Committee on Armed Services, *Policy Implications of Lifting the Ban*, 1993; House Committee on Armed Services, *Assessment of the Plan to Lift the Ban on Homosexuals in the Military, Hearings Before the Military Forces and Personnel Subcommittee of the Committee on Armed Services, House of Representatives*, 103rd Cong., 1st sess., 1993.
52. Ibid.; House Committee on Armed Services, *Policy Implications of Lifting the Ban*, 1993.
53. Melissa Sheridan Embser-Herbert, *The U.S. Military's "Don't Ask, Don't Tell" Policy: A Reference Handbook* (Westport, CT: Praeger Security International, 2007).
54. House Committee on Armed Services, *Policy Implications of Lifting the Ban*, 1993.
55. Ibid.
56. Ibid.
57. Mixner, *Stranger Among Friends*, 301–10.
58. Ibid., 301; Elizabeth Drew, *On The Edge: The Clinton Presidency* (New York: Simon and Schuster, 1994), 250.
59. Les Aspin, "Policy on Homosexual Conduct in the Armed Forces, Memorandum for the Secretary of the Army, Secretary of the Navy, Secretary of the Air Force, Chairman, Joint Chiefs of Staff," Office of the Secretary of Defense, Weekly Compilation of Presidential Documents, vol. 29, July 19, 1993; a "senior administration official" briefing reporters about the final policy on July 16, days before it was officially announced, said, "It's fair to call this policy 'don't ask, don't tell, don't pursue'": "Background

Briefing on Gays in the Military," U.S. Newswire, July 16, 1993; Les Aspin used the policy's full name in December 1993. See "News Conference," December 22, 1993.

60. Aspin, "Policy on Homosexual Conduct."

61. 10 USC 654, *Policy Concerning Homosexuality in the Armed Forces;* Clifford Krauss, "With Caveat, House Approves Gay-Troops Policy," *New York Times,* September 29, 1993.

62. Paul Quinn-Judge, "Senate OK's Tougher Version of Policy on Gays in Military," *Boston Globe,* September 10, 1993; "Senate's Policy on Gays Tougher than Clinton's," *Bergen Record,* September 10, 1993; Krauss, "With Caveat, House Approves Gay-Troops Policy"; Martin Kasindorf, "Gay Rights Lose in Military Bill," *Newsday,* September 29, 1993.

63. Krauss, "With Caveat, House Approves Gay-Troops Policy"; Kasindorf, "Gay Rights Lose in Military Bill."

64. Ibid.; Charles Doe, "New Pentagon Policy on Gays in Military Now in Effect," United Press International, March 1, 1994.

5. THE EVIDENCE

1. Eric Schmitt, "Pentagon Speeds Plan to Lift Gay Ban," *New York Times,* April 16, 1993.

2. National Defense Research Institute, *Sexual Orientation and U.S. Military Personnel Policy: Options and Assessments* (Santa Monica, CA: Rand Corporation, 1993).

3. "Study Would Allow Sodomy, Integrate Gays in Military," *St. Louis Post-Dispatch,* June 6, 1993; Eric Schmitt, "Pentagon Keeps Silent on Rejected Gay Troop Plan," *New York Times,* July 23, 1993.

4. Author interview with Charles Moskos, February 17, 2000; Eric Schmitt, "Months After Order on Gay Ban, Military Is Still Resisting Clinton," *New York Times,* March 23, 1993; Schmitt, "Pentagon Speeds Plan to Lift Gay Ban."

5. Author interview with Minter Alexander, February 20, 2008; William J. Clinton, "Memorandum on Ending Discrimination in the Armed Forces," January 29, 1993.

6. Author interview with Alexander.

7. Author interview with Vincent Patton, February 28, 2008.

8. U.S. Department of Defense, Office of the Secretary of Defense, *Summary Report of the Military Working Group,* July 1, 1993.

9. Kate Dyer, ed., *Gays in Uniform: The Pentagon's Secret Reports* (Boston: Alyson Publications, 1990).

10. Theodore Sarbin and Kenneth Karols, *Nonconforming Sexual Orientations and Military Suitability,* Defense Personnel Security Research and Education Center, December 1988; Michael McDaniel, *Preservice Adjustment of Homosexual and Heterosexual Military Accessions: Implications for Security Clearance Suitability,* Defense Personnel Security Research and Education Center, January 1989; Dyer, *Gays in Uniform.*

11. Sarbin and Karols, *Nonconforming Sexual Orientations;* Michael Frisby, "Military Seeks Third Study of Policy on Gays," *Boston Globe,* November 2, 1989.

12. Ibid.

13. McDaniel, *Preservice Adjustment;* La Tricia Ransom and Mary Ann Hu, "Pentagon's Own Reports Refute Military Stand on Gays," *Oregonian,* January 29, 1993.

14. Dyer, *Gays in Uniform;* Frisby, "Military Seeks Third Study"; Senate Committee on Armed Services, *Policy Concerning Homosexuality,* 1993, 291–349; Donna Cassata, "Studies Estimating Military 10 Percent Gay Said Dumped by Pentagon," Associated Press, April 1, 1993.

15. Craig Alderman, "Memorandum for Director DOD Personnel Security Research and Education Center," January 18, 1989; Craig Alderman, "Memo for Mr. Peter Nelson Through Mr. Maynard Anderson," February 10, 1989; Frisby, "Military Seeks Third Study."

16. Carson Eoyang, "Memorandum for the Deputy Undersecretary of Defense (Policy)," January 30, 1989; Frisby, "Military Seeks Third Study"; Frisby, "Military Seeks Third Study."

17. Randy Shilts, "Pentagon Memo Urged Reversing Ban on Gays in Military," *San Francisco Chronicle*, June 25, 1991.

18. "Defense Force Management: DOD's Policy on Homosexuality," U.S. Government Accountability Office (GAO), June 12, 1992, http://archive.gao.gov/d33t10/146980.pdf (accessed March 8, 2008).

19. Ibid.

20. Ibid.

21. Author interview with Lawrence Korb, June 15, 2000.

22. Lawrence Korb, "Evolving Perspectives on the Military's Policy on Homosexuals: A Personal Note," in Wilbur Scott and Sandra Carson Stanley, eds., *Gays and Lesbians in the Military: Issues, Concerns, and Contrasts* (New York: Aldine de Gruyter, 1994), 220–21; U.S. Department of Defense, Office of the Assistant Secretary of Defense, Directive No. 1332.14, Enlisted Administrative Separations, January 28, 1982.

23. Author interview with John Hutson, February 19, 2008; "Defeating 'Don't Ask, Don't Tell,' " panel discussion, Yale Law School, October 5, 2006.

24. Ibid.

25. Ibid.

26. Ibid.

27. Rand, *Sexual Orientation*, 210; Senate Committee on Armed Services, *Policy Concerning Homosexuality*, 1993, 430.

28. *Dronenburg v. Zech*, 241 U.S. App. D.C. 262 (U.S. App. 1984); *Steffan v. Cheney*, 780 F. Supp. 1 (U.S. Dist. 1991).

29. Melissa Wells-Petry, *Exclusion: Homosexuals and the Right to Serve* (Washington, D.C.: Regnery Gateway, 1993), 90–91; Marc Wolinsky and Kenneth Sherrill, eds., *Gays and the Military: Joseph Steffan Versus the United States* (Princeton University Press, 1993).

30. *Lawrence v. Texas*, 539 U.S. 558 (2003).

31. Senate Committee on Armed Services, *Policy Concerning Homosexuality*, 1993, 9; Eric Schmitt, "Military Cites Wide Range of Reasons for Its Gay Ban," *New York Times*, January 27, 1993.

32. "Women in Combat: Hearing of the Manpower and Personnel Subcommittee, Senate Armed Services Committee," Federal News Service, June 18, 1991.

33. Senate Committee on Armed Services, *Policy Concerning Homosexuality*, 1993, 428; Charles Moskos, "The Folly of Comparing Race and Gender in the Army," *Washington Post*, January 4, 1998.

34. "DOD's Policy on Homosexuality."

35. Laura L. Miller, "Fighting for a Just Cause: Soldiers' Views on Gays in the Military," in Scott and Stanley, *Gays and Lesbians in the Military*, 70; Steve Berg, "Is Military Service a Right or Privilege," *Minneapolis Star Tribune*, July 18, 1993; the research was conducted by the private group American Security Council Foundation, which opposed gay service.

36. Senate Committee on Armed Services, *Policy Concerning Homosexuality*, 1993, 594–97; Bob Zelnick, " 'Don't Ask, Don't Tell' Flawed from the Start," *Boston Globe*, January 3, 2000.

37. Joyce Price, "GOP Vows to Fight Clinton Plan to End Gay Ban," *Washington Times*, July 18, 1993; House Committee on Armed Services, *Policy Implications of Lifting the Ban*, 1993.

38. *Lambda Report*, no. 2, June and July 1993; "DOD's Policy on Homosexuality."

39. "DOD's Policy on Homosexuality."

40. Author interview with Judith Stiehm, March 23, 2000; author interview with Aaron Belkin, March 28, 2000.

41. Charles Moskos, "From Citizens' Army to Social Laboratory," in Scott and Stanley, *Gays and Lesbians in the Military,* 53–65; American Sociological Association, *Footnotes* (newsletter), 1997; e-mail from Chuck Loebbaka to author, February 20, 2008; *The Connection,* National Public Radio, December 20, 1999.

42. Edward Shils and Morris Janowitz, "Cohesion and Disintegration in the Wehrmacht in World War II," *Public Opinion Quarterly* 12, no. 2 (1948): 280–315.

43. See, for example, Charles Moskos, *The American Enlisted Man: The Rank and File in Today's Military* (New York: Russell Sage Foundation, 1970), 146; John Downey, *Management in the Armed Forces: An Anatomy of the Military Profession* (London: McGraw-Hill, 1977), 196.

44. U.S. Department of Defense, Office of the Secretary of Defense, *Summary Report of the Military Working Group,* July 1, 1993; Senate Committee on Armed Services, *Policy Concerning Homosexuality,* 1993, 708.

45. Robin Williams, "The American Soldier: An Assessment, Several Wars Later," *Public Opinion Quarterly* 53, no. 2 (1989): 165; Omer Bartov, "Daily Life and Motivation in War: The Wehrmacht in the Soviet Union," *Journal of Strategic Studies* 12 (1989): 200–14; James Griffith, "Measurement of Group Cohesion in U.S. Army Units," *Basic and Applied Social Psychology* 9, no. 2 (1988): 149–71; Guy Siebold and Dennis Kelly, *Development of the Combat Platoon Cohesion Questionnaire* (Alexandria, VA: U.S. Army Research Institute for the Behavioral and Social Sciences, 1988); Brian Mullen and Carolyn Copper, "The Relation Between Group Cohesiveness and Performance: An Integration," *Psychological Bulletin* 115, no. 2 (1994): 210–27; Robert MacCoun, "What Is Known About Unit Cohesion and Military Performance," in National Defense Research Institute, *Sexual Orientation and U.S. Military Personnel Policy,* 283–331; Elizabeth Kier, "Homosexuals in the U.S. Military: Open Integration and Combat Effectiveness," *International Security* 23, no. 2 (1998): 5–39; Robert MacCoun, Elizabeth Kier, and Aaron Belkin, "Does Social Cohesion Determine Motivation in Combat? An Old Question with an Old Answer," *Armed Forces and Society* 32, no. 4 (2006): 646–54.

46. Author interviews with Moskos.

47. Mullen and Copper, "The Relation Between Group Cohesiveness and Performance," 210–27; MacCoun, "What Is Known About Unit Cohesion," 293; Kier, "Homosexuals in the U.S. Military," 17; Judith Hicks Stiehm, "Managing the Military's Homosexual Exclusion Policy: Text and Subtext," *University of Miami Law Review* 46 (1992): 693.

48. Robert MacCoun, "Sexual Orientation and Military Cohesion: A Critical Review of the Evidence," in Gregory Herek, Jared Jobe, Ralph Carney, eds., *Out in Force: Sexual Orientation and the Military* (Chicago: University of Chicago Press, 1996), 160.

49. For more on comradeship and friendship in the military, see, for example, Sarah Cole, "'My Killed Friends Are with Me Where I Go': Friendship and Comradeship at War," in *Modernism, Male Friendship, and the First World War* (Cambridge: Cambridge University Press, 2003), 138–84; and Desiree Verweij, "Comrades or Friends? On Friendship in the Armed Forces," *Journal of Military Ethics* 6, no. 4 (2007): 280–91. Also, John Muirhead, *Those Who Fall* (New York: Random House, 1986), 6; Phyllis Moen, Donna Dempster-McClain, and Henry Walker, eds., *A Nation Divided: Diversity, Inequality, and Community in American Society* (Ithaca, NY: Cornell University, 1999), 210.

50. For more on the inverse correlation between social cohesion and combat performance, see, for example, Kier, "Homosexuals in the U.S. Military," 15–18.

51. James Kahan, Noreen Webb, Richard Shavelson, and Ross Stolzenberg, *Individual Characteristics and Unit Performance: A Review of Research and Methods* (Santa Monica, CA: RAND, R-3194-MIL, 1985), 81; Department of Military Psychiatry, *Evaluating the Unit Manning System: Lessons Learned to Date* (Washington, D.C.: Walter Reed Army Institute of Research, 1987), 1; Faris Kirkland and Linette Sparczino, eds., *Unit Manning System Field Evaluation: Technical Report No. 5* (Washington, D.C.:

Walter Reed Army Institute of Research, 1987), 2; Department of Military Psychiatry, "Unit Reconstitution in a Wartime Scenario," in David Marlow, ed., *Unit Manning System Field Evaluation: Technical Report No. 4* (Washington, D.C.: Walter Reed Army Institute of Research, 1986), 57.

52. Author interviews with Moskos.

53. Shils and Janowitz, "Cohesion and Disintegration in the Wehrmacht," 286; Kier, "Homosexuals in the U.S. Military," 15; Nora Kinzer Stewart, *Mates and Muchachos: Unit Cohesion in the Falklands/Malvinas War* (Washington, D.C.: Brassey's, 1991), 18.

54. William Claire Menninger, *Psychiatry in a Troubled World: Yesterday's War and Today's Challenge* (New York: Macmillan, 1948), 224; Catherine Manegold, "The Odd Place of Homosexuality in the Military," *New York Times*, April 19, 1993; Allen Frantzen, *Before the Closet: Same-sex Love from* Beowulf *to* Angels in America (Chicago: University of Chicago Press, 1998), 297–98; Allan Bérubé, *Coming Out under Fire: The History of Gay Men and Women in World War Two* (New York: Free Press, 1990), 38, 188.

55. Senate Committee on Armed Services, *Policy Concerning Homosexuality*, 1993, 354–65, 446–53.

56. Ibid.

57. Ibid.

58. Ibid.; author interviews with Moskos.

59. Senate Committee on Armed Services, *Policy Concerning Homosexuality*, 1993, 446–48.

60. Ibid., 450.

6. GAYS IN FOREIGN MILITARIES

1. Aaron Belkin and Jason McNichol, "Effects of the 1992 Lifting of Restrictions on Gay and Lesbian Service in the Canadian Forces: Appraising the Evidence," white paper, Palm Center, University of California, Santa Barbara, 2000.

2. Ibid.

3. Aaron Belkin and Jason McNichol, "The Effects of Including Gay and Lesbian Soldiers in the Australian Defence Forces: Appraising the Evidence," white paper, Palm Center, University of California, Santa Barbara, 2000.

4. Ibid.

5. Ibid.

6. Aaron Belkin and Melissa Levitt, "Homosexuality and the Israel Defense Forces: Did Lifting the Gay Ban Undermine Military Performance?" *Armed Forces and Society* 27, no. 4 (2001): 541–65.

7. Jay Bushinsky, "Gays in Israeli Military Take U.S. Cue," *Chicago Sun-Times*, February 8, 1993; Dan Izenberg, "Gays Speak Out for Equality at Knesset Meeting," *Jerusalem Post*, February 3, 1993.

8. Ethan Bronner, "Israeli Army Move to End Gay Bias Hailed," *Boston Globe*, June 12, 1993.

9. Reuven Gal, "Gays in the Military: Policy and Practice in the Israeli Defence Forces," in Wilbur Scott and Sandra Carson Stanley, eds., *Gays and Lesbians in the Military: Issues, Concerns, and Contrasts* (New York: Aldine de Gruyter, 1994), 182–83; Emily Bazelon, "Gay Soldiers Leave Their Uniforms in the Closet," *Jerusalem Post*, March 16, 1994.

10. Bazelon, "Gay Soldiers Leave Their Uniforms."

11. Bronner, "Israeli Army Move to End Gay Bias Hailed."

12. "Homosexuals in the Military: Policies and Practices of Foreign Countries," U.S. Government Accountability Office (GAO), June 1993; for more on mandatory service in Israel, see Amia Lieblich, *Transition to Adulthood During Military Service: The Israeli Case* (Albany: State University of New York Press, 1989).

13. Aaron Belkin and R. L. Evans, "The Effects of Including Gay and Lesbian Soldiers in the British Armed Forces: Appraising the Evidence," white paper, Palm Center, University of California, Santa Barbara, 2000.

14. Sue Leeman, "European Court Ruling Reopens British Debate on Gays in Forces," Associated Press, September 27, 1999; Helen Branswell, "U.K.'s Ban on Gays in Army Discriminatory," *Toronto Star,* September 28, 1999.

15. Edmund Hall, *We Can't Even March Straight: Homosexuality in the British Armed Forces* (London: Vintage, 1995).

16. Edmund Hall, "Gay Ban Is Based on Bias Alone," *Independent,* March 5, 1996.

17. Ibid.

18. Sarah Lyall, "European Court Tells British to Let Gay Soldiers Serve," *New York Times,* September 28, 1999; Sue Leeman, "European Court Ruling."

19. "Britain to Act After Ruling on Gays in Military," *Irish Times,* September 28, 1999; Belkin and Evans, "British Armed Forces."

20. 2000 Ministry of Defence Report, quoted in Belkin and Evans, "British Armed Forces"; Ministry of Defence, quoted in Aaron Belkin, "Don't Ask, Don't Tell: Is the Gay Ban Based on Military Necessity?" *Parameters* (Summer 2003): 111.

21. Belkin and Evans, "British Armed Forces."

22. Ibid.

23. Belkin and McNichol, "Canadian Forces."

24. National Defense Research Institute, *Sexual Orientation and U.S. Military Personnel Policy: Options and Assessments* (Santa Monica, CA: Rand Corporation, 1993); Belkin and McNichol, "Canadian Forces," 2000; F. C. Pinch, "Perspectives on Organizational Change in the Canadian Forces," U.S. Army Research Institute for the Behavioral and Social Sciences, Alexandria, VA, 1994.

25. "Policies and Practices of Foreign Countries"; Belkin and McNichol, "Australian Defence Forces," citing United Kingdom Ministry of Defence; see also Belkin and Levitt, "Israel Defense Forces."

26. Belkin, "Is the Gay Ban Based on Military Necessity?"

27. Sean Rayment, "Air Force Enlists Stonewall in Drive for Gay Recruits," *Sunday Telegraph,* December 31, 2006.

28. *Ask Not,* directed by Johnny Symons (Oakland, CA: Persistent Visions, 2008); citation is to an early version of the film, viewed on February 15, 2008.

29. Belkin and Evans, "British Armed Forces." Reports also suggested a decrease in harassment as a result of the lifting of the gay ban.

30. Edmund Hall, quoted in Belkin and Evans, "British Armed Forces."

31. Author interview with Robb Nunn, May 11, 2007.

32. Belkin and McNichol, "Canadian Forces."

33. Belkin and McNichol, "Australian Defence Forces"; Renshaw, quoted in Belkin and McNichol, "Australian Defence Forces."

34. Stuht, quoted in Belkin and McNichol, "Australian Defence Forces."

35. Belkin and McNichol, "Australian Defence Forces."

36. *The O'Reilly Factor,* FNC, June 18, 2003.

37. Laura Rehrmann, "Retired Colonel Says Military Men Will Never Accept Gays," Associated Press, April 1, 1993.

38. Belkin and Evans, "British Armed Forces"; Rand, *Sexual Orientation,* 74; David Segal, Paul Gade, and Edgar Johnson, "Social Science Research on Homosexuals in the Military," in Scott and Stanley, *Gays and Lesbians in the Military,* 33–51.

39. Geoffrey Bateman, "Is the U.S. Military Unique? 'Don't Ask, Don't Tell' and the (Ir)relevance of Foreign Military Experiences," white paper, Palm Center, University of California, Santa Barbara, 2005.

40. Senate Committee on Armed Services, *Policy Concerning Homosexuality,* 1993, 399–400.

41. Ibid.

42. Ibid., 349–52.

43. Chris Reidy, "Just Saying No," *Boston Globe,* January 31, 1993.

44. Senate Committee on Armed Services, *Policy Concerning Homosexuality,* 1993, 349–52; Charles Moskos, "From Citizens' Army to Social Laboratory," in Scott and Stanley, *Gays and Lesbians in the Military; World Affairs Council Weekly Broadcast,* NPR, May 1, 2000; *The Connection,* NPR, December 20, 1999.

45. Gal, "Gays in the Military," 181–89.

46. Belkin and Levitt, "Israel Defense Forces," 2001; Belkin, "Is the Gay Ban Based on Military Necessity?"

47. Belkin and Levitt, "Israel Defense Forces," 2001; Belkin, "Don't Ask, Don't Tell," *Parameters* (Summer 2003).

48. Gal, "Gays in the Military," 181–89.

49. Geoffrey Bateman and Sameera Dalvi, "Multinational Military Units and Homosexual Personnel," white paper, Palm Center, University of California, Santa Barbara, 2004.

50. Nile Gardiner, "Great Britain and the International Coalition in Iraq," Heritage Foundation, June 6, 2007, http://www.heritage.org/Research/MiddleEast/hl1028.cfm (accessed January 6, 2008); Ivo H. Daalder, "The Coalition That Isn't," Brookings Institution, March 24, 2003, http://www.brookings.edu/opinions/2003/0324iraq_daalder.aspx (accessed January 6, 2008).

51. Jason Straziuso, "Heat Becomes Enemy in Afghanistan," Associated Press, June 23, 2006; Matthew Pennington, "NATO Gears Up for Mission in Afghanistan," Associated Press, July 29, 2006; "More Dutch Troops for Afghanistan," *BBC News,* February 3, 2006, http://news.bbc.co.uk/1/hi/world/europe/4673026.stm (accessed January 6, 2008); "Australia Outlines Afghan Force," *BBC News,* May 8, 2006, http://news.bbc.co.uk/2/hi/south_asia/4983540.stm (accessed January 6, 2008).

52. Straziuso, "Heat Becomes Enemy"; Pennington, "NATO Gears Up"; Resource News International, "Canada at a Glance," November 16, 2000; Jim Garamone, "NATO Commander Says Troops Proved Toughness over Summer," American Forces Press Service, October 17, 2006, http://www.defenselink.mil/news/newsarticle.aspx?id=1652 (accessed April 30, 2008).

53. Bateman and Dalvi, "Multinational Military Units," 2004; Charles Moskos, John Allen Williams, and David Segal, *The Postmodern Military: Armed Forces After the Cold War* (Oxford: Oxford University Press, 2000).

54. Ibid.

55. Ibid.

56. Belkin, "Is the Gay Ban Based on Military Necessity?"

57. Rand, *Sexual Orientation.*

58. Elizabeth Kier, "Rights and Fights: Sexual Orientation and Military Effectiveness," *International Security* 24 (Summer 1999): 195.

59. See David Segal, Paul Gade, and Edgar Johnson, "Social Science Research on Homosexuals in the Military," in Scott and Stanley, *Gays and Lesbians in the Military,* 47; Aaron Belkin and Jason McNichol, "Pink and Blue: Outcomes Associated with the Integration of Open Gay and Lesbian Personnel in the San Diego Police Department," white paper, Palm Center, University of California, Santa Barbara, 2001; Rand, *Sexual Orientation;* John Bicknell, "Study of Naval Officers' Attitudes Toward Homosexuals in the Military," master's thesis, Naval Postgraduate School, March, 2000.

60. Aaron Belkin, "'Don't Ask, Don't Tell': Does the Gay Ban Undermine the Military's Reputation?" *Armed Forces and Society* 34, no. 2 (2008): 276–91; Laura Miller, "Fighting for a Just Cause," in Scott and Stanley, *Gays and Lesbians in the Military,* 80.

61. Belkin, "Is the Gay Ban Based on Military Necessity?"; see also Segal, Gade, and Johnson, "Social Science Research on Homosexuals in the Military," 42; Belkin and McNichol, "Pink and Blue." Segal *et al.* report a "consensus that most homosexuals in the military do not come out, but rather keep their sexual orientation a private matter,

even where policy and practice allow them to serve." Their report is from 1994, and evidence since then suggests that, while most gays use discretion in deciding when and whether to come out, most are known to be gay by at least some peers and often by supervisors.

62. Rand, *Sexual Orientation.*
63. Belkin, "Is the Gay Ban Based on Military Necessity?"; see also Gregory Herek and Aaron Belkin, "Sexual Orientation and Military Service: Prospects for Organizational and Individual Change in the United States," in Thomas Britt, Amy Adler, and Carl Andrew Castro, eds., *Military Life: The Psychology of Serving in Peace and Combat* (Westport, CT: Praeger Security International, 2005), 4:119–42; Belkin and Evans, "British Armed Forces."
64. Herek and Belkin, "Sexual Orientation and Military Service," in Britt et al., *Military Life.*
65. Belkin and Evans, "British Armed Forces."
66. Ibid.; author interview with Christopher Dandeker, May 9, 2007; Herek and Belkin, "Sexual Orientation and Military Service," in Britt et al., *Military Life.*
67. E-mail from Patrick Lyster-Todd to author, April 11, 2007; Herek and Belkin, "Sexual Orientation and Military Service," in Britt et al., *Military Life.*

7. "DON'T ASK, DON'T TELL" DON'T WORK

1. Charles Doe, "New Pentagon Policy on Gays in Military Now in Effect," United Press International, March 1, 1994.
2. Figures are from Servicemembers Legal Defense Network (SLDN), who compiled them from official Pentagon data; "Financial Analysis of 'Don't Ask, Don't Tell': How Much Does the Gay Ban Cost?" white paper, Blue Ribbon Commission Report, University of California, Santa Barbara, 2006.
3. "Military Personnel: Financial Costs and Loss of Critical Skills Due to DOD's Homosexual Conduct Policy Cannot Be Completely Estimated," U.S. Government Accountability Office (GAO), February 2005; "Uniform Discrimination: The 'Don't Ask, Don't Tell' Policy of the U.S. Military," report, Human Rights Watch, 2003; job specialty classifications and statistics come from the Department of Defense and the Defense Manpower Data Center and were analyzed by the Palm Center, University of California, Santa Barbara, in June 2004; see also "Conduct Unbecoming: The Ninth Annual Report on 'Don't Ask, Don't Tell,'" report, Servicemembers Legal Defense Network, 2003.
4. "Remarks by the Joints Chiefs of Staff and Coast Guard Commandant Following Statement by President Clinton Announcing Policy on Gays in the Military Introduced by Secretary of Defense Les Aspin," news conference, July 19, 1993.
5. Ibid.; Senate Committee on Armed Services, *Policy Concerning Homosexuality*, 1993, 709; "Remarks Announcing the New Policy on Gays and Lesbians in the Military," Weekly Compilation of Presidential Documents, vol 29, July 19, 1993.
6. Les Aspin, "Policy on Homosexual Conduct in the Armed Forces, Memorandum for the Secretary of the Army, Secretary of the Navy, Secretary of the Air Force, Chairman, Joint Chiefs of Staff," Office of the Secretary of Defense, Weekly Compilation of Presidential Documents, vol. 29, July 19, 1993. The clause regarding priests is in a policy attachment; it designates the "priest-penitent relationship" as one that is protected against intrusions of privacy; "News Conference: Secretary of Defense Les Aspin, Jamie Gorelick, General Counsel, Department of Defense Regarding the Regulations on Homosexual Conduct in the Military," press conference, December 22, 1993.
7. U.S. Department of Defense, Office of the Assistant Secretary of Defense, Directive No. 1332.14, Enlisted Administrative Separations, and "Enclosures" 1–4, December 21, 1993, incorporating changes from March 4, 1994, certified current as of November 21, 2003.

8. "News Conference."

9. Ruth Marcus, "Administration Rewords Military Rules on Gays," *Washington Post,* February 11, 1994.

10. Navy Manpower Analysis Center, "Homosexual Administrative Discharge Board/ Show Cause Hearings," memorandum of Department of the Navy, June 1994.

11. "Conduct Unbecoming: The Fifth Annual Report on 'Don't Ask, Don't Tell,'" report, Servicemembers Legal Defense Network, 1999, 35–36; "Conduct Unbecoming: The Tenth Annual Report on 'Don't Ask, Don't Tell,'" report, Servicemembers Legal Defense Network, 2004, 16.

12. "Conduct Unbecoming: The First Annual Report on 'Don't Ask, Don't Tell,'" report, Servicemembers Legal Defense Network, 1995, ii; "Conduct Unbecoming: The Tenth Annual Report," 16; DOD Directive 1332.14 and "Enclosures," November 21, 2003.

13. Author interview with Zoe Dunning, March 10, 2008; Rhonda Evans, "U.S. Military Policies Concerning Homosexuals: Development, Implementation and Outcomes," white paper, Palm Center, University of California, Santa Barbara, 2001.

14. Ibid.

15. Ibid.

16. Judith Miller, General Counsel of the Department of Defense, "Memorandum for the General Counsels of the Military Departments, the Judge Advocate General of the Army, the Judge Advocate General of the Navy, the Judge Advocate of the Air Force, the Staff Advocate to the Commandant of the Marine Corps: Policy on Homosexual Conduct in the Armed Forces," August 18, 1995.

17. Thomas Friedman, "Compromise Near on Military's Ban on Homosexuals," *New York Times,* January 29, 1993; in announcing the implementing regulations for the new policy, Defense Secretary Les Aspin said, "We were able to get it to happen in a way in which that [*sic*] we didn't have to divert resources away from other fights —on NAFTA, on the economic programs and all the other things that we needed political capital on this year"; see "News Conference."

18. "News Conference."

19. Senate Committee on Armed Services, *Policy Concerning Homosexuality,* 1993, 713, 772.

20. Reno quoted in Janet Halley, *Don't: A Reader's Guide to the Military's Anti-Gay Policy* (Durham, NC: Duke University Press, 1999), 61, 136; author communication with Kathi Westcott, attorney, Servicemembers Legal Defense Network; author communication with Bridget Wilson, attorney, Rosenstein, Wilson & Dean.

21. "Joint Chiefs of Staff Chairman Gen. Colin Powell Remarks to the U.S. Naval Academy," Annapolis, MD, January 11, 1993.

22. Senate Committee on Armed Services, *Policy Concerning Homosexuality,* 1993, 709.

23. "Conduct Unbecoming: The First Annual Report"; "Conduct Unbecoming: The Second Annual Report on 'Don't Ask, Don't Tell,'" report, Servicemembers Legal Defense Network, 1996; "Conduct Unbecoming: The Third Annual Report on 'Don't Ask, Don't Tell,'" report, Servicemembers Legal Defense Network, 1997; "Conduct Unbecoming: The Ninth Annual Report on 'Don't Ask, Don't Tell,'" report, Servicemembers Legal Defense Network, 2003.

24. "Conduct Unbecoming: The First Annual Report"; "Conduct Unbecoming: The Fifth Annual Report"; "Conduct Unbecoming: The Second Annual Report"; "Conduct Unbecoming: The Third Annual Report."

25. "Conduct Unbecoming: The Second Annual Report"; "Conduct Unbecoming: The Third Annual Report."

26. "Conduct Unbecoming: The Fifth Annual Report."

27. "Conduct Unbecoming: The Third Annual Report."

28. Carolyn Lochhead, "Defense Secretary Says He Will Correct Treatment of Gays," *San Francisco Chronicle,* February 27, 1997; "Conduct Unbecoming: The Third Annual Report"; "Conduct Unbecoming: The Fifth Annual Report."

29. "Conduct Unbecoming: The Second Annual Report"; "Conduct Unbecoming: The Fifth Annual Report."
30. "Conduct Unbecoming: The Second Annual Report."
31. "Conduct Unbecoming: The Third Annual Report."
32. J. Jennings Moss, "Losing the War," *The Advocate,* April 15, 1997; "Conduct Unbecoming: The Third Annual Report."
33. "Conduct Unbecoming: The Third Annual Report"; see Norman Kempster, "Pentagon Survey Finds Much Sex Harassment," *Los Angeles Times,* July 3, 1996.
34. "Conduct Unbecoming: The Fifth Annual Report"; Tobias Barrington Wolff, "Political Representation and Accountability Under Don't Ask, Don't Tell," *Iowa Law Review* 89 (2004):1633; Tobias Barrington Wolff, "Compelled Affirmations, Free Speech, and the U.S. Military's Don't Ask, Don't Tell Policy," *Brostelza Law Review* 63 (1997): 1141.
35. Bonnie Moradi, "Perceived Sexual-Orientation-Based Harassment in Military and Civilian Contexts," *Military Psychology* 18, no. 1 (2006): 39–60; Sharon Terman, "The Practical and Conceptual Problems with Regulating Harassment in a Discriminatory Institution," white paper, Palm Center, University of California, Santa Barbara, 2004; see also T. S. Nelson, *For Love of Country: Confronting Rape and Sexual Harassment in the U.S. Military* (New York: Hayworth Press, 2002); "Conduct Unbecoming: The Third Annual Report."
36. Author interview with Melissa Sheridan Embser-Herbert, October 3, 2003; Halley, *Don't.*
37. Author interview with anonymous, 2004.
38. Author interview with Brian Muller, February 20, 2004, and subsequent follow-up communications.
39. Ibid.
40. Author interview with anonymous, 2004.
41. Ibid.
42. Ibid.
43. Ibid.
44. See http://www.deomi.org/deomi.htm (accessed May 11, 2008); author phone call to DEOMI, 2004.
45. Reichen Lehmkuhl, *Here's What We'll Say: Growing Up, Coming Out, and the U.S. Air Force Academy* (New York: Carroll & Graf, 2006), 78–100.
46. Senate Committee on Armed Services, *Policy Concerning Homosexuality,* 1993, 283–84.
47. "Conduct Unbecoming: The Fifth Annual Report."
48. Ibid.
49. Ibid.
50. "Conduct Unbecoming: The First Annual Report."
51. Ibid.; "Conduct Unbecoming: The Second Annual Report"; "Conduct Unbecoming: The Ninth Annual Report."
52. Chris Bull, "No More Evasive Actions: Former Navy Officer Timothy McVeigh Interview," *The Advocate,* December 8, 1998.
53. Author interview with Alex Nicholson, September 18, 2007.
54. Ibid.
55. Ibid.; *Ask Not,* directed by Johnny Symons (Oakland, CA: Persistent Visions, 2008).
56. See, for instance, Chad Carter and Antony Barone Kolenc, "'Don't Ask, Don't Tell': Has the Policy Met Its Goals?" *University of Dayton Law Review* 31, no. 1 (2005): 1–24; Charles Moskos suggested, in as late as 2007, that Arabic linguists might be revealing they are gay solely in order "to seek employment by civilian contractors" (letter from Charles Moskos to Sam Nunn, October 6, 2007, in author's possession).
57. "Conduct Unbecoming: The Third Annual Report."
58. "Conduct Unbecoming: The Third Annual Report"; "Conduct Unbecoming: The Sev-

enth Annual Report on 'Don't Ask, Don't Tell,'" report, Servicemembers Legal Defense Network, 2001.
59. "Conduct Unbecoming: The Third Annual Report."
60. "Conduct Unbecoming: The Sixth Annual Report on 'Don't Ask, Don't Tell,'" report, Servicemembers Legal Defense Network, 2000, 48–54.
61. *CBS Morning News,* CBS, July 18, 2000.
62. *NBC Nightly News,* NBC, June 17, 2003.
63. *Nightline,* ABC, June 23, 2000.
64. Office of the Under Secretary of Defense (Personnel and Readiness), "Report to the Secretary of Defense: Review of the Effectiveness of the Application and Enforcement of the Department's Policy on Homosexual Conduct in the Military," April 1998; "Conduct Unbecoming: The Fifth Annual Report."
65. "Conduct Unbecoming: The Seventh Annual Report."
66. Department of Defense Working Group, *Anti-Harassment Action Plan* (July 21, 2000).
67. "DOD Issues Review of Efforts to Curb Anti-Gay Harassment," PR Newswire, June 29, 2004; "Conduct Unbecoming: The Ninth Annual Report"; "Conduct Unbecoming: The Tenth Annual Report."
68. *Good Morning, America,* ABC, September 9, 2002.

8. A FLAWED POLICY AT ITS CORE

1. See Chad Carter and Antony Barone Kolenc, "'Don't Ask, Don't Tell': Has the Policy Met Its Goals?" *University of Dayton Law Review* 31, no. 1 (2005): 1–24.
2. Servicemembers Legal Defense Network, *The Survival Guide: A Comprehensive Guide to "Don't Ask, Don't Tell" and Related Military Policies,* fifth edition (2007).
3. On standards of evidence, see, for example, "Board of Inquiry on Lt. Paul Thomasson, USN, Held on 23–24 May 1994 at Naval Legal Service Office Capitol Region," http://thomasson.info/trans.htm (accessed March 10, 2008); on punishment of command violations, see "Conduct Unbecoming: The Second Annual Report on 'Don't Ask, Don't Tell,'" report, Servicemembers Defense Fund Network, 1996, 13.
4. Philip Shenon, "Armed Forces Still Question Homosexuals," *New York Times,* February 27, 1996; "Conduct Unbecoming: The First Annual Report on 'Don't Ask, Don't Tell,'" report, Servicemembers Defense Fund Network, 1995; "Conduct Unbecoming: The Second Annual Report"; Shenon, "Armed Forces Still Question Homosexuals," February 27, 1996.
5. Lincoln Caplan, "'Don't Ask, Don't Tell'—Marine Style," *Newsweek,* June 13, 1994.
6. "Conduct Unbecoming: The Fifth Annual Report on 'Don't Ask, Don't Tell,'" report, Servicemembers Defense Fund Network, 1999; Conduct Unbecoming: The First Annual Report"; "Conduct Unbecoming: The Third Annual Report on 'Don't Ask, Don't Tell,'" report, Servicemembers Defense Fund Network, 1997.
7. Author interview with Fred Fox, February 26, 2008; *Ask Not,* directed by Johnny Symons (Oakland, CA: Persistent Visions, 2008).
8. Benefits are listed and explained on the Web sites of the four major branches; for example, see http://www.goarmy.com (accessed January 12, 2008) and http://www.navy.com (accessed January 12, 2008); see also Charles Moskos, "Preliminary Report on Operation Iraqi Freedom," December 14, 2003; Statement of Derek Stewart, Director, Defense Capabilities and Management, United States General Accounting Office Testimony Before the Senate Subcommittee on Personnel, Armed Services Committee, April 11, 2002.
9. Statement of Derek Stewart.
10. See http://www.sldn.org/templates/law/record.html?section=89&record=1709 (accessed May 11, 2008).
11. Author interview with anonymous, 2004.

12. Kathi Westcott and Rebecca Sawyer, "Silent Sacrifices: The Impact of 'Don't Ask, Don't Tell' on Lesbian and Gay Military Families," *Duke Journal of Gender Law & Policy* 14 (2007).
13. Ibid.
14. Ibid.
15. Author interview with anonymous, 2004.
16. Author interview with Austin Rooke, July 13, 2004.
17. Ibid.; author interview with Wendy Biehl, April 28, 2004, and subsequent follow-up communications.
18. Author interview with Brian Hughes, March 7, 2004, and subsequent follow-up communications.
19. Author interview with Ian Finkenbinder, September 5, 2003, and subsequent follow-up communications; author interviews with anonymous, 2004.
20. Author interviews with Brian Muller, various dates.
21. Author interview with Robert Stout, March 7, 2005, and subsequent follow-up communications.
22. Ibid.
23. Ibid.
24. Ibid.
25. Ibid.
26. Malia Rulon, "Wounded Gay Soldier Wants to Continue Serving," Associated Press, April 8, 2005; author interview with Robert Stout, various dates.
27. Rulon, "Wounded Gay Soldier," April 8, 2005.
28. Author interview with anonymous, 2004.
29. Author interview with anonymous, 2004.
30. Author interview with Alan Steinman, May 14, 2004; John Files, "Gay Ex-Officers Say 'Don't Ask' Doesn't Work," *New York Times,* December 10, 2003; Symons, *Ask Not.*
31. Author interviews with anonymous, various dates.
32. Ibid.; author interview with Finkenbinder.
33. Author interview with anonymous, 2004.
34. Author interviews with anonymous.
35. Author interview with Finkenbinder.
36. Author interview with anonymous.
37. Author interview with Finkenbinder.
38. Author interview with anonymous.
39. Ibid.
40. Author interview with Rooke.
41. Author interview with Finkenbinder; author interview with anonymous.
42. Author interviews with anonymous.
43. USC, Sec. 654, "Policy Concerning Homosexuality in the Armed Forces"; Les Aspin, "Policy on Homosexual Conduct in the Armed Forces, Memorandum for the Secretary of the Army, Secretary of the Navy, Secretary of the Air Force, Chairman, Joint Chiefs of Staff," Office of the Secretary of Defense, Weekly Compilation of Presidential Documents, vol. 29, July 19, 1993; author interviews with anonymous, 2004, 2008.
44. Jim Drinkard, "Gay-Rights Backers Not That Harsh on McCain," *USA Today,* January 19, 2000.

9. BRAIN DRAIN: ARABIC LINGUISTS

1. Walter Pincus and Dana Priest, "Sept. 10 Messages Spoke of 'Zero Hour,'" *Toronto Star,* June 20, 2002.
2. Nahal Toosi, "Try Saying It in Arabic," *Milwaukee Journal Sentinel,* February 20, 2005; Paul Simon, "Beef Up the Country's Foreign Language Skills," *Washington Post,* October 23, 2001.

3. Alison Mitchell, "Intelligence Activities: House Panel Calls for 'Cultural Revolution' in F.B.I. and C.I.A.," *New York Times,* October 3, 2001; Ahmed Rashid, "CIA Tries to Recruit Native Speakers by Email," *Daily Telegraph* (London), September 29, 2001.

4. Council on Foreign Relations, "America—Still Unprepared, Still in Danger," report, October 2002; Alex Berenson, "The World: Arms and Aims; the Art of War vs. the Craft of Occupation," *New York Times,* November 2, 2003.

5. "Foreign Languages: Human Capital Approach Needed to Correct Staffing and Proficiency Shortfalls," U.S. General Accounting Office (GAO), January 2002.

6. Rajiv Chandrasekaran, "Attack on Bridge Part of Perilous Routine for Troops," *Washington Post,* July 9, 2003; David Ignatius, "Tongue-Tied in the Arab World," *Washington Post,* July 11, 2003.

7. Ann Scott Tyson, "Uzbek or Dari? Military Learns New Tongues," *Christian Science Monitor,* January 2, 2004; National Commission on Terrorist Attacks upon the United States, *The 9/11 Commission Report* (New York: W. W. Norton, 2004); Chuck McCutcheon, "Calls for Reform of Spy Agencies Echo Past Efforts," *Times-Picayune* (New Orleans), July 25, 2004; Pentagon Advisory Panel reported in *St. Louis Post-Dispatch,* December 13, 2004; Justice Department Inspector General Report cited in *Washington Post,* September 28, 2004.

8. Walter Pincus and Dana Priest, "Bush Orders the CIA to Hire More Spies: Goss Told to Build Up Other Staffs, Too," *Washington Post,* November 24, 2004; Susan Schmidt and Allan Lengel, "Help Still Wanted: Arabic Linguists; Agencies Rushed to Fill Void, but Found Screening New Hires Takes Time," *Washington Post,* December 27, 2002; "Nominee Promises Tighter Control over U.S. Intelligence Agencies," *New York Times,* April 13, 2005.

9. Author interview with Ian Finkenbinder, September 5, 2003, and subsequent follow-up communications.

10. Ibid.

11. Ibid.

12. The data are contained in two letters from David S. C. Chu, Under Secretary of Defense for Personnel and Readiness, to the Honorable Marty Meehan, December 2, 2004, and May 3, 2005, in author's possession.

13. "Financial Costs and Loss of Critical Skills," GAO, February 2005.

14. Author interviews with Finkenbinder; author interviews with Alastair Gamble, October 24, 2002, and subsequent follow-up communications; Nathaniel Frank, "Stonewalled," *New Republic,* January 24, 2005.

15. "Financial Costs and Loss of Critical Skills," GAO, February 2005; the figures come from government data and published sources aggregated with knowledge of additional discharges confirmed in personal interviews.

16. Anne Hull, "How 'Don't Tell' Translates," *Washington Post,* December 3, 2003; Tyson, "Uzbek or Dari?"

17. Author interviews with Gamble.

18. Ibid.; author interview with Patricia Ramirez, October 25, 2002; Carl Nolte, "Wanted: Speakers of Arabic, Farsi; People Fluent in the Languages Are in Short Supply in the U.S.," *San Francisco Chronicle,* September 19, 2001; National Commission, *9/11 Commission Report.*

19. Author interview with Ramirez; Lou Chibbaro, "Nine Arabic Linguists for Army Discharged for Being Gay," *Washington Blade,* November 8, 2002.

20. Author interview with Ramirez.

21. Ibid.

22. Ibid.

23. Ibid.

24. Ibid.

25. Ibid.

26. Ibid.

27. Ibid.
28. Ibid.
29. Ibid.
30. Ibid.
31. Author interviews with Gamble; Nathaniel Frank, "Perverse: Don't Ask, Don't Tell v. the War on Terrorism," *New Republic,* November 18, 2002.
32. Ibid.
33. Ibid.
34. Ibid.
35. Ibid.
36. Margie Mason, "Military Boots 6 Gay Arabic Linguists Despite Shortage," Associated Press, November 14, 2002.
37. Author interviews with Gamble.
38. Author interview with Harvey Perritt, October 30, 2002.
39. Christopher Heredia, "Gay, Lesbian Troops Can Serve Openly—For Now," *San Francisco Chronicle,* September 19, 2001.
40. David Kirby, "Think Before You Tell," *The Advocate,* December 4, 2001.
41. Regulation 500-3-3, vol. 3, "Reserve Component Unit Commanders Handbook," U.S. Army, 1999, Table 2.1: "Personnel Actions During the Mobilization Process," in author's possession.
42. Lou Chibbaro, "Out Gay Soldiers Sent to Iraq," *Washington Blade,* September 23, 2005.
43. E-mail from Major Nate Flegler, Media Division, FORSCOM Public Affairs, to author, October 6, 2005.
44. Senate Committee on Armed Services, *Policy Concerning Homosexuality,* 1993, 17– 18.
45. Joseph Giordono, "Discharged Gay Sailor Is Called Back to Active Duty," *Stars and Stripes,* May 6, 2007; Joseph Giordono, "Navy Bars Outed Gay Sailor from Return to Service," *Stars and Stripes,* June 10, 2007.
46. Bryan Bender, "Military Retaining More Gays," *Boston Globe,* March 19, 2006.
47. Allan Bérubé, *Coming Out Under Fire: The History of Gay Men and Women in World War Two* (New York: Free Press, 1990), 172.
48. Ibid., 262; Randy Shilts, *Conduct Unbecoming: Gays and Lesbians in the U.S. Military* (New York: Ballantine Books, 1994), 70.
49. Randy Shilts, "Military May Defer Discharge of Gays," *San Francisco Chronicle,* January 11, 1991.
50. Randy Shilts, "Army Discharges Lesbian Who Challenged Ban," *San Francisco Chronicle,* January 19, 1991; Wade Lambert and Stephanie Simon, "US Military Moves to Discharge Some Gay Veterans of Gulf War," *Wall Street Journal,* July 30, 1991; Doug Grow, "Captain Did Her Duty, Despite Military's Mixed Messages," *Minneapolis Star Tribune,* March 16, 1993; Randy Shilts, "Gay Troops in the Gulf War Can't Come Out," *San Francisco Chronicle,* February 18, 1991; Shilts, *Conduct Unbecoming,* 735–38.
51. Department of Defense, "Defense Language Transformation Roadmap," report, January 2005.
52. Ibid.
53. Department of Defense, Office of the Under Secretary of Defense for Personnel and Readiness, the National Language Conference, "A Call to Action for National Foreign Language Capabilities," white paper, February 1, 2005; Department of Defense, "DoD Issues Call for National Foreign Language Capabilities," press release, April 27, 2005.
54. National Language Conference, "A Call to Action."
55. Ibid.
56. Department of Defense, "DoD Issues Call"; Department of Defense, "DoD Announces Plan to Improve Foreign Language Expertise," press release, March 30, 2005.
57. Tim Weiner, "Titan Corp. to Pay $28.5 Million in Fines for Foreign Bribery," *New*

York Times, March 2, 2005; John Mintz, "Army Veteran, Arab Linguist Is Forced Out in Crossfire," *Washington Post,* April 21, 2002.

58. Senate Judiciary Committee Hearing, Subcommittee on Terrorism, Technology and Homeland Security, October 14, 2003; Peter Grier and Faye Bowers, "Guantánamo Probe Stirs Wider Security Concerns," *Christian Science Monitor,* October 23, 2003; Nathaniel Frank, "Why We Need Gays in the Military," *New York Times,* November 28, 2003.

59. Duncan Mansfield, "Army Dismisses Gay Arabic Linguist," Associated Press, July 27, 2006.

60. Author interview with Stephen Benjamin, May 21, 2007; "U.S. Military Continues to Discharge Gay Arab Linguists," Associated Press, May 23, 2007.

61. Ibid.

62. Ibid.

63. Ibid.

64. E-mail from Stephen Benjamin to author, May 22, 2007.

65. Author interview with Jarrod Chlapowski, February 28, 2008; *Ask Not,* directed by Johnny Symons (Oakland, CA: Persistent Visions, 2008).

66. Author interview with Chlapowski.

10. GAYS OUT, EX-CONVICTS IN

1. Nathaniel Frank, "Revolving Door for Troops," *Washington Post,* July 12, 2004.

2. Senate Committee on Armed Services, *Policy Concerning Homosexuality,* 1993, 690–91.

3. A 2005 GAO report states that "from the passage of the homosexual conduct policy statute, in fiscal year 1994, through fiscal year 2003 the military services separated about 9,500 servicemembers for homosexual conduct. This represents about 0.40 percent of the 2.37 million members separated for all reasons during this period": "Financial Costs and Loss of Critical Skills," GAO, February 2005; Charles Moskos writes that homosexual separations represent 0.1 percent of military personnel: Charles Moskos, "The Law Works—and Here's Why," *Army Times,* October 27, 2003, cited in David Burrelli and Charles Dale, "Homosexuals and U.S. Military Policy: Current Issues" Congressional Research Services Report, March 13, 2006, 8.

4. "Military Reserves Falling Short in Finding Recruits," *New York Times,* August 28, 2000.

5. Justin Brown and Kent David-Packard, "Military Captures Recruits, at Last," *Christian Science Monitor,* August 9, 2000; David Wood, "U.S. Military Engages in Dramatic Image Building," *Minneapolis Star Tribune,* April 1, 2001; Tony Perry, "Aircraft Carrier Trolls for Future Navy Recruits," *Los Angeles Times,* May 21, 2000; Dave Moniz, "'Army of One' Recruits a New Generation of Soldiers," *USA Today,* January 10, 2001.

6. Wood, "U.S. Military Engages in Dramatic Image Building"; Ron Hutcheson and Jonathan Landay, "Bush Urging Military Pay Raise," *Milwaukee Journal Sentinel,* February, 13, 2001.

7. "Attacks Inspire Rise in Army Recruits," *Boston Herald,* September 22, 2001; "National Guard Triples Bonuses for Some Recruits," *USA Today,* December 17, 2004.

8. Jamie Wilson, "U.S. Army Lowers Standards in Recruitment Crisis," *The Guardian,* June 4, 2005; "Applications Drop at Military Academies," Reuters, June 14, 2005; Eric Schmitt, "Army Likely to Fall Short in Recruiting, General Says," *New York Times,* July 24, 2005; "Conflict in Iraq Hampers Enlisting," *St. Petersburg Times,* March 28, 2005; "For Recruiters, a Distant War Becomes a Tough Sell," *USA Today,* April 6, 2005; "Military Offering More, and Bigger, Bonuses," *USA Today,* February 21, 2005; Ann Scott Tyson, "Army Aims to Catch Up on Recruits in Summer," *Washington Post,* June 11, 2005; James Gordon, "It's Slim Pickin's: War Forcing Army to Accept Less-Qualified Recruits," *Daily News,* March 15, 2005.

9. Author interview with Gary Gates, August 3, 2006; Gary Gates, "Lesbians and Gay Men in the U.S. Military: Estimates from Census 2000," white paper, the Williams Institute, University of California, Los Angeles, October 2005; Gary Gates, "Effects of 'Don't Ask, Don't Tell' on Retention Among Lesbian, Gay, and Bisexual Military Personnel," research brief, Williams Institute, University of California, Los Angeles, October 2005.

10. Schmitt, "Army Likely to Fall Short in Recruiting, General Says."

11. Ibid.; Dan Ephron, "Peter Pace Called Homosexual Acts 'Immoral' Last Week. It Wasn't the First Time He'd Weighed In on the Matter," *Newsweek*, March 26, 2007; Aamer Madhani, "Top General Calls Homosexuality 'Immoral,'" *Chicago Tribune*, March 12, 2007; "Joint Chiefs Nominee Indicates It Is Appropriate for Congress to Revisit 'Don't Ask, Don't Tell,'" *PR Newswire*, August 1, 2007.

12. Damien Cave, "Army Recruiters Say They Feel Pressure to Bend Rules," *New York Times*, May 3, 2005.

13. Jim Dwyer and Robert Worth, "Accused G.I. Was Troubled Long Before Iraq," *New York Times*, July 14, 2006; Michael Boucai, "Balancing Your Strengths Against Your Felonies: Considerations for Military Recruitment of Ex-Offenders," white paper, Palm Center, University of California, Santa Barbara, September 2007.

14. "U.S. Army, Marines Allow More Convicts to Enlist," Reuters, April 21, 2008.

15. Gordon, "It's Slim Pickin's"; Tom Bowman, "Army Worries About Quality: More High School Dropouts, Low Scores Recruited," *Baltimore Sun*, March 7, 2005. The discharge figures are compiled by the Servicemembers Legal Defense Network from official Department of Defense and other government figures.

16. Jamie Wilson, "U.S. Army Lowers Standards in Recruitment Crisis," *Guardian*, June 4, 2005.

17. See "Financial Costs and Loss of Critical Skills," GAO, February 2005; Moskos, "The Law Works"; Wilson, "U.S. Army Lowers Standards in Recruitment Crisis"; Greg Jaffe, "To Fill Ranks, Army Acts to Retain Even Problem Enlistees," *Wall Street Journal*, June 3, 2005; Phillip Carter and Owen West, "Dismissed! We Won't Solve the Military Manpower Crisis by Retaining Our Worst Soldiers," *Slate*, June 2, 2005.

18. Bowman, "Army Worries About Quality"; Boucai, "Balancing Your Strengths"; "Military Recruiting: New Initiatives Could Improve Criminal History Screening," GAO, February 1999.

19. Suzanne Goldenberg, "Former U.S. Private Charged with Rape and Killing Victim's Family in Iraq," *Guardian*, July 4, 2006; Dwyer and Worth, "Accused G.I. Was Troubled."

20. Ibid.

21. David Cloud, "Starkly Contrasting Portraits of G.I. in Iraqi Abuse Retrial," *New York Times*, September 22, 2005; Eric Schmitt, "Officer in Charge of Questioning Iraqi Inmates Had No Interrogation Training," *New York Times*, June 9, 2004; "Latest Report on Abu Ghraib: Abuses of Iraqi Prisoners 'Are, Without Question, Criminal,'" *New York Times*, August 26, 2004.

22. National Gang Intelligence Center, "Gang-Related Activity in the US Armed Forces Increasing," intelligence assessment, January 12, 2007; Claudia Núñez, "Gang Members Get Trained in the Army," *Opinión*, March 9, 2008.

23. Author interview with Derek Sparks, April 25, 2004.

24. Author interview with Beth Schissel, November 27, 2005.

25. Ibid.

26. Christopher Bond and Patrick Leahy, "United States Senate National Guard Caucus: Report by Caucus Co-Chairs Senators Christopher S. Bond and Patrick J. Leahy on National Guard and Army Reservists on Medical Hold at Ft. Stewart, Georgia," Senate report, October 24, 2003, http://leahy.senate.gov/press/200310/102403a.html (accessed May 12, 2008).

27. Senate Appropriations Committee, Defense Subcommittee, *Defense Subcommittee Hearing on the FY2006 Defense Medical Health Program*, May 10, 2005.

28. Ibid.
29. "Military Personnel: DOD Needs Action Plan to Address Enlisted Personnel Recruitment and Retention Challenges," GAO, November 2005; House Committee on Armed Services, Subcommittee on Military Personnel, *Defense Health Programs Overview: Statement of Joseph G. Webb, Jr., Deputy Surgeon General, United States Army,* 109th Cong., 1st sess., October 19, 2005; Bryan Bender, "U.S. Military Struggles to Recruit Medical Professionals," *Boston Globe,* October 20, 2005.
30. Frank, "Revolving Door for Troops"; also see Gregg Zoroya, "Army Allows Reserve Officers to Quit Rather Than Go to War," *USA Today,* December 20, 2005.
31. Frank, "Revolving Door for Troops"; figures are from Servicemembers Legal Defense Network; Rep. Marty Meehan quote contained in e-mail from Sandra Solstrum (December 22, 2005) in author's possession.
32. Author interview with Schissel.
33. Scott Greenberger, "One Year Later, Nation Divided on Gay Marriage," *Boston Globe,* May 15, 2005.
34. Tim Reid, "From A-Bomb to Gay Bomb," *Times* (London), June 14, 2007; U.S. Department of Defense, *Physical Disability Evaluation,* DOD Instruction 1332.38, November 14, 1996, certified current as of 2003.
35. Keely Savoie, "Military Dumb in Any Language," editorial, *Charleston Gazette* (West Virginia), December 8, 2002; "Anti-Gay Military Asks for Trouble," *Atlanta Journal-Constitution,* June 25, 2004; "Let Gay Soldiers Serve Openly," *USA Today,* April 28, 2005; Max Boot, "Gay or Female, Uncle Sam Should Want You," *Los Angeles Times,* May 26, 2005.
36. Senate Committee on Armed Services, *Hearing on the Status of the U.S. Army and Marine Corps in Fighting the Global War on Terrorism,* 109th Cong., 1st sess., June 30, 2005.
37. Susan Milligan, "Military Recruiters Getting a Foot in Door: Federal Education Bill Requires High Schools to Share Student Data," *Boston Globe,* November 21, 2002; Steven Carter, "Military Recruits in Schools, but It Gets No Welcome Mat," *Oregonian,* December 18, 2003; Erika Hayasaki, "Districts Taking On Recruiters," *Los Angeles Times,* February 13, 2003; author interview with anonymous staff member, House Armed Services Committee, 2001; "Easier Access for Military Recruiters," *Tampa Tribune,* July 6, 2000; Aaron Belkin, "'Don't Ask, Don't Tell': Does the Gay Ban Undermine the Military's Reputation?" *Armed Forces & Society* 34, no. 2 (January 2008): 276–91.
38. House Committee on Armed Services, *Report of the House Committee on Armed Services, National Defense Authorization Act for FY 2000,* 106th Cong., 1st sess., May 24, 1999.
39. Ibid.
40. Congressional study cited in brief of Professors William Alford et al. in support of appellants and in support of reversal, *Forum for Academic and Institutional Rights v. Rumsfeld,* 390 F.3d 219.
41. Ibid.
42. Marcella Bombardieri, "Harvard Law Ends Its Ban on Military," *Boston Globe,* August 27, 2002.
43. Department of Defense, Office of the Under Secretary of Defense for Personnel and Readiness, the National Language Conference, "A Call to Action for National Foreign Language Capabilities," white paper, February 1, 2005; Department of Defense, "DoD Issues Call for National Foreign Language Capabilities," press release, April 27, 2005.
44. David Burrelli and Charles Dale, "Homosexuals and U.S. Military Policy: Current Issues," Congressional Research Service Report, May 27, 2005.
45. Ibid.
46. "Conference Report on H.R. 1119, National Defense Authorization Act for Fiscal Year 1998," *Congressional Record,* 105th Cong., 2nd sess., October 23, 1997.

47. Burrelli and Dale, "Homosexuals and U.S. Military Policy."
48. H. Con. Res. 36, 109th Cong., 1st sess., February 2, 2005.
49. Burrelli and Dale, "Homosexuals and U.S. Military Policy."
50. Cave, "Army Recruiters Say They Feel Pressure"; Frank Main, "More Army Recruits Have Records," *Chicago Sun-Times,* June 19, 2006.

11. RAINBOW WARRIORS

1. "Conduct Unbecoming: The Second Annual Report on 'Don't Ask, Don't Tell,'" report, Servicemembers Legal Defense Network, 1996; Andrea Stone, "Many Troops Openly Gay, Group Says," *USA Today,* January 8, 2008.
2. Eric Schmitt, "Military Cites Wide Range of Reasons for Its Gay Ban," *New York Times,* January 27, 1993; "Conduct Unbecoming: The Third Annual Report on 'Don't Ask, Don't Tell,'" report, Servicemembers Legal Defense Network, 1997; "Conduct Unbecoming: The Tenth Annual Report on 'Don't Ask, Don't Tell,'" report, Servicemembers Legal Defense Network, 2004.
3. Margarethe Cammermeyer, *Serving in Silence* (New York: Penguin, 1994); Lincoln Caplan, "'Don't Ask, Don't Tell'—Marine Style," *Newsweek,* June 13, 1994; "Conduct Unbecoming: The Third Annual Report"; "Conduct Unbecoming: The Tenth Annual Report."
4. Author interview with Steve Clark Hall, Feburary 15, 2008; Steve Estes, *Ask and Tell: Gay and Lesbian Veterans Speak Out* (Durham: University of North Carolina Press, 2007), 107–9.
5. Ibid.
6. Ibid.
7. Ibid.
8. Nathaniel Frank, "Gays and Lesbians at War: Military Service in Iraq and Afghanistan Under 'Don't Ask, Don't Tell,'" white paper, Palm Center, University of California, Santa Barbara, 2004; author interviews with anonymous, 2004.
9. Author interview with Ian Finkenbinder, September 5, 2003, and subsequent follow-up communications; author interviews with anonymous, 2004; author interview with Austin Rooke, July 13, 2004: Rooke followed his statement with an indication that others had more trouble than he did: "However, I don't think that's the norm. I still come into contact with people in the military who have been in for years and are absolutely terrified" that they will be outed. Consistent with evidence reported earlier, the difficulty appears to result from the policy, rather than the presence of known gays; author interview with Wendy Biehl, April 28, 2004, and subsequent follow-up communications; observations are based on author field visits to various U.S. military installations.
10. Author interview with Biehl, a lesbian and former army specialist, who noted that women tend to socialize in the showers without incident. "We all talk in the showers," she said. "We sort of point and say, 'Oh my god, I have a bruise here,' and everybody just looks."
11. Author interview with anonymous, 2004.
12. Author interviews with anonymous, 2004.
13. Author interview with anonymous, 2004.
14. Author interview with anonymous, 2004.
15. Author interview with anonymous, 2004.
16. Author interview with anonymous, 2004.
17. Zogby International, "Opinions of Military Personnel on Sexual Minorities in the Military," December 2006; Jim Drinkard, "Gay-Rights Backers Not That Harsh on McCain," *USA Today,* January 19, 2000.
18. Author interviews with anonymous, 2004.
19. Ibid.

20. Ibid.
21. Ibid.; author interview with Biehl, who reported seeing a rainbow sticker on a duffel bag placed by someone with "no shame."
22. Author interview with anonymous, 2004.
23. Author interviews with anonymous, 2004; author interviews with Brian Muller, February 20, 2004, and subsequent follow-up communications.
24. Author interviews with anonymous, 2004.
25. Ibid.
26. Ibid.
27. Ibid.
28. Author interview with Fred Fox, February 26, 2008.
29. Author interview with anonymous, 2004.
30. *Morning Edition,* NPR, January 29, 1993; also see, for example, David Tuller, "Gays Say Debate Could Be Beneficial," *San Francisco Chronicle,* January 28, 1993; Howard Goldberg, "Public Split on Gays in Military, Poll Finds," Associated Press, December 17, 1992; "Newsweek/Gallup Profile American Voters on Gay Rights," *Hotline,* September 8, 1992.
31. Aaron Belkin, "'Don't Ask, Don't Tell': Does the Gay Ban Undermine the Military's Reputation?" *Armed Forces & Society* 34, no. 2 (January 2008); *Bowers v. Hardwick,* 478 U.S. 186 (1986); *Lawrence v. Texas,* 539 U.S. 558 (2003).
32. Richard Goldstein, "The Gathering Storm over Gay Rights," *Village Voice,* August 6, 2003.
33. Scott Greenberger, "One Year Later, Nation Divided on Gay Marriage," *Boston Globe,* May 15, 2005; Lydia Sadd, "Tolerance for Gay Rights at High-Water Mark," Gallup Poll News Service, May 29, 2007; Kyle Dropp and Jon Cohen, "Acceptance of Gay People in Military Grows Dramatically," *Washington Post,* July 19, 2008.
34. David Dunlap, "Gay Images, Once Kept Out, Are Out Big Time," *New York Times,* January 21, 1996.
35. Richard Huff, "New Season Will Set Record for Gay Roles, Group Says," *Daily News,* August 14, 1997; "42 Million Tune In to Watch a Coming Out," *New York Times,* May 2, 1997.
36. Bernard Weinraub and Jim Rutenberg, "Gay-Themed TV Gaining a Wider Audience," *New York Times,* July 29, 2003; Rick Kissell, "'Queer' Looks Fabulous," *Daily Variety,* July 17, 2003.
37. Rupert Smith, "Amazing, Grace" *Guardian,* April 7, 2003; David Teather, "Gay Team Flings TV Closet Door Wide Open," *Guardian,* August 11, 2003; Weinraub and Rutenberg, "Gay-Themed TV," July 29, 2003.
38. Matthew Gilbert, "'Will' Brought Attitude, but More Important, It Changed Ours," *Boston Globe,* May 14, 2006; Gail Shister, quoting Suzanna Walters, "'Will & Grace' Bids Goodbye but Leaves a Big Mark," *Philadelphia Inquirer,* May 18, 2006.
39. Author interviews with Muller; author interviews with Finkenbinder; author interview with anonymous, 2004.
40. Lawrence Korb, "Evolving Perspectives on the Military's Policy on Homosexuals: A Personal Note," in Wilbur Scott and Sandra Carson Stanley, eds., *Gays and Lesbians in the Military: Issues, Concerns, and Contrasts* (New York: Aldine de Gruyter, 1994), 219–29.
41. Gerald Garvey and John DiIulio, "Only Connect?" *New Republic,* April 26, 1993.
42. Author interview with Gerald Garvey, March 20, 2000.
43. Sonya Ross, "Clinton: Military Gay Policy Failing," Associated Press, December 11, 1999; "Transcript of July 5 Interview of President Clinton by Joe Klein of The New Yorker Magazine," U.S. Newswire, October 11, 2000; "Clinton: Gay Ban 'Diminishes Our Security,'" *Express Gay News,* October 13, 2003.
44. Charles Moskos and Michelle Benecke, "Suffering in Silence," *Washington Post,* July 18, 2000.

45. Tarak Barkawi, Christopher Dandeker, Melissa Wells-Petry, and Elizabeth Kier, "Rights and Fights: Sexual Orientation and Military Effectiveness," *International Security* 24, no. 1 (Summer, 1999): 181–201.

46. Aaron Belkin and Geoffrey Bateman, eds., *Don't Ask, Don't Tell: Debating the Gay Ban in the Military* (Boulder, CO: Lynne Rienner Publishers, 2003), 133; author interviews with Christopher Dandeker, February 21, 2001, and May 9, 2007.

47. *Lawrence v. Texas*, 539 U.S. 558 (2003); author interview with Cass Sunstein, 2000.

48. Author interviews with John Hutson, August 19, 2003, and February 19, 2008; John Hutson, "Retire a Bad Military Policy," *National Law Journal*, August 4, 2003; "Senior Admiral Says Lifting Gay Ban Would Strengthen Military," news release, Palm Center, University of California, Santa Barbara, August 21, 2003; "Defeating 'Don't Ask, Don't Tell,'" panel discussion, Yale Law School, October 5, 2006.

49. Ibid.

50. Ibid.

51. Ibid.

52. John Hutson, unpublished op-ed, in author possession.

53. Bryan Bender, "Military Retaining More Gays," *Boston Globe*, March 19, 2006; Nathaniel Popper, "Backroom Battler for Rumsfeld and Bronfman Finds Himself Centerstage in High-Stakes Struggle," *Jewish Daily Forward*, March 30, 2007.

54. John Shalikashvili, "Second Thoughts on Gays in the Military," *New York Times*, January 2, 2007.

55. Ibid.

56. Author interview with Aaron Belkin, August 25, 2008.

57. Zogby, "Opinions of Military Personnel," December 2006; Melissa Healy, "The Times Poll: 74% of Military Enlistees Oppose Lifting Gay Ban," *Los Angeles Times*, February 28, 1993; Laura Miller, "Fighting for a Just Cause: Soldiers' Views on Gays in the Military," in Scott and Stanley, *Gays and Lesbians in the Military*, 70; John W. Bicknell, "Study of Naval Officers' Attitudes Toward Homosexuals in the Military," master's thesis, Naval Postgraduate School, March 2000.

58. Zogby, "Opinions of Military Personnel," December 2006; "The Military Index," *Foreign Policy*, March/April 2008.

59. *Meet the Press*, NBC, June 15, 2003; National Annenberg Election Survey, *NEAS 04*, 2004.

60. Author interview with Brett Keen, March 11, 2008.

61. Ibid.

62. Author interview with Sean May, October 10, 2007.

63. Author interview with anonymous, USS *Ronald Reagan*, January 13, 2008.

64. Author interview with Stephen Jay Vossler, March 4, 2008.

65. Author interview with Dan Rossi, February 18, 2008; New York City Council, Committee on Civil Rights and Committee on Veterans, *Joint Hearing on Proposed Resolution 1170-A*, January 25, 2008.

66. Bob Barr, "Don't Ask, Who Cares," *Wall Street Journal*, June 13, 2007

67. Alan Simpson, "Bigotry That Hurts Our Military," *Washington Post*, March 14, 2007.

68. "Twenty-eight Generals and Admirals Call for End to Military's Gay Ban," news release, Palm Center, University of California, Santa Barbara, November 29, 2007; "Media Reporting 50+ Generals Now Oppose Gay Ban," news release, Palm Center, University of California, Santa Barbara, July 23, 2008.

69. Brigadier General Hugh Aitken, Lieutenant General Minter Alexander, Lieutenant General Robert Gard, and Vice Admiral Jack Shanahan, "Report of the General/Flag Officers' Study Group," Palm Center, University of California, Santa Barbara, 2008.

70. House Armed Services Committee, Subcommittee on Personnel, *Statement of Brian Jones, Sergeant Major USA (RET.), CEO, Adventure Training Concepts,* 110th Cong., 2nd sess., July 23, 2008; *Hearsay*, WHRV-FM, August 13, 2008.

71. House Armed Services Committee, Subcommittee on Personnel, *Statement of Elaine Donnelly, President, Center for Military Readiness,* 110th Cong., 2nd sess., July 23, 2008; House Armed Services Committee, Military Personnel Subcommittee, *Don't Ask Don't Tell Review: Hearing of the Military Personnel Subcommittee of the House Armed Services Committee,* 110th Cong., 1st sess., 2008.

72. Ibid.; Elaine Donnelly, "Constructing the Co-Ed Military," *Duke Journal of Law & Policy* 14, no. 2 (May 2007): 815–952.

73. House Armed Services Committee, *Don't Ask Don't Tell Review.*

74. Frank, "Gays and Lesbians at War," 2004.

75. Lee Nichols, *Breakthrough on the Color Front* (Colorado Springs: Three Continents Press, 1993); *Meet the Press,* NBC News, June 10, 2007; *GPS,* CNN, December 14, 2008.

76. Letter from Sam Nunn to Alan Simpson, October 18, 2007.

77. Memo from Charles Moskos to Sam Nunn, October 6, 2007; author interview with Charles Moskos, March 13, 2008.

INDEX